AFFECT AND LEGAL EDUCATION

Emerging Legal Education

Emerging Legal Education is a forum for analysing the discourse of legal education and creating innovative ways of learning the law. The series focuses on research, theory and practice within legal education, drawing attention to historical, interdisciplinary and international characteristics, and is based upon imaginative and sophisticated educational thinking. The series takes a broad view of theory and practice. Series books are written for an international audience and are sensitive to the diversity of contexts in which law is taught, learned and practised.

Affect and Legal Education
Emotion in Learning and Teaching the Law

Edited by

PAUL MAHARG
Northumbria University, UK

and

CAROLINE MAUGHAN
University of the West of England, Bristol, UK

Routledge
Taylor & Francis Group
LONDON AND NEW YORK

First published 2011 by Ashgate Publishing

Published 2016 by Routledge
2 Park Square, Milton Park, Abingdon, Oxfordshire OX14 4RN
711 Third Avenue, New York, NY 10017, USA

First issued in paperback 2016

Routledge is an imprint of the Taylor & Francis Group, an informa business

British Library Cataloguing in Publication Data
Affect and legal education : emotion in learning and
teaching the law.
1. Law--Study and teaching--Psychological aspects.
2. Affect (Psychology)
I. Maharg, Paul. II. Maughan, Caroline.
340'.07-dc22

Library of Congress Cataloging-in-Publication Data
Affect and legal education : emotion in learning and teaching the law / by Paul Maharg, and Caroline Maughan.
p. cm. -- (Emerging legal learning)
Includes bibliographical references and index.
ISBN 978-1-4094-1026-3 (hardback)
1. Law--Study and teaching--Methodology. 2. Law and ethics. 3. Emotions. I. Maharg, Paul. II. Maughan, Caroline.
K100.A52 2011
340.071'1--dc22

2011016676

ISBN 13: 978-1-138-24715-4 (pbk)
ISBN 13: 978-1-4094-1026-3 (hbk)

Contents

PART III: AFFECT AND LEARNING

List of Figures and Tables

Figures

Tables

Notes on Contributors

Karen Barton A Senior Lecturer at the Centre for Professional Legal Studies, University of Strathclyde Law School, Karen is Co-director of the Diploma in Legal Practice, the postgraduate qualification required by all Scottish Law graduates prior to commencing their two-year traineeship. At the same time she continues to develop her interests in professional education and training and is involved in two leading-edge projects in professional legal education based at GGSL: the Standardised Client Initiative in Interviewing Skills; and a JISC/HEA-funded Portfolio Pilot Project involving diploma students, trainees and trainers within a number of Scottish legal firms.

Karen was one of the first UKCLE Associates appointed in 2006 and is a member of the BILETA Executive. She is also a member of the CELTS Conference Organising Committee, and a founder member of eLit (www.elit-conf.org/index.html). She helped set up and blogs at the UKCLE's Blog for Law Teachers, Digital Directions (www.warwick.ac.uk:9180/ukcle/associates/digital-directions), and also at Zeugma, where there are links to a number of her papers.

Lorraine Boran is a Lecturer in Psychology, School of Nursing, Dublin City University. She holds a PhD in Psychology, a first class honours PG Diploma in Statistics and a first class honours BA in Psychology from Trinity College Dublin. She also holds a PG Diploma in Legal Studies from The Honorable Society of Kings Inns and is currently completing her final year in an honours LLB Degree in Irish Law in Griffith College Dublin/Nottingham University. She also lectures in Statistics and Research Methods on the MSc programme in the Department of Clinical Speech and Language Studies in Trinity College Dublin. She previously was a programme director of two postgraduate programmes in Equality Studies and Leadership in Carlow College. She is currently conducting several research projects in the areas of working memory and cognition. She has a number of journal articles in preparation arising from her doctorate research and has given a number of podium presentations at international conferences.

Anthony Bradney is Professor of Law at Keele University. He was previously Professor of Law at the universities of Leicester and then Sheffield. His research has mainly been into the relationship between religions and law where his publications include *Law and Faith in a Sceptical Age* (Routledge 2009), theories of legal pluralism, where his publications include *Living without Law: An Ethnography of Dispute Avoidance and Resolution in the Religious Society of Friends* (with Fiona Cownie, Ashgate 2000), and university legal education, where his publications include *Conversations, Chances and Choices: The Liberal Law School in the Twenty-first Century* (Hart Publishing 2003). In addition to this, over the last five years he has published a series of articles and essays as well as given conference papers on images of law and legal institutions in the television programmes *Buffy the Vampire Slayer* and *Angel*. He is a co-author of two textbooks, *How to Study Law* (Sweet and Maxwell), which is currently in its sixth edition, and *The English Legal System in Context* (Oxford University Press), which is currently in its fifth edition.

Sara Chandler is Professor of Clinical Legal Education at the College of Law, and a former Director of Pro Bono at the College's Legal Advice Centre, Bloomsbury, London. Before joining the College of Law in 2003 Sara worked for 15 years in law centres and for five years in legal aid private practices. She is a specialist in housing law (landlord and tenant).

Sara has worked with law societies and bar associations in African jurisdictions as part of the Law Society of England and Wales' international programme, particularly in capacity building programmes for legal aid and access to justice. Her special interest is in the teaching of ethics and clinical legal education, and she has collaborated with Nigel Duncan in an international investigation of the teaching of ethics at undergraduate and vocational level. Her current role in the Law Societies' International Human Rights Committee is responsibility for supporting human rights lawyers in Colombia. She represents solicitors in the voluntary sector on the Council of the Law Society, and is also a member of the Global Alliance for Justice Education Steering Committee.

David Delany currently works as an Academic Developer in Trinity College Dublin's Centre for Academic and Student Learning (CAPSL), where he runs an innovative accelerated learning course for academics. This course is based on research in cognitive science into the nature of superior performance and is rationally designed from first principles to accelerate the development of elite levels of insight, problem-solving and innovation. On this advanced thinking skills course, participants learn how to use novel deep learning and adaptive problem-solving techniques to accelerate the transition from novice to expert, and from expert to elite expert.

Maksymilian Del Mar is Lecturer in Legal and Social Philosophy at the Department of Law, Queen Mary, University of London, United Kingdom. He completed undergraduate studies in law, philosophy and literature at the University of Queensland, Australia, and a PhD in Law at the School of Law, University of Edinburgh, United Kingdom. While in Edinburgh, he was a member of the AHRC Beyond Text in Legal Education project. Until recently, he was a Swiss National Science Foundation Researcher at the Institute of the Social Sciences, University of Lausanne, Switzerland.

Nigel Duncan is Principal Lecturer, The City Law School (formerly the Inns of Court School of Law). He had earlier established the first Law Access course in the UK and taught on undergraduate courses. He is the co-ordinator of Case Preparation, Negotiation and the FRU option and he also teaches Advocacy, Opinion Writing, Legal Research, Professional Development and Employment Law on the BVC and Criminal Procedure on the LLM in Criminal Litigation. He is Academic Lead for Assessment for City University.

Nigel is also editor and main contributor to *Employment Law in Practice* (9th ed., Oxford University Press 2010), editor of *Opinion Writing and Case Preparation* (Oxford University Press 2010) and is, with H. Brayne and R. Grimes, author of *Clinical Legal Education: Active Learning in Your Law School* (Blackstone 1998). He is editor of the refereed journal *The Law Teacher* and is currently conducting research into professional and judicial ethics. He is the author of many articles, predominantly in the field of legal education, professional development and ethics. He has designed an innovative website to act as a forum and resource for those interested in teaching legal ethics.

Nigel is a National Teaching Fellow of the Higher Education Academy. He is a regular presenter at conferences both in the UK and internationally. He is an Honorary Fellow of the Society of Advanced Legal Studies, a Teaching and Learning Fellow at City University, has acted as Chair of the Association of Law Teachers and is a founder member of the Clinical Legal Education Organisation and of the Global Alliance for Justice Education. He is a Fellow of the Higher Education Academy and sits on the Advisory Board and Strategy Committee of the UK Centre for Legal Education.

Graham Ferris is a Reader in Law at Nottingham Trent University where he teaches Critical Legal Thinking on the LLB, and Corporate Property, Banking and Restitution, and the Law of the World Trade Organisation at master's level. He also teaches legal theory to PhD students.

Graham has published extensively in the field of property law. He has also published, or given papers, on legal history, and legal theory and legal education. Graham has co-authored work with Professor Graham Battersby and Catherine Williams, both of the University of Sheffield. Graham is currently working on the application of legal theory to the design and delivery of legal education and property law in the context of development.

Rebecca Huxley-Binns is a Reader in Legal Education at Nottingham Trent University. Amongst other teaching commitments, she teaches on LLB (Hons) Law (distance learning) and the LLB (Hons) Law (full-time), and is the Module Leader for criminal law, the law of evidence and is Mistress of the Moots. She also teaches Critical Legal Thinking.

Rebecca has published a number of law textbooks and numerous journal articles. She was awarded the British Academy Grant for Overseas Conferences and Research, summer 2005 (for ALSB Conference, San Francisco – to present a paper on corporate manslaughter) and was awarded the Law Teacher of the Year in 2010. She was also Principal Examiner for the Institute of Legal Executives (Higher Professional Diploma, Level 6) in Criminal Law, External Examiner for London South Bank University and for Bristol Law School. She also serves as a Committee Member for the Association of Law Teachers.

Alan M. Lerner was Practice Professor of Law at the University of Pennsylvania, where he had been based since 1993. Previously he was a partner at Cohen, Shapiro, Shiekman and Cohen and worked for a few years as a Law Clerk in the US District Court. He taught Interdisciplinary Child Advocacy Clinic, Civil Practice Clinic, Advanced Civil Practice Clinic, Law and Lawyering in the Workplace, and Employment Discrimination Law. His research interests included lawyering and clinical supervision (including professional responsibility), child advocacy, child welfare law, employment discrimination law.

Alan taught the Interdisciplinary Child Advocacy Clinic from 2002, teaming law students, upper-level medical students and graduate social work students to study society's responses to child maltreatment, and represent children for whom dependency petitions have been filed in court.

Paul Maharg is Professor of Legal Education in the School of Law, University of Northumbria. Prior to this he was a Professor of Law in the Glasgow Graduate School (GGSL), University of Strathclyde, where he was Director of the Innovative Learning Technologies Development Unit at the GGSL, as well as Director of the two-year, JISC/UKCLE-funded project, SIMPLE (SIMulated Professional Learning Environment (http://simplecommunity.org). He is the author of *Transforming Legal Education: Learning and Teaching the Law in the Early Twenty-first Century* (Ashgate 2007, www.transforming.org.uk), co-editor of and contributor to *Digital Games and Learning* (Continuum Press 2011, with Sara de Freitas) and has published widely in the fields of legal education and professional learning design (http://ssrn.com/author=272987). His specialisms include interdisciplinary educational design and the use of digital simulations. He was recently appointed a Senior Fellow of the Higher Education Academy and a Fellow of the RSA (www.thersa.org). He blogs at http://www.paulmaharg.com.

Chris Maguire is Dean of Academic Affairs at BPP University College. Chris joined BPP in 2005 as its first Director of Quality Assurance and Enhancement. He is responsible for developing and managing the regulatory infrastructure and cultural ethos that underpin the BPP's quality standards. Before joining BPP Chris was the principal officer for education and training for the Bar Council, where his degrees in English and European Literature, and the Renaissance, together with his background in theatre, were considered a sound preparation for joining the legal world. His formal education continues at King's College London, where he is doing a doctorate in education.

Chris has held a number of external appointments, including: Chair of the Association of Law Teachers; consultant to the Nigerian Council of Legal Education; consultant on legal education to the Cypriot Government; member of the Lord Chancellor's standing conference on legal education; Phineas Gage Group on neuroscience; UK Centre for Legal Education Advisory Committee member; Association of Personal Injury Lawyers Advisory Committee member and European Stage Experts Committee member.

Caroline Maughan is a Visiting Fellow and a former Director of Teaching and Learning at Bristol Law School, University of the West of England. She studied linguistics and taught languages in further education before qualifying as a barrister, and has since taught law in further and higher education, specialising more recently in skills-based learning. She currently teaches on the Bar Professional Training Course and a runs a skills/process module on LLB year 3, which is based around simulated casework in the 'virtual' town of Brigstowe. Her research interests include skills-based, experiential and collaborative learning. With Julian Webb she co-edited *Teaching Lawyers' Skills* (1996) and co-wrote the student text *Lawyering Skills and the Legal Process* (CUP Law in Context series, 2nd ed., 2005). She has facilitated a number of workshops at conferences and staff development events across the UK.

External appointments past and present include: Fellow of the Higher Education Academy; member of the Lord Chancellor's Standing Conference on Legal Education; Associate of the UK Centre for Legal Education; external examiner, Bar Council; peer reviewer, *Law Teacher* journal. She has also worked as a mentor on the UWE PGCE programme.

Richard Roche is a lecturer in Psychology at the National University of Ireland, Maynooth. Prior to his appointment at NUI Maynooth, he obtained his BA in Psychology at Trinity College, Dublin (graduating with First Class honours and as a Scholar of TCD), where he also completed his PhD, Postgraduate Diploma in Statistics and Postdoctoral Fellowship. His research interests include the neuroscience of learning and memory; spatial memory and navigation; memory consolidation and reconsolidation; memory and ageing; and human electrophysiology.

Richard's current research involves three main areas of interest: the neurocognitive processes underlying human financial decision-making and neuroeconomics; electrophysiological markers of cognitive recovery following stroke; and EEG indices of abnormal processing in children at risk for developing psychosis. To date he has published 13 journal articles, and has co-authored one book, *Pioneering Studies in Cognitive Neuroscience*, with Seán Commins.

Julian Webb is Professor of Legal Education at the University of Warwick and Director of the Higher Education Academy's UK Centre for Legal Education. Julian has published widely on legal education, the legal profession and lawyers' ethics, with a particular focus on legal education policy, and the teaching of ethics and values. He is the co-author, with Donald Nicolson, of *Professional Legal Ethics: Critical Interrogations* (Oxford University Press 1999) and general editor of the *Penguin Dictionary of Law* (2009). With John Paterson, he also edits the 'Law, Science and Society' book series published by Routledge-Cavendish. His current teaching involves undergraduate modules on the English Legal System and Introduction to Legal Theory, and a postgraduate Foundations of Socio-Legal Theory course.

Julian has been an education adviser to the General Council of the Bar, and has undertaken research and consultancy for a number of professional bodies, including the Lord Chancellor's Advisory Committee for Legal Education and Conduct, the Dutch Council of the Judiciary, the Law Society of England and Wales and the New Zealand Council of Legal Education.

Fiona Westwood qualified as a solicitor in 1976 and practised for more than 20 years as a commercial lawyer, latterly as an equity partner of a large Glasgow and Edinburgh firm with particular responsibilities for business development across the whole business. Since 2000, she has been involved in postgraduate vocational skills development, as part-time tutor at Edinburgh and Strathclyde Universities and then Senior Lecturer in Legal Practice at Glasgow Graduate School of Law. Her particular areas of responsibility and academic publications relate to practice management and the development of professionalism. She has also served on the Law Society of Scotland Working Parties on Education and Training and Professional Standards.

Fiona runs her own management consultancy, Westwood Associates, which specialises in providing support to the professional sector. She has researched and written three books on professionals, their organisations and their skill development. Her first two, *Achieving Best Practice – Shaping Professionals for Success* and *Accelerated Best Practice – Implementing Success in Professional Firms*, concentrated on practice and business development. Her third book, *Developing Resilience – The Key to Professional Success*, tackles personal and professional development from undergraduate to mastery.

In memory of Alan M. Lerner

Introduction

Paul Maharg and Caroline Maughan

Affect

As a novelist and social critic, Dickens was an acute observer of professional life, its construction, its power and its effect on society. In *Great Expectations*, a classic *Bildungsroman* of social education, he explored the corrosive power of legal action separated from feeling in the professional lives of the lawyer Jaggers and his clerk, Wemmick, as seen through the eyes of Pip. Wemmick's strategy for survival in Jaggers' legal world is schizoid: the complete separation of feeling from professional acting, and this is enacted in almost every representation of him in the novel. Wemmick takes his cue from his capable employer, Jaggers, who throughout the novel eradicates all feeling from the law. 'Get out of this office', he tells a client at one point who is pleading that he can't help his emotions, 'I'll have no feelings here. Get out' (Dickens 1999: 524).

The collection of chapters that make up this volume can be seen as a response to Jaggers. To our knowledge *Affect and Legal Education* is the first book-length study of the subject in legal education. It's long overdue. The book's subject is an essential part of almost every aspect of education, and yet in legal educational literature it is relatively invisible. There are four reasons for this. First there is a problem with the subject's interdisciplinarity: finding the research in other disciplines, understanding it and then using it as a lever (Schaffer and Squire 2006) is difficult. How does one adapt other disciplines' methodological canons to law on this topic? Second, affect as a topic for research cuts across what might be termed the current technicisation of legal education – its deployment as outcomes, for example, organised into matrices, gridded into modules. This approach has a place in curriculum thinking, but often says little about the educational 'lifeworld' of situations, communities, actors and interactions. Third, and following on from the first two points, the lack of a recognisable body of research makes a topic relatively invisible, not just to academics and researchers but to funding bodies as well. It is significant that Beyond Text, one of the recent projects in law to focus on affect, was funded by the arts via AHRC (Arts and Humanities Research Council) as part of the funding body's wider Beyond Text initiatives. Fourth, affect itself is problematic because it is often seen as irrational, and antithetical to core Western ideals of rationality. As a result it is under-theorised, and the principal result of this is that legal education has operated principally in the domain of knowledge and reasoning and ignored the effect of feelings, attitudes and values in the learning process.

But what exactly do we mean by affect? What does it comprise? Martin and Briggs (1986), wryly admitting that the phrase 'affective domain' has become a 'catch-all phrase' for aspects of behaviour, list:

> self-concept, motivation, interests, attitudes, beliefs, values, self-esteem, morality, ego development, feelings, need achievement, locus of control, curiosity, creativity, independence, mental health, personal growth, group dynamics, mental imagery, and personality. (Martin and Briggs 1986: 12)

Price, writing on educational technology and affect, defined the subject more generally:

> the affective domain involves the study of emotions: how they are expressed, how they are learned, how they arise, how they are experienced consciously and unconsciously, how they are influenced by and influence behaviour, how they relate to intelligence, language, reason and morality. (Price 1988: 19)

Price could have added that we are born with some of them – it is now accepted that some emotions are not learned but are biologically determined and can be identified across cultures, and in non-human species, too. He could also have noted that the affective domain (as Martin and Briggs' list makes clear) involves much more than the term 'emotion' implies. Nevertheless, his definition is impressively comprehensive, and we have adopted it as the definition of the term that applies to work in this volume. The editors have not sought to impose this definition upon the work of authors (some distinguish between emotion and affect, others treat the terms as interchangeable); but we do believe that in many respects the volume as a whole examines aspects of the domain that are described by Price.

Background to the Book

Around 10 years ago, a group of legal educators shared their disillusionment with some aspects of law learning – the arrival of first-year students, highly motivated, for instance, and their subsequent crash of confidence. The group obtained evidence of this from interviews with students that seemed to parallel critiques of US legal education from the 1980s. In April 2002 an expanded group of us began a three-year research project, known as the 'Gage project',[1] funded by

1 Phineas Gage was perhaps the most famous patient to have survived serious brain damage after an industrial accident. He was a foreman managing a gang of men building railroads in the US in the 1840s. His job was to bore holes in which dynamite was placed. This was then 'tamped' into the hole to push it well down. One day in 1848 the charge

UKCLE (UK Centre for Legal Education). Its brief was to review modern research in the biological and behavioural sciences, to identify any possible influence on theories of adult professional learning and to disseminate findings to the wider legal education community.[2] This was achieved through the UKCLE conference workshops and elsewhere, and resources for the project can be found at www.ukcle.ac.uk/projects/past-projects/maguire/.

From the original workshops of the Gage Project it was clear that there was a growing interest in the subject of affect and emotion, and out of that interest the idea for this book was born. To help crystallise ideas, Maharg and Maughan organised a new conference genre at the 2009 ALT Conference in Amsterdam – a plenary poster workshop where, at the start of the conference, authors presented their ideas via posters in a workshop setting and discussed them with conference participants. From that poster workshop the structure of the book became fairly clear to us. What was also clear, again, was the interest stimulated by the topic.

Structure and Outline of the Book

Part I: Affect, Legal Education and Neuroscience

Teachers involved in adult learning – and perhaps particularly those involved in skills learning – are constantly asking: why does a skilled professional do things in a particular way at a particular time? Professionals themselves can offer some insight into their expertise but are not always able to articulate the tacit action theories they are using. Lately the biological and behavioural sciences have been giving us new insights into the function of brain activity in the learning process. The science is making us rethink some of our socially constructed categories of knowledge. Intelligence for instance was traditionally measured by observations of what happens in terms of observable outputs. Now that we can see much of what is going on inside the brain, the concept of an intelligence quotient as a measure of general intelligence is looking more fluid.

---

exploded while it was being tamped. The three-foot-long tamping iron shot through Phineas' skull, entering under the left cheekbone and exiting through the top of his head. Most of the front part of the left side of his brain was destroyed. Before the accident Gage had been a reliable, sociable, conscientious and popular worker. Afterwards he became 'fitful, irreverent, and grossly profane, … impatient and obstinate, yet capricious and vacillating, unable to settle on any of the plans he devised for future action. His friends said he was "no longer Gage"' (Macmillan 2009). Consequently he was unable to hold down a job. He died in 1861.

2 The project was titled 'Applying Behavioural Science to Legal Education'; group members were Hugh Brayne, Chris Maguire, Caroline Maughan, Mike Maughan and Julian Webb.

Maughan's chapter is at once introduction and a chapter in its own right. She opens with a brief example of the power and accuracy of the emotional brain and briefly summarises some of the recent approaches to research on our emotional selves. She then describes how the affective domain has largely been ignored in higher education (and especially at curriculum design level), in contrast to both primary and secondary education, where it is an integral part of teacher training and practice. She presents evidence from students and from academics (e.g. Peter Goodrich) talking of their experiences of legal education; and she comments on the relative lack of literature in the UK on the subject, in comparison with the research that has been carried out in the last 20 years in US law schools. Maughan argues the case for expanding our horizons in at least three directions: aligning student and tutor expectations, reviewing our attitudes and roles as tutors, and rethinking curriculum design.

Influenced by the matter of the original Gage Project, the editors invited two pieces from neuroscientists – the first (by Richard Roche) a summary of the latest research on brain science, and the second demonstrating the contribution of neuroscience to one aspect of the affective domain (Lorraine Boran's and David Delany's chapter). In addition to demolishing some common myths about the brain, Roche gives us a useful overview of our understanding of brain activity that contradicts many of our accepted linguistic formulations regarding memory. The summary of Elizabeth Loftus' work, and its important consequences for court testimony, calls to mind not just the work of other memory researchers working within the domain of law such as Amina Memon, but also the work of jurists such as Goodrich (1990), Jackson (1995) and Cotterill (2002). His final sections, on emotion and memory, with some practical guidelines arising therefrom, lead neatly to Chapter 2, where Boran and Delany discuss one aspect of the neuroscientific contribution to the study of emotion, namely the literature on self-control. They frame it in terms of 'attentional control' – the brain mechanisms by which we 'filter, process and analyse events'. Their analyses include impulse control, delay of gratification, self-control in academic performance and coping mechanisms (e.g. resilience in the face of stress); and they wind up with a helpful review of attentional training tools arising from neuroscientific literature. Their review holds valuable insights for legal educationalists in the areas of attentional control, fluid intelligence and academic performance.

Part II: Affect and Legal Educators

The second part of the book focuses on law teachers and the affective context within which they live and work. Collier (2002), Cownie (2004) and others have described aspects of this in the lives of academics. Part II opens with a study of a hitherto neglected cadre, namely law teachers at the professional end of legal education – more specifically, those involved as practitioner-supervisors in clinical legal educational programmes (Chandler). The study is, in effect, a pilot for more substantial analysis of this group of legal educators, and it is included here because even at pilot stage it contains insights into the role that affect plays in the professional legal domain. Within her cohort of clinicians, Chandler focuses on how the feelings of clinic supervisors altered as their roles changed from being litigators to becoming educators. She reveals the conflicted role of the clinician and the responses to that of practitioner-supervisors who have, *inter alia*, duties to the client as regards legal service, and duties to the student as regards experience and education; and she describes their coping mechanisms. She points to the conflicted identities of these teachers, working as they do in the inter-tidal zones between the academy and legal practice.

By contrast, Bradney focuses his attention on the research that legal academics carry out, for its own sake, and in his construction of the academic as artist explores the consequences that the relationship between work and art in their lives has for them and others around them. He draws instances from Eliot's *Daniel Deronda*, Charles Lamb, Gabriel García Márquez and Montaigne, and describes some of the 'complexities and contradictions' that are unique to the academic condition. The final chapter in this section analyses what academics think and feel about a single concept, namely quality. Maguire explores the 'field of battle' that quality has become in higher education, quoting Power (1997: 123) to describe its trivial certificates and 'shallow rituals of verification'. Arguing against approaches such as total quality management and adducing Lyotard and Bourdieu, he describes the ritualised nature of quality events. The respondents in his study, though, do not echo the classic critiques of quality cultures: there is a more nuanced approach to the concept. As Maguire points out, what is important, particularly from an affective point of view, is that academics feel the environment is 'safe and supportive'.

Part III: Affect and Learning

Part III opens with Lerner's eloquent critique of the Langdellian orthodoxy in the US. Basing it upon a neuroscience approach together with an analysis of the role of emotions and values in judicial decision-making, Lerner claims that our belief that 'emotions and reason are entirely separate functions' is profoundly mistaken. He traces the research on implicit and explicit memory, citing Damasio and others, to show how our decision-making powers are affected by memory and emotion. He concludes that taking emotion into account is critical for the teaching process.

Del Mar, reaching the same conclusion, comes to it from a direction that is more jurisprudential and language-based, referencing the Hart/Fuller debate, Austinian approaches to speech acts and the like. Analysing the relation between understanding and imagination, and proceeding from the inherent ambiguity of language, he argues that imagination is critical to creative and active exploration of concepts, not least legal concepts; and that affect is integral to imagination. He puts this to the test in the second part of his chapter by taking the example of 'concerted action' in the domain of competition law. As he puts it, 'The life of the law is, to a great extent, about the emotional life of a community; about its emotional relationships, its troubles and temptations, its conflicts and forms of resolving them'. Del Mar finishes with some examples of what 'affective teaching' might be, drawing upon the work of Andy Clark, Martha Nussbaum and others.

Ferris and Huxley-Binns take a slightly different line, arguing for the hypothesis that 'legal education is most effective and enjoyable when reason and emotion co-operate'. Drawing upon the work of Harry Frankfurt, Damasio and the body of literature on law school distress that has been developed in the US, they focus on the issue of (quoting Frankfurt) 'what to care about'. The process is not simply cognitive: as they put it, 'reason without purpose is not a viable proposition'. In doing so they claim that Frankfurt can give teachers a way of understanding how to transfer the positive effects of educational initiatives such as clinic to elsewhere in the curriculum. The result of not paying attention to what students might care about, and more generally in not paying attention to affect, they argue, is evident in the research on student distress in the US. Their summary of the self-determination literature and cognitive evaluation theory points to interesting possibilities for the use of affect in the classroom: as they put it, 'what we care about determines both what we do and how we feel about it'.

Webb takes another tack. Starting on varieties of classrooms where students engage in activities from the visual and performing arts, he calls for the realisation of '*humane* professionalism' through student-centred curricula and methods of learning. He also argues for an embodied approach that will refocus students on 'actively caring about what they are learning, and its consequences', not least because (quoting Prinz) 'emotions command attention and facilitate memory'. He proposes pointers to improving the situation – helping students to think somatically, so that they reason better and care about what they are learning, providing experiential and clinical opportunities for students in the law school curriculum; and the use of performance-based learning. Throughout his chapter there is an emphasis on the social aspects of legal learning, and the shift from teacher-centred activities to student and student-group activities.

Barton and Westwood's chapter gives examples of Webb's embodied approach, and the role that affect plays in the development of professional character. They note the relationship between personal value system and professional value system, observing that this has been a theme in recent work on legal education, such as the Carnegie Report on Legal Education (2007). Their chapter offers a model for the development of professional character through social learning, where students work in 'firms' on transactions and other tasks, and updates earlier work carried out on this approach.

Duncan begins his chapter with a graphic illustration of ethics in practice, and the values that underpinned the choices made by the respondents to an ethical issue. His chapter analyses the part that emotion plays in ethical choices made by law professionals and students. He notes how the division of undergraduate and postgraduate legal programmes in England and Wales (and other jurisdictions in the UK, too) has too often stranded the study of ethics in the professional stage, where the dominant approach has been a 'didactic, code-compliance approach'. He outlines alternative methods in use and, drawing upon neuroscientific as well as more classical experimental literature, he points out how powerful the role of empathy can be in the learning of ethics, though acknowledging it is not without its problems. Emphasising the place of moral courage in the development of ethics, he concludes by outlining approaches that use affect in the curriculum.

In the final chapter of the book Maharg outlines an approach to curriculum design less as a process of building modules and knowledge structures and more as the creation of spaces, gaps and absences. Drawing on music and approaches to text and narrative such as *rezeptionaesthetik*, he illustrates through two case studies (one on writing conferences, the other on games and simulations) how affect may be embedded as an integral part of the curriculum by creating space for student dialogue and creativity.

Theme and Variations

If, to adopt a musical metaphor, Price's definition of affect above is our theme and the findings of neuroscience our ground base, the chapters are variations upon both. And indeed the connections between the chapters are many and rich. Boran and Delany's focus on fluid intelligence is useful for most chapters in this book. Their chapter, read in the context of the remarks made about legal practice by Chandler's respondents, point us to the necessity to make more of continuities between the learning experiences of legal education and legal practice.

Attentiveness surfaces as a key component of affect. For Boran and Delany it is critical; Bradney sees it as essential to friendship. Similarly, self-control became a theme in a number of chapters – Ferris and Huxley-Binns, for instance, in their use of Frankfurt's concept of second-order desires, cast an interesting light on the research outlined by Boran and Delany. The relations between acts of choosing and self-determination theory, important to Ferris and Huxley-Binns' chapter, is also the focus of Lerner's. Care and caring as constructs in legal education emerge as critical in a number of chapters (Webb, Ferris and Huxley-Binns). The volume (and this is a deliberate strategy of the editors for the book as a whole) reveal the contact points and continuities between different stages of the legal educational process and between the academy and practice.

Inevitably there are disagreements between authors. Bradney's concept of quality audit as measuring the unmeasurable is contested by the findings of Maguire's study, for instance. But overall what is striking about the chapters is the extent to which they agree on a broad range of approaches, often based upon variants of experiential learning theory that the authors discuss. The book also draws upon practical projects, on a variety of recent projects and initiatives. Del Mar's approach, for instance, is part of the theoretical underpinning of the Beyond Text project at Edinburgh University, which sought to explore extra-textual ways of understanding law and justice, drawn from a variety of visual and performing arts; and Webb draws upon the project in his chapter on embodiment.

These are some ways in which the book can be read by readers. For us editors, reading and re-reading the chapters, the dominant metaphor for the book was of a pressure valve opening. There were more authors who wanted to contribute than we could accommodate in the volume. Much more can be written on the subject, and we are sure that this book is but the first of many to explore the topic. If our book serves to illuminate how important affect is to a broad range of approaches to legal education, and to legal academics as well as law students, then it will have served its pioneering purpose. As Lerner points out, 'If we want our law students to make the most of their cognitive powers, we need to help them understand the power of their emotional minds'. The same applies to staff and staff development.

And it is fitting to draw to a close with a mention of Alan M. Lerner. He was a superb clinician, a wonderful teacher, witty, generous, living in the moment, utterly committed to learning, teaching and its research. He died soon after completing his chapter. This book is dedicated to his memory.

References

Collier, R. 2002. The Changing University and the (Legal) Academic Career: Rethinking the Relationship between Women, Men and the 'Private Life' of the Law School, *Legal Studies* 22(1): 1–32.

Cotterill, J. (ed.) 2002. *Language in the Legal Process*. Basingstoke: Palgrave Macmillan.

Cownie, F. 2004. *Legal Academics: Culture and Identities*. Oxford: Hart Publishing.

Dickens, C. 1999. *Great Expectations*, edited with an introduction by E. Rosenberg. New York: W.W. Norton & Co.

Goodrich, P. 1990. *Languages of Law: From Logics of Memory to Nomadic Masks*. London: Weidenfeld and Nicolson.

Jackson, B.S. 1995. *Making Sense in Law: Linguistic, Psychological and Semiotic Perspectives*. Liverpool: Deborah Charles Publications.

Macmillan, M. 2009. *The Phineas Gage Information Page*. [Online] Available at: http://www.deakin.edu.au/hmnbs/psychology/gagepage/ [accessed 28 October 2010].

Martin, B.L. and Briggs, L.J. 1986. *The Affective and Cognitive Domains: Integration for Instruction and Research*. Englewood Cliffs, NJ: Educational Technology Publications.

Power, M. 1997. *The Audit Society: Rituals of Verification*. Oxford: Oxford University Press.

Price, E.A. 1998. Instructional Systems Design and the Affective Domain, *Educational Technology* 38(6): 17–24.

Schaffer, D.W. and Squire, K.D. 2006. The Pasteurization of Education, in *Technology and Education: Issues in Administration, Policy, and Applications in K12 Schools, Advances in Educational Administration*, Vol. 8, edited by S.Y. Tettegah and R.C. Hunter. Oxford: Elsevier.

PART I
Affect, Legal Education and Neuroscience

Chapter 1
Why Study Emotion?[1]

Caroline Maughan

How Your Mind Makes Decisions without You: The Story of Lieutenant Commander Michael Riley[2]

It is early morning on 24 February 1991. Michael Riley is monitoring the radar screens on the British destroyer HMS Gloucester. He's been staring at blips all night. Suddenly a new radar trace appears on the screen. There's something about it that makes him suspicious. It seems to be heading straight for a battleship in a Coalition convoy located within 20 miles of the Kuwait coast. Is it an Iraqi missile? Or is it one of those A6 American jet fighters which fly regularly in that same airspace? His heart's racing, his palms are clammy. If it's a missile, Riley needs to act on his fear and shoot it down immediately to prevent the deaths of hundreds of sailors. But what if it's an American plane? Riley gives the order to fire, the target is hit.

On debriefing, Riley said he knew it was a missile. He was used to watching A6 jets, and this blip just didn't feel right. However, later analysis of the radar tapes showed it was impossible to distinguish between a missile and an A6 blip. So what made Riley act as he did?

Detailed analysis of the tapes by a cognitive psychologist 20 or so years later eventually yielded the secret: timing. The planes and the missiles flew at different altitudes, which meant that a missile trace would have appeared on the screen eight seconds after an A6 one. Without knowing he was doing so, Riley was assessing the altitude of the blip. Hence his panic when he stared at this scary thing on the screen – it just didn't feel like an A6.

But how did Riley unconsciously distinguish the apparently identical blips? What was happening in his brain to cause his fear?

Brain cells communicate with one another via neurotransmitters, one of which is dopamine. It was most probably Riley's dopamine neurons that told him the blip was a missile. Dopamine is known as the brain chemical which produces

---

1 The sources of material for some of this chapter were sessions run at UK conferences 2000–4 in collaboration with Mike Maughan, Julian Webb, Chris Maguire, Berni Bell and Hugh Brayne. My thanks to them for permission to use these materials.

2 An incident of the first Gulf War, adapted from Lehrer (2009: 34–41).

feelings of happiness. It does more than that, however – it helps to regulate all our emotions:

> It is the common neural currency of the mind, the molecule that helps us decide among alternatives. By looking at how dopamine works inside the brain, we can see why feelings are capable of providing deep insights. While Plato disparaged emotions as irrational and untrustworthy – the wild horses of the soul – they actually reflect an enormous amount of invisible analysis. (Lehrer 2009: 40–41)

When things don't go according to plan and something unexpected turns up, like the slightly odd radar blip, the dopamine cells stop firing and instead send a strong alert signal to the neocortex, the thinking part of the brain. At that point the brain emits a powerful emotion: surprise, shock, fear, panic; adrenaline pours into the bloodstream, your pulse races, your heart thumps, your palms sweat. In other words, your mind forces you to take notice and act immediately. It didn't feel like an A6, so Riley did what felt right – he gave the order to fire.

The point here is that this hits you as a feeling, not a process of reasoning. Let's imagine you are in your car, overtaking on a narrow road. Suddenly a car is coming straight towards you at speed. To avoid the crash you have to make a split-second decision. The conscious part of your brain can't possibly take in all the information necessary for you to take avoiding action; by the time it has, it's too late. Fortunately, your emotional brain will have assessed the situation and the alternatives to enable you to make a decision long before you are even aware there's a problem (Le Doux 1998: 163–5; Blakemore and Frith 2005: 178). Your implicit kinaesthetic memory – the totality of your awareness of the things around you – has solved the problem for you.

These errors of expectation which generate the fear responses are translated into long-term lessons – a crucial aspect of decision-making. As Lehrer says, our brains incorporate the lessons of the past into our future decision-making; if this were not the case, then we would be endlessly repeating our mistakes:

> We can now begin to understand the surprising wisdom of our emotions. The activity of our dopamine neurons demonstrates that feelings aren't simply reflections of hard-wired animal instincts. Those wild horses aren't acting on a whim. Instead human emotions are rooted in the highly flexible brain cells, which are constantly adjusting their connections to reflect reality. Every time you make a mistake or encounter something new, your brain cells are busy changing themselves. Our emotions are deeply empirical. (2009: 46)[3]

3 Lehrer cites physicist Niels Bohr's definition of an expert: 'a person who has made all the mistakes that can be made in a very narrow field' to stress how important it is to develop the capacity to learn from one's mistakes. He cites psychologist Carol Dweck's experiments with school children in New York, which showed that those who were praised for being 'smart' began to see their mistakes as signs of stupidity and were reluctant to take

Of course this is not to say that our emotional brain always gets it right. Our emotions have evolved to play the percentages; over the millennia our emotional responses have got us out of trouble often enough to enable us to pass them on through our genes. In contrast, our cognition is able to work in the here and now, to evaluate present situations in terms of what's happened before and how that fits with what we should do now. For example, if I have a row with my boss, I have a choice: I can succumb to the 'fight or flight' emotional response (hit him, or run away) or I can take some time to consider the situation rationally.

It is perhaps counter-intuitive to imagine that emotions may be essential to rational thinking and decision-making. Nevertheless, brain science seems to be telling us that pure reason is a myth. We are not the rational beings we think we are. The evolutionary expansion of the frontal cortex has not turned us into rational, dispassionate, deliberative beings. A large part of our frontal cortex is involved with emotion; reason and emotion are co-dependent.

Much of the work in this area involves the study of brain-damaged patients. One day in 1982 neurologist Antonio Damasio began to treat a patient called Elliot. Elliot had had a small tumour removed from the front of his brain, in the neocortex. He was found to be incapable of making any decision; if he wanted to eat out, he would look carefully at menus, seating plans, lighting arrangements. He would even drive to each restaurant to have a look at it – but still couldn't decide which one to eat at. Yet his intellect was in all other respects normal. Damasio records: 'I never saw a tinge of emotion in my many hours of conversation with him: no sadness, no impatience, no frustration' (1994: 41). Damasio attached Elliot to a machine which would measure sweat gland activity in his palms. He showed him photos which would normally arouse an emotional response such as a naked woman, a severed foot, a gun. No response, no sweaty palms. Elliot felt nothing.

Damasio's work with Elliot and similar patients showed that the function of the part of Elliot's brain that was missing connects the emotional brain centres with the thinking part of the brain. When the connection is severed, so that we can't grasp our emotions, we don't know what to think and so can't make up our minds about anything.

---

on harder tasks for fear of making mistakes and appearing not so smart after all. In contrast, those who were praised for their effort were more willing to take risks and persevere with harder tasks. They saw their mistakes as the building blocks of knowledge and wanted to understand and learn from them. As Lehrer notes:

> the problem with praising kids for their innate intelligence … is that it misrepresents the neural reality of education. It encourages kids to avoid the most useful kind of learning activities, which is learning from mistakes. Unless you experience the unpleasant symptoms of being wrong, your brain will never revise its models. Before your neurons can succeed, they must repeatedly fail. There are no shortcuts for this painstaking process (2009: 57).

Carol Dweck's work is discussed later in this chapter.

The Historical Separation of Cognition and Emotion

If it is true that we cannot reason without emotions or feelings, the accepted wisdom of centuries will have been turned on its head. Historically in Western culture emotion has been split from cognition. Early philosophers divided mental processes into three separate parts – affect, cognition and conation (feeling, knowing and willing). Kant noted 'Pure reason corresponds to intellect or cognition, practical reason to will, action or conation, and judgment to feeling pleasure or pain, hence affection' (cited in Hilgard 1980: 109). Plato viewed human emotion as a potentially out of control chariot, held in check by its driver, the intellect.[4] The French mathematician and philosopher Descartes, on declaring '*Cogito ergo sum*', asserted a sharp separation of the mind from the body and decisively influenced modern science. The mind, he maintained, is indivisible, insubstantial and permanent. The body, on the other hand, is subject to the mind, is divisible into its component parts and is subject to the ravages of mortality (Descartes 1641/1967).[5]

The Romantics took the mind–body division for granted, albeit that they saw the emotions as the 'source of wisdom, innocence, authenticity and creativity' and reason as potentially repressive:

> the emotions come from nature and live in the body. They are hot, irrational impulses and intuitions, which follow the imperatives of biology. The intellect comes from civilisation and lives in the mind. It is a cool deliberator that follows the interest of self and society by keeping the emotions in check. (Pinker 1998: 369)[6]

In the 20th century, Freud believed he saw several 'ghosts in the machine'.[7] Indeed the whole thrust of psychoanalysis is to discover the nature of the ghost to see why and how it is damaging us. The mind–body dualism is evident in classifications

---

4 Plato describes the horse which represents emotions as 'of an ignoble breed. He has a short bull neck, a pug nose, black skin, and bloodshot white eyes; companion to wild boasts and indecency, he is shaggy around the ears – deaf as a post – and just barely yields to horsewhip and goad combined' (cited in Lehrer 2009: 17).

5 Cited in Popkin (1967). Where has this led? Can we see this dualism in the distinction between academic and vocational studies? Or in the conceptual separation of knowledge and behaviour in skills learning?

6 The Romantic movement bucked the trend in stressing emotion as central to how we experience the world and respond to it. Moreover, the separation of affect from cognition had not gone unchallenged. Enlightenment thinkers Hume, Reid and Adam Smith saw emotion as working with reason and consequently as deserving of study and classification. See Smith (1759), in which he proposed that emotions were the thread that wove the fabric of society together: noted by Evans (2001: xi).

7 The philosopher Gilbert Ryle coined this expression to ridicule the notion that mental states can be separated from physical states (Ryle 1949).

such as his 'id' and 'ego', and more recent neuromythologies such as 'left brain' and 'right brain' hemispheres (Pinker 1998: 370).

In mid-20th-century psychology, duality persisted in various forms; the behaviourists emphasised observable behaviour, rejecting subjective inner states of mind such as emotion, intention and perceptions as areas incapable of investigation. The behaviourist model of learning focused on changing or conditioning observable behaviour through repeated practice and reinforcement. Rather, the mind is a blank slate[8] waiting to be crammed with knowledge transferred from expert to novice – an essentially teacher-controlled approach which renders students passive and dependent.

In contrast, cognitivists explored the inner processes of the mind, but with an almost exclusive emphasis on cognition to the exclusion of the emotions. The cognitivist paradigm replaced behaviourism as the dominant influence in the latter part of the 20th century.[9]

More recently still, cognitive psychologists developed the idea of the mind as a computer. Whilst their research led to important work in the field of artificial

---

8 The *tabula rasa* metaphor is thought to have originated with John Locke in the 17th century. It proposes a view of human nature which is entirely constructed by the relationship of the individual with their environment. This empiricist approach was influential in British and American intellectual movements in the late 19th and early 20th centuries, such as social constructionism (Durkheim 1895/1962) and social Darwinism (Pinker 2002: 15–17). Later, in 1974, behaviourist psychologist B.F. Skinner wrote that 'studying the brain was just another misguided quest to find the causes of behaviour inside the organism rather than out in the world' (Pinker 2002: 20). These intellectual threads have had a profound influence on educational policy and theories about teaching and learning; are we seeing the *tabula rasa* view operating when tutors suggest to new law students that they need to stop thinking in ways they had formally been used to thinking and start learning how to 'think like a lawyer'?

Similarly, if you take an exercise as ordinary and straightforward as a legal problem in which there are two parties and where the student is asked to advise one of the parties, we can see the influences of behaviourism. That is to say that the stimulus of presenting a properly formed legal problem will elicit the response of applying the appropriate legal rules and knowledge to the situation so that the student will arrive at an appropriate solution. We might also see in this more than a hint of social constructionism: we enjoin our students to ignore their previous experience, because the ways in which they need to think and reach conclusions have already been developed (socially constructed by legal educators). It only remains for them to adopt this way of discoursing to become effective lawyers.

9 The cognitivist paradigm is a very broad one, encompassing aspects of the mind to do with attention, language and development, memory, perception. It is often associated with constructivism – a learning theory generally attributed to Jean Piaget – which is highly influential in adult learning today. Learning is seen as a process of change and development rather than mere knowledge acquisition. Learners create meaning for themselves from new information by applying and relating it to previously acquired knowledge; in other words, a deep understanding of subject matter is acquired from knowledge construction and transformation rather than information absorption and accumulation.

intelligence, researchers largely sidestepped the emotions because these would need to be simulated.[10]

The 20th-century reluctance to study emotion is summed up by Damasio:

> Throughout most of the twentieth century emotion was not trusted in the laboratory. Emotion was too subjective, it was said. Emotion was too illusive and vague. Emotion was at the opposite end from reason, easily the finest human ability, and reason was presumed to be entirely independent from emotion. In the end, not only was emotion not rational, even studying it was probably not rational. (1999: 55)

A substantial body of research is now contributing to the decline of the mind–body dualism. A variety of theories of the mind have been proposed and debated, based on brain research and borrowing from a range of disciplines in the biological, behavioural and social sciences.[11] The modern view seems to be that it is the synergy of reason and emotion rather than reason alone that helps us set our goals. As social psychologist Robert Emmons notes:

> It is clear … that goal-directed action cannot be understood apart from affect … at a minimum, affect is related to goals in the following ways: it plays a role in determining one's commitment to goals; it energizes goal-directed behaviour; and it serves as feedback informing a person of the status of their goals. (1996: 313, cited in Turner et al. 2002: 79)

What modern thinking is telling us is that there is no reasoning without an emotional framework of goals and sub-goals; and there is no effective expression of emotion (except in life-threatening situations) if it is not regulated by our powers of reason (Pinker 1998: 373).

If our emotional selves are so much part of our whole being, surely learning can be no different. If it is not, then how should we take account of the affective in our

10 But note the relatively new field of 'affective computing'; see, for example, Picard (2000).

11 See, for example, sociologist J. Barbalet: 'all actions, and indeed reason itself, require appropriate facilitating emotions if successful action or reason at all are to be achieved. How could a person deal competently with any practical problem without the emotion of confidence in their actions, without the emotion of trust in the actions of enabling others, without the feeling of dissatisfaction with failure to encourage success, without the envy of competitors to spur the pursuit of interests, and so on' (2002: 1). On emotion theory in philosophy Ronald de Sousa offers a helpful introduction (2007); see also Evans 2001; also a review by Jesse Prinz which compares evolutionary psychology and social constructionism perspectives of emotion and proposes a unified theory on the basis that emotions are 'fundamentally alike', the product of both nature and nurture (in Evans and Cruse 2004: 69–87). For emotion theory in psychology see for example Richard Lazarus (1991); also social psychologists Robert Zajonc (1980) and Robert Emmons (1996).

teaching and learning strategies? How can we provide the environment which will allow all learners the opportunity to attain their individual goals in a way which is motivating, exciting and satisfying? And to what extent have professional and higher education acknowledged the role played by emotion in formal learning?

The Exclusion of the Affective Domain in Higher Education

In higher education the role of emotions in learning has largely been ignored and certainly under-theorised. Yet all participants in the educational process recognise, both explicitly and implicitly, the significance of the non-cognitive and its influence on student learning and behaviour.[12] Our experience tells us that highly motivated students tend to do better; that as our student numbers are rising, feelings of isolation and insecurity are on the increase; that today's students are assessment-driven more than ever before; that some students, turned off by law early on in their studies, become bored, lose motivation; that fear of failure can lower self-confidence and self-esteem.[13]

Any group of tutors, discussing any group of students, will predictably spend some of the time discussing personality, attitudes and demeanour as well as intellectual ability. In a recent workshop undergraduate law teachers were asked to list the characteristics of 'good' and 'weak' students. Attributes and qualities listed were by no means confined to cognitive abilities, indicating the extent to which we rely on affective issues when making judgements about students:

'Good' Student	**'Weak' student**
Interested	Lazy
Motivated	Uncommunicative
Intellectually able	Never there
Conscientious	Unreflective
Working to their full potential	Cannot cope with the course
Able to engage with people and issues	Uninterested
Prepared	Lacks motivation
Enthusiastic	Passive consumer
Reflective	Too easily distracted

12 See, for example, Brayne: 'Such recognition is in fact implicit in the work of all good law teachers: when they try to motivate the students, try to challenge them, getting them to role play, try to grab attention with exciting information, they are appealing for an emotional response, a response which can become a launching pad for the emergence of the intellectual response' (2002: 297).

13 The importance of self-esteem is explained in evolutionary terms by Nigel Nicholson: 'the idea of failure strikes at our most vital interests. Among social creatures, failing publicly, or being seen as a failure, is one of the most threatening kinds of loss' (2000: 151).

Wouldn't rather be somewhere else
Goes beyond what we give them
Gains something from being there
Is subject to inappropriate peer pressure
Disruptive[14]

Moreover, much tutor time is spent writing references for their students to satisfy the recipient's interest in areas other than propositional knowledge.

The role of affect has long been recognised in primary and secondary education. In professional and higher education we accept that cognition and behaviour are inter-related; we see the former as informing the latter. We assess cognitive ability through the products of our students' behaviour (essays, presentations, exams, etc.). However, the affective domain has traditionally been ignored at the curriculum design level. When we come to look at the formal design of our programmes we seek in vain for mention of those aspects of humanity which are not in the realm of understanding and manipulating propositional reasoning. While the development and assessment of cognitive abilities have become highly formalised, feeling and emotion remain the private business of the learner and of any tutor who cares to engage with them.

It is not hard to see why:

1. Affect has no place in the academy. Dominated by Cartesian dualism, universities traditionally regarded themselves as centres of pure rationality, their purpose being the objective and dispassionate search for truth (Leathwood and Hey 2009: 429). Modern echoes of this position are evident in the opinions of, for example, Furedi, and Ecclestone and Hayes, who warn of an increasing 'therapy culture' in higher education which threatens the academy's detached pursuit of truth (Furedi 2003; Ecclestone and Hayes 2009). These arguments are strongly resisted by Leathwood and Hey, amongst others:

14 That some teachers blame students for their lack of motivation and poor performance is noted in the educational literature, for example:

> there are two kinds of [weak students]: the downright indolent [or those who put efforts into other than academic work] and … Some not very well motivated; he takes the courses largely because he likes other courses even less. He may be doing his degree on that basis … Only attending university because there's nothing else more intelligent occurred to him to do (Marton et al., cited by Entwhistle in Brown et al. 1998: 15).

See also Hativa (2002); and Rubin Henderson: 'Rather than consider how law school practices mesh with student goals, experiences, and abilities, some claim the real problem is law students' sense of entitlement, lack of work ethic and generally whiny attitude' (2003: 50). Studies suggest it is teachers who use an information transmission approach and have a limited view of how teaching affects learning who shift the blame in this way (see for example Van Driel, Verloop, Van Werven et al. 1997: 105–22). The blame-the-student attitude has been noted, too, by this author at conferences.

> Both resistance to the affective turn in HE and resistance to the incursion of the masses draw on a discourse of dumbing down, a pollution of the ivory tower, and evoke a powerful binary: purity/danger, pristine/contaminated, rational/irrational. … Fear, threat and the mourning of and yearning for, a lost world of higher education (in which women and others had no place) infuse a moral panic about declining standards. (2009: 435)

2. Affect is hard to incorporate into a learning programme. With the cognitive domain we are very experienced and have all kinds of methods for teaching and measuring its outputs.
3. Affect is hard to pin down, categorise or put into learning outcomes. As Yorke and Knight point out:

> Learning in higher education seems to have taken something of a rational-instrumental turn in recent years, with notions of self and emotion being backgrounded. This may be related to the skills-based instrumentalism being encouraged by governments that press human capital theory upon their higher educational systems, to the detriment of the conception of 'learning as growing as a person'. A 'learning outcomes' approach to higher education seems to risk underemphasizing the importance of the personal dimension of student learning, in that the focus veers towards the delivery of measurable task outcomes. (2004: 34)

4. Affect is difficult to measure. The package of attitudes, values and feelings varies from one individual to another and influences successful learning outcomes, whilst the aims of assessment are usually normative. Can or should we be 'assessing' the affective domain in order to rank individuals?
5. Affect threatens to alter the tutor's role, forcing us to deal with aspects of the learner we may be uncomfortable with. We are not trained or equipped to play the role of counsellor.
6. Affect threatens the primacy of propositional knowledge and the ponderous reasoning system that underpins it. Affect is more akin to intuition, gut feeling. These kinds of tacit knowledge are difficult, impossible and unnecessary to reason through slowly and deliberately – hence the use of the word 'ponderous'. Propositional knowledge is typically seen as something we spread on virgin ground to bring forth the fruits of understanding; what is to be learned is seen as something largely outside ourselves. However, if we agree that learning is about how we construct the world, then that is as much to do with our feelings and our attitudes as it is to do with what we know. My intention here is not to denigrate the importance of propositional knowledge – unlike unconscious knowledge it is a valuable means of categorising and understanding the exterior world. Nevertheless

> it represents only a threshold or starting point for an individual learner who has to internalise it and personalise it in order to fit it into their frameworks of understanding.

So we collude in avoiding discussion of the affective domain in course and assessment design, and all too often in delivery, too. Add to this the historical separation of the cognitive from the affective and we have in place a collective mindset which confers prestige on the cognitive and either ignores or throws up despairing hands at the affective. Is this true of legal education, too, or do law teachers take account of affect's influence on learning?

The Student Experience of Law School

> 'Before I started the degree I thought I'd enjoy every single part of law that I studied. In fact, over the 3 years I've enjoyed about 50% of it. About half of it I've found, in all truth, slightly mundane. And that's one of the main shocks I've had from the law degree. I thought I'd enjoy it all'.
>
> 'I knew it was going to be hard work, but I expected to come out knowing about law, knowing everything I needed to know. But I know nothing. I reckon I could do the course ten times over and still not know enough'.
>
> 'If I'm honest and I could turn back the clock, I'd probably have done a different degree. What makes it a struggle is the thought that you always have at the back of your head: it's the 2:1 profession, it's the elite profession. It's how well you do and where you come from. I think you always have that at the back of your head and that's always there. It's not really the degree, it's the whole profession ...'
>
> 'The attitude of the teachers is a key thing. Their attitude to the subject and their attitude to you. You can see the ones who don't want to be there and it's really obvious, and yet if they're there and excited, then that's the best you can get'.[15]

Those students came to law with enthusiasm, excitement, interest and determination. They were very clear about their intentions and goals, as many of our students are. Of course, I am by no means saying that all experiences of learning law are negative. What I am suggesting is that we have a system that satisfies only *some* of our students. So what is it about our institutions, our programmes, our teaching and learning strategies and our students that makes studying law a stultifying, demotivating and disaffecting experience for a number of them? And thinking back ... how was it for you?

Peter Goodrich recalls what could only be described as a crushing of the spirit:

15 Taken from interviews with third-year UK law students.

> Law school stole my hopes of change and robbed me of any surviving sense of the relevance of my inner world, of poetry, desire or dream, to the life of the institution. My experience of law school was the denial of the relevance of my experience of law school. The irony of that paradox, of the experience of repression as a mode of knowing, of the embodiment of denial as a mode of being, is the secret of the school's success as a rite of reproduction: an institutionally managed trauma gives birth to a conforming or believing soul. (1996: 59)

At a rather more mundane level – though it didn't seem at all mundane at the time – I can recall the feeling of elation when after a long struggle with contract law it finally began to sink in and 'come together' in time for the end-of-year exam. I thought myself lucky – some fellow students didn't get it in time, and possibly never did. Some 'got it' sufficiently to get through the exam, then promptly forgot it. From time to time we students doubted our ability to 'see the wood for the trees',[16] but there were so many trees.[17] Our capacity for understanding was being undermined by an approach to learning best described as absorb-rote-learn-regurgitate, which placed emphasis on the rules at the expense of the concepts and completely ignored the economic and social foundations of the subject.

I admit to being long in the tooth and this was quite a while ago, however it is sad to note that the 'banking' approach[18] identified by Paolo Freire in the 1970s has yet to be banished entirely from UK undergraduate legal education. I suppose we should not be surprised if heavy workloads, large student numbers, seven core subjects to 'cover', commodification of learning and a culture of instrumentalism generally in UK university education combine to crush teachers' spirits and curb their enthusiasm and imagination (Bleackley 1998: 166). So it should be no surprise to us if students lose theirs.

To date there appears to be a distinct lack of interest and research in the UK on the affective side of studying law. In contrast, the US literature reflects a concern about the psychological distress of law students and lawyers in practice that goes back at least as far as the 1980s.[19] Legal education as an attack on self is vividly described below:

> I dreamed that it was the first day of school, and all the first-year law students were invited to a big picnic on a lovely sloping lawn outside the law school. The grills were fired up, frisbees were flying, it was a beautiful fall day. We were all aware that, one by one, our classmates were being taken into the building,

16 A common criticism made of law students by their teachers.

17 Cp Kennedy (1982: 54): 'the trade-school mentality, the endless attention to trees at the expense of forests ...'.

18 'in which the scope of action allowed to the students extends only as far as receiving, filing and storing of the deposits' (Freire 1974: 58).

19 See Ferris and Huxley-Binns, Chapter 9 this volume, for a more detailed review of US law school experience.

> but we were not at all clear about what was going on inside. There might have been a slight sense of unease and anxiety about the goings-on inside, but mostly we were all enjoying the sunshine and fresh air. I was approached by someone who told me it was my turn to go in. I went, apprehensive but willing. I was escorted to a small room, squarish, with a tall window facing into a basement window well. There was a small desk that filled most of the room. I was seated in a chair on the side of the desk and put my arm on the desk, almost as though I were to have blood drawn. A professor, a gruff man, asked me a question about interpretation of contracts. Having had no previous legal training or background, I simply said I didn't know the answer. The professor nodded and smiled, and then chopped my arm off. Then I was ushered out of the room. (An American law student quoted in Iijima 1998: 524)

Scott Turow describes damaging effects of law school in his memoir *One L*:

> They're turning me into someone else … they're making me different.
>
> [the students] … were limited, harmed, by the education, forced to substitute dry reason for emotion, to cultivate opinions which were 'rational' but which had no roots in experience, the life they'd had before. They were being cut away from themselves …

And thinking like a lawyer, a process of logic and reason which suppresses emotion:

> is a grimly literal, linear, step-by-step process of thought, makes one suspicious and distrustful. (Turow 1977, cited in Elkins 1985: 30–31)

In requiring new students to develop the capacity to 'think like lawyers' we deny the value of their previous experience and in so doing may alienate them from their values and ideals, suggests Bethany Rubin Henderson. Furthermore, there is no consensus on what this concept actually means (2003: 49). In a review of empirical and anecdotal evidence of the 'dark side' of US law school education, Lawrence Krieger (2002), confirming the experience of those of us in the UK who experience 'the undoing' of our students' collective energy, enthusiasm, and engagement after only a few months of law school, offers an explanation:

> Thinking 'like a lawyer' – defining people (or 'parties') primarily according to their legal rights, and trying to understand, prevent, or resolve problems by linear application of legal rules to those rights, usually adopting a zero-sum competitive approach to outcomes. This process requires the closest scrutiny of spoken and written thought to identify any defect that may undermine an adversary's position or create future problems for one's client. Thinking 'like a lawyer' is fundamentally negative; it is critical, pessimistic, and depersonalising. It is a damaging paradigm in law schools because it is usually conveyed, and

> understood, as a new and superior way of thinking, rather than an important but strictly limited legal tool. (2002: 117)[20]

Trained to 'think like lawyers' and act as agents for others, students risk 'losing contact with their authentic selves' (2002: 119).

As a consequence of absorbing the culture of competition, what starts out as high intrinsic motivation – desire for personal growth and fulfilment, to build strong relationships, doing work you enjoy and believe in – may swiftly switch to more extrinsically motivated goals and values: 'acting for reasons outside of oneself, such as to relieve guilt or anxiety, please others, or gain rewards' (2002: 121–2) with their attendant loss of satisfaction, security and well-being.

If some law schools uphold – consciously or unconsciously – the competitive paradigm that stresses individual effort at the expense of community and collaboration, if they fail to recognise the degree to which learning is a social process, then we should not be surprised if some individuals feel isolated.[21] We know that building supportive relationships with peers and tutors will increase positive affect, but high staff–student ratios and large classes, particularly in year one, can make it difficult if not impossible for tutors to know their students' names, let alone form any kind of meaningful relationship with them.[22] Recently, two first-year students reported:

---

20 The limitations of the Socratic case-dialogue method are noted by the Carnegie Foundation for the Advancement of Teaching:

> the process of enabling students to 'think like lawyers' takes place not only in a compressed period of time but primarily through the medium of a single form of teaching: the case-dialogue method. Compared to other professional fields, which often employ multiple forms of teaching through a more prolonged socialization process, legal pedagogy is remarkably uniform across variations in schools and student bodies. With the exception of a few schools, the first-year curriculum is similarly standardized, as is the system of competitive grading that accompanies the teaching and learning practices associated with case dialogue. The consequence is a striking conformity in outlook and habits of thought among legal graduates (Sullivan et al. 2007: 7).

21 Educationist Frank Coffield notes two current models/metaphors of learning: the acquisition metaphor – common in formal education settings – where learning is focused on the individual gaining knowledge, skills, qualifications, the 'direct result of teaching which is seen as a simple, technical process' and the participative metaphor, which shifts the focus from the individual to learning through participating in communities of practice: 'groups of people informally bound together by shared expertise and passion for a joint enterprise' (Wenger and Snyder 2000: 139). Key words for this model are community, identity, meaning, practice, dialogue, co-operation and belonging. 'Learning is viewed as a process of participation in a variety of social worlds' (Coffield 2008: 8–9).

22 This can produce negative outcomes for both intrinsically and extrinsically motivated students – the latter whose goals are centred around making useful contacts, earning the respect of their tutors, cue-seeking for good grades, getting the best possible reference, etc.

> It seems like unless you're in trouble and you actually make an effort to go and see someone, you don't have any individual personal contact with a lecturer or a tutor … you don't go and see them unless you're in trouble, do you, you don't go and see them because you feel like you're doing well. The onus is on you to approach them and if you are feeling down, you might not even make that contact – I felt like I'd lost my way with the work, and confidence – I was still doing the work, I was still motivated, but it just wasn't going that well, really …

> If you never came for 3 months no one would know.

This is disheartening stuff for law teachers and their institutions. Since it is beyond argument that our teaching generates affective responses whether we intend it or not, and that we and our students are well aware of this, what ways are there, as the old song goes, to 'accentuate the positive and eliminate the negative'?

Reviewing our Attitudes and our Practice

In the educational literature of the last decade or so there has been a move away from teachers' perspectives towards a welcome emphasis on how students learn. This has come about in part because of the scarcity of resources to cope effectively with the massification of higher education and a corresponding anxiety about our ability to continue to offer high-quality learning. With some exceptions, analysis of the theories of emotion that underpin student-centred pedagogies is lacking (Beard, Clegg and Smith 2007; Varlander 2008). However, for some researchers, focusing on the student experience has inevitably brought with it recognition of the importance of the affective domain. It is now widely accepted that students' worries and fears about studying are not necessarily only to do with course content; often they are about motivation, feelings about self-esteem, self-efficacy, fear of failure, security, fitting in, well-being, boredom, and so on.

When reviewing our practice there are two things I would like us to bear in mind. First, motivation is critical.[23] Motivation to learn is a fundamental human drive. It sits firmly in the affective domain, influencing the learner's behaviour through a dynamic interaction between perceptions of self and reading of context. It is motivation which underpins everything I am going on to discuss. As Vygotsky explains, it is the first step in the process that shapes our thoughts and ultimately our actions:

23 Is it part of our job to motivate students? 'Whether or not staff believe it is their job to motivate students, research findings make it very clear that their ways of teaching and designing assessment will, nevertheless, have strong influences on student motivation. And these ways of teaching and assessing reflect lecturers' beliefs about the nature of teaching and learning' (Marton, Hounsell and Entwhistle 1997: 20).

> Thought has its origins in the motivating sphere of consciousness, a sphere that includes our inclinations and needs, our interests and impulses, and our affect and emotion. The affective and volitional tendency stands behind thought. Only here do we find the answer to the final 'why' in the analysis of thinking. (Cited in Rieber and Carton 1987: 282)[24]

Second, we cannot ignore the wider context in which we operate. This will doubtless influence any action we might want to take. Clearly there are key factors that impinge on our ability to change and develop our approaches to teaching and learning: the climate of our institution and our relationship with the professions, for example. Others are tutor workload, resources, student numbers, management styles. Our influence in these arenas is not great and change is more likely to come about through collective micro-political action. Nevertheless, there are arenas in which we as tutors can influence what is done and how it is done. So what ways might we find to expand our own and our students' horizons which could offer a more pleasurable and satisfying experience for everybody?

Expanding Horizons (1): Align Student and Tutor Expectations?

We know students have different reasons and motivations for entering law school, different learning preferences, and different levels of ability. However, once they are with us, it is the levels of ability that we tend to concentrate on. This 'one size fits all' approach deals predominantly and almost exclusively, in the formal sense, with cognition – we focus on grades and rank, ordering students according to intellectual ability, yet we know that affective issues such as motivation, confidence, well-being and security have a major influence on successful learning. Our students' individualised packages of expectations and wide variety of experiences form the basis of their intrinsic motivation to learn law. How, then, can we sustain this intrinsic motivation?

As noted earlier, some teachers put the blame for poor motivation squarely on the shoulders of the student. It seems these teachers see motivation as a fixed trait: some students are highly motivated, others are not. However, research tells us that it is a lot more complex than that. Nor is motivation determined only by extrinsic factors; on the contrary, it is influenced by what students perceive as important to them based on their needs, values and what they think they can accomplish. This in turn is influenced by their expectations of success or failure. If this is so, are there opportunities to engage in dialogue with students about their aspirations, goals, fears, anxieties? Might they welcome discussion with us about their learning experiences, their learning preferences, their expectations of tutors, challenges to their values presented by the study of law, sources of stress

24 These thoughts on the significance of motivation for learning are taken from Julian Webb's contribution to our earlier conference presentations on affect and legal education 2000–1.

and pressure, what excites them, what bores them and why?[25] Would they want to hear about *our* expectations and what motivates *us*, or could this be burdensome for student and teacher alike?

Students have expectations about what learning law is going to be like. Disappointed expectations about this could possibly decrease intrinsic motivation and lead to failing experiences. So, for example, what if you want to introduce facilitation methods to a group happy and secure with didacticism and dependency? This could be deeply unsettling for some students.

Research by Carol Dweck and her colleagues shows that learners who lack resilience are reluctant to take risks and would rather stick with what they know and feel comfortable with. (Might this also be the case with some teachers?) Restricted learning choices may be made by those who lack resilience – who may be feeling good while things are going smoothly but who tend to fall apart when the going gets tough (Chiu, Hong and Dweck 1994; Claxton 1997). Motivation theory tells us that people are most highly motivated by tasks that are challenging yet achievable, and jointly negotiated (Riggio 2003). Moreover, assuming we would like our students to become better learners, not mechanistic information processors, it is perhaps not a good idea to leave understanding of what is involved in learning to chance. In the past I have had to learn from my mistakes on this one: it is a much better idea to discuss in advance the approach, its rationale and how it works.[26]

Expanding Horizons (2): Review our Attitudes and Roles as Tutors?

Of course, building a supportive, meaningful relationship with our students may mean rethinking our attitudes to staff–student relations – and the tutor's role. What kind of relationship do you want with your students; what kind of relationship do they want with you – inside and outside class? In conversations with students my colleagues and I were struck by how even informal interaction with tutors can affect student motivation; it increases if they are 'noticed':

> I failed two exams in the first year, that was really disheartening, I didn't think I'd make it to the third year, and when I came back in the summer to revise, I was stood on the stairs and someone who didn't lecture me at all … a lecturer, she just came up and asked me how I was getting on with my revision and wished me luck. And I think that was the biggest thing which had an impact on my getting into the second year. … I said I didn't even know you knew my name,

25 Timothy Seifert suggests that tutor–student interaction is the critical factor in the learning process: 'Teachers who are perceived as nurturing, supportive and helpful will be developing in students a sense of confidence and self-determination which will be translated into the learning-oriented behaviours of the intrinsically motivated student' (2004: 148).

26 We discuss this particular experience in some detail in Maughan and Webb (1996: 265–81).

> and she said you'd be surprised what we know, and yet she made the effort to wish me well and I passed ... that's why I'm here today [laughs]![27]

Research indicates that teachers' self-perceptions and beliefs about their roles can influence how they handle emotional situations in the classroom, such as whether they suppress or address students' emotions.[28] So what kind of relationships do you have, and are they what you want? How important is it to you that students perceive you as an expert? Is this how you see yourself, or have you a range of roles? Much of adult education theory (Knowles 1985; Boud 1995; Brookfield 1995) and the experience of those of us who have done it, tell us that students are generally much more engaged by active, independent, facilitated learning – although surface and unconfident learners may feel happier with dependency. Deep learners, already intrinsically motivated, can experience the pleasure and intellectual challenge that comes from independent enquiry and having some control over both the outcome and the process of learning that facilitative approaches offer.

Expanding Horizons (3): Rethink Curriculum Design?

This third arena goes to the very nature of what we do and why we do the things we do. Just for a moment, imagine you want to design a new law module – undergraduate or master's. What will be your starting point? Learning and teaching methodology? Course content? Maximum size of group? Kinds of assessment? None of these?

Law teachers are sometimes accused of being obsessed with content; indeed, the strongly positivistic orientation of some law teaching, when combined with the continuing expansion and ubiquity of law, means that William Twining's famous 'dragon of coverage', condemned to the slaughter over 20 years ago, may still be lurking in the darker corners of a law school somewhere near you (Twining 1988: 12).[29] A coverage approach, of course, risks the law school not even fulfilling its potential adequately to develop students' higher cognitive abilities, never mind the affective. The effect of this may well be to demotivate students.

And on the subject of demotivation, to what extent can the negative affect associated with formal assessment remain unacknowledged? The literature on

---

27 Extracts from conversations with third-year law students (see note 15).

28 For example, a study by Williams-Johnson et al. (2008) into school teachers' perceptions found that those who believed that addressing emotions was part of the job addressed them so as to create a nurturing and sensitive environment.

29 English law schools are under pressure to meet the expectations of external bodies – Solicitors' Regulation Authority, Bar Standards Board, QAA – each of which, to some extent, has its own agenda for the curriculum. This adds considerably to the risk that the curriculum becomes over-full of different kinds of content, encouraging our students to engage in symbolic and strategic rather than deep forms of learning.

this – backed up by our experience, surely – is unequivocal. In the UK we are familiar with the surveys that consistently report student dissatisfaction with feedback arrangements more than anything else in their studies.[30] In law, much time and energy is devoted to assessed tasks such as exams, from which there is often little or no feedback. For many students assessment is a threatening, painful process, engendering anxiety, uncertainty, defensiveness, fear of failure, shame – hardly an environment conducive to successful and pleasurable learning. Moreover, talk to any teacher and they will tell you how dismal aspects of the assessment process can be.

What is the real purpose of our formal assessment systems? Are they primarily designed for rank-ordering students in terms of achievement, or to help them learn and improve? If the former, do we need so much of it? Are we in the habit of assessing everything? If so, why?[31]

Should some of the time and effort devoted to coverage and summative assessment be traded off against using that time to offer opportunities for students to improve their understanding of how their law studies relate to their experience of the world? And how new learning modifies this understanding? Louis Rubin suggests, drawing on Dewey, that abstract, rational, unadulterated thought is not the way most people make sense of their world. Its value is not grasped until the learner feels it has a bearing on their existence – what is real, what is experiential, what is of concern is half-learned already:

> To 'learn from experience' is to make a backward and forward connection between what we do to things and what we enjoy or suffer from things in consequence. Under such conditions, doing becomes a trying; an experiment with the world to find out what it is like; the undergoing becomes instruction – discovery of the connection of things … Experience is primarily an active-passive affair; it is not primarily cognitive. (Dewey 1964: 140, cited in Rubin 1974)

There are a number of implications here for curriculum design and our teaching and assessment strategies which will now be explored: *ways of knowing; one size fits all approaches;* and *the learning environment.*

---

30 Every year the National Student Survey (NSS) asks UK final-year undergraduates to comment on their courses. Overall satisfaction is usually high (82% in 2010) but there is consistently less satisfaction in the areas of assessment and feedback (67% in 2010).

31 In their discussion of student resilience, Walker et al. note that the present stress on providing ever broader 'transparent accounts' of learning places heavy burdens on students. They query the usefulness of assessment 'products' in terms of learning, labelling them the 'monotonous construction of unproductive work', and cite Sidorkin's comment: 'If we create ourselves through producing things, what sort of self can be created by producing useless things?' (Walker, Gleaves and Grey 2006; Sidorkin 2004: 254). Are these thoughts relevant to the law curricula?

Ways of knowing To what extent do our pedagogies have to engage with the whole repertoire of ways of knowing other than the technical-rational? As noted above, the 'thinking like a lawyer' notion is based on a competitive paradigm, a narrow definition of success and limited ways of knowing. Instead, should we perhaps put more value on and expand experiential, creative, imaginative, intuitive ways of knowing?[32] Talk to any experienced practising lawyer and she will tell you she uses her experiential knowledge and intuition as well as her propositional knowledge when framing and solving problems. Does ignoring students' understanding of how the world works and their intuitions about how law fits into it encourage them to 'learn' a body of knowledge, rather than to think like lawyers actually think?

Presumably we would like our students to develop a creative approach to lawyering, too; one that extends beyond that which is merely technical/mechanical. Creativity involves moving beyond the limits of linear thinking into forms of lateral thinking and intuitive problem-solving. It encompasses the more imaginative, non-linear techniques of problem framing and solving.[33] However, you need a certain amount of confidence in your abilities to feel able to go beyond the technical/mechanical solution, as well as the motivation to search out new methods and techniques. A learning environment with opportunities to experiment and exchange ideas freely could play an important part in creating such confidence.

And how likely are we to underestimate the impact of the unconscious ways of knowing – our tacit, or implicit, memory processes we use to acquire new knowledge?[34] After all, we are nothing without our memory. Joseph Le Doux (2002) claims that the concept of self is founded on and maintained and developed through memory. When we develop our memory, we are developing our sense of self. When we learn, we are making memories.

Knowledge is not possible without the means of selecting, making sense of, storing, retrieving and applying information. To understand how these processes work requires an understanding of how memory works. We can conceptualise memory as 'dynamic knowing'. By this we mean that our minds are not simply

---

32 Claxton notes:

> We know that knowledge makes itself known through sensations, images, feelings and inklings, as well as through clear, conscious thoughts. Experiments tell us that just interacting with complex situations without trying to figure them out can deliver a quality of understanding that defies reason and articulation. Other studies have shown that confusion may be a vital precursor to the discovery of a good idea. To be able to meet the uncertain challenges of the contemporary world, we need to heed the message of this research, and to expand our repertoire of ways of learning and knowing to reclaim the full gamut of cognitive possibilities (1997: 203).

33 For discussion of one type of creative approach – visual imagery learning techniques – see Blakemore and Frith 2005: 153–9.

34 The good news is, our students will learn despite what we do with them and to them.

filing systems, that is, information is taken down, dusted off and made use of as and when we need it. Because our mental structures change as we learn, the information we store also changes to adapt to our developing understanding.

We operate according to a number of schemata, or patterns of what is important and appropriate in different contexts. A mind that formed a memory of a particular experience with a particular understanding of the world at that time will recall it and evaluate it according to a schema that has since been modified.[35]

We create most new memories unconsciously:

> … brain research brings to light new insights about a form of long-term memory that has long been overlooked, that of implicit memory, which receives, stores and recovers outside the conscious awareness of the individual. From implicit memory emerges habits, attitudes and preferences inaccessible to conscious recollection but these are nonetheless shaped by former events, influence our present behaviour, and are an essential part of who we are. (Taylor 2001: 218)[36]

As we saw with Michael Riley, such memories are capable of influencing our behaviour even though we are not aware of why we are acting in a certain way. For example, in the early part of the 20th century the physician Edouard Claparede treated a brain-damaged patient who had apparently lost the ability to create new memories. Each time Claparede walked in the room he had to reintroduce himself to her as she had no recollection of having seen him before – even if he left the room and came back a few minutes later. One day he entered the room, and as on every other day, held out his hand to greet her. And as usual, she shook his hand. But when their hands met, she quickly drew hers back; Claparede had hidden a sharp nail in his hand and had pricked her with it. The next time he returned to the room to greet her, she still did not recognise him, but refused to shake his hand. She couldn't tell him why she wouldn't shake hands with him.

---

35 This is in line with constructivist models of learning: see Jarvis and Parker 2005: 90–91. In recent years experiential, self-directed and transformative learning theories of adult learning have grown in importance. The notion of transformative learning developed by Mezirow seeks to engage learners in critical reflection on their experience so that their schemata and perspectives are changed (1994). But if Mezirow sees critical reflection as the predominant process in learning, how does this square with brain science research that puts unconscious learning at the heart of it? See Taylor (2001), below.

36 Taylor's thesis is that transformative learning theory relies too heavily on rational discourse and critical reflection at the expense of emotion and unconscious ways of knowing. Taylor's argument may strike a chord with those of us who have searched in vain for deep, honest reflection from students about their reasoning processes. It also raises questions about whether we should be formally assessing the 'quality' of such reflection.

Implicit memory contrasts with explicit (declarative) memory: the kind of memory we have in mind when we use the term 'memory' in everyday usage: conscious recollection; to be aware of some past experience, and knowing facts. They can be brought to mind and described verbally (declared). See Roche, Chapter 2 and Lerner, Chapter 7 (this volume).

Although she didn't have a conscious memory of the situation, subconsciously she had learned that shaking his hand could cause her harm, and her brain used this stored information, this memory, to prevent the harm occurring again. This case illustrates the point that this memory system forms implicit memories about dangerous or otherwise threatening situations (Le Doux 1998: 180–81). It shows that these implicit memories are capable of influencing our behaviour even though we are not consciously aware of why we are doing something.

What does this tell us about our teaching? There is unintended learning which we are not in control of, and of which students are not aware. This kind of learning is important to the individual for the development of their schemata and may well show itself in student levels of anxiety, motivation, enthusiasm or boredom.

Since implicit memory primarily evaluates incoming information at the level of gut feeling, we don't become aware of these emotions until they are imprinted into our consciousness as feelings. Imagine an unconfident or unprepared student asked a difficult question in a seminar. His initial response may well be one of fear. There will be physiological responses such as increased heart rate, blood rushing to the muscles, sweating, dilated pupils. This will lead to a strong tendency to act in an instinctive way, rather than the conscious, deliberate reasoning process that the tutor is looking for. These responses are quite outside the student's control, but he becomes aware of what his body is telling him through feelings of anxiety and stress. A student may exhibit outward signs of this inner anxiety. Equally, he may have devised strategies for masking this emotional state, say, by appearing arrogant or laid back.

It seems that the implicit system is less forgetful and inaccurate than the explicit (conscious) memory system.[37] So it would seem likely that the frightened student will remember the fear of the event rather than the intended learning points.

When students are in lectures, seminars, writing essays, working in groups, revising for exams, they are using their working and long-term memory and developing their own personal schemata. These are not going to be objective, measurable knowledge structures, but will be closely tied in to the individual's personal experiences, feelings, values and beliefs. All of these will be brought to bear not only on what the content of what is learned but on the whole process of learning it.

There is a lot that is not yet known about memory, however it seems to be agreed that the brain has a distinct set of memory systems which all interact with one another and with the external world, and all work in parallel. In its interactivity and self-organisation properties this represents a small but critical part of the overall complex system of learning. And this brings us to:

37 If explicit memory is forgetful and inaccurate, does it help to encode and retrieve new knowledge if you first encounter it in a memorable learning episode? If so, how can we create such episodes?

'One size fits all' approaches to learning Learning is a lot more complex than some essentially behaviourism-based 'outcomes approaches'[38] would have us believe. All teachers know that what we teach is not necessarily what is learned; yet linear models of learning, still prevalent in higher education, view learning as a simple information processing system: information is fed into the system, learning 'takes place', and is measured by comparison with predetermined outcomes.

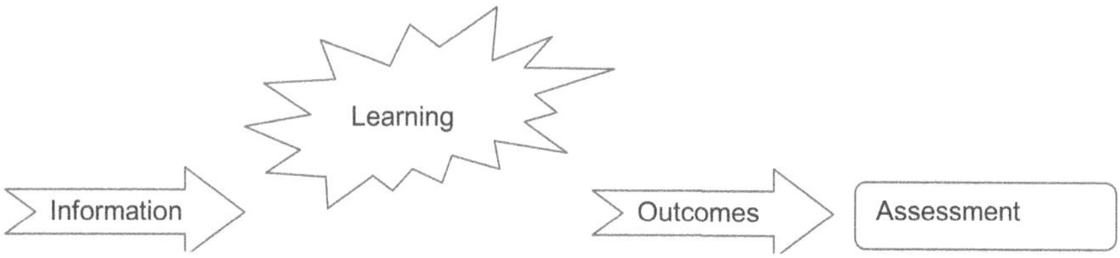

Figure 1.1 Simple linear system of learning

This simple system approach does not come anywhere near providing an adequate explanation of what is involved. Too much attention is paid to the inputs and outputs of the learning process, and too little to what actually goes on in the 'black box' of the mind and the transformations necessary to move from input to output. It ignores the emotional dimension in learning and the physiological changes that take place in the brain when we learn.

Moreover, it is often said that our students learn in spite of us. Established educational theories and processes tend to focus on the conscious thinking part of our brain, yet much, if not most of our learning occurs at the unconscious level. A lot of information is processed and dealt with before any of it arrives at the neocortex – the point at which we consciously decide what to do with that information (Le Doux 1997).

38 In their discussion of the misuse of learning outcomes, Hussey and Smith note:

> ... armed with learning outcomes written in ... precise language, we can ... state clearly what will be learned during a given unit of teaching, and exactly how it can be assessed. In designing our courses or modules we now have a useful guide to what is expected from a learning activity, both for the teachers and the taught. The progress of the student, the suitability of the teaching method and the effectiveness of the teacher, can all be determined objectively: the entire enterprise can be 'tracked' and audited, even by someone completely ignorant of the discipline concerned (2002: 224).

However, not all outcomes approaches are as reductionist; Eisner suggested the outcomes of a learning experience should be subject-specific, student-specific and teacher-specific: student-specific outcomes he defined as 'personalised learning', which would include what a student has learned which was not directly taught (see Allan 1996: 100–1 and Eisner 1979).

As we have seen, at the unconscious level we respond to everything in terms of the pleasure it offers or anxiety it may cause. If learning is so highly individualised, a 'one size fits all' simple approach to teaching and learning law is surely inappropriate. Strategies are required which cater for a variety of learning needs and preferences.

The learning environment How do you, your colleagues, or your students view mistakes? To what extent is it possible, or desirable, to cultivate a climate in which mistakes are seen as learning opportunities, rather than one in which students perceive making mistakes as a sign of stupidity or failure?[39] Is ability a fixed trait? Or capable of change? If we want to encourage positive affect and intrinsic motivation, how useful is it for us to know about the self theories that students bring to their learning experiences?

Self theories are the beliefs we hold about our personal attributes and capabilities. They have a powerful influence over our attitude to performing tasks, building and maintaining relationships, achieving goals. Understanding how they work can help us answer vexing questions such as why some students who perform poorly on set tasks and assignments react positively, remain motivated and put in extra effort to improve, whilst others lose motivation and may even switch off from a module or their course of study. What can we teachers do to encourage the former response and discourage the latter? Three areas of research into people's perceptions in the face of failure are briefly outlined below. As you will see, there is plenty of overlap.

Self-efficacy theory

Albert Bandura defines self-efficacy as: 'People's judgments of their capabilities to organize and execute courses of action required to attain designated types of performances. It is concerned not with the skills one has but with judgments of what one can do with whatever skills one possesses' (1986: 391). Self-efficacy: 'influences individual choices, goals, emotional reactions, effort, coping, and persistence. Self-efficacy also changes as a result of learning, experience and feedback' (Gist and Mitchell 1992: 186). Students who believe they are capable of resolving a complex problem are more likely to put the effort into resolving it, whereas those who believe they will ultimately fail at the task will be less likely to persist with it (Brannick, Miles and Kisamore 2005: 474).

Moreover, students with high self-efficacy are better at organising their own learning and do better academically than those who have doubts about their intellectual abilities (Bandura 1997: 239). They view hard tasks as challenges to be overcome rather than threats to be avoided. This view encourages 'intrinsic interest and deep engrossment in activities' (Bandura 1994: 73, cited in Jernigan 2004). Nevertheless, we all know students whose opinion of their ability is low yet who use the negative impact of a poor performance or grade to work harder and do better (for an example, see Jernigan 2004).

---

39 See above, note 3.

Studies suggest that people with high and low self-efficacy interpret feedback on a task similarly when they've done well, but dissimilarly when performance has been poor. When a person with high self-efficacy and one with low self-efficacy both do well, they attribute that success to their ability. Where performance is poor, people with high self-efficacy attribute it to insufficient effort or to task difficulty, whereas people with low self-efficacy attribute it to lack of ability. So if you get a poor mark in an assessment and get negative feedback from your tutor, what could happen? If your self-efficacy is high, you are more likely to take note of the feedback and work to improve your grades. But if it is low, then your self-efficacy, motivation, coping strategies and effort may decline with each subsequent performance. A negative spiral like that can be difficult to reverse (Gist and Mitchell 1992: 202).

In our experience students enter academic and professional law courses with high expectations. Disappointment and frustration when progress is not as fast as expected may lower self-efficacy so that students put in less effort or give up. We would imagine that their teachers have high self-efficacy: we know we're articulate, intelligent and good at law. Because of this we may forget that others might not be able to grasp it as quickly and easily as we did. So what happens when our expectations of students aren't met? Could our disappointment and frustration reduce our self-efficacy? Is it possible we put in less effort with some students, especially those we label 'persistent failures'? Hopefully not, as Bandura notes that teachers with low self-efficacy tend to take a pessimistic view of student motivation, invoking poor ability as the reason why their students can't be taught (1997: 242, citing Ashton and Webb 1986).

Students' implicit theories about personal attributes

In the 1980s Dweck and Leggett formulated a model to predict when positive or negative responses to failure are likely to occur (1988). They proposed that people's responses are primarily based on the implicit theories they hold about personality. They identified two typical orientations: 'entity theorists' and 'incremental theorists'. Entity theorists believe that personal attributes such as ability are fixed. These people are performance-oriented, in that when given a task or assignment, they want to demonstrate how good they are at it; they are 'more motivated to prove themselves than to improve themselves' (El-Alayli and Baumgardner 2003: 120). They therefore tend to attribute poor performance to lack of ability, which they can't do anything about. Failure at a task may therefore be accompanied by feelings of helplessness, reduced effort and lack of desire to improve – likely to result in poor performance in the future.[40]

---

40 But El-Alayli and Baumgardner's study showed that entity theorists were motivated to work harder after they discovered they had low ability, whereas incremental theorists did the opposite. Their explanation is that entity theorists, in a performance-oriented environment (which this was), may try harder to demonstrate their competence by scoring more highly against their more able 'competitors' when the next opportunity

In contrast, incremental theorists are challenged rather than threatened by failure. They are learning-oriented, motivated by a desire to improve themselves. They believe that personal attributes can be changed and perceive performance of a task as a stage in the development of skills and abilities. They therefore tend to attribute a poor performance to lack of effort rather than low ability and will respond to negative feedback with increased motivation, effort and persistence.

The learning environment has been shown to have a bearing on these different responses. A competitive environment, which values success in terms of outperforming others, may encourage the perception that success lies in high ability. Putting in a lot of effort may be seen as a sign of poor ability, precisely because you need to work harder. On the other hand, a learning-oriented environment values success in terms of personal development, effort and challenge (El-Alayli and Baumgardner 2003: 121).

And what of our learning environments? There seems little doubt that with our strong emphasis on performance, grades, normative assessment and feedback, we encourage the perception that high ability is valued above all other factors. If this is so, we need to be aware that negative feedback given to students with an entity theory perspective could block their learning.

Dweck's research shows us how powerful these self-beliefs are in determining how students approach and carry out tasks and how responses to feedback are governed by these beliefs. By acknowledging the importance of positive attitudes and emotions for student learning,[41] we can search for ways to promote incrementalism.[42] Implicit theories can be changed by our approach to assessment and feedback. And do we need to check our own theories? Yorke and Knight offer an illuminating thought:

---

arises. However, they noted that although their motivation was strong, the entity theorists had a worse emotional response than incremental theorists, whether they were successful or unsuccessful. The authors offer an explanation: 'Perhaps entity beliefs make individuals feel bad, in general, because they are uncomfortable with their apparent lack of control' (2003: 130).

41 For example:

> Students who attribute success and failure to internal, controllable causes are more likely to feel pride, satisfaction, confidence and have a higher sense of self-esteem. Consequently, these students will choose to work on more difficult tasks, persist longer in the face of failure, display higher levels of cognitive engagement and produce work that is of higher quality. Students who attribute failure to internal, uncontrollable stable factors (inability) are more likely to feel shame and humiliation and will show little effort or cognitive engagement (Seifert 2004: 140).

42 If we agree that is what we want to do. Yorke and Knight (2004) asked 2,269 undergraduates and 70 academic staff if they agreed/tended to agree or disagreed/tended to disagree with the statement 'An individual can't change their intelligence by much'. 70–75% of both students and staff tended towards the incremental view of intelligence – although responses will presumably depend on how respondents define 'intelligence'.

> the beliefs that teachers hold about students are likely to have an impact on the latter's learning. To hear, floating out into a corridor, phrases like 'You are a 2.1 student' leaves the adventitious listener wondering whether the teacher concerned was making a pre-emptive (and fixed) judgement, or making a comment on the quality of the work that had apparently been submitted. In either case the critically important issue is what kind of self-theory the student brings to bear when construing such a remark. (2004: 30)

Fairness

Studies confirm that perceptions of fairness influence the extent to which feedback on poor performance is accepted. Students are naturally concerned about fairness because of the importance of grades for their future life and work. They tend to focus on their mark when they get an assignment back, and the mark may determine whether they read the feedback and take it on board. Perceived discrepancies between the mark expected and the mark received can lead to negative perceptions about the fairness of the mark received, and the process used to decide it. In such circumstances students may develop negative feelings towards their teachers, the course and the institution.

Research in employment and educational settings has centred on *distributive justice*: perceptions of the fairness of outcomes; and *procedural justice*: perceptions of the fairness of the evaluation methods.[43]

Students' perceptions of injustice may be influenced not only by a performance/expectation discrepancy, but also by what they felt they deserved, given the amount of effort they put in, or a comparison of their grades with other students' grades and the amount of effort these others put in. It seems that students value effort more highly than lecturers (Adams 2005), who often aren't aware of the amount, urgency and intensity of effort put in by their students, particularly at exam time, and who are concerned to judge a piece of work on its merits (Nesbit and Burton 2006: 657). Moreover, if a lot of time and effort is expended on an assignment, students may overestimate the marks they are likely to get.

If the grade is what is expected given the amount of effort put in and in comparison with what other students were awarded, given their efforts, the outcome is perceived to be fair.[44] Moreover, evaluation procedures are regarded as fair when they correspond to set standards, for example, 'consistency, suppression

43 The literature on fairness is reviewed in Tata 1999; Chory-Asad 2002; Nesbit and Burton 2006. Chory-Assad's study showed that student concerns about procedural fairness reduced the motivation to learn, encouraged negative attitudes towards the course and aggressive feelings towards lecturers.

44 Equity is said to exist, i.e. we estimate what is a just reward for the amount of effort we have put in. Nesbit and Burton add that those who feel unfairly under-rewarded may well be dissatisfied and angry (2006: 656). Higgins et al. note the emotional investment made in an assignment and the expectation of some 'return' on that investment (2001: 272). For a discussion of equity theory, see Adams (1965, cited in Chory-Assad).

of personal bias, use of accurate information, voice, and congruity with prevailing standards or ethics' (Tata 1999: 265). Studies on 'interactional justice' – the interpersonal component of procedural justice – have found that negative feedback is more likely to be accepted if it is delivered with interpersonal fairness, i.e. if recipients feel they were treated with respect, dignity and without bias, and their personal needs and concerns were taken into account.[45]

Moreover, clear, accurate, non-ambiguous communication has been shown to increase perceptions of procedural fairness and so encourage positive responses and motivation and reduce the likelihood of aggression towards teachers (Hong et al. 1999: 567).[46] Although the power relationship obviously influences how feedback is received and acted upon (or not), much of what goes wrong with feedback is to do with the communication process itself; whether the message we want to get across is understood as we intended. First, simply 'telling' (usually in writing) the recipient what is right or wrong 'ignores the active role the student must play in constructing meaning from feedback messages' (Juwah, Macfarlane-Dick, Matthew et al. 2004: 7). Second, we may *assume* it has been understood in the way it was intended. 'We have discussed the assessment criteria with the students, and they understand them', we may say. But are we sure they fully grasp the niceties and nuances of our academic discourse? For example, let us take the word 'reflection'. Do they understand the word in the same way you and your colleagues do?[47] As Higgins et al. acknowledge, communication only 'works' when based on shared understandings (2001: 273). There may well be implicit messages – 'we know what we mean by …' – which will prevent the feedback being taken on board.

To what extent will encouraging students to look inwards for reasons for failure rather than attributing it to external causes help them and us to understand a self-theory and its influence on their learning? Chris Argyris (1991) thinks we are mistaken if we think getting people to learn is about attitudes – i.e. that with the right commitment and motivation, learning will automatically come about. In his view this will only happen if we teach students how to reason through their

45 See the discussion in Leung, Su and Morris 2001. Further, Bryson and Hand note: 'Sensitivity to students' sense of equity and justice appears to be a key element in developing and maintaining trust and creating a more conducive environment for teaching and learning' (2007: 358).

46 All well and good but there are issues of discourse and power which can interfere with communication. Students may not fully understand the discourse used by tutors in feedback: 'the use of discourse is a means by which tutors, wittingly or unwittingly, exert power over students. The ideology of universities demarcates novice students from authoritative academics, and this is often reinforced by the role of correcting and judging scripts rather than engaging in debate on them' (Carless 2006: 221, citing Ivanic, Clark and Rimmershaw in Lea and Tierer 2000; see also Lea and Street 1998).

47 And do you and your colleagues agree about its meaning? There appear to be no widely accepted definitions of 'reflection', nor is there agreement about methods of identifying it: Sumsion and Fleet (1996: 121); Hatton and Smith (1995: 33).

behaviour and its causes. There's a human tendency to blank out negative feedback and blame anything but ourselves when we experience failure; this 'defensive reasoning' blocks learning and we may not even be aware it is happening. Questioning students about their beliefs and perceptions may help to uncover their reasoning processes and pinpoint the real causes of substandard performance.[48]

A strong note of caution: some of the studies cited are based on subjects' reactions to hypothetical scenarios; behaviour in real situations may be different. Other studies are based on self-reporting of actual experiences, but we can't be certain that recall is always accurate. Also, these studies can't take into account the quality of the staff–student relationship – the trust that may or may not exist and the effect this might have on students' perceptions about their goals and abilities. Nevertheless, much of the discussion may chime with your intuitions and experience of what it is like to be human. Moreover, consideration of students' self theories can open the door to an examination of our own implicit theories about learning.

If students are anxious to avoid poor performance and are preoccupied with thoughts of failure, they will not want to risk making any mistakes or to involve themselves in challenging activities. A safe, secure, trusting environment for experimentation and risk-taking may be both more meaningful in terms of cognitive engagement, and more pleasurable in terms of affective engagement. But can we surmount the problems of the 'creeping core'? And what of the 'hidden curriculum'? Yorke and Knight warn of its dangers:

> The implicit 'message' the students pick up is that they should play safe and not take the opportunity to learn through taking on challenging (and hence risky) tasks. Here is an aspect of the 'hidden curriculum' which may prove very difficult to dislodge from the students' unconscious. Wherever grades count towards a final award, students are implicitly discouraged from risking poor grades. In a society in which complex learning and employability are officially desired outcomes of the educational process, a higher education should surely not prompt students to avoid complexity and the taking of risks in their learning. (2004: 36)

48 Argyris would add that the starting point is for us teachers to look inwards and critically examine our own reasoning processes about our behaviour. Do we reason defensively? If so, why and how does this happen? What are the consequences? Are there inconsistencies between the kinds of behaviour we espouse and what we actually do? For example, take the rules of feedback: it should be positive, constructive, timely, sensitive, etc. Do we follow the rules consistently? Are you, or am I, 'dispositionally a critical person', who has trouble sticking to the rules? (Leung et al. 2001: 1158).

Summing up ...

The research I have described in this chapter is intended to demonstrate the critical significance of the non-cognitive in learning, not least in learning the law. The difficulties in dealing with many of these issues are perhaps highlighted by their being formally ignored in the discourse on learning in higher education. Nevertheless their informal recognition can be attested by almost any off-the-record conversation held with students or tutors.

The research described constitutes but a small part of what is out there and offers not much more than an introduction to subject matter which extends over a number of disciplines. From the perspective of the individual learner, what makes learning a complex adaptive system is that there are potentially an infinite number of inputs and transformations that relate specifically to any one given individual which are qualitatively and quantitatively different from the inputs and transformations made by any other individual. So we can say with confidence that learning is individual; a whole lot of learning happens which is additional to, or instead of, the intended learning outcomes. The framework of understanding individuals construct for themselves is going to be different at a deep level, even if they use the same words, concepts, rules, etc., in their studies and professional lives. So we can say that you can start by defining learning outcomes, but a complex system means everyone gets there in their own way. What is critical is to design a learning environment that enriches the learning opportunities for those with a multitude of learning styles, preferences, attitudes and feelings.

In conclusion I offer a definition of human learning which just *feels* right:

> – the combination of processes whereby the human person (knowledge, skills, attitudes, emotions, values, beliefs and the senses) enters a social situation and constructs an experience which is then transformed through cognitive, emotional and practical processes, and integrated into the person's biography – is the driving force behind the emerging humanity, and this is lifelong. Human beings are, therefore, both being and becoming, and these are inextricably intertwined, since growth and development in the one affects the growth and development of the other. Learning is, therefore, existential and experiential. (Jarvis 2005: 2)

References

Adams, J.B. 2005. What Makes a Grade? Faculty and Student Perceptions, *Teaching of Psychology* 32(1): 21–5.

Adams, J.S. 1965. Inequity in Social Exchange, in *Advances in Experimental Social Psychology*, Vol. 2, edited by L. Berkowitz. New York: Academic Press, 267–99.

Allan, J. 1996. Learning Outcomes in Higher Education, *Studies in Higher Education* 21(1): 93–108.

Argyris, C. 1991. Teaching Smart People How to Learn, *Reflections* 4(2): 4–15.

Ashton, P.T.I. and Webb, R.B. 1986. *Making a Difference: Teachers' Sense of Efficacy and Student Achievement*. White Plains, NY: Longman.

Bandura, A. 1986. *Social Foundations of Thought and Action*. Englewood Cliffs, NJ: Prentice-Hall.

Bandura, A. 1994. *Self-efficacy: Encyclopedia of Human Behavior*. Vol. 4. New York: Academic Press, 71–81.

Bandura, A. 1997. *Self-efficacy: The Exercise of Control*. New York: W.H. Freeman.

Barbalet, J. 2002. *Emotions and Sociology*. Oxford: Blackwell.

Beard, C., Clegg, S. and Smith, K. 2007. Acknowledging the Affective in Higher Education, *British Education Research Journal* 33(2): 235–52.

Blakemore, S.-J. and Frith, U. 2005. *The Learning Brain: Lessons for Education*. Oxford: Blackwell.

Bleackley, A. 1998. Learning as an Aesthetic Practice: Motivation through Beauty in Higher Education, in *Motivating Students*, edited by S. Brown, S. Armstrong and G. Thompson. London: RoutledgeFalmer, 165–72.

Boud, D.J. 1995. *Enhancing Learning through Self-assessment*. London: Kogan Page.

Brannick, M.T., Miles, D.E. and Kisamore, J.L. 2005. Calibration between Student Mastery and Self-efficacy, *Studies in Higher Education* 30(4): 473–83.

Brayne, H. 2002. Learning to Think like a Lawyer – One Law Teacher's Exploration of the Relevance of Evolutionary Psychology, *International Journal of the Legal Profession* 9(3): 283–311.

Brookfield, S. 1995. *Becoming a Critically Reflective Teacher*. San Francisco: Jossey-Bass.

Bryson, C. and Hand, L. 2007. The Role of Engagement in Inspiring Teaching and Learning, *Innovations in Education and Teaching International* 44(4): 349–62.

Carless, D. 2006. Differing Perceptions in the Feedback Process, *Studies in Higher Education* 31(2): 219–33.

Chiu, C., Hong, Y. and Dweck, C.S. 1994. Toward an Integrative Model of Personality and Intelligence: A General Framework and Some Preliminary Steps, in *Personality and Intelligence*, edited by R.J. Sternberg and P. Ruzgis. Cambridge: Cambridge University Press, 104–36.

Chory-Asad, R.M. 2002. Classroom Justice: Perceptions of Fairness as a Predictor of Student Motivation, Learning and Aggression, *Communication Quarterly* 50(1): 458–78.

Claxton, G. 1997. *Hare Brain, Tortoise Mind: Why Intelligence Increases when You Think Less*. London: Fourth Estate.

Coffield, F. 2008. *Just Suppose Teaching and Learning Became the First Priority*. London: Learning and Skills Network.

Damasio, A. 1994. *Descartes' Error: Emotion, Reason and the Human Brain*. New York: Grosset/Putnam.

Damasio, A. 1999. *The Feeling of What Happens: Body and Emotion in the Making of Consciousness*. New York: Harcourt Brace.

de Sousa, R. 2007. *Emotion*. [Online] Available at: http://plato.stanford.edu/entries/emotion [accessed 5 July 2010].

Descartes, R. 1641/1967. Meditations on the First Philosophy, in *The Philosophy of the 16th and 17th Centuries*, edited by R.H. Popkin. New York: Free Press, 121–80.

Dewey, J. 1964. *Democracy and Education*. New York: Macmillan.

Durkheim, E. 1895/1962. *The Rules of the Sociological Method*. Glencoe, Illinois: Free Press.

Dweck, C.S. 1999. *Self-theories: Their Role in Motivation, Personality, and Development*. Ann Arbor, MI: Edwards Bros.

Dweck, C.S. and Leggett, E.L. 1988. A Social-cognitive Approach to Motivation and Personality, *Psychological Review* 95(2): 256–73.

Ecclestone, K. and Hayes, D. 2009. *The Dangerous Rise of Therapeutic Education*. Abingdon: Routledge.

Eisner, E. 1979. *The Educational Imagination*. New York: Macmillan.

El-Alayli, A. and Baumgardner, A. 2003. If at First You Don't Succeed, What Makes You Try, Try Again? Effects of Implicit Theories and Ability Feedback in a Performance-oriented Climate, *Self and Identity* 2, 119–135.

Elkins, J.R. 1985. Rites of Passage: Law Students 'Telling their Lives', *Journal of Legal Education* 35, 27–55.

Emmons, R. 1996. Striving and Feeling: Personal Goals and Subjective Well-being, in *The Psychology of Action: Linking Cognition and Motivation to Behaviour*, edited by P.M. Gollwitzer and J.A. Bragh. New York: Guildford, 314–37.

Evans, D. 2001. *Emotion: The Science of Sentiment*. Oxford: Oxford University Press.

Freire, P. 1974. *Pedagogy of the Oppressed*. New York: Seabury Press.

Furedi, F. 2003. *Therapy Culture: Cultivating Vulnerability in an Uncertain Age*. London: Routledge.

Gist, M.E. and Mitchell, T.R. 1992. Self-efficacy: A Theoretical Analysis of its Determinants and Malleability, *Academy of Management Review* 17(2): 183–211.

Goodrich, P. 1996. Of Blackstone's Tower: Metaphors of Distance and Histories of the English Law School, in *What are Law Schools For? Vol. 2: Pressing Problems in the Law*, edited by P. Birks. Oxford: Oxford University Press, 59–68.

Hativa, N. 2002. Becoming a Better Teacher: A Case of Changing the Pedagogical Knowledge and Beliefs of Law Professors, in *Teacher Thinking, Beliefs and Knowledge in Higher Education*, edited by N. Hativa and P. Goodyear. The Hague: Kluwer Academic Publishers.

Hatton, N. and Smith, D. 1995. Reflection in Teacher Education: Towards Definition and Implementation, *Teaching & Teacher Education* 11(1): 33–49.

Higgins, R., Hartley, P. and Skelton, A. 2001. Getting the Message Across: The Problem of Communicating Assessment Feedback, *Teaching in Higher Education* 6(2): 269–74.

Hilgard, E.R. 1980. The Trilogy of Mind: Cognition, Affection and Conation, *Journal of the History of the Behavioural Sciences* 16: 107–17.

Hong, Y.Y., Chiu, C.Y., Dweck, C.S. et al. 1999. Implicit Theories, Attributions and Coping: A Meaning System Approach, *Journal of Personality and Social Psychology* 77(3): 588–99.

Hussey, Y. and Smith, P. 2002. The Trouble with Learning Outcomes, *Active Learning in Higher Education* 3: 220–33.

Iijima, A. 1998. Lessons Learned: Legal Education and Law Student Dysfunction, *Journal of Legal Education* 48(4): 524–38.

Ivanic, R., Clark, R. and Rimmershaw, R. 2000. What am I Supposed to Make of This? The Messages Conveyed to Students by Tutors' Written Comments, in *Student Writing in Higher Education: New Contexts*, edited by M.R. Lea and B. Stierer. Buckingham: Oxford University Press, 47–65.

Jarvis, P. 2005. Towards a Philosophy of Human Learning: An Existentialist Perspective, in *Human Learning*, edited by P. Jarvis and S. Parker. Abingdon: Routledge, 1–15.

Jernigan, C.G. 2004. *What do Students Expect to Learn? The Role of Learner Expectancies, Beliefs and Attributions for Success and Failure in Student Motivation.* [Online] Available at: http://cie.asu.edu/volume7/number4/index.html [accessed 5 July 2010].

Juwah, C., Macfarlane-Dick, D., Matthew, B. et al. 2004. *Enhancing Learning through Effective Formative Feedback.* York: Higher Education Academy Generic Centre.

Kennedy, D. 1982/1998. Legal Education as Training for Hierarchy, in *The Politics of Law*, edited by D. Kairy. [Online] Available at: www.duncankennedy.net/bibliography/alpha/html [accessed 21 July 2010].

Knowles, M. 1985. *The Modern Practice of Adult Education.* Cambridge: Cambridge University Press.

Krathwohl, D.R., Bloom, B.S. and Masia, B.B. 1964. *Taxonomy of Educational Objectives: The Classification of Educational Goals Handbook 2: The Affective Domain.* New York: David McKay Co.

Krieger, L.S. 2002. Institutional Denial about the Dark Side of Law School, and Fresh Empirical Guidance for Constructively Breaking the Silence, *Journal of Legal Education* 52: 112–29.

Lazarus, R. 1991. *Emotion and Adaptation.* New York: Oxford University Press.

Lea, M.R. and Street, B. 1998. Student Writing in Higher Education: An Academic Literacies Approach, *Studies in Higher Education* 23(2): 157–72.

Leathwood, C. and Hey, V. 2009. Gender/ed Discourses and Emotional Sub-texts: Theorizing Emotion in UK Higher Education, *Teaching in Higher Education* 14(4): 429–40.

Le Doux, J. 1997. *Parallel Memories: Putting Emotions Back into the Brain – A Talk with Joseph Le Doux.* [Online] Available at: http://www.edge.org/3rd_culture/ledoux/ledoux_p1.html [accessed 5 July 2010].

Le Doux, J. 1998. *The Emotional Brain.* London: Orion Books.

Le Doux, J. 2002. *Synaptic Self.* New York: Viking Penguin.

Lehrer, J. 2009. *The Decisive Moment: How the Brain Makes up its Mind.* Edinburgh: Cannongate Books.

Leung, K., Su, S. and Morris, M.W. 2001. When is Criticism not Constructive? The Roles of Fairness Perceptions and Dispositional Attributions in Employee Acceptance of Critical Supervisory Feedback, *Human Relations* 54(9): 1155–87.

Locke, J. 1690/1947. *An Essay Concerning Human Understanding.* New York: EP Dutton.

Marton, F., Hounsell, D. and Entwhistle, N. 1997. *The Experience of Learning: Implications for Teaching and Studying in Higher Education.* Edinburgh: Scottish Academic Press.

Maughan, C. and Webb, J. 1996. Taking Reflection Seriously: How Was It For Us?, in *Teaching Lawyers' Skills*, edited by J. Webb and C. Maughan. London: Butterworth, 265–81.

Mezirow, J. 1994. Understanding Transformation Theory, *Adult Education Quarterly* 44: 222–32.

Nesbit, P.L. and Burton, S. 2006. Student Justice Perceptions Following Assignment Feedback, *Assessment & Evaluation in HE* 31(6): 655–70.

Nicholson, N. 2000. *Managing the Human Animal.* New York: Crown Publishers.

Picard, R.W. 2000. *Affective Computing.* Cambridge, Mass: MIT Press.

Pinker, S. 1998. *How the Mind Works.* London: Allen Lane.

Pinker, S. 2002. *The Blank Slate: The Modern Denial of Human Nature*. London: Allen Lane.

Prinz, J. 2004. Which Emotions are Basic? in *Emotion, Evolution and Rationality*, edited by D. Evans and P. Cruse. Oxford: Oxford University Press, 69–87.

Riggio, R.E. 2003. *Introduction to Industrial/Organizational Psychology.* New Jersey: Prentice Hall.

Rubin, L.J. 1973. *Facts and Feelings in the Classroom.* East Grinstead, West Sussex: Ward Lock Educational.

Rubin Henderson, B. 2003. Asking the Lost Question: What is the Purpose of Law School? *Journal of Legal Education* 53(1): 48–79.

Ryle, G. 1949. *The Concept of Mind.* Chicago: University of Chicago Press.
Seifert, T. 2004. Understanding Student Motivation, *Educational Research* 46(2): 137–49.
Sidorkin, J. 2004. In the Event of Learning: Alienation and Participative Thinking in Education, *Educational Theory* 54(3): 251–62.
Skinner, B.F. 1974. *About Behaviourism.* New York: Knopf.
Smith, A. 1759/2007. *The Theory of Moral Sentiments.* New York: Cosimo Classics.
Sullivan, W.M., Colby, A., Wegner, J.W. et al. 2007. *Educating Lawyers: Preparation for the Profession of Law. Summary.* Stanford, California: The Carnegie Foundation for the Advancement of Teaching. [Online] Available at: http://www.carnegiefoundation.org/sites/default/files/publications/elibrary_pdf_632.pdf [accessed 2 August 2010].
Sumsion, J. and Fleet, A. 1996. Reflection: Can We Assess It? Should We Assess It? *Assessment & Evaluation in Higher Education* 121(2): 121–9.
Tata, J. 1999. Grade Distributions, Grading Procedures, and Students' Evaluations of Instructors: A Justice Perspective, *The Journal of Psychology* 133(3): 263–72.
Taylor, E.W. 2001. Transformative Learning Theory: A Neurobiological Perspective of the Role of Emotions and Unconscious Ways of Knowing, *International Journal of Lifelong Education* 20(3): 218–36.
Turner, J.E., Husman, J. and Schallert, D. 2002. The Importance of Students' Goals in their Emotional Experience of Academic Failure: Investigating the Precursors and Consequences of Shame, *Educational Psychologist* 37(2): 79–89.
Turow, S. 1977. *One L.* New York: Farrar, Straus and Giroux.
Twining, W. 1988. Legal Skills and Legal Education, *The Law Teacher* 22(1): 4–13.
Van Driel, J.H., Verloop, N., Van Werven, H.I. et al. 1997. Teachers' Craft Knowledge and Curriculum Innovation in Higher Engineering Education, *Higher Education* 34: 105–22.
Varlander, S. 2008. The Role of Students' Emotions in Formal Feedback Situations, *Teaching in Higher Education* 13(2): 145–56.
Vygotsky, L. 1987. Thinking and Speech, in *The Collected Works of L S Vygotsky, Volume 1*, edited by R.W. Rieber and A.S. Carton. New York: Plenum Press.
Walker, C., Gleaves, A. and Grey, J. 2006. Can Students within Higher Education Learn to be Resilient, and Educationally Speaking, Does it Matter? *Educational Studies* 32(3): 251–64.
Wenger, E.C. and Snyder, W.M. 2000. Communities of Practice: The Organizational Frontier, *Harvard Business Review* Jan–Feb, 139–45.
Williams-Johnson, M., Cross, D., Hong, J. et al. 2008. There are No Emotions in Math: How Teachers Approach Emotion in the Classroom, *Teachers College Record* 110(8): 1574–610.
Yorke, M. and Knight, P. 2004. Self-theories: Some Implications for Teaching and Learning in Higher Education, *Studies in Higher Education* 29(1), 25–37.
Zajonc, R. 1980. Feeling and Thinking: Preferences Need No Inferences, *American Psychologist* 35, 151–75.

Chapter 2
Learning and the Brain – An Overview

Richard Roche

Introduction

Learning takes place as a result of discrete and long-lasting changes in the physical structure of the brain, and understanding the nature of, and mechanisms behind, such changes has been one of the major topics in the history of neuroscience. This chapter will present a brief overview of what is currently known about the way in which learning is represented in the human brain, and specifically how emotional responses can influence this learning process. Initially, a summary of the brain's structure (on both macro- and microscopic levels) will be presented, outlining how brain cells communicate and the basic functions of the lobes of each hemisphere. In so doing, some common misconceptions and widely accepted myths about the brain will be dispelled. Following this, an overview of learning and memory will detail what has been learned by neuroscientific approaches to the study of how information is retained in the brain. Next, how the brain processes emotion will be discussed, and the impact of emotion on reasoning, decision-making and memory will be explored. Finally, different methods of teaching and learning will be compared in the light of neuroscientific knowledge in order to identify potentially the most appropriate and effective methods of conveying information in a learning environment.

An Introduction to the Brain: Truth and Myth

Inside the skull of every reader of these words, safely encased within thick bone and floating in impact-absorbing fluid-filled sacs, lies the most complex object in the known universe. The brain is an organ of such immense complexity, such staggering potential, that it is capable of generating more thoughts than there are atoms in all the cosmos. Weighing approximately the same as a bag of sugar, and boasting a texture described as similar to a variety of desserts (from jelly to blancmange), it is responsible for every thought, action, sensation, emotion, memory and intention which we experience, and it carries out the majority of these functions with such speed and efficiency that we are largely unaware of their presence. In fact, often it is only when some aspect of its function is damaged that we become aware of its myriad operations at all, and we have learned much about the functioning of the normal brain from the study of damaged ones. More recently, with the advent of modern brain-imaging techniques, it has become possible to study the intact, healthy brain *in vivo* as it executes complex cognitive tasks. Such has been the impact of such technology that we have learned more about this enigmatic organ in the last 50 years than we had gleaned in the previous 2,000. The brain has finally begun to reveal some of its secrets.

There are many myths associated with the brain and its functioning – false beliefs like the notion that the brain is grey in colour; that we only use 10% of our brains; that brain damage is irreversible; that the larger your brain, the more intelligent you are. Some of these myths may have roots in actual fact, while others have no sound scientific basis whatsoever. It is likely that the majority of these common misconceptions have arisen because, due to the enormous complexity of this organ, some of its operations have been oversimplified for ease of explanation to a wider audience. Such simplifications, through a process of 'Chinese whispers', inevitably become confused and, in many cases, the resultant 'fact' evolves into something which is fundamentally inaccurate. Before we begin to outline the structure of the brain and some of its major functions, we will first attempt to dispel some of these erroneous beliefs.

The Brain is Grey

One of the most common misconceptions regarding the brain involves its basic physical appearance; whether in visual representations, written references or verbal descriptions, the brain is consistently (and incorrectly) depicted as being grey in colour. Perhaps most famously, the fictional Belgian detective Hercule Poirot was often known to comment on exercising the 'little grey cells' in order to identify a murderer. While this myth does contain a kernel of truth in the fact that much of the brain *is* grey (specifically the *grey matter*, which includes neurons), there are also large portions of brain tissue which are white in colour. These *white matter* regions are composed of fibre tracts which connect neuron bundles to each other. Furthermore, the brain contains black tissue: the *substantia nigra* ('black substance') is one of five subcortical nuclei which form the basal ganglia, a set of structures which are associated with motor control and have been implicated in Parkinson's disease. Finally, the many veins and arteries which regulate blood flow to and from the brain mean that there are significant areas of red to be found in the brain. As such, the brain is a far more colourful organ than the monochrome grey with which it is so often portrayed.

We Only Use 10% of Our Brain

The idea that humans only use one-tenth of their brain is a very common, and utterly inaccurate, story which has made its way into popular culture. Variants of this statement have been attributed to such figures as Albert Einstein, and despite many public refutations of the 'fact', the idea persists. This myth seems to convey an image of one small portion of the brain working away furiously while the remaining 90% of cortical tissue sits dormant, waiting for us to tap its potential. Another popular interpretation of this myth is to claim it hints at as yet undiscovered psychic abilities such as telekinesis or extrasensory perception which humans have not yet been able to master. The truth is that we use all of our brain, not just 10% of it. In the past 200 years, neuroscientists have been able to identify the cognitive, motor or perceptual operations of each section of the cerebral cortex, as we will see in the next section, and (as we will also see), there is no area to which a specific function has not been attributed. Even in cases of blindness, when one would expect the now redundant visual cortices to be inactive, it has been shown that this is not what happens – the cells in this region appear to be 'co-opted' into other functions such as auditory processing or, in Braille readers, tactile perception. The brain is constantly active – if we were to translate brain cell firing into auditory signals, we would hear the constant crackle of hundreds of thousands of cells communicating each second, even when we think ourselves to be inactive, or 'doing nothing'. Even in our sleep, the brain continues to work tirelessly.

Brain Damage is Always Permanent

Many cases of brain injury – e.g. from a car crash, a stroke or a degenerative disorder – result in the loss of large numbers of brain cells (neurons), and frequently the aftermath of such damage can be devastating for the person affected. Symptoms can include speech problems, memory impairment, paralysis, perceptual disturbances or even personality changes, depending on the location of the injury and the extent of brain tissue damaged. And while these impairments are often long-lasting or even permanent, the prognosis after brain injury is not always hopeless. The brain's structure is not fixed – it is a very plastic organ; it has a remarkable capacity to repair itself from injury and to reorganise itself to bridge gaps in damaged circuits. In this way, areas of damage or cell loss can be repaired, and in some cases most of the impaired cognitive functions can be regained with time. It is this same remarkable plasticity, this ability to form new connections between assemblies of cells, that allows us to retain information for long periods of time in the form of memories.

The Structure of the Brain

Having dispelled some of these misconceptions about the nature, qualities and usage of our brains, it will be instructive next to take a brief look at the physical structure of the cortex. To do this, we must look at both the *gross anatomy* – the larger structures, subdivisions and areas of interest in the brain – and the *microanatomy* – the discrete elements and populations of neural cells that combine to carry out the functions of these regions. Providing such a simple overview will better arm the reader for the discussion of the neural substrates of learning and memory which follows later in this chapter. Finally, a very famous case study will be described in order to demonstrate how much of what we know about the normal functioning of the brain, particularly in relation to memory, comes from the study of people in whom it is damaged.

Gross Anatomy of the Human Brain

If we look at the surface of the brain, we see a familiar pattern of deep grooves and bumps which creates a convoluted topography of crevices and protrusions. These grooves are known as *sulci* (singular: *sulcus*) and the protrusions are referred to as *gyri* (singular: *gyrus*). The human brain consists of two cerebral hemispheres, two large lumps of brain tissue separated by the longitudinal sulcus, a long, deep groove that runs the length of the cortex, making it look (from above) a bit like a walnut. While each hemisphere contains a number of subdivisions which are all associated with different functions (see Figure 2.1), in general it can be said that the left hemisphere is concerned with language function while the right hemisphere is more concerned with visuo-spatial relations. More specifically, each of the two hemispheres is divided into four lobes; the *frontal lobe* resides at the front of the brain, beneath the forehead; the *parietal lobe* occupies the area behind this, beneath the crown of the skull; further back again lies the *occipital lobe*, sitting at the very back of the head; at the side of the brain, around the area beneath the ear, sits the *temporal lobe*. Contained in these eight lobes, across the two cerebral hemispheres, lie all the perceptual, intellectual, emotional, attentional, memory and motor-related functions a human being is capable of producing. In addition to these lobes, the brain also contains the *cerebellum* (literally, the '*little brain*'), which sits below the occipital lobes and deals with motor behaviours which have become automatic through practice, such as driving a car or juggling, and the *brain stem*, the long tube which connects the brain, via the spinal cord, to the rest of the body, allowing the signals from the brain to be turned into action. However, it is to the lobes of the cortex that we will turn our attention.

The *frontal lobes* occupy one-third of the mass of the whole brain, and were the last regions of the cortex to develop in evolutionary terms. As such, most of the higher-order functions which we associate with being human are housed here. Separated from the parietal lobes by the central sulcus, the frontal region consists of the *motor strip*, which is responsible for generating motor signals to be sent to the limbs to carry out actions, and the *pre-motor* and *supplementary motor* areas which deal with organising and integrating these action plans before the motor strip is activated. The *prefrontal cortex*, which can be considered the seat of higher intelligence, problem-solving, planning and abstract reasoning, sits just ahead of these motor areas; damage to this region can have catastrophic consequences such as perseveration (the inability to disengage from an ongoing action, such as slicing bread – a person with prefrontal injury may slice through the breadboard), disinhibition (where inappropriate or profane things may be blurted out) and problems maintaining attention. Other frontal regions include the *orbitofrontal* cortex, a region just behind the eyes which may be related to social behaviour and judging the appropriateness of actions, and the *cingulate gyrus*, which is implicated in executive functions such as coordinating behaviours and action plans. The speech production region, called Broca's Area, is also located in the fronal cortex; damage to this structure can leave people unable to generate coherent speech.

The *parietal lobes* contain a *sensory strip* which mirrors the motor strip of the frontal cortex – whereas the motor strip sends signals *to* the muscles, skin and joints, the sensory region receives messages back *from* each of these areas, informing the brain about the extent of movement and displacement of the body. Behind this lies the *posterior parietal cortex* (PPC), where information from the sensory strip is integrated into a representation of where the body (and body parts) resides in space at any given time. Damage to parietal regions (which often happens in stroke) can result in problems with body image such as paralysis, or (in rare cases) the feeling that a limb may not actually belong to the person. Problems with attending to the space around the body can also result from parietal damage, as in the case of spatial neglect.

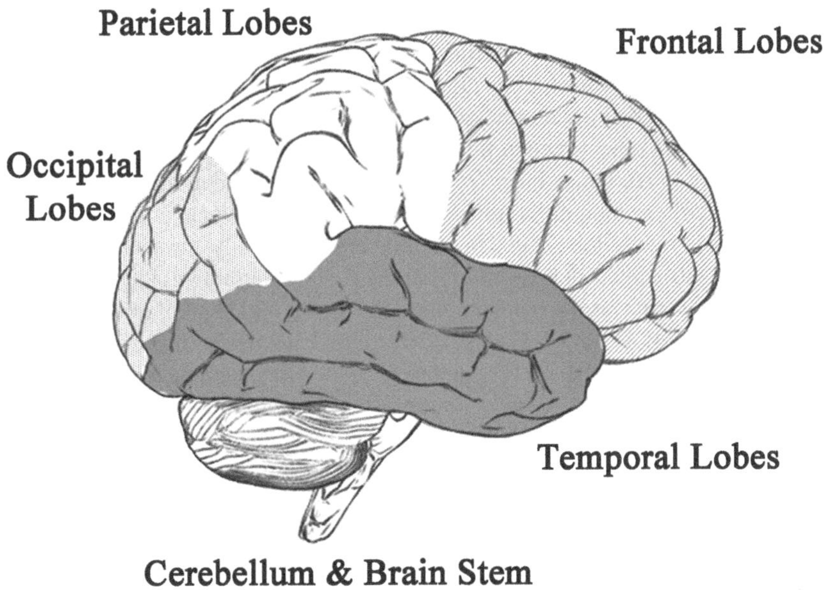

Figure 2.1 Lobes of the brain including frontal (top-right), parietal (top-centre), occipital (left) and temporal lobes (bottom), as well as the cerebellum and brain stem

The *occipital lobes* are concerned with vision. All signals which enter the eye are sent to the occipital regions at the back of the head, where the visual signal is processed. Early visual areas V1 and V2 process all aspects of the visual scene, shape, colour, orientation, curvature, movement, etc. From area V2 onwards, however, we see a division of labour in the visual cortex – information about shape (and some movement) is processed in area V3; colour information is computed in area V4 and motion information is dealt with in area V5 (also called area MT). Next, visual information separates into two pathways, one containing movement information which is concerned with *where* objects are in space (which projects to the parietal cortex), and one carrying colour and shape information associated with *what* the object is (which projects to the temporal cortex). Damage to these visual areas can lead to widespread visual deficits such as blindness is part of the visual field (following damage to V1 or V2), or more discrete deficits such as a lack of colour vision (*cerebral achromatopsia*, following damage to area V4) or a lack of motion perception (*cerebral akinetopsia*, following V5 damage).

The *temporal lobes*, which are separated from the occipital, frontal and parietal areas by the Sylvian Fissure, receive sound information from the ears; they therefore contain the primary and secondary auditory cortices, which are housed in the *superior temporal sulcus*. Also located in this region is Wernicke's Area, which is complementary to Broca's Area in that it is associated with language comprehension – damage to Wernicke's Area can result in an inability to understand language. The ventral (underside) portion of the temporal lobes receive information from the so-called 'what' visual pathway, and is therefore concerned with visual object recognition; damage to ventral temporal areas can lead to deficits in object recognition (termed *agnosia*), which can be as specific as an inability to recognise faces (*prosopagnosia*). Long-term memory may also be subserved by the temporal regions, and of particular interest is a region buried deep in each temporal lobe called the *hippocampus* (literally, the seahorse; plural: *hippocampi*; so named due to its appearance). Considerable evidence suggests that the hippocampus is a crucial structure for the laying down of new memories, as damage to this structure leads to *anterograde amnesia* (discussed in more detail later in this section). Directly adjacent to the hippocampus in each temporal lobe sits the amygdala, a roughly almond-shaped structure which is associated with feelings of fear or anger, and which has direct access to the hippocampus. As we will see later, this anatomical fact has major implications for the retention of some memories.

From this, we can see that the brain is composed of many different areas (up to 50 according to some systems of division), each of which are responsible for a particular aspect of thought and cognition, and damage to which can result in some very specific and debilitating deficits. How these functions are carried out is the result of the action of billions of tiny brain cells, or neurons, which are connected into complex networks and circuits, more complicated than the most sophisticated super-computer yet created. It is to these tiny cells that we next turn our attention.

Microanatomy of the Human Brain

The brain is composed of between 10 and 100 *billion* cells, or neurons. Each of these cells makes connections (up to 200 or more) with other cells, creating complex circuits and networks which form the basis of our ability to see, hear, feel, move, think, remember and solve problems. While there are several types of neurons, the majority share a set of common physical features (see Figure 2.2): a bulbous (or sometimes pyramid-shaped) cell body called the *soma*; an area of branch-like projections called *dendrites*; a long tube-like aperture, the *axon*, which extends from the soma from a point called the *axon hillock*; the terminating end of the axon, termed the *synaptic terminal*.

Signals pass between these neurons to create processing circuits. These messages, lightning-fast electro-chemical impulses, are sent from the axon of one neuron (the output area of the cell) to be picked up at the dendritic tree (input part) of the next neuron. The message this signal carries is very simple – it effectively instructs the next neuron either to fire (pass on the signal) or not to fire.

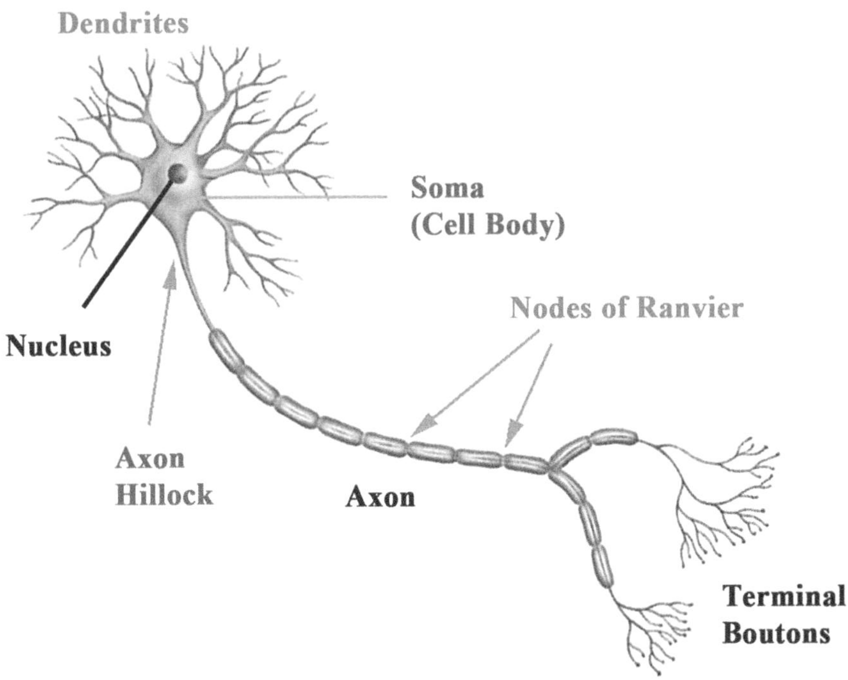

Figure 2.2 **Structure of a neuron, depicting the dendrites, soma, axon hillock, axon and terminal boutons; nodes of Ranvier are tiny gaps between areas of insulation (myelin) along the axon**

For many years, it was assumed that neurons were all physically connected to each other, and that signals passed between them by virtue of this physical linkage. However, following some pioneering work by Sir Charles Sherrington in 1932, it was revealed that neurons do not, in fact, touch each other – they are separated by tiny gaps, referred to as synaptic clefts. The impulse is able to pass to the next cell because the neuron sending the signal (the *pre-synaptic* neuron) releases a chemical – *neurotransmitter* – into the synaptic cleft. This neurotransmitter binds to special receptive areas in the receiving, or *post-synaptic*, cell, causing that cell to either fire, passing on the message, or not to fire, effectively ending that processing chain. At any moment, one cell might receive multiple signals from other neurons, some telling it to fire, others urging it not to; whether or not the cell will fire is determined by the summation of these input signals.

The signal itself is called an *action potential*, and it is a rapid change in the voltage potential of a neuron. It comes about as a result of the concentrations of positively and negatively charged ions which are inside and outside the cell at a given time. Ions are simply charged particles, such as potassium (K+) and sodium (Na+, both of which carry positive charges), which float around inside and outside neurons. Some ions, such as chloride (Cl-), can pass into and out of cells at will through small pores in the neuron's cell wall or membrane, while others, such as sodium and potassium, can only pass through the membrane under certain conditions (which we will not discuss here).

This system of signalling between neurons operates throughout the brain in the *same way* – regardless of whether the activity of these cells translates into perception, attention, memory, movement or emotion, this is how the signals are passed among the cells. The specific nature of the type of processing (perception, memory, emotion, attention) depends on which part of the cortex the cells are located in. Many cognitive operations involve circuits which span multiple regions of cortex. Consider the simple act of catching a ball – visual cortex in the occipital lobes will first be required to perceive the moving ball, with ventral stream areas required to identify the object, and dorsal stream areas needed to compute its location and trajectory. Parietal cortex will then be employed to generate the relevant co-ordinate system for arm-centred movements required to intercept the ball, while frontal pre-motor and motor areas will be recruited in order to turn these action plans into signals for the limbs to move accordingly. And this account fails to include areas involved in motivation or intention to catch the ball, memories of previous successful/failed catching attempts or emotions associated with success/failure. Clearly, even the simplest acts involve complex processes to be accomplished properly – this is why damage to the brain can have far-reaching implications for some unexpected capacities. Later, we will consider a very famous example which emphasises this point in relation to memory; the case of patient H.M.

The way in which these networks and circuits of neurons might represent a memory has been a topic of discussion for decades. One of the most convincing (and elegant) theories of the cellular basis of learning and memory came from

Donald Hebb in 1949. Hebb suggested that, if two neurons in a circuit were repeatedly involved in firing together, then some change must take place – maybe the growth of new connections, or the release of more neurotransmitter, or the presence of more receptors – that will make these cells more likely to fire again in synchrony in the future. This proposal, which came to be known as Hebb's Law, can be paraphrased thus: 'Cells that fire together, *wire* together'. The suggestion that some physical change takes place between cells during the encoding of a memory trace was later supported by the discovery of long-term potentiation (LTP) by Bliss and Lømø in 1973; their experiments showed that, when a cell was repeatedly induced to fire by high-frequency stimulation, it became more likely to fire in future in response to such stimulation. They also showed that this effect was long-lasting. Beautifully mirroring what Hebb had predicted over 20 years earlier, the process of LTP has been shown in various parts of the brain, most notably in the hippocampus, and remains the most compelling cellular model of learning and memory currently proposed.

Learning, Memory and the Brain

There are many forms of memory: we can remember our own name and address, how to write and ride a bicycle, we know the capital of France, and we can remember to post a letter on the way to work. Each of these types of memory is separate and distinct, subserved by differing brain regions. Much has been learned about some of these systems; short-term (or 'working') memory seems to deal with relatively short-lived retention of information, and appears to be underpinned primarily by the prefrontal cortex. Procedural memory, the ability to acquire motor skills like juggling and writing, relies on the basal ganglia, a collection of subcortical nuclei governing movement (although the cerebellum appears to be involved when such skills become automatic, as in driving). Prospective memory, the ability to remember to do something in the future, is different again, and appears to be driven by prefrontal and parietal areas. But it is long-term memory (LTM), the retention of facts and personally experienced events, that we are most concerned with in this chapter; from this point onwards, the term 'memory' will refer to long-term memory unless specifically stated otherwise.

Even long-term memory itself is not unitary, but divided into several different forms. The most common division in LTM, proposed by Squire and Zola-Morgan (1991), is between *episodic* and *semantic* long-term memories. Episodic memory, also known as autobiographical or declarative memory, is our recollection of events which happened to us personally; specific events from our childhoods, recent years or just yesterday. The distinguishing feature of these memories is that we ourselves were present for these events. This differentiates them from semantic memory, which consists of our store of knowledge and facts about the world; this is information for which we were not personally present – capital cities of countries, historical events, important dates and meanings of words. Both of these forms of LTM are extremely enduring, and some may even last for a lifetime. And while this type of retention is clearly among the most important (particularly in terms of education and learning), it has also been one of the most problematic to study. In the next section, we will provide a brief overview of some of the main research findings on LTM; but first, we must address some common biases in the way we think about how memory works.

Memory is Not a Place

If we consider how we think about memory, or examine the language we use to describe it, we notice a consistent pattern – we seem to view memory as a place. We talk about 'storing' information, so that it can later be 'retrieved' or 'recalled'. We speak of 'recollection', as if our experiences are somehow kept in a great mental repository, catalogued and shelved for later (re)collection when we wish to 'bring' this event to mind. There is a clear implication that our memories are discrete objects which are sent from one place to another when we learn something, and later brought back from this mysterious storehouse when we remember it. This spatial metaphor is further supported by the fact that many mnemonic techniques are based on spatial imagery – for example, the Method of Loci, wherein one associates different items to be remembered with distinct locations in a mental journey. Research has shown us, though, that memory does not work this way, and there is no 'library in the brain' where our memories are stored.

Another influential way of thinking about memory relates to information processing and computers. It is convenient to think of our memory as acting like a computer's hard drive – information is encoded to this location, which has a finite amount of space in which to store items; later, when we require this information again, we engage in search processes which retrieve the item and bring it back (onto the screen/into our minds) so that we can interact with it again: to examine it, manipulate it or otherwise utilise the information contained therein. In this analogy, forgetting would imply a failure of these search processes. This information processing conception of memory has proven just as influential as the spatial metaphor, providing terms such as 'encoding', which have become common in models of how memory works. And, like the spatial metaphor, the implication here is, again, that memory is a place in which things (memories) are kept.

One further implication, common to both of these analogies of memory, is that when a memory is 'retrieved', its contents will be identical to those at the time of encoding; the file you saved to your hard drive and the book you return to its shelf in the library will be the same every time you retrieve them in the future. However, as we will see, this view is very inaccurate and, like both of the analogies outlined above, to think about memories in this way would be extremely misleading.

A Famous Case Study – Patient H.M.

Until the middle of the last century, relatively little was known about how the brain actually represents memories. However, in the mid-1950s, an unexpected consequence of a pioneering surgical procedure was to cast a previously overlooked region of the medial temporal lobes into the research spotlight as a key structure in memory formation. The operation would also transform a young epilepsy sufferer into one of the most important contributors to our understanding of memory in history.

The famous neurosurgical patient H.M. underwent surgery in 1953 for intractable and severe epilepsy that was centred on his temporal lobes (particularly the hippocampal formation and amygdala) – a procedure which was described at the time as a '… frankly experimental operation' (Scoville and Milner 1957). He had suffered a road traffic accident at the age of nine and finally underwent surgery at 21, as his epilepsy was largely refractory to the ongoing drug treatment during this time. The surgery reduced his epileptic seizures in frequency and severity, but an unexpected surgical consequence was a severe and intractable amnesia, one which never resolved – it remained for more than 50 years to the end of his life on 2 December 2008. H.M. is perhaps the most tested neuropsychological patient ever; the profound amnesia he suffered as a result of his surgery proved a fertile source of theory, hypothesis and data since the 1950s. H.M.'s amnesia was not global – it did not appear to affect his capacity to recall events from earlier in his life, prior to the surgery ('remote' memories). Neuropsychological studies indicated that his amnesia was related to a specific type of memory.

H.M. appeared to have lost the ability to retain information about personally experienced events that occurred *since his surgery*. For example, he would quickly forget people he had met moments previously, he could not recall what he had eaten at a recent meal; put simply, he was unable to learn or retain *new information*. Other types of memory seemed largely unaffected. His short-term memory appeared to be normal: he could, for example, rehearse word lists or number strings at a slightly lower range than the norm. Furthermore, he could also learn a variety of motor skills and habits. He could not, of course, remember learning these tasks. His IQ also remained unchanged and was in the normal range. H.M. once reflected thus on a life without memory:

> Every day is alone in itself, whatever enjoyment I've had, and whatever sorrow I've had … Right now, I'm wondering. Have I done or said anything amiss? You see, at this moment everything looks clear to me, but what happened just before? That's what worries me. It's like waking from a dream; I just don't remember. (Milner 1970: 37)

The subsequent neuropsychological investigations of H.M. by Milner and her colleagues inaugurated a revolution regarding the biological substrates of memory. A very substantial body of data has since been generated suggesting that the hippocampal formation plays a critical role in the biological processes underlying at least some forms of memory. Patients and animals with damage limited to the hippocampal formation typically do not present with deficits in their short-term memory capacities; nor do they show deficits in their capacity to access information previously acquired prior to their having sustained such damage. They do, however, show a marked deficit in their capacity to acquire and retain at least some types of *new information*. The essence of the deficit appears to be the loss of the capacity to store and subsequently retrieve new personally experienced information, or autobiographical memory. Other types of memory, however, were preserved and a variety of terms have been applied to these types of preserved mnemonic functions, such as 'implicit', 'procedural' or 'non-declarative memory'. It is reasonably certain, therefore, that the hippocampal formation does *not* act as either a short- or long-term memory store, because patients with extensive hippocampal lesions can both rehearse information in short-term memory and can access remote memories of various sorts.

Theories of Long-term Memory and the Brain

The case of H.M. shifted focus to the hippocampus as an important structure involved in memory formation, yet even today, the precise role for the hippocampus (and the medial temporal lobes which encompass it) is still unclear. Recent conceptions suggest that the medial temporal lobes link together different cortical sites that represent a memory (Squire and Zola-Morgan 1991). More specifically, it is suggested that, initially, storage takes place within the medial temporal lobes or the hippocampus (Treves and Rolls 1994; McClelland et al. 1995; Alvarez and Squire 1994), where the hippocampus effectively acts as *a temporary memory storage site*. Gradually over time, the hippocampus repeatedly reactivates representations in the neocortex, leading to stronger connections between these cortical sites and eventually allowing the neocortex to store the memory *independent of hippocampal involvement*. These key ideas form the basis for what is termed the 'Standard Model' of memory formation, and can be found in several of the major theories of recent decades. The standard model is possibly best epitomised by Squire's **Classic Consolidation Theory**. The most compelling challenger to the standard view to date has been the **Multiple Trace Theory** of Nadel and Moscovitch. These two influential theories are discussed and compared in detail in Frankland and Bontempi (2005).

How Memory Works – Remembering and Forgetting

We have learned much in recent decades about how memory works; our current understanding of the memory process has arisen thanks to a combination of experimental investigations, patient case studies and informed theorising. In this section, some of the key discoveries pertaining to memory will be outlined; some of these will highlight optimal strategies for the learning of new information, while others will demonstrate how memories should not be thought of as infallible and stable in their content.

Memory is More like Watching a Play than a DVD

One of the most important findings to emerge from neuroscientific research into memory is that memories *are not the same every time they are retrieved*; rather, they are malleable and subject to change over time. We now know that recalling a visual image from memory activates many of the brain areas that would have been active during the original visual experience of that event; as such, memories constitute a re-activation of brain structures which were active during the original experience. Indeed, remembering an event really constitutes an internal 're-living' of that event, as the entire complex neural circuit involved at the time of learning will become activated again; it is this reactivation that corresponds to our subjective experience of 'remembering'. But we have also discovered that remembered events are not exact carbon copies of the original event. Research into the phenomenon of *memory reconsolidation* has shown that a retrieved memory is in a labile state, and during this labile phase, the contents of the memory can be modified (e.g. new information incorporated), weakened or even, in some cases, eradicated (for a review see Moore and Roche 2007). As such, when we think of recalling a memory, it is more correct to imagine it as viewing a play rather than a DVD; with a DVD movie, every time you play it, it will be identical. But with a play, each new performance will be slightly different to the last; subtle aspects or nuances will change, even though the lines and the themes remain roughly the same. In some cases, even major details may change. This fallibility is demonstrated next in the case of eyewitness testimony.

Eyewitness Testimony: The Fragility of Recollection

The reliability of memory is crucial in situations involving eyewitness testimony; the ability to recount important details about an event will often prove pivotal in enabling the jury to reach a decision. However, even in cases where witnesses purport to have a 'good memory' and may even claim to have 100% confidence in their recollections, the contents of their memories can be erroneous and, in some circumstances, even manipulated. Professor Elizabeth Loftus has devoted more than four decades to memory research, specifically relating to the quality of eyewitness testimony. In one of her (many) seminal studies (Loftus and Palmer 1974), she showed videos of a car accident to two groups of people; both groups viewed the clip in which two cars collided. Later, one group was asked 'Did you see much broken glass when the cars collided?' while the other group was asked the same question, but with 'when the cars smashed into each other' substituted in place of 'collided'. Even though there was no broken glass present in the video clip, the second ('smashed') group reported seeing broken glass significantly more often than did the first ('collided') group. This dramatic demonstration of how the contents of memory could be manipulated by something as simple as the phrasing of a question reveals the fragility of our memory system, and how we should treat the contents of our recollections with caution, even if we think we are sure of our facts.

Unforgettable – Why We Forget and How to Prevent It

The flipside of memory is forgetting, and much research has been devoted to how and why we forget information that we once knew. Two main theories of forgetting have been proposed to explain the mechanism of memory failure: the **decay theory** claims that, as a memory ages, the neural trace underpinning it becomes weaker so that, over time, the trace itself is no longer strong enough to be reactivated. By contrast, **interference theory** proposes that the presence of new information (especially if it is similar to older information) may render older memories more difficult to access. As a result, they are inaccessible to retrieval and effectively 'forgotten'. It is likely that both of these processes contribute to the loss of information from memory.

Other scientists have studied the process of forgetting and how it might be prevented. Early pioneer of experimental psychology Herrman Ebbinghaus studied lists of nonsense syllables (such as 'zof' and 'wid'; he generated more than 2,000 such words) and monitored how long it took to forget them.

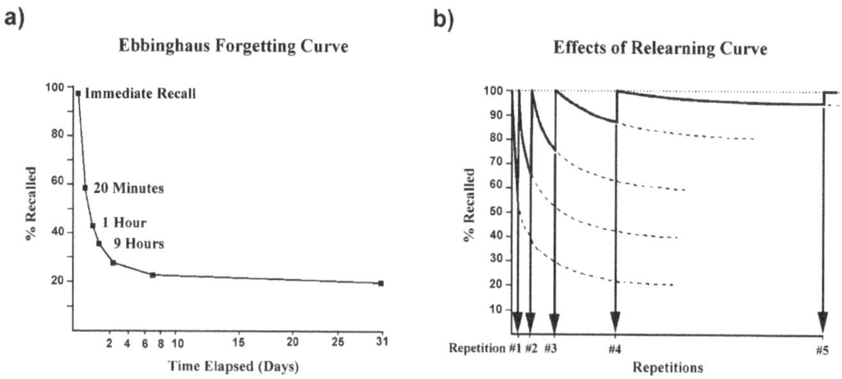

Figure 2.3 **a) Ebbinghaus' Forgetting Curve, showing the normal rate of decay of information in memory – note that maximum loss occurs within two days of learning, after which the curve asymptotes at ~20%; b) Effects of re-learning information on the normal forgetting curve – dotted lines show normal forgetting curve trajectory in the absence of repetition of information**

In this way, he was able to create a 'forgetting curve' which illustrated how retention of items dropped off in the hours and days following initial learning (see Figure 2.3a). Furthermore, he then went on to study the effects of subsequent instances of re-learning and how these might impact on his retention of the words. By doing this, he demonstrated that even one additional learning session increased the asymptote (where the graph levels off) of forgetting by 20%, increasing from 20% of items to 40% (Figure 2.3b). Further, four sessions of re-learning brought this asymptote to over 90% recall, demonstrating that each subsequent instance of re-learning had dramatic effects on recall and, most importantly, on forgetting.

Emotion Processing and the Brain

How the brain processes emotion – which can be defined as the psychological and/or physiological reaction to stimuli – has proven to be considerably more difficult to study and understand than have many of the cognitive processes such as learning and memory which are referred to in this chapter and elsewhere.

Part of this difficulty may stem from the fact that emotion encompasses a wide range of behaviours and reactions, and as such it should not be thought of as a unitary construct. Consider some of the processes that the term *emotion* entails. We may first think of the internal psychological and physiological experiences which go hand in hand with an emotional experience: the subjective feeling of being 'happy' or 'sad', and the accompanying behaviours or physiological reactions which are typically associated with these feelings – smiling, frowning, crying or sobbing, the sensation of feeling unwell, or that our 'heart is breaking'. Such processes would be difficult enough to operationalise and study in the laboratory, but the problem is compounded by the fact that emotion also involves processes regarding the *appraisal* of stimuli – if we encounter a tiger in the street, we may experience fear or terror, whereas experiencing the same stimulus (the tiger) while visiting a zoo or wildlife park will elicit a different reaction. Clearly, emotion involves much more than merely how we react to stimuli – context seems important. Furthermore, the ability to recognise, interpret and respond accordingly to the expression of emotion in others is another key aspect of emotion processing, as these abilities are closely tied to issues of empathy and social behaviour. Other important elements of emotional processing involve how we handle or deal with our own emotions, such as breathing techniques or distraction – termed *emotion regulation* – or strategies to cope better with them – *emotional suppression*. Unsurprising, then, that we cannot point to one area in the brain and say 'this is the emotion centre' – rather, the processes described above are carried out by a variety of brain structures, many of which form distributed and interacting systems. For a comprehensive review of these systems and their role in emotion processing, see Rosen and Levenson (2009).

In very crude terms, we may divide the regions of the brain which are involved in emotion processing into three broad areas and categories: 'older' deep brain structures such as the diencephalon, thalamus and hypothalamus appear to be involved in emotions such as anger and rage; areas of the medial temporal lobes (specifically the amygdala, Greek for 'almond', which it resembles in shape) appear to underpin fearful reactions; and areas of the frontal cortex (such as the prefrontal and orbitofrontal cortices) may serve functions more closely related to the social aspects of emotion, such as speech, context and empathy. In addition, there is some evidence for a hemispheric difference in emotional processing, with the right hemisphere more involved in emotional reactions to (especially visual) stimuli, while the left hemisphere may have more of a role in linguistic and social aspects.

In addition, an interesting subset of frontal neurons have been discovered which show fascinating firing properties in relation to observed and self-executed actions (di Pellegrino et al. 1992; Rizzolatti et al. 1996). These cells, which have been dubbed 'mirror neurons', fire maximally when a monkey observed another monkey or a human raising food to its mouth, and also fire maximally when the monkey mimics this behaviour itself (for an account of the discovery of mirror neurons and the impact their discovery has had, see Roche and Commins (2009). Such discoveries as those outlined above have paved the way for the emergence of a new sub-discipline in neuroscience called *social neuroscience.*

Decision-making and Reasoning: Emotion and Other Biases

One characteristic which singles out primates from other species is our ability to make decisions about complex issues, to mentally solve a problem or reason out a solution. As such, it is not surprising to learn that the brain regions thought to be responsible for these complex reasoning processes lie in the most recently evolved (or 'youngest') areas of the brain, the prefrontal cortex. Considerable evidence has shown that the PFC region is activated while people engage in complex reasoning tasks, which damage to this part of the frontal lobe can lead to significant impairments on such tasks in humans and monkeys. The integrity of the prefrontal cortices allows us to carry out complicated calculations, follow a set of rules, compare alternatives and arrive at a reasoned judgement or solution, sometimes involving an ingenious approach or piece of insight. However, despite being 'good problem-solvers', we should not congratulate ourselves too much on our reasoning ability – a considerable literature exists which suggests that, while we may be able to arrive at the correct solution most of the time, the *way* in which we go about solving a problem is less than ideal, and far from logical.

Studies by Wason (1960, 1966) were among the first to demonstrate that we are particularly poor at seeking out evidence that disconfirms, or *falsifies*, our hypotheses; this is particularly problematic because the only way we can truly verify the truth of a hypothesis is to attempt to disprove it. For example, if we believe that a particular 'virus X' is responsible for causing a disease, say H1N1 (swine flu), we can either seek out cases where sufferers of swine flu have 'virus X' (*confirmation*), or we can seek to disconfirm the hypothesis by looking for cases where swine flu is present but 'virus X' is not (*disconfirmation/falsification*). While we may find thousands or millions of confirmatory cases, it will only take *one instance* of disconfirming evidence to disprove the theory. Using an ingenious '2-4-6 task' in which people had to test a rule by generating number sequences, he showed that very few people spontaneously generated disconfirming number sequences, while they had no difficulty producing confirming ones. He called this tendency *confirmation bias*, and it represents a common failure of humans to engage in rational decision-making. Various other biases (including belief bias, conversion errors and atmosphere pattern) were later discovered from studies of syllogisms and other types of reasoning.

Another major source of bias in human reasoning comes from emotions. We are all anecdotally aware that, when emotions are running high, our reasoning may not be completely sound: we have probably all arrived at false conclusions or made rash judgements when there have been strong emotions involved. When we are calm, relaxed and in an emotionally stable state, we seem to be somehow better equipped to reason out the solution to a problem, assemble all the facts, consider each element in turn and arrive at a carefully considered answer. When we are angry, or sad, or excited, however, these processes seem to disappear, only to be replaced by judgements made on limited evidence, flawed logic or even irrational beliefs. Kahneman (2003) described this contrast as the difference between rule-based reasoning (the former case) and heuristic reasoning (the latter example). He claimed that, under ideal conditions, we engage in decision-making based on a set of logical rules which allow us to arrive at a well-reasoned conclusion. However, under certain circumstances (e.g. when we are experiencing strong emotions), we abandon this approach in favour of relying on 'tried-and-tested' heuristic, rules of thumb or intuitions about what the likely solution might be based on experience. So, when we are calm, we use rule-based reasoning, which allows us to make decisions and solve problems in a logical way (although, as we have seen above, perhaps '*what seems* a logical way' might be more accurate), but when we are angry or upset or elated, we fall back on our well-worn heuristics and rules of thumb; it is the use of these heuristics which may lead us to the wrong conclusion, or to make a bad decision.

Others have shown that, even when processing the same visual stimulus, the introduction of emotion can cause a different brain area to be activated. In an early study of this phenomenon, Goel and Dolan (2003) referred to this as 'hot versus cold cognition' – when people thought about some cognitive aspect of a stimulus, the ventro-medial PFC was activated for such 'cold' cognition; by contrast, thinking about the emotional aspects of the same stimulus resulted in activation of a 'hot cognition' area, the lateral PFC.

In a more recent example, Piech et al. (2010) asked participants to consider which of a series of meals they would prefer, either on the basis of which would taste best ('hot cognition') or which would be most difficult to prepare ('cold cognition'). As expected, different frontal areas were activated in each condition, with the medial PFC implicated in the 'hot' or affective choices, while the lateral OFC was active for the ‘cold’ cognitive decision. As these and other such studies demonstrate, the introduction of emotion into a decision-making situation will not only influence the behavioural outcome of the process, it will also lead to the involvement of an entirely different set of brain structures in arriving at that solution.

Memory and Emotion

Some memories are special – whether it might be the birth of our first child, the assassination of John F. Kennedy, the 11 September 2001 attacks on the World Trade Centre – there are certain episodes which retain their clarity and detail regardless of how much time passes. They seem to be indelibly etched into our minds like a high-resolution photograph, a snapshot in time, perfectly preserved, never surrendering their contents to the slow decay of forgetting. Such *flashbulb memories*, as they are termed, usually share one common element – the presence of strong emotional content. Why is it the case that such specific occurrences have this special status in memory, and why are they so resistant to erosion and loss? The answer, once again, lies in anatomy.

As we have already discovered, the amygdala (plural: amygdalae) is a key structure for processing emotion in the brain. It seems particularly involved in emotions such as fear, anger and shock – surgical removal of the amygdala in experimental animals leads to an inability to show a fearful reaction to stimuli associated with traumatic events such as a mild electric shock. The amygdala’s anatomical location, positioned immediately anterior to the hippocampus in each hemisphere (and being densely connected therewith), appears to give it a role of special significance in memory. It seems that events which are emotionally salient, such as those listed above, effectively have – thanks to the amygdala’s proximity and connectivity to the hippocampus – a direct route into long-term memory. These flashbulb memories achieve a special status in the brain, whereby they are not subject to the normal decay and loss which is often the fate of other memories.

Teaching and Learning Strategies – How Best to Engage the Brain

Taking all of the above into account, can we identify particular learning strategies that are most effective in promoting the long-term retention of memories? And furthermore, can we tailor our teaching strategies to best accommodate these learning techniques? In this section, we outline some of the best approaches to learning and memory formation, with the intention that knowledge of these strategies can guide our teaching styles in a way that will maximise the likelihood of retention over the long term. Various memory techniques exist, including mnemonics such as the ‘method of loci’ or the ‘pegword’ system (many such techniques involve visual imagery, though some are verbal), mind maps, concept trees and others. While some of these approaches may be useful for enhancing the long-term recall of information, often the most effective strategy for a student will be determined by: a) the *content* of the to-be-learned information; and b) the *preferred learning style* of the student. What we present here are some general guidelines which may be applied to the learning process, regardless of information type or personal preference.

Context is Crucial

One key finding to have emerged from the past 60 years of hippocampal research is that context is a crucial aspect of memory formation. The hippocampus itself is essentially a context machine, receiving convergent input from all the senses: visual, auditory, olfactory – all the elements necessary to provide a contextual background to any piece of information. Studies have repeatedly shown that new information is better remembered when it entails a rich context – imagery, associations, details, salient points: all of these factors will lead to better retention. Other experiments show that new facts display enhanced recall if they can be incorporated into a person's stored knowledge base. As such, rich and evocative examples which relate to students' prior experience are likely to promote improved retention of the facts. Also, elaborative processing of the information, wherein people focus on the meaning of material rather than superficial features, leads to better recall. These approaches have been shown to be significantly superior learning strategies to rote rehearsal and repetition. Finally, it has been demonstrated that memory recall is best when the physical environment at the time of testing matches that in which the learning took place: i.e. those who study in the library are more likely to recall the information if they are tested in the library.

Massed versus Spaced Learning – Cramming Doesn't Work in the Long Run

A common tactic of students in the lead-up to an examination is to learn large amounts of information at the last minute; this strategy often goes hand in hand with foregoing sleep in order to make the most of the dwindling time before the test. While such 'cramming' has frequently saved the proverbial bacon of many a despairing undergraduate, as a long-term memory technique, it has been shown to be poor. This *massed learning* leads to adequate retention over the short term (a matter of days); the long-term recall of such crammed information is very poor relative to *spaced learning*, wherein the information has been rehearsed and re-learned over a space of weeks or months. When the number of repetitions of information is matched using both techniques, spaced learning results in greatly improved long-term retention over massed. For anyone intending to pursue a career in the legal profession, retention of the facts far beyond the exam period will clearly be essential. Furthermore, the practice of 'pulling an all-nighter' can be even more detrimental to long-term recall, as it has been repeatedly shown that sleep (during which memory consolidation takes place) is a crucial aspect of the long-term memory process. As such, lack of sleep combined with cramming will lead to disastrously poor long-term recollection of the learned information.

Re-learning and Savings – Lessons from Ebbinghaus

A cursory look at the Ebbinghaus Forgetting Curve (Figure 2.3b) reveals the dramatic impact re-learning can have on subsequent retention. Even just one episode of re-learning already studied information increases the asymptote of the forgetting curve from ~20% to closer to 45%, while a third learning session increases the cut-off to over 60%. Obviously, the more times material is learned, the greater its long-term recollection is likely to be. When this re-learning approach is combined with the strategy of spaced learning described above, long-term retention of the information will be significantly facilitated.

Conclusion

Thanks to neuroscientific research and experimental investigation, we now know more about how our memory works than we have at any previous point in human history. Our understanding of the brain's complex architecture and interconnectivity has informed our conceptualisations of how the memory process operates, how we learn new information and why some events are preserved for decades while others are forgotten in minutes. Such evidence has allowed us to rethink our view of memory, not as a sort of mental warehouse of facts, but as *an active and constructive process* whereby every act of recall is really an internal re-experiencing of events, subject to subtle change and distortion. Such research has also helped us to discover the optimal learning strategies that allow for the greatest chance of accurate long-term recall. And while these findings can inform the strategies employed by both the teacher and the student, it remains inescapable that optimal learning outcomes will only be achieved with the application of motivation, attention and application on the part of the learner.

References

Alvarez, P. and Squire, L.R. 1994. Memory Consolidation and the Medial Temporal Lobe: A Simple Network Model, *Proceedings of the National Academy of Science of the USA* 91: 7041–5.

Bliss, T.V. and Lømø, T. 1973. Long-lasting Potentiation of Synaptic Transmission in the Dentate Area of the Anaesthetised Rabbit Following Stimulation of the Perforant Path, *Journal of Physiology* 232(2): 331–56.

di Pellegrino, G., Fadiga, L., Fogassi, L., Gallese, V. and Rizzolatti, G. 1992. Understanding Motor Events: A Neurophysiological Study, *Experimental Brain Research* 91(1): 176–80.

Frankland, P.W. and Bontempi, B. 2005. The Organization of Recent and Remote Memories, *Nature Reviews Neuroscience* 6(2): 119–30.

Goel, V. and Dolan, R.J. 2003. Reciprocal Neural Response within Lateral and Ventral Medial Prefrontal Cortex during Hot and Cold Reasoning, *NeuroImage* 20(4): 2314–21.

Hebb, D.O. 1949. *The Organization of Behavior: A Neuropsychological Theory.* New York: Wiley.

Kahneman, D. 2003. A Perspective on Judgment and Choice: Mapping Bounded Rationality, *American Psychologist* 58(9): 697–720.

Loftus, E.F. and Palmer, J.C. 1974. Reconstruction of Auto-mobile Destruction: An Example of the Interaction between Language and Memory, *Journal of Verbal Learning and Verbal Behaviour* 13: 585–9.

McClelland, J.L., McNaughton, B.L. and O'Reilly, R.C. 1995. Why there are Complementary Learning Systems in the Hippocampus and Neocortex: Insights from the Successes and Failures of Connectionist Models of Learning and Memory, *Psychological Review* 102(3): 419–57.

Milner, B. 1970. *Memory and the Medial Temporal Regions of the Brain. Biology of Memory.* New York: Academic Press, Inc.

Moore, J.L. and Roche, R.A.P. 2007. Reconsolidation Revisited: A Review and Commentary on the Phenomenon, *Reviews in the Neurosciences* 18(5): 365–82.

Nadel, L. and Moscovitch, M. 1997. Memory Consolidation, Retrograde Amnesia and the Hippocampal Complex, *Current Opinion in Neurobiology* 7: 217–27.

Piech, R.M., Lewis, J., Parkinson, C.H., Owen, A.M., Roberts, A.C., Downing, P.E. and Parkinson, J.A. 2010. Neural Correlates of Affective Influence on Choice, *Brain and Cognition* 72(2): 282–8.

Rizzolatti, G., Fadiga, L., Gallese, V. and Fogassi, L. 1996. Premotor Cortex and the Recognition of Motor Actions, *Cognitive Brain Research* 3(2): 131–41.

Roche, R.A.P. and Commins, S. 2009. *Pioneering Studies in Cognitive Neuroscience.* Maidenhead: McGraw-Hill.

Rosen, H.J. and Levenson, R.W. 2009. The Emotional Brain: Combining Insights from Patients and Basic Science, *Neurocase* 15(3): 173–81.

Rosenbaum, R.S., Priselac, S., Köhler, S., Black, S.E., Gao, F., Nadel, L. and Moscovitch, M. 2000. Remote Spatial Memory in an Amnesic Person with Extensive Bilateral Hippocampal Lesions, *Nature Neuroscience* 3: 1044–8.

Scoville, W.B. and Milner, B. 1957. Loss of Recent Memory after Bilateral Hippocampal Lesions, *Journal of Neurology, Neurosurgery and Psychiatry* 20: 11–21.

Squire, L.R. and Zola-Morgan, S. 1991. The Medial Temporal Lobe Memory System, *Science* 253: 1380–86.

Treves, A. and Rolls, E.T. 1994. A Computational Analysis of the Role of the Hippocampus in Memory, *Hippocampus* 4: 374–91.

Viskontas, I.V., McAndrews, M.P. and Moscovitch, M. 2000. Remote Episodic Memory Deficits in Patients with Unilateral Temporal Lobe Epilepsy and Excisions, *Journal of Neuroscience* 20(15): 5853–7.

Wason, P.C. 1960. On the Failure to Eliminate Hypotheses in a Conceptual Task, *Quarterly Journal of Experimental Psychology* 12: 129–40.

Wason, P.C. 1966. Reasoning, in B.M. Foss (ed.), *New Horizons in Psychology*. Harmondsworth: Penguin.

Chapter 3
Enhancing Self-Control: Insights from Neuroscience

Lorraine Boran and David Delany

> A man who is master of himself can end a sorrow as easily as he can invent a pleasure.
>
> Oscar Wilde (1890/1988: 85)

> This is your thirty-fifth attempt to elicit an emotional response from me.
>
> Young Spock in *Star Trek* (2009)

Introduction

Self-control refers to our ability to manage natural, reflexive responses to events, and thereby shape our sensory, behavioural and emotional experiences. High self-control predicts successful relationships, academic performance, effective decision-making and coping under stress and uncertainty, emotion regulation, and mental well-being. Central to the notion of self-control is impulse control and delay of gratification. Crucially, self-control can also be understood in terms of attentional control. Attention is a key tool in our cognitive mental kit that allows us to filter, process and analyse events. Uncovering the brain mechanisms of attentional control and understanding how these attentional processes can be improved have considerable value for its application to enhancing self-control.

In this chapter, we review self-control in terms of how individuals regulate and influence their thoughts, emotions, impulses and performance. In particular, we describe various facets of self-control, including impulse control and delay of gratification; affect regulation, in particular emotion regulation; coping and defence mechanisms; and also self-control outcomes in terms of academic performance. Following this, self-control will be analysed in terms of the brain's ability to regulate attention, and neural (brain) models of attentional control will be considered. Finally, we review powerful new attentional training tools that have been developed using insights from the neuroscience of self-regulation. Attentional training tools create novel opportunities for enhancing self-regulation with significant implications for academic performance.

Self-control

Rigid emotional control and cold logic are prized cognitive traits attributed to Spock, the humanoid Vulcan in *Star Trek*. Emotional suppression and even ritual purging of emotions are some of the techniques used to gain emotional control. Contrary to common belief, among Vulcans at least, thought or emotional suppression does not result in greater emotional or self-control. Recent studies suggest that the mental effort expended attempting to suppress unwanted emotional responses temporarily leads to a loss of self-control and mental resilience as measured by how long one can resist fatigue in a test of grip strength (Muraven, Tice and Baumeister 1998). Moreover, this form of effortful control can lead to a resurgence of the unwanted thought or emotion (Wegner et al. 1987).

Nevertheless, in our daily lives we attempt to regulate our normal responses, by asserting control over immediate or dominant impulses, behavioural tendencies and habits that disrupt our current goals. We try to resist the urge to eat yet another chocolate in the service of our longer-term goal of looking good; we attempt to avoid inappropriate sexual or intimate contact that could threaten our marriage or long-term partnerships; we wrestle with our performance anxiety at the thought of sitting an exam or giving a public presentation. The degree to which we self-regulate and influence our thoughts, emotions, impulses, performance and relationships varies among individuals and between situations (Tangney, Baumeister and Boone 2004). It is critical in the pursuit of long-term goals. So what is self-control?

Self-control is an adaptive mental capacity used to serve the long-term best interests of the individual across the lifespan (Barkley 1997) and to ensure congruence between the individual and environment (Rothbaum, Weisz and Snyder 1982). It is a process that regulates our normal responses 'so as to bring them in line with ideals, moral values, social norms, laws' (Baumeister et al. 2006: 1796). It shapes our sensory, emotional, cognitive (thought) and behavioural experience in a number of domains including response tendencies (impulse control, emotions), performance (e.g. academic), psychological adjustment, mental well-being (e.g. self-esteem and psychopathology) and interpersonal skills, including attachment to others, relationships and communication skills (Tangney, Baumeister and Boone 2004).

Self-control also refers, more narrowly, to the regulation of automatic, impulsive and dominant responses (Miyake et al. 2000). An impulse is a specific internally or externally generated trigger of a more general motivational tendency to behave in a certain way (Hofmann, Friese and Strack 2009). Impulses are associated with pleasure or relief (Metcalfe and Mischel 1999), and are concerned with immediate rather than future prospects (Lieberman 2007). Impulse behaviours linked to low self-control have been widely documented in a number of domains, including binge eating and drinking (Rush, Becker and Curry 2009), abuse of alcohol (Cook et al. 1998) and gambling (Grant and Kim 2003). Low impulse-control is also a risk factor in developing anti-social, aggressive and delinquent behaviours (Gottfredson and Hirschi 1990).

Self-control can also be described in terms of how easily an individual can delay gratification by resisting an immediate reward in return for a preferred future reward (Mischel, Shoda and Rodriguez 1989). Mechanisms that enhance the importance of the immediate reward, such as paying attention to or thinking about it, shorten the length of time it takes to delay gratification. On the other hand, orienting attention away from the immediate reward, either consciously or unconsciously, lengthens the delay period (Mischel, Shoda and Rodriguez 1989). Metcalfe and Mischel (1999) suggest that a 'hot' emotional process must be controlled by a 'cold' cognitive process if willpower is to win out, and the individual is to succeed at resisting an impulse and delaying gratification.

The dichotomy of regulated and impulsive behaviour is reflected in dual process theories of information processing in the brain. Dual process theories differentiate between two fundamental processing modes; one is controlled and effortful, the other automatic and effortless (Schiffrin and Schneider 1977). This taxonomy has been described using various terms such as the aforementioned cold versus hot cognition (Metcalfe and Mischel 1999), reflective versus impulsive processing (Strack and Deutsch 2004), and endogenous versus exogenous processing (Posner 1980). Reflective, endogenous or cold processing is responsible for higher-order thinking (Strack and Deutsch 2004), is goal-oriented, strategic, requires awareness and voluntary control, and inhibits or overrides pre-potent behavioural tendencies, such as impulses and habits.

Control resources support the reflective system, when recruited to monitor and correct ongoing behaviour in accordance with specified goals or standards. On the other hand, impulsive, exogenous or hot processing is automatically activated by spontaneous memories or environmental triggers (Strack and Deutsch 2004) through experience-dependent learning. Hofmann, Friese and Strack (2009: 165) cite the example of a learned association between chocolate and the positive feelings associated with chocolate where the external trigger of chocolate may co-activate the learned response to approach the chocolate bar and eat it. Overriding this impulsive act and altering the learned response requires reflective, endogenous or cold control.

The division in processing is thought to reflect two separate systems in the brain: one supporting top-down control from the frontal cortex (the brain's 'conductor' or 'CEO'), involving dorsal posterior parietal regions that respond to advance information about future events, and the other supporting bottom-up processing of salient and relevant sensory immediate events, recruiting ventral frontal and temporoparietal regions (Corbetta and Shulman 2002). Bechara (2005) identified similar neural systems in the study of addiction to drugs. The impulsive system is dependent on the amygdala (a brain structure central to emotional processing), which signals hedonic feelings or pain associated with immediate prospects. On the other hand, the reflective system relies on the orbitofrontal cortex, an area of the brain heavily involved in planning, and forethought.

Baumeister and Heatherton (1996: 3) argue that an individual's capacity to self-regulate, although limited, is 'renewable over time and can be increased or decreased as a result of gradual developments or practice'. The authors prefer to use the term 'strength' rather than 'capacity' when describing self-control; and argue for a transient deficit or reduction in self-control following initial effortful exertion in any type of task. So, for example, when faced with stressors that tax one's self-regulatory capacity in one domain, such as college, a breakdown in self-regulation may be observed in other unrelated domains, such as overeating, increased irritability and depression, substance abuse, etc. (Muraven and Baumeister 2000).

Baumeister et al. (2006) review experimental tests of self-control depletion in a number of domains. In most of the studies reviewed, self-control is manipulated, by randomly assigning one group of individuals to a condition that requires effortful self-control (such as thought suppression: don't think about a white bear! (Wegner et al. 1987)), while the other group completes a task that does not tax self-control (such as completing math puzzles). A follow-up task is then given to each group to examine the effects of manipulating self-control; the prediction being that those who have to assert self-control in the initial task by suppressing their thoughts will find it more difficult to re-assert self-control in a follow-up task due to 'ego-depletion' (Baumeister et al. 1998). Muraven, Collins and Neinhaus (2002) used this design to examine whether thought suppression made individuals less able to resist the temptation to take an alcoholic beverage before completing a simulated driving test. It was assumed that individuals were motivated to avoid drinking too much alcohol as successful driving performance attracted a reward. The authors found that those who actively suppressed their thoughts in the initial task consumed more alcohol than those who did not.

Moreover, regulatory depletion has been documented in a wide variety of social domains including aggression (e.g. DeWall et al. 2007), attitude change (e.g. Burkley 2008) and interracial interactions and stereotype threat (e.g. Richeson and Trawalter 2005). Recently, Clarkson et al. (2010) showed that perceived levels of self-resource depletion predicted levels of self-control, regardless of actual levels of resource depletion. This supports the argument that behaviour is the result of controlled and automatic processing systems working together with situational and dispositional factors (Hofmann, Friese and Strack 2009). Problems with self-control emerge when controlled processes no longer inhibit or override impulsive or automatic processes (Carver 2005) and are implicated in myriad personal and social problems (Baumeister, Heatherton and Tice 1994). In particular, and of interest in the current review, is the link between self-control and emotion regulation. Evidence will be presented throughout the chapter supporting the argument that this relationship is important in predicting effective learning and academic performance.

Self-control and Affect Regulation

An important facet of self-control is the regulation of emotional states over both short (e.g. an emotional state such as happiness or anger) and long (e.g. an emotional episode such as dealing with negative feedback on an exam; or mood, such as depression or euphoria) time frames (Gross 1998). An emotion is a behavioural, physiological and experiential response tendency (Wadlinger and Isaacowitz 2011) triggered by internal or external events that serves an adaptive purpose (Keltner and Gross 1999). The meaning attributed to events related to ongoing or goal-oriented activity gives rise to an emotion. Emotion regulation refers to 'processes by which individuals influence which emotions they have, when they have them, and how they experience and express these emotions' (Gross 1998: 275); and these processes may be conscious or unconscious (Bargh and Williams 2007). Other definitions of emotion regulation focus on the occurrence, type, duration and intensity of physiological, attentional, experiential (e.g. motivational states) and behavioural outcomes of internal feeling states (Eisenberg and Spinrad 2004). A primary goal of emotion regulation is the reduction of negative emotions, or the increase in positive emotions or relief (Wadlinger and Isaacowitz 2011).

Certain areas in the brain have been identified in emotional responding and decision-making including the orbitofrontal cortex at the cortical level (e.g. Beer et al. 2006). The emotional circuitry at the subcortical level includes the amygdala and hippocampal formation – crucial in memory formation. Emotional experience is mediated by activity in the amygdala, hippocampal formation and hypothalamus (see Kolb and Whishaw 2008, for a general introduction). The autonomic system is part of the peripheral nervous system that controls internal glands and organs by connections to the central system (brain and spinal cord). Both central and autonomic systems are involved in emotion regulation (e.g. Kreibig 2010). The neural systems involved in generating an emotional response and regulating emotion are thought to be distinct, although this is still a subject of debate.

Tangney, Baumeister and Boone (2004) report that low levels of self-control predict poor psychological adjustment (high levels of psychopathology) and less optimal emotional responses. That is, poor self-control is correlated with poor emotion regulation and psychopathology. Psychopathology refers to psychological disorders that include anxiety, depression and addictive or substance-abuse disorders. A central component of these disorders is deficient self-control and emotion regulation (Aldao, Nolen-Hoeksema and Schweizer 2010). A number of emotion regulatory strategies have been identified, and some of these are predictive of psychopathology, including emotional suppression, avoidance of negative experiences and rumination (Aldao, Nolen-Hoeksema and Schweizer 2010). As already mentioned, emotional suppression can lead to a depletion of self-control (Muraven, Tice and Baumeister 1998). Similarly, avoidance of experiences that produce negative emotions, such as panic and anxiety, are risk factors for the development of psychopathology. For example, Holahan et al. (2005) found that avoidance coping predicted depressive symptoms a decade later. Rumination has also been linked to depression, anxiety, binge eating and drinking disorders (Nolen-Hoeksma, Wisco and Lyubomirsky 2008).

Emotion regulation strategies that promote good psychological adjustment and mental well-being include reappraisal, problem-solving and mindfulness (Aldao, Nolen-Hoeksema and Schweizer 2010). Reappraisal involves interpreting a stressor in a positive light (Gross 1998), while problem-solving refers to a more controlled attempt at eliminating the sources of negative emotion. Mindfulness, a form of meditation training involving acceptance of emotions (Segal, Williams and Teasdale 2002) and also selective attention to positive information (Waddlinger and Isaacowitz 2011), has been found to improve mood and quality of life and reduce depression (Godfrin and van Heeringen 2010).

Emotion regulation strategies: coping and defences Within the coping literature, self-control (including emotional control) is crucial in developing resilience in the face of stress. For the purpose of this chapter, resilience can be understood in terms of mental hardiness, which has been operationally defined as a pattern of attitudes and skills that equip an individual with the cognitive tools to deal with challenges and setbacks, and turn them into growth opportunities (Maddi 2002). Maddi and colleagues have been researching hardiness since the mid-1970s, when they first began profiling employees of Illinois Bell Telephone, who were about to undergo major stress and challenges as the company responded to federal regulation. These stresses and challenges manifested in different ways – some individuals were in constant fear of losing their job, others were let go, and still others were required to alter their work practice and duties to accommodate high-level changes in organisational structures and practice during a time of uncertainty. The latter stress often meant that both employees and supervisors alike were unsure of their job responsibilities. A triad of hardy attitudes including control, commitment and challenge were identified as a protective buffer in the face of stress; individuals expressing these attitudes experienced less stress-related illness (Maddi 2002). Control refers to the attitude that it is preferable if an individual attempts to control events; commitment to solving the problem is also important, and challenge refers to the belief that every experience is a learning experience, be it good or bad. In other domains, hardiness not only provides a buffer effect against stress, but can also enhance performance, such as innovativeness and creativity in university students (Maddi et al. 2006).

So, can we conclude that whatever doesn't kill you makes you stronger?[1] Maddi et al. (2009) show that hardiness can indeed be trained, and is not something with which one is born or must acquire in early life following trauma or upheaval. The authors successfully trained hardy attitudes and skills, including effective emotion regulation, self-regulation and social support seeking in undergraduates. Improvements were observed in hardiness ratings and crucially generalised to

1 Adapted from Nietzsche 1968: 254.

improved academic performance. The authors argue that increased hardiness helps students recognise stresses in an objective way and react appropriately so that stresses can be turned into opportunities.

As noted above, certain emotion regulation strategies such as emotional suppression, avoidance of negative experiences and rumination are counterproductive and are risk factors for developing psychopathology. Similarly, certain coping mechanisms such as defensiveness and avoidant cognitions and behaviours are counterproductive (Hodgins, Yacko and Gottlieb 2006). Individuals who do not rewrite history or distort reality but approach experience in an open manner, are less defensive, experience greater control (dispositional and/or situational) and use less avoidant strategies to protect negative self-attributions and feedback.

One defensive strategy that is relevant in the present discussion and linked to academic performance is self-handicapping behaviour, which refers to a set of cognitive and behavioural responses that allows an individual to externalise failure and internalise success (Hirt, Deppe and Gordon 1991). This particular strategy is well documented in college students who fear academic failure. In an attempt to manufacture an excuse for any potential failure, these students focus on task-irrelevant events, thereby creating a barrier to achievement. There are cognitive and behavioural components to self-handicapping strategies, including so-called counter-factual thoughts we have (e.g. 'If I had studied more, I definitely would have gotten a first') and behaviours we enact (e.g. 'I haven't seen the girls in ages, I'll go out for one drink and then get up early tomorrow to start on the assignment) to excuse failure, threat of failing or falling below an expected standard (Hendrix and Hirt 2009).

Self-handicapping thoughts regulate our emotional responses. For example, downward self-handicapping thoughts (e.g. 'I passed the assignment, others didn't; at least I got a pass'), compared to upward handicapping thoughts (e.g. 'If I had prepared more for my presentation, I could have answered that question') can result in more positive or optimal feelings (Roese 1994). By deliberately creating obstacles to success or withdrawing effort, the probability of upward self-handicapping thoughts is increased, which protects against negative feelings (McCrae 2008). Using upward self-handicapping thoughts allows the individual to attribute failure externally to the obstacle and not internally to self-ability or intelligence (Elliot and Church 2003), but at a cost because it reduces the probability of achieving (McCrae 2008).

The problem with self-handicapping cognition and behaviour is that students using these strategies are less academically successful than their peers who use emotion regulation strategies that promote optimism, such as reappraisal (Eronen, Nurmi and Salmela-Aro 1998). Optimistic students show strong belief in their competence and have high performance expectations based on positive past experiences. As self-regulated learners, they stay on task, monitor performance, take credit for success and attribute failure to outside environmental factors (see Seligman 2006). Interestingly, students who adopt defensive pessimistic coping strategies can initially experience academic success, even though they also experience academic-related performance anxiety and have low performance expectations (Cantor 1990). Instead of a self-fulfilling prophecy, this strategy provides motivation and attributional protection to students, often leading to academic success (Eronen, Nurmi and Salmela-Aro 1998: 160). However, it's important to note that in the long run, an optimistic strategy is more beneficial compared with defensive, pessimistic or self-handicapping coping strategies (Eronen, Nurmi and Salmela-Aro 1998).

Reappraisal is also a powerful emotion regulation strategy used to protect against the threat of negative stereotypes that impair the performance of members of groups stereotyped to lack that ability. For example, stereotypes abound that women struggle with maths, Black people struggle academically and men struggle linguistically (see Alter et al. 2010). Performance is thought to be impaired following activation of the negative stereotype because of the individual's attempt to suppress negative emotions triggered by the stereotype, which ultimately depletes cognitive resources available to complete the task. Johns, Inzlicht and Schmader (2008) demonstrated that when individuals regulate negative emotions triggered by stereotypes by using reappraisal strategies, they in fact restore cognitive resources supporting successful performance, and thus improve performance. This finding has obvious implications for the effects of emotion regulation in response to stereotype threat on academic performance.

We turn now to the role of attention in self-regulation, and more particularly, emotion regulation.

Self-control as Attentional Control

Attention is thought to be an important component of self-control or self-regulation such that problems paying attention predict self-regulation failure (Derryberry 2002). For the purpose of this review, we define attention as the ability to maintain an aroused and alert brain state long enough to select events (e.g. internal, external) and responses (e.g. thoughts, behaviours) that are relevant to the goals of the individual (Corbetta and Shulman 2002). Individuals vary in their ability to pay attention over time, also referred to as temporal, vigilant or sustained attention. Vigilance is supported by an attentional network predominantly in right fronto-parietal regions of the brain (Robertson et al. 1997), and damage to these regions results in problems with maintaining attention (as in attention deficit disorder) and impulse control – crucial components of self-control.

In this section we review attentional control of two forms of self-control: one is emotion regulation, and the other is executive function, such as impulse control.

Attentional control of emotion regulation Self-control in terms of attentional regulation begins to break down when problems manifest in regulating attentional focus, response and behavioural tendencies. Problems with attentional regulation can be easily observed in cases of psychopathology. For example, individuals with social anxiety and low self-esteem automatically and unconsciously monitor their environment for signs of disapproval (e.g. frowning faces, any behavioural sign of rejection from others), and once identified, find it difficult to pull their attention away from signs of rejection or negative feedback (Dandeneau and Baldwin 2004).

The emotional stroop is a task used to measure how much an individual's attention is captured by emotion-related words. Individuals are asked to name the ink colour of emotionally significant words (e.g. frown, bad, etc., for individuals with social anxiety) and neutral words (e.g. town, lad, etc.). Emotionally significant words capture the socially anxious individual's attention on an unconscious level and interfere with their ability to name the colour of the ink; attention is stuck on the word and it takes longer to reorient attention away from the word to the colour of the ink (Wadlinger and Isaacowitz 2011).

A number of training techniques have been used in psychopathology to re-train attention away from emotionally significant events. For example, Dandeneau and Baldwin (2004) showed that low self-esteem individuals trained to repeatedly override the urge to focus on frowning faces and refocus on a smiling face were better able to deal with negative social information and showed less interference on the rejection Stroop (used rejection words such as unwanted, excluded, etc.).

Wadlinger and Isaacowitz (2011) also note that this type of attentional training technique can be used to enhance emotional and behavioural self-control. The authors make connections between various forms of emotional coping strategies (Gross 1998) and attentional mechanisms that may support them. For example, they note that tasks such as Dandeneau's attentional training require little cognitive effort and train individuals to unconsciously override impulsive, dominant or pre-potent response tendencies to emotionally significant cues. This is similar to distraction (Gross 1998), which involves shifting attention from one event to another, and can help an individual focus on positive aspects of an experience, which may in turn positively affect mood and esteem (e.g. Tamir and Robinson 2007). This attentional mechanism may also support other emotional regulatory strategies such as reappraisal and problem-solving (Wadlinger and Isaacowitz 2011: 77), which have been shown to predict academic achievement (Eronen, Nurmi and Salmela-Aro 1998).

Other emotion regulatory strategies such as meditation and mindfulness training are supported by attentional processes (Chambers, Gullone and Allen 2009). Meditation is a form of attention training and extensive practice in meditation leads to better impulse control, sustained attention, less depression and rumination (Chambers, Lo and Allen 2008). Extensive meditative practice drives physical changes in the brain, such as increases in the thickness of prefrontal regions responsible for attention and control (Lazar et al. 2005).

Concentration meditation is one type of meditative practice where the individual focuses and sustains attention on either a visual stimulus or the breath. Imaging results suggest that expert practitioners of concentration meditation show less activation in emotion-related areas in the brain and greater activation in impulse control and sustained attention areas of the brain, compared with novice practitioners, when presented with a distraction (Brefczynski-Lewis et al. 2007). The authors reason that seasoned meditators do not experience as many intrusive thoughts and emotions as novice meditators when presented with distracters, hence lower levels of activity in brain areas responsible for these functions.

Additionally, a qualitative study of the long-term effects of deep breathing meditation on academic and test anxiety in medical students reported reduced academic anxiety and self-doubt and improved academic performance (Paul, Elam and Verhulst 2007). Similarly, increased self-control and improved academic performance have been reported in adolescent students who practise transcendental meditation (Rosaen and Benn 2006).

Attentional control of executive function The fronto-parietal system controls executive function and is responsible for inhibiting impulsive, pre-potent and dominant responses; monitoring events, updating information and switching between multiple tasks (see Miyake et al. 2000). These functions are critical in self-control (Derryberry 2002) because they are heavily involved in regulating attentional focus, response and behavioural tendencies.

One measure of executive function is working memory – a limited capacity cognitive system that can temporarily monitor and manipulate up to four items (Luck and Vogel 1997), that relies heavily on attentional control. That is, individuals with high working memory capacity are better at impulse control (e.g. better control of inhibition on the stroop task) and attentional orienting (Engle 2002). Additionally, poor emotion regulation, such as suppression of negative emotions, can lead to a reduction of working memory capacity (Johns, Inzlicht and Schmader 2008).

Klingberg, Forssberg and Westerberg (2002) developed a working memory training programme for children with attention deficit hyperactivity disorder (ADHD) with the aim of improving their ability to sustain attention, control impulses and reduce hyperactivity. Training led to significant improvements in working memory performance and, crucially, it also generalised to better performance on attentional control and fluid intelligence (IQ). Once thought to be fixed, it is now established that IQ can be improved following working memory training, even in young adults (Jaeggi et al. 2008).

Given that attentional control and IQ are both important predictors of academic performance (Rohde and Thompson 2007), other researchers have examined whether working memory training can generalise to improvements in academic performance. Working memory is crucial in supporting learning and is thought to be a more powerful predictor of academic achievement later in life, compared with IQ (Alloway and Alloway 2010). As noted above, a number of papers have shown that working memory can indeed be trained and benefits of such training extend to general attention abilities (Klingberg, Forssberg and Westerberg 2002). More importantly, and of interest to educators, is the observed post-training improvement in fluid intelligence, which is linked to higher-level thinking such as problem-solving and reasoning (Jaeggi et al. 2008). Another recent exciting finding is the improvement in academic performance in children following working memory training (Holmes, Gathercole and Dunning 2009). More work needs to be done to uncover the mechanisms that explain improvements in academic performance following working memory training and whether this finding can be replicated in university students.

We have reviewed a number of self-control processes in terms of attention orienting (emotion regulation strategies) and executive function training (working memory). We now turn to the question of how self-control, in particular emotion regulation, as well as general attentional control, is linked to academic performance.

Self-control and Academic Performance

A self-regulated learner is one who is 'able to set task-related, reasonable goals, take responsibility for his or her learning, and maintain motivation' (Heikkilä and Lonka 2001: 101). Many researchers have examined the sociocultural, environmental and individual factors that predict effective learning and academic success in learners. Among those predictors most researched are intelligence (e.g. Minnaert and Janssen 1998), self-regulation (e.g. Zimmerman and Schunk 2008), and emotion regulation (e.g. Robbins et al. 2009). The ability to self-regulate, as well as other psychological factors, such as self-efficacy and anxiety, predicts academic performance in young children (Graziano et al. 2007) and university students (Perry et al. 2001; Zimmerman and Schunk 2008). Similarly, the ability to delay gratification (an important aspect of self-control) also predicts academic performance in children (Mischel, Shoda and Rodriguez 1989) and university students (Bembenutty 1999). This may be due to the fact that students who delay gratification are more disciplined, manage time effectively, manage exam anxiety and stay on task, thus increasing the probability of academic success (Duckworth and Seligman 2005).

Impulse control and the ability to delay gratification are executive functions linked to working memory. Both Klingberg et al. (2002, 2005) and Jaeggi et al. (2008) have shown that working memory can be trained, leading to significant improvements in impulse control and, crucially, to significant increases in IQ – an important predictor of academic performance (Rohde and Thompson 2007). A more promising finding is the significant improvement in academic performance following working memory training in young children (Holmes, Gathercole and Dunning 2009).

Emotion regulation is also a critical factor in the learning process and shapes how the student monitors goals, progress and feedback (Robbins et al. 2009). Effective coping strategies such as resilience (Maddi et al. 2009), reappraisal and optimism (Eronen, Nurmi and Salmela-Aro 1998) are strongly predictive of academic success. Attentional training in the social anxiety domain has shown that individuals can learn to override and move their attention away from anxiety-provoking events, resulting in improved emotion regulation (Wadlinger and Isaacowitz 2011). Given the crucial role of emotion regulation in academic achievement, more research needs to be done to uncover the mechanisms that can be used to train emotion regulation strategies that can drive improvements in academic performance.

Conclusion

Self-control has been viewed as a muscle (Muraven and Baumeister 2000) that can be trained. This is exciting as training can produce generalised improvement in self-control in other untrained domains (Baumeister et al. 2006). Moreover, self-control can be trained in a number of ways by targeting the attentional system. Emotion regulation can be facilitated by attentional orienting programmes (Wadlinger and Isaacowitz 2011) and executive function (impulse control, monitoring, response inhibition) can be improved using targeted working memory training (Klingberg et al. 2002, 2005; Jaeggi et al. 2008). Self-control and emotion regulation, informally referred to as 'emotional intelligence' (EQ), are strongly correlated with quality of relationships, impulse control levels, mental health status, degree of psychological adjustment and academic performance (Tangney, Baumeister and Boone 2004).

We have reviewed evidence suggesting that customised attentional training can remodel specific dysfunctional automatic attentional patterns – with positive implications that extend across the clinical domains of emotional psychopathologies and potentially to non-clinical domains of academic achievement. We have also seen how executive function training can drive substantial improvements in attentional control, fluid intelligence (IQ) and academic performance.

The obvious next step is the combined application of these distinct, but interrelated strands of applied neurocognitive research, in the form of 'IQ-EQ training': the integrated application of attentional retraining and executive function training. The nascent IQ-EQ approach raises the remarkable prospect of developing customised software-based training interventions that give individuals an unprecedented ability to maximise their intellectual capacities, fine-tune their emotional health, rationally modulate their attitudes and beliefs on any topic, and deliberately enhance their capacity for self-control.

References

Aldao, A., Nolen-Hoeksema, S. and Schweizer, S. 2010. Emotion-regulation Strategies Across Psychopathology: A Meta-analytic Review, *Clinical Psychology Review* 30(2): 217–37.

Alloway, T.P. and Alloway, R.G. 2010. Investigating the Predictive Roles of Working Memory and IQ in Academic Attainment, *Journal of Experimental Child Psychology* 106: 20–29.

Alter, A.L., Aronson, J., Darley, J.M., Rodriguez, C. and Ruble, D.N. 2010. Rising to the Threat: Reducing Stereotype Threat by Reframing the Threat as a Challenge, *Journal of Experimental Social Psychology* 46(1): 166–71.

Bargh, J.A. and Williams, L.E. 2007. The Nonconscious Regulation of Emotion, *Handbook of Emotion Regulation*: 429–45.

Barkley, R.A. 1997. Behavioral Inhibition, Sustained Attention, and Executive Functions: Constructing a Unifying Theory of ADHD, *Psychological Bulletin* 121(1): 65–94.

Baumeister, R.F., Bratslavsky, E., Muraven, M. and Tice, D.M. 1998. Ego Depletion: Is the Active Self a Limited Resource? *Journal of Personality and Social Psychology* 74: 1252–65.

Baumeister, R.F., Gailliot, M., DeWall, C.N. and Oaten, M. 2006. Self-regulation and Personality: How Interventions Increase Regulatory Success, and How Depletion Moderates the Effects of Traits on Behavior, *Journal of Personality* 74(6): 1773.

Baumeister, R.F. and Heatherton, T.F. 1996. Self-regulation Failure: An Overview, *Psychological Inquiry* 7(1): 1–15.

Baumeister, R.F., Heatherton, T.F. and Tice, D.M. 1994. *Losing Control: How and Why People Fail at Self-Regulation*. San Diego: Academic Press.

Bechara, A. 2005. Decision Making, Impulse Control and Loss of Willpower to Resist Drugs: A Neurocognitive Perspective, *Nature Neuroscience* 8(11): 1458–63.

Beer, J.S., John, O.P., Scabini, D. and Knight, R.T. 2006. Orbitofrontal Cortex and Social Behavior: Integrating Self-monitoring and Emotion-cognition Interactions, *Journal of Cognitive Neuroscience* 18(6): 871–9.

Bembenutty, H. 1999. Sustaining Motivation and Academic Goals: The Role of Academic Delay of Gratification, *Learning and Individual Differences* 11(3): 233–57.

Brefczynski-Lewis, J.A., Lutz, A., Schaefer, H.S., Levinson, D.B. and Davidson, R.J. 2007. Neural Correlates of Attentional Expertise in Long-term Meditation Practitioners, *Proceedings of the National Academy of Sciences* 104(27): 11483–8.

Burkley, E. 2008. The Role of Self-control in Resistance to Persuasion, *Personality and Social Psychology Bulletin* 34(3): 419.

Cantor, N. 1990. From Thought to Behaviour: 'Having' and 'Doing' in the Study of Personality and Cognition, *American Psychologist* 45: 735–50.

Carver, C.S. 2005. Impulse and Constraint: Perspectives from Personality Psychology, Convergence with Theory in Other Areas, and Potential for Integration, *Personality and Social Psychology Review* 9(4): 312.

Chambers, R., Gullone, E. and Allen, N.B. 2009. Mindful Emotion Regulation: An Integrative Review, *Clinical Psychology Review* 29(6): 560–72.

Chambers, R., Lo, B. and Allen, N. 2008. The Impact of Intensive Mindfulness Training on Attentional Control, Cognitive Style, and Affect, *Cognitive Therapy and Research* 32(3): 303–22.

Clarkson, J.J., Hirt, E.R., Jia, L. and Alexander, M.B. 2010. When Perception is More than Reality: The Effects of Perceived versus Actual Resource Depletion on Self-regulatory Behavior, *Journal of Personality and Social Psychology* 98(1): 29–46.

Cook, M., Young, A., Taylor, D. and Bedford, A.P. 1998. Personality Correlates of Alcohol Consumption, *Personality and Individual Differences* 24(5): 641–7.

Corbetta, M. and Shulman, G.L. 2002. Control of Goal-directed and Stimulus-driven Attention in the Brain, *Nature Reviews Neuroscience* 3(3): 201–15.

Dandeneau, S.D. and Baldwin, M.W. 2004. The Inhibition of Socially Rejecting Information among People with High versus Low Self-esteem: The Role of Attentional Bias and the Effects of Bias Reduction Training, *Journal of Social and Clinical Psychology* 23(4): 584–603.

Derryberry, D. 2002. Attention and Voluntary Self-control, *Self and Identity* 1(2): 105–11.

DeWall, C.N., Baumeister, R.F., Stillman, T.F. and Gailliot, M.T. 2007. Violence Restrained: Effects of Self-regulation and its Depletion on Aggression, *Journal of Experimental Social Psychology* 43(1): 62–76.

Duckworth, A.L. and Seligman, M.E. 2005. Self-discipline Outdoes IQ in Predicting Academic Performance of Adolescents, *Psychological Science* 16(12): 939.

Eisenberg, N. and Spinrad, T.L. 2004. Emotion-related Regulation: Sharpening the Definition, *Child Development* 75(2): 334–9.

Elliot, A.J. and Church, M.A. 2003. A Motivational Analysis of Defensive Pessimism and Self-handicapping, *Journal of Personality* 71(3): 369–96.

Engle, R.W. 2002. Working Memory Capacity as Executive Attention, *Current Directions in Psychological Science* 11(1): 19.

Eronen, S., Nurmi, J.E. and Salmela-Aro, K. 1998. Optimistic, Defensive-Pessimistic, Impulsive and Self-handicapping Strategies in University Environments, *Learning and Instruction* 8: 159–77.

Godfrin, K.A. and van Heeringen, C. 2010. The Effects of Mindfulness-based Cognitive Therapy on Recurrence of Depressive Episodes, Mental Health and Quality of Life: A Randomized Controlled Study, *Behaviour Research and Therapy* 48(8): 738–46.

Gottfredson, M.R. and Hirschi, T. 1990. *A General Theory of Crime*. Stanford, CA: Stanford University Press.

Grant, J.E. and Kim, S.W. 2003. Comorbidity of Impulse Control Disorders in Pathological Gamblers, *Acta Psychiatrica Scandinavica* 108(3): 203–7.

Graziano, P.A., Reavis, R.D., Keane, S.P. and Calkins, S.D. 2007. The Role of Emotion Regulation in Children's Early Academic Success, *Journal of School Psychology* 45(1): 3–19.

Gross, J.J. 1998. The Emerging Field of Emotion Regulation: An Integrative Review, *Review of General Psychology* 2: 271–99.

Heikkilä, A. and Lonka, K. 2001. Studying in Higher Education: Students' Approaches to Learning, Self-regulation and Cognitive Strategies, *Studies in Higher Education* 31(1): 99–117.

Hendrix, K.S. and Hirt, E.R. 2009. Stressed out Over Possible Failure: The Role of Regulatory Fit on Claimed Self-handicapping, *Journal of Experimental Social Psychology* 45(1): 51–9.

Hirt, E.R., Deppe, R.K. and Gordon, L.J. 1991. Self-reported versus Behavioral Self-handicapping: Empirical Evidence for a Theoretical Distinction, *Journal of Personality and Social Psychology* 61(6): 981–91.

Hodgins, H.S., Yacko, H.A. and Gottlieb, E. 2006. Autonomy and Nondefensiveness, *Motivation and Emotion* 30(4): 283–93.

Hofmann, W., Friese, M. and Strack, F. 2009. Impulse and Self-control from a Dual-systems Perspective, *Perspectives on Psychological Science* 4(2): 162.

Hofmann, W., Gschwendner, T., Friese, M., Wiers, R.W. and Schmitt, M. 2008. Working Memory Capacity and Self-regulatory Behavior: Toward an Individual Differences Perspective on Behavior Determination by Automatic versus Controlled Processes, *Journal of Personality and Social Psychology* 95(4): 962–77.

Holahan, C.J., Moos, R.H., Holahan, C.K., Brennan, P.L. and Schutte, K.K. 2005. Stress Generation, Avoidance Coping, and Depressive Symptoms: A 10-year Model, *Journal of Consulting and Clinical Psychology* 73(4): 658–66.

Holmes, H., Gathercole, S.E. and Dunning, D.L. 2009. Adaptive Training Leads to Sustained Enhancement of Poor Working Memory in Children, *Developmental Science* 12(4): F9–F15.

Jaeggi, S.M., Buschkuehl, M., Jonides, J. and Perrig, W.J. 2008. Improving Fluid Intelligence with Training on Working Memory, *Proceedings of the National Academy of Sciences* 105(19): 6829.

Johns, M., Inzlicht, M. and Schmader, T. 2008. Stereotype Threat and Executive Resource Depletion: Examining the Influence of Emotion Regulation, *Journal of Experimental Psychology: General* 137(4): 691–705.

Keltner, D. and Gross, J.J. 1999. Functional Accounts of Emotions, *Cognition & Emotion* 13(5): 467–80.

Klingberg, T., Forssberg, H. and Westerberg, H. 2002. Training of Working Memory in Children with ADHD, *Journal of Clinical and Experimental Neuropsychology* 24(6): 781–91.

Klingberg, T., Fernell, E., Olesen, P.J., Johnson, M., Gustafsson, P., Dahlström, K., Gillberg, C.G. et al. 2005. Computerized Training of Working Memory in Children with ADHD – A Randomized, Controlled Trial, *Journal of the American Academy of Child & Adolescent Psychiatry* 44(2): 177–86.

Kolb, B. and Whishaw, I.Q. 2008. *Fundamentals of Human Neuropsychology*. New York: Worth Publishers.

Kreibig, S.D. 2010. Autonomic Nervous System Activity in Emotion: A Review, *Biological Psychology* 84: 394–421.

Lazar, S.W., Kerr, C.E., Wasserman, R.H., Gray, J.R., Greve, D.N., Treadway, M.T., McGarvey, M., et al. 2005. Meditation Experience is Associated with Increased Cortical Thickness, *Neuroreport* 16(17): 1893–7.

Lieberman, M.D. 2007. The X-and C-systems: The Neural Basis of Automatic and Controlled Social Cognition, *Fundamentals of Social Neuroscience*: 290–315.

Luck, S.J. and Vogel, E.K. 1997. The Capacity of Visual Working Memory for Features and Conjunctions, *Nature* 390(6657): 279–80.

Maddi, S.R. 2002. The Story of Hardiness: Twenty Years of Theorizing, Research and Practice, *Consulting Psychology Journal: Practice and Research* 54: 173–85.

Maddi, S.R., Harvey, R.H., Khoshaba, D.M., Fazela, M. and Resurreccion, N. 2009. Hardiness Training Facilitates Performance in College, *The Journal of Positive Psychology* 4(6): 566–77.

Maddi, S.R., Harvey, R.H., Khoshaba, D.M., Lu, J.L., Persico, M. and Brow, M. 2006. The Personality Construct of Hardiness, III: Relationships with Repression, Innovativeness, Authoritarianism, and Performance, *Journal of Personality* 74: 575–98.

McCrae, S.M. 2008. Self-handicapping, Excuse Making, and Counterfactual Thinking: Consequences for Self-esteem and Future Motivation, *Journal of Personality and Social Psychology* 95(2): 274–92.

Metcalfe, J. and Mischel, W. 1999. A Hot/Cool-system Analysis of Delay of Gratification: Dynamics of Willpower, *Psychological Review* 106(1): 3–19.

Minnaert, A. and Janssen, P.J. 1998. The Additive Effect of Regulatory Activities on Top of Intelligence in Relation to Academic Performance in Higher Education, *Learning & Instruction* 9(1): 77–91.

Mischel, W., Shoda, Y. and Rodriguez, M.I. 1989. Delay of Gratification in Children, *Science* 244(4907): 933–8.

Miyake, A., Friedman, N.P., Emerson, M.J., Witzki, A.H., Howerter, A. and Wager, T.D. 2000. The Unity and Diversity of Executive Functions and their Contributions to Complex, *Cognitive Psychology* 41(1): 49–100.

Muraven, M. and Baumeister, R.F. 2000. Self-regulation and Depletion of Limited Resources: Does Self-control Resemble a Muscle? *Psychological Bulletin* 126(2): 247–59.

Muraven, M., Collins, R.L. and Neinhaus, K. 2002. Self-control and Alcohol Restraint: An Initial Application of the Self-control Strength Model, *Psychology of Addictive Behaviors* 16(2): 113–20.

Muraven, M., Tice, D.M. and Baumeister, R.F. 1998. Self-control as Limited Resource: Regulatory Depletion Patterns, *Journal of Personality and Social Psychology* 74(3): 774–89.

Nietzsche, F. 1968. *The Will to Power*, edited by W. Kaufmann. New York: Vintage.

Nolen-Hoeksema, S., Wisco, B.E. and Lyubomirsky, S. 2008. Rethinking Rumination, *Perspectives on Psychological Science* 3(5): 400–24.

Paul, G., Elam, B. and Verhulst, S.J. 2007. A Longitudinal Study of Students' Perceptions of Using Deep Breathing Meditation to Reduce Testing Stresses, *Teaching and Learning in Medicine* 19(3): 287–92.

Perry, R.P., Hladkyj, S., Pekrun, R.H. and Pelletier, S.T. 2001. Academic Control and Action Control in the Achievement of College Students: A Longitudinal Field Study, *Journal of Educational Psychology* 93(4): 776–89.

Posner, M.I. 1980. Orienting of Attention, *Quarterly Journal of Experimental Psychology* 32(1): 3–25.

Richeson, J.A. and Trawalter, S. 2005. Why Do Interracial Interactions Impair Executive Function? A Resource Depletion Account, *Journal of Personality and Social Psychology* 88(6): 934–47.

Robbins, S., Oh, I., Le, H. and Button, C. 2009. Intervention Effects on College Performance and Persistence, Mediated by Motivational, Emotional, and Social Control Factors: Integrated Meta-analytic Path Analyses, *Journal of Applied Psychology* 94: 1163–84.

Robertson, I.H., Manly, T., Andrade, J., Baddeley, B.T. and Yiend, J. 1997. Oops! Performance Correlates of Everyday Attentional Failures in Traumatic Brain Injured and Normal Subjects, *Neuropsychologia* 35(6): 747–58.

Roese, N.J. 1994. The Functional Basis of Counterfactual Thinking, *Journal of Personality and Social Psychology* 66(5): 805–18.

Rohde, T.E. and Thompson, L.A. 2007. Predicting Academic Achievement with Cognitive Ability, *Intelligence* 35(1): 83–92.

Rosaen, C. and Benn, R. 2006. The Experience of Transcendental Meditation in Middle School Students: A Qualitative Report, *Journal of Science and Healing* 2(5): 422–5.

Rothbaum, F., Weisz, J.R. and Snyder, S.S. 1982. Changing the World and Changing the Self: A Two-process Model of Perceived Control, *Journal of Personality and Social Psychology* 42(1): 5–37.

Rush, C.C., Becker, S.J. and Curry, J.F. 2009. Personality Factors and Styles Among College Students who Binge Eat and Drink, *Psychology of Addictive Behaviors: Journal of the Society of Psychologists in Addictive Behaviors* 23(1): 140–45.

Schiffrin, R.M. and Schneider, W. 1977. Controlled and Automatic Human Information Processing: I Detection, Search and Attention, *Psychological Review* 84: 1–66.

Segal, Z., Williams, J.M.G. and Teasdale, J. 2002. *Mindfulness-based Cognitive Therapy for Depression: A New Approach to Preventing Relapse.* New York: Guilford Press.

Seligman, M.E.P. 2006. *Learned Optimism: How to Change your Mind and your Life*. New York: Vintage Books.
Strack, F. and Deutsch, R. 2004. Reflective and Impulsive Determinants of Social Behavior, *Personality and Social Psychology Review* 8: 220–47.
Tamir, M. and Robinson, M.D. 2007. The Happy Spotlight: Positive Mood and Selective Attention to Rewarding Information, *Personality and Social Psychology Bulletin* 33(8): 1124.
Tangney, J.P., Baumeister, R.F. and Boone, A.L. 2004. High Self-control Predicts Good Adjustment, Less Pathology, Better Grades, and Interpersonal Success, *Journal of Personality* 72(2): 271–324.
Wadlinger, H.A. and Isaacowitz, D.M. 2011. Fixing our Focus: Training Attention to Regulate Emotion, *Personality and Social Psychology Review* 15(1): 75–102.
Wegner, D.M., Schneider, D.J., Carter, S.R. and White, T.L. 1987. Paradoxical Effects of Thought Suppression, *Journal of Personality and Social Psychology* 53(1): 5–13.
Zimmerman, B.J. and Schunk, D.H. 2008. Motivation: An Essential Dimension of Selfregulated Learning, *Motivation and Self-regulated Learning: Theory, Research, and Applications* 141–68.

PART II
Affect and Legal Educators

Chapter 4

Can Litigators Let Go? The Role of Practitioner-supervisors in Clinical Legal Education Programmes

Sara Chandler

Do We Experience Joy Every Day in Our Clinical Lives?

In my recent survey of clinicians a respondent remarked that she experienced joy every day with her students. The survey shows that clinicians experience a variety of feelings in their clinical work, some not as positive as joy. This chapter examines the impact of the transition undergone by clinical legal practitioners on leaving the city or the high street for the campus in their journey from litigator to educator. Corporate or high street practices are familiar settings for the majority of legal practitioners in whichever jurisdiction. The future of the legal profession depends on training institutions providing valid teaching for the preparation of future entrants to the profession and many choose to do so by employing practising lawyers as faculty staff. In institutions where clinical legal education is offered to law students, legal practitioners take on new clinical roles as they teach their student apprentices. Do these clinicians have time to care about their changing roles? The results of the international survey I carried out in spring 2010 indicate that they do.

Practitioner-supervisors

Clinical legal education has given rise to a role in the legal profession which I call the 'practitioner-supervisor'. In England and Wales, 'training principals' and 'pupil masters' play this role in the apprenticeship period, during which pre-qualification candidates undertake a training contract (solicitor) or pupillage (barrister). At these stages the candidate is supervised by a practitioner who is also fully engaged in their own legal practice. In addition to that, some institutions offer clinical programmes as part of the academic and/or vocational stages of study which precede apprenticeship. The practitioner-supervisor trains law students in the practical skills they will go on to use during pupillage or the training contract. During the vocational training stage, the practitioner gives up some or all of their practice to become an educator. This chapter will examine how practitioners feel about their new role as practitioner-supervisors in the vocational training context, the challenges of the new role and whether practitioner-supervisors find their roles rewarding.

Clinical Legal Education

Philip Plowden (2004) defines clinical legal education in clear terms as teaching law through exposure to real clients and their problems. In addition to learning law, clinic provides the forum for developing legal skills and the values, attitudes and behaviour necessary for ethical legal practice. Plowden identifies a key challenge for practitioners:

> clinical work vests the ownership of the learning experience firmly with the students – and one of the challenges for staff working in this environment is to find a balance between maintaining that ownership at every level, but at the same time guiding the student, and protecting the interests of the client. The work becomes a partnership, with the relationship changing as students become more able and more autonomous. (2004)

Furthermore, the clinical experience provides students with the opportunity to learn more than the law, legal processes and skills. It exposes students to emotional settings not normally experienced in law school; the challenge of handling their own and other people's emotions in difficult and sometimes harrowing situations: 'the learning is broader than simply the development of key black letter law skills. Clinical work puts the emotional content back into law. It is in part this which engages students by revivifying law' (Plowden 2004). In order to achieve effective clinical practice the profession needs clinicians who can inspire students as apprentices and in doing so promote and acknowledge change in apprentices' behaviour, particularly in their values, attitudes, beliefs, feelings and emotions towards their clients and other participants they encounter in their practice.

Transitional Roles in the Clinical Experience

The transition from practitioner to educator in the clinical legal education context thus gives rise to a number of affective issues. The responsibility of supervisory practice with all the professional duties of the practitioner to their clients and the Court, as well as the duty to their students places the practitioner in positions of potential conflict.

Questions of training methods may be regarded by some as less significant during pupillage or the training contract; however, in the clinical legal education context, training methods offer a number of challenges to the practitioner. In an educational context discussion about how students learn arises frequently. The framework in which skills training is carried out has evolved considerably in the last 30 years. The growth and acceptance in the UK of experiential and problem-based learning, along with clinical experience for law students – referred to in Webb and Maughan (1996) and Brayne, Duncan and Grimes (1998) – have given rise to a discussion of the effectiveness of such methods in practice. In examining effectiveness, practitioner-supervisors need to examine their role in the process.

Practitioner-supervisors have recognised this themselves. Cath Sylvester and Jonny Hall, who practise in Northumbria University's Student Law Clinic (now nearly 30 years old), observed of the supervisor's role that: 'the demands of clinical work often make it very tempting to take a very interventionist role in casework' (2004: 51). This dilemma is at the centre of the practitioner's role when they become educators. The practitioner is the expert and the student can learn as an apprentice does by following in their footsteps. David Cruikshank writes: 'The teacher remains the expert who eventually provides a solution to the problem. Students may learn by imitating the expert's steps some problem-solving skills' (1996: 190–91).

For some practitioners there is a practical difficulty in finding the balance necessary for the student to learn from their experience without putting the client at risk. Can students learn effectively without experiencing some risk, enabling them to learn from their mistakes?

Mike Norwood recommends a series of best practices in relation to in-house clinical courses on observing clinical legal education in the USA. He examines the dichotomy between the goal of giving students responsibility and the goal of protecting clients' interests and writes:

> Deciding when and how to intervene in a student's representation of a client is one of the most difficult decisions faced by clinical teachers. When a supervisor intervenes too early in the process, the student is not afforded the opportunity to learn from approaching the problem by herself ... Furthermore, a clinical teacher who is constantly 'rescuing' a student is likely to undermine the student's confidence in her ability to become a capable lawyer. At the other extreme, a supervisor who provides little or no intervention when it is apparent the student is beyond his or her own capabilities risks real harm to the client. (2007: 195)

How might the dilemma of balancing control with autonomy affect the practitioner-supervisor's feelings about their role? As practitioners relocate from private practice offices to the law school and postgraduate college, they find themselves in a new environment which encourages new attitudes, values and goals in relation to the teaching and training of their students. Practitioners may experience a development in their own practice which may reward them in ways they may not have expected before entering an educational environment. They may discover new objectives in their work which give them satisfaction and pleasure in the role they have undertaken.

Of course, practitioners not only relocate their practice in terms of environment, but also give up the daily practical experience, the excitement of litigation, the satisfaction of successful transactions, client contact and pleasure in achieving successful outcomes and access to justice for their clients. New experiences as practitioner-supervisors give rise to a variety of emotions that may not be quite as pleasurable and exciting. Perhaps the recognition that feelings influence the perception of the practitioner-supervisor's role forms part of a learning process for the practitioner-supervisor. Work Based Learning,[1] the Law Society's proposed apprenticeship period, will run alongside the training contract for those Legal Practice Course graduates who cannot obtain a training contract but do work as para-legals. The title implies a greater focus on trainee-centred learning and may challenge the traditional master–apprentice role of the solicitor and trainee solicitor. Training principals can make the learning process easier for the trainee by having a greater understanding of how to facilitate their learning. Giving a greater degree of independence and responsibility to the trainee may enable young lawyers to develop their capabilities to a greater extent, as long as they receive appropriate guidance and supervision.

Developing a conscious theory of learning and an understanding of teaching methods can enable practitioner-supervisors to derive greater satisfaction from their work, and as a consequence greater motivation. Posing questions about the nature of their practice, the style of their supervision, and their feelings about their work may enable a practitioner-supervisor to have a greater understanding of their role and their identity. In gaining greater understanding of their role practitioner-supervisors can understand how to make better lawyers of their students.

In Chapter 12 Nigel Duncan recommends increasing the opportunities for repetition of the practical experience in order to increase learning and enable students to develop their capacity for empathy and in turn for ethical legal practice. Those opportunities, together with the development of reflective practice in students, can present the practitioner-supervisor with an alternative to the satisfaction derived from their own experience as a litigator. A simple explanation of reflective practice is that we question what we already know and identify what we need to know in order to progress our understanding and improve our practice. Schön (1983, 1987) writes that the reflective practitioner:

> allows himself to experience surprise, puzzlement, or confusion in a situation which he finds uncertain or unique. He reflects on the phenomenon before him, and on the prior understandings which have been implicit in his behaviour. He carries out an experiment which serves to generate both a new understanding of the phenomenon and a change in the situation. (1983: 68)

1 Current pilot by the Solicitors Regulation Authority (SRA) to evaluate an alternative assessment practice to the Training Contract.

The supervisor's role is to engender this reflection in their students by enabling students to process feedback on the current experience and build on their previous experience. We do this in order to guide the direction for future learning.

Practitioners new to clinic supervision do not generally address their practical work in terms of the theory of learning. Running a practice in the context of an educational environment is a sufficient challenge for most new clinic supervisors without adding the consideration of how their students are learning. However, the development of clinical legal practice can be enriched by the development of theories of teaching and learning.[2]

In their 2004 study of five clinical programmes in the UK, Hugh Brayne and Richard Grimes commented that experiential learning has been long established as effective pedagogy. They observed:

> clinical programmes can exist to achieve a range of objectives, and each participant is likely to have their own additional personal motive. For example, teachers report greater satisfaction from their closer and, they feel, more effective personal involvement in the students' learning. Students obtain satisfaction at achieving something both on behalf of others and in their own development of skill and understanding, plus, of course, an enhanced CV. (2004: 14)

Developing Conscious Supervisory Skills

Paolo Freire's contribution to the theory of learning was the theme of the *International Journal of Clinical Legal Education* (IJCLE) annual conference in July 2006. In an unpublished paper to the conference a theme was developed in the examination of the role of the practitioner-supervisor in providing a safety blanket, while enabling student advisors to experiment and develop their skills by taking ownership of their cases and assisting their own clients (Chandler and Robotham 2006). However, 'educational practice, whether it be authoritarian or democratic, is always directive' (Freire 1994/2004: 66). Freire discusses how the educator's 'directivity' interferes with the creative, investigative capacity of students and can become manipulative and authoritarian. Practitioner-supervisors share this situation. Like Freire we recognise that the role of the supervisor is often directive and we seek to understand how we can encourage creativity within our students. Freire takes issue with the 'banking' concept of education in which the educator makes 'deposits' in the receiver-student, who has a passive role in receiving information. In a clinic setting supervisors can choose to work alongside their students, giving them the respect of a colleague and enabling them to take a fully active and creative role.

---

2 The discussion of clinical legal practice has been developed in the USA to a greater extent than in the UK where these issues are coming to the surface as more universities and colleges adopt clinic as part of their practice.

The Survey of Clinic Supervisors 2010

The aim of the survey was to find out how the feelings of the clinic supervisors changed as they changed their role from litigator to educator. I then sought to identify issues arising from their responses. I contacted practitioner-supervisors in 30 universities and postgraduate colleges,[3] 15 from the UK and 15 from other countries. The criteria for selection for the sample were that the institution has a clinical legal education programme and that the students are supervised by qualified legal practitioners. Sixty-eight clinic supervisors responded to the questionnaire with comments on their roles in educating students.

Framework for Examining the Role of Practitioner-supervisor

I developed a basic framework for examining the transition from practitioner to educator, by reviewing the practical tasks involved in the stages of development of a case. The questions in the survey were designed to assess the degree of intervention in the casework process by the practitioner-supervisor and the impact that had on their emotions – levels of satisfaction, pleasure, anxiety, and so on. I hope to examine how more or less risk taken by the practitioner-supervisor affects the satisfaction gained as educators when students are allowed to take on more or less responsibility for their cases. The criteria for choosing stages of development were based on steps in the practical casework timetable and usually form the basis for interaction between supervisor and student such as supervision, assessment and feedback, and meetings for encouraging reflection by students on their development.

There are a number of stages in the case timetable where the practitioner-supervisor may discuss the case with students, explore students' feelings, the development of their practical skills and their developing confidence in becoming lawyers. These stages are also markers at which the practitioner-supervisor may assess the degree to which students may take responsibility for cases and the risk involved in allowing students ownership of cases.

Practitioner-supervisors may develop different styles in their role such as coach, mentor, colleague and role model to apprentice. They may observe in their students a growing confidence in preparing for and conducting client interviews;

3 University of Northumbria, College of Law, City Law School, Nottingham Law School, Monash University, University of Kent, University of Strathclyde, University of Cape Town, University of Tennessee, Istanbul Bilgi University, Nelson Mandela University, Palacky University, Ohio State University, University of Hertfordshire, Queen Mary University, BPP Law School, University of East London, Sheffield Hallam University, Cardiff University, Leeds University, University of Glamorgan, University of Toronto, De Montfort University, Warsaw University, University of Memphis, University of Westminster, Abia State University, Nigeria, Ebonyi State University, Nigeria, Adekunle Ajasin University, Nigeria, Nigeria Law School.

in the imagination and knowledge they bring to developing the case plan; and in their competence in growing research skills. Further, they may observe the enthusiasm with which students employ problem-solving skills. Discussion with students enables positive and negative emotional experiences which have emerged in respect of these stages to be examined in context, giving opportunities for the supervisor to give positive and immediate feedback to students. Students can be challenged on the degree of their commitment to clients, and in the ensuing discussion the practitioner-supervisor can feel more or less satisfaction as they assess the degree to which students have developed. These approaches emerged in the participants' responses to the survey.

At every stage the practitioner-supervisor faces a challenge in managing risk in student activity. A question arises as to the risk we are assessing, that is: risk of what or to whom. The practitioner's duty to their client is balanced against two other duties: their supervisor/educator's duty to their students and their duty to their employer, the educational institution, and their insurers. There are other duties, such as the duty to the Court, the regulatory authority, the legal aid funder and to society in general, which involve more or less aspects of the practitioner's role in developing the future members of the profession to a satisfactory degree of competence[4] and with a level of ethical practice that enhances the student's understanding and commitment to the rule of law, access to justice and respect for human rights.[5]

In order to develop an understanding of the role of the practitioner-supervisor I ran a group discussion of clinic supervisors to identify issues around which feelings arise, and from this I devised the questions for the survey. Some of the questions put to participants in the survey touch directly on the detail of their role, for example in supervising the development of drafting skills, how much guidance does a supervisor give? Does the supervisor amend the draft in their own words, expressing their own drafting skills? This approach is a familiar master–apprentice role and has the benefit of enabling the student to read good examples drafted into their own work. Other questions then arise: for example, to what extent does the document remain the student's own work? Does the practitioner-supervisor refrain from drafting, and confine themselves to suggestions and await the student's own amendment of the document? To what extent can a student say: 'This is all my own work'? Is there a valuable educational experience in the practitioner-supervisor

4 For England and Wales: Day One Outcomes: Training Framework Review, Solicitors Regulation Authority 2007. Six outcomes should be demonstrated by candidates for qualification as a solicitor as follows: (A) Core knowledge and understanding of the law applied in England and Wales; (B) Intellectual, analytical and problem-solving skills; (C) Transactional and dispute resolution skills; (D) Legal, professional and client relationship knowledge and skills; (E) Personal development and work management skills; (F) Professional values, behaviours, attitudes and ethics.

5 For England and Wales: Solicitors Regulation Authority Solicitors Code of Conduct 2007; Bar Standards Board Barristers Code of Conduct 2004.

producing an amended document with a sense of 'Here's one I prepared earlier'? The practitioner's experience is there to be harnessed to the learning experience of the student and the practitioner has to develop the capacity to hold back and allow the case timetable to be dictated by the learning speed of the student if the student is to benefit fully from their clinical experience.

Types of Model in the Survey

The survey showed that there are a number of clinic models where there is greater or lesser degree of intervention by supervisors. A campus-based legal advice centre[6] or a community-based law centre[7] model with practitioner-supervisors from the faculty supervising students who give oral or written advice, and who undertake casework and representation was the most frequent, though some campus-based services were supervised by private practice pro bono lawyers. Other models included:

- campus based telephone helplines,[8] supervised by private practice pro bono lawyers;
- a prison service supervised by the faculty;[9]
- remote supervision (by e-mail) by project supervisors (such as the National Centre for Domestic Violence[10]);
- cross departmental supervision in the Innocence Project;[11]
- supervision on and off campus of representation at Tribunals, such as the Free Representation Unit (FRU).[12]

Practice supervision in the USA is different from the UK because of the ABA Model Student Practice Rule 1969. Students from in-house clinics and placed in

6 Northumbria University Student Law Office; Sheffield Hallam University Law Clinic; Kent University Student Law Clinic; Queen Mary University Legal Advice Centre; The College of Law has Legal Advice Centres at five centres (York, Chester, Birmingham, London Bloomsbury and Guildford).

7 For example, Springvale Monash Legal Service (35 years of service to the community); and Downtown Legal Services, Toronto (10 years of service to the community).

8 The College of Law helplines in Birmingham, Chester, Guildford and London Bloomsbury and the BPP Law School helplines are supervised by pro bono lawyers through Lawworks (see http://www.lawworks.org.uk).

9 Abia State University.

10 Students take instructions by phone, draft documents and send them by e-mail for supervision, meet their client at Court to issue applications for emergency injunctions and assist their clients in Court as 'MacKenzie friends' – unqualified assistants without rights of audience who may assist the Court (see http://www.ncdv.org.uk).

11 http://www.innocencenetwork.org.uk.

12 http:www.freerepresentationunit.org.uk and City University, London.

externships must be accompanied and supervised by their practice supervisor in the Courts of most of the states where the practice rule applies.[13]

Survey Findings

Type of student activity supervised by respondents The first variation between respondents was on whether they hold practising certificates. Nearly every respondent held a practising certificate (79.4%), and most of the activities undertaken by students required that they were supervised by a practising lawyer.

The greatest number of respondents undertook supervision of students doing casework (85.3%), followed closely by supervision of advocacy (82.4%); 67.7% supervise advice-only services, 55.9% supervised students in representation of their clients, 32.4% supervised streetlaw, and only 20.6% supervised mediation.

Central to the supervision of these activities is the duty owed to the client. 64.7% said their duty to their client was more important to them than duty to their students. More than one respondent identified this dichotomy as central to the role of supervisor. A variety of emotions were expressed by participants about this issue: the majority (55.9%) felt conflicted, 54.4% felt concern, 32.4% confusion, 25% frustration, 22.1% satisfaction, 13.2% irritation and 11.8% impatience.

Supervision styles The main set of questions concerned the degree of intervention by supervisors throughout the life of a case, and participants responded to tick boxes according to their own style of supervision.

Approval and amendment

In response to questions about style of supervision, 88.2% of participants approved every piece of written work done by students for the client, and 88.2% gave students suggestions for amendments to documents, though one respondent said this was done by hints rather than suggestions, and another said it depended on the experience of the student. 14.7% of supervisors asked students to amend drafts without suggestions. Most (91.2%) asked students to research the law and prepare a first draft of an advice letter, pleadings or a document on their own, and 38.2% asked students to prepare skeleton arguments for representation at hearings without supervisor suggestions, and 47.1% asked students to prepare skeleton arguments with supervisor suggestions.

Most participants wanted to avoid prescription:

> I view the role as largely facilitative and prefer not to take a prescriptive approach where possible. I feel students get more out of a clinical experience if they feel they have ownership of a case and have responsibility for progressing it as long as they know support and guidance is available and the supervisor is approachable and responsive. (Rebecca Parker, College of Law)

13 For a description of the rule see Joy and Kuehn (2002–3).

Observation

Some supervision included observation of the student/client interview (25%), with a view to assessing student development of competence, or simply being on hand in case of need to assist the students. 16.7% of participants listened in to phone calls made by students with the client, 14.7% listened to phone calls made by students with the other party, and 14.7% listened to calls made by students to the Court or Tribunal.

Students who undertake advocacy on behalf of their clients, for example in the College of Law's Tribunal Representation Service or the Free Representation Unit, have a greater opportunity to develop their skills independently if they attend court or tribunal without their supervisor. For the practitioner-supervisor, however, this presents a considerable risk in that the student may not be able to succeed in winning outcomes that are to the client's satisfaction. The practitioner-supervisor has to assess the risk of failure for the client alongside the effect of failure on the student.

30.9% of participants observed their students when they represented their clients, and in most US state jurisdictions students may not represent at Court unless their supervisor is present, since students are licensed to practise only under the supervision of a licensed advocate through the Student Practice Rule. One respondent from Ohio State University commented that he would not be compliant with the practice rule if he failed to accompany students to Court. The learning experience of success or failure in representation is greatly enhanced by the supportive practitioner-supervisor who enables students to reflect upon the experience, with feedback from the supervisor's observation. The degree of support offered by the practitioner-supervisor can be affected by their understanding of their role, and support can be undermined by the practitioner-supervisor who is not prepared to allow the student to represent the client even in the face of failure.

One participant wrote:

> Supervision of students is completely different to running your own case load. You now have to deal with a range of students with different abilities and they are a bridge between you and the needs of the client. You have to ensure that the bridge has solid foundations and you must constantly ensure that the students are doing work correctly under your strict guidance to avoid any risk of negligence. (Nicholas Ross, College of Law)

Supervisor–student meetings

Most supervisors conducted meetings with their students throughout the stages of the case, 79.4% met before client interviews to prepare, and 79.4% met after the interview for de-briefing with students. 64.7% of participants reviewed the client file regularly and gave written feedback to the students. 76.5% of the participants engaged in reflective meetings with their students. One commented:

> The post-case reflection meeting is the most important meeting of the clinical experience when the students look back and really understand the learning process they have been through, and how they will use the experience when they are in practice unsupervised. (Stephen Illingworth, College of Law)

Choices of supervision styles

Making choices can be stressful for the practitioner-supervisor and can affect the practitioner-supervisor in their role. One clinician referred to several constant pressure points on the practitioner-supervisor: pressure from peers, from students, from university management, from clients, from SRA, and from within 'wanting to do more but with limited resources and little support losing inclination and desire to maintain energy and effort – it feels like an uphill struggle and thankless task sometimes' (Anon.).

Another referred to 'constant uncertainty about the extent and level of supervision' and wrote:

> It is tremendously rewarding although fraught with difficulty in that one often feels as though one should rewrite the document be it letter of advice or application, whilst knowing that that does not help the student. I believe because I regard myself as an 'educator' first, that I am more concerned with my students' experience, process of, and understanding than a Principal engaged with trainees in a law firm would be and consequently more aware of the denigrating effect that non-constructive criticism can have. The self-reflective element of Law Clinic is crucial. (Anon.)

Table 4.1 shows the percentage of time participants spent in contact with their students, or supervising students' written work.

Table 4.1 Percentage of time participants spent in contact with their students, or supervising students' written work

Hours per week	**Up to 7**	**Up to 14**	**Up to 21**	**Up to 28**	**Up to 35**
Contact	42.6	25	11.8	11.8	5.9
Supervision of written work	57.4	27.9	8.8	4.4	2.9

There is always the feeling of ultimate responsibility regardless of the hours. One respondent observed:

> I think the role of supervisor is very difficult because ultimately if something goes wrong in a case I am responsible, subsequently I work very hard to ensure that as far as possible student casework is carried out expeditiously and competently … allowing the students to have conduct of the case – it is a more active role than observation. (Anon.)

Mixed feelings at case outcomes The positive benefit of the supervisory role to the practitioner-supervisor emerged from the responses of the survey participants. Participants referred to seeing their students under their guidance develop their skills, especially those students who presented as unlikely candidates for success as advisors, negotiators or advocates. 69.1% of participants described their feelings of pride on students achieving a successful outcome for their clients, and a larger percentage, 82.4%, described themselves as satisfied. 91.1% were happy with their students and 85.3% were happy for their clients. One participant commented:

> It is definitely the best part of my job yet the most stressful! I love the interaction it allows with students. It's a pleasure to be able to see them develop. You do feel proud of their achievements – rather like a parent might a child. (Victoria Murray, Northumbria University)

Participants identified the rewards of the role clearly:

> The most rewarding part of being a supervisor is watching the students 'mature' almost from their first encounter with the public. Without exception they express a sense of responsibility and pride when reflecting on the experience of hearing and unravelling a problem for the first time. For many it is their first taste of dealings with the many ethical issues which lawyers encounter daily. (Anon.)

Another commented:

> I find the role deeply satisfying in terms of both student and client response and benefit. I also find it stressful and I can spend the occasional night in fitful sleep worrying about a particular case. (Pat Brand, Cardiff University Law School)

Practitioner-supervisors could gain satisfaction from their educator role, having reduced their practitioner role, though other tensions arose. One commented:

> Supervising students is very different to running cases yourself as a practitioner. I had almost 200 cases in practice and knew every case inside out. In the clinic I can have up to 40 cases on the go, but keeping tabs on them all and making sure

> the students are on track is a stressful juggling act. (Carol Boothby, Northumbria University)

Finding a balance between intervention and giving students responsibility was difficult:

> It can be stressful keeping watch over so many cases at any one time whilst ensuring that the students are doing a good job and benefitting from the experience. (Anon.)

There was also a degree of frustration expressed by practitioner-supervisors with students who do not benefit from the clinical experience because they work below expectation, or withdraw from the clinic. The most common emotion fed back by participants was concern (52.9%), closely followed by frustration (38.2%), and then annoyance (35.3%). Only 2.94% felt any anger, and a small proportion (20.6%) felt sympathy for students who withdraw, depending on the circumstances:

> If a student has to withdraw from the scheme because they recognise they are not yet at a stage where they can cope with the case and their studies at the same time then I feel sympathy for the student as they are missing out on the pro bono experience. (Stephen Illingworth, College of Law)

Where a practitioner-supervisor is able to assist students to realise their potential in the face of lack of interest, absence or difficult team members there is satisfaction in meeting these challenges and overcoming them. Using task evaluation and formative assessment to give students feedback on their developing skills gives the supervisor the context in which to coach their students into positive behaviour, understanding and skills development.

On being asked about their feelings if students make a major error on a case, the majority (79.4%) felt concern for the client and 63.2% felt confident that they use the situation as a learning experience for the student. 48.5% felt concerned for the students and 38.2% felt stressed. 32.4% felt nervous, 32.4% felt anxiety and 32.4% felt guilt. One commented: 'For those who make a mistake I use it as a learning experience to enable their future development' (Sally Gill, College of Law).

There were a small number who felt guilt, however one respondent commented:

> I feel a lot more helpless rather than guilt, whenever my students perform poorly. Guilt will come in because I feel I can invest a lot more of my time, helpless because the frustrating condition and environment of service can be helpless at times. (Anon.)

In order to understand their changing and developing role, practitioner-supervisors need to engage in reflective practice about their own work. In the same way that students learn from reflection upon their developing skills, supervisors can benefit from the same. However, does the supervisor have the space available in a busy clinic timetable to reflect upon their supervisory and educative skills? One participant who teaches and supervises in clinic commented: 'I get more satisfaction from supervision than any other aspect of teaching. I laugh a lot when supervising, which rarely happens outside of clinical learning' (Kevin Kerrigan, Northumbria University). Another commented, 'joy is an emotion experienced everyday with our students' (Matilda Smith, University of Cape Town); another wrote that the role is 'a privilege (and a challenge to stay on top of developments in the law)' (Adrian Evans, Monash Law School). Lastly:

> Though highly challenging, it's exciting to work and supervise students who are eager to learn. Sometimes it could be frustrating when your supervisory instructions are not followed. By and large, it's a wonderful experience. (Amari Omaka, Ebonyi State University)

Are some tasks more satisfying than others? The practitioner-supervisor is able to observe and assess the transition of law students from recent degree graduates to junior lawyers. In taking on the values of educators, practitioners may gain more or less satisfaction from seeing this transition, by encouraging and managing the transition of their students.

The quality of discussion between practitioner-supervisor and student may bring varying degrees of satisfaction. A low level of discussion with student advisors about the practicalities of file management as opposed to issues of justice in society, or the tactics of a litigation case may give rise to more or less satisfaction. One participant commented:

> Accepting constructive criticism and correction early on is an important lesson for lawyers and is part of the learning process. I want students to know that lawyers should not be working in isolation but that they should be supported in everything they do and that supervision should be a feature of their working life. (Pamela Robotham, College of Law)

One respondent observed, 'It is rewarding seeing the pleasure students get out of their initial interviewing. It is also rewarding seeing some students who do not excel academically excel at clinical work' (Richard Owen, University of Glamorgan).

Greater variety of tasks undertaken by students may make the supervisory role more interesting for the practitioner. For example guiding students in their legal research can be less satisfying than enabling students to undertake advocacy. In supervising students who undertake advocacy at hearings, whether at tribunals or courts, the practitioner is handing over their own role to the student:

> It is very important that the supervisor resists the temptation to take over the case at times – this defeats the purpose. *In extremis* the supervisor has to act

> where the client's case would be harmed – but to do so routinely takes away part of the learning for the students. The student advisors need to take responsibility for the case, and therefore for their own learning. (Stephen Illingworth, College of Law)

Practitioner-supervisors find this frustrating:

> I often find the role frustrating as it is necessary to hand over a certain amount of control and responsibility to the students. I have to decide whether it is better to maintain a higher level of control over the casework but take on fewer clients, or allow more students to take on casework but relinquish some of the control I have due to time constraints. (Anon.)

One participant commented:

> I find myself very conflicted in my role as supervisor. I want the students to receive the best experience and training. However I find that sometimes the students' best interests conflicts with the client's. (Caroline Foster, Northumbria University)

There are different approaches to the degree of supervision given to students who represent at tribunals or in court as McKenzie Friends. Some practitioner-supervisors attend and observe their students and others do not see their students until they return from the hearing. Some supervisors assess the reflective journals of their students after they have completed representation of clients at tribunals, but do not see them in action. Observation of students at tribunals can sometimes defeat the supervisor's purpose if the Tribunal Chair addresses questions to the supervisor and ignores the student representative, a situation reported to me in discussion.

Roles, line management and teamwork Teaching can sometimes be an isolating experience which may also affect the practitioner-supervisor. Though many participants comment on the positive rewards, there other aspects:

> It is hard work and often very scary. I often feel alone and not supported by colleagues. The most rewarding experience is seeing the students grow in confidence and become ethical, reflective and professional young adults. (Colleen Smith, Sheffield Hallam University)

Line management and teamwork help to overcome the isolation that can sometimes lower the levels of satisfaction, but only if management works in a positive way to motivate and support the practitioner-supervisor. Rather like the isolation of the sole practitioner, a lone practitioner-supervisor lacks colleagues with whom to discuss their work, whether that be work as an educator or as a practitioner. Working in a team in a student law clinic provides the practitioner-supervisor with support, and a forum for discussion of cases and of the educational issues that arise in the course of their supervision.

A question for the practitioner-supervisor is: how do they see themselves? In the survey 39.7% identified themselves as educators, 26.5% as clinicians, 20.6% as legal practitioners, 11.8% as lecturers, 11.8% as academics and 2.9% as trainers. One participant wrote, 'It is a very satisfying role; it is mixture of teaching and practising as a lawyer, whilst delivering useful services to various impoverished communities' (Bev Bird, University of Cape Town).

Some participants who supervise clinic do not hold practising certificates and identify themselves as academics:

> For us academics who don't practise law, it is the only opportunity to get to the real case law. At the same time seeing all the young students excited about the cases and their solutions makes me feel really happy knowing that I have done a good job both for them and for the client. (Blanka Tomankacova, Palacky University)

Supervision is valued for contact with practice:

> My work as a supervisor helps me to stay in contact with 'live law'. From a general point of view I appreciate and prefer this system (holding the position of supervisor by academics), which helps to build the inter-connection between legal academia and legal practice. (Ondrej Hamulak, Palacky University)

It is not a static role, one participant wrote:

> I aim to be a clinician but often find that there is a tension between that and being a legal practitioner. At the start of the year I try to put the student first; however often, as cases progress, the client becomes more important. (Anon.)

Another commented:

> I think the role is very consistent with being a higher education educator. I am occasionally frustrated that the students don't get that I don't know the answers and I need to rely on them to some extent to answer the questions clients raise. I'm happy to take responsibility for what goes out, and will check thoroughly to satisfy myself we've fulfilled our duty to the client – but sometimes I won't make that clear to the students. (Nicholas Johnson, Nottingham Law School)

Each member of a team can be assisted in their role visualisation by a line manager. This is not unlike private practice or in-house legal teams who operate under a system of line management designed to encourage teamworking and job satisfaction. Members of the team may have their own subjective view of their role, and the line manager may challenge or reinforce that view and encourage development. Team members may feel more or less confidence when knowing their role in a team and what they bring to a team. The line manager is in a position to give feedback to team members about their role that can facilitate the transition from practitioner to educator. Through the use of appraisal, training and career development reviews line managers can enable practitioners to make the transition to educators.

There is a degree of role memory that remains during the transition to educator. This may be affected by the experience a practitioner has already had in supervising trainee solicitors while in private practice or working in-house. If a practitioner is already aware of issues in supervision, particularly in enabling trainee solicitors more or less responsibility, and more or less ownership of cases, then they are more likely to understand and internalise the educational value in allowing the same to students. In bridging the two roles the practitioner-supervisor may continue membership of practitioner associations such as local Law Societies, Bar Associations and specialist practitioner associations or sections in order to maintain self-identity as a practitioner, access training and networking.

Identity is important for the practitioner-supervisor among their feelings about themselves. Professional status helps to define roles, so for example: the contractual job title, the titles given at the end of a letter, in fact the choice of who signs a letter, all contribute to the sense of identity the practitioner-supervisor has. Identification of the advisors is important for the client as well as the supervisor and student advisors, and the student law clinic must be very clear with the client about the different roles of the practitioner-supervisor and their student advisor-apprentices. A respondent commented: 'It can be very satisfying if both the student and the client are clear about the roles undertaken and the service provided. Unfortunately this is not always the case!' (Anon.).

Clients need to know that they are advised by students who are supervised by practising lawyers. However, most supervisors will not be directly available to them and client interaction will be with the students. Sometimes clients are not happy with this and want direct contact with the supervisors. This throws up a dilemma for the supervisor, who is faced again with ensuring they only play a role in the background.

Conclusions

I return to the central question that participants in the survey referred to in their comments: the duty to their clients and to their students. Though the large majority of participants felt conflicted at this dual duty, they also felt it gave rise to the greatest satisfaction. Some respondents felt their supervision of students did not conflict with their duty to the client as their duty to their clients was shared by the students. Commitment to their students was very clear in the comments made by participants and the educational benefit to students is prioritised clearly by respondents. Throughout the responses there is reference to the learning and development of students, and there is satisfaction in adding to their practitioner role that of student supervisor and educator.

There is a clear commitment from participants to a style of supervision which is enabling rather than constraining, though some found this stressful, particularly if they lacked support, whether formal or otherwise. Most developed a style of supervision in their approval and amendment of student advice work and observation of advocacy that allowed students to own the case and to work with a degree of independence. However, to do so the practitioner-supervisors needed to feel confident of professional and institutional support. Support from faculty management was required, and support from peers through faculty and practitioner organisations helped to alleviate the stress felt by some respondents.

Above all practitioner-supervisors developed their strengths through their own reflective practice in order to combine teaching and practice roles that not only gave them satisfaction but also gave their students the best of learning experiences. The findings showed some use of reflective practice but only by a minority of respondents. Reflective practice is a method which practitioner organisations can assist in developing in practitioner-supervisors.

Different methods of supervision, coaching, training, mentoring, direction and guidance all provide choices that practitioner-supervisors can reflect upon and develop in their work. Among other organisations in the clinical education field, the UK-based Clinical Legal Education Organisation (CLEO) aims to support clinicians and has published model standards for clinics giving guidance on setting learning outcomes, supervision, evaluation and assessment (2007).[14] The educational aims of live client clinics as set out in the CLEO model standards are designed to develop and enhance the students' learning experience and understanding of substantive law and legal process; professional responsibility and ethics; legal and transferable skills and the role of law and justice in society (2007: 4). The standards are there to provide guidance for practitioner-supervisors.

The way forward for practitioner-supervisors is to look for networks of support within their institutions and from the larger profession. These networks can not only provide support for the new or isolated practitioner but are forums of best practice and guidance. They also provide a voice for the practitioner-supervisor, as I hope that this survey has done in a practical way.

14 CLEA (Clinical Legal Education Association) in the USA has the same purpose.

References

Amsterdam, A.A. 1984. Clinical Legal Education: A 21st Century Perspective Report on Legal Education and Professional Development, *Association of American Law Schools Journal of Legal Education* 34: 612–18.

Andrusyszun, M.A. 1989. *Clinical Evaluation of the Affective Domain*. Brandon, Manitoba: Department of Nursing and Health Studies, Brandon University.

Brayne, H., Duncan, N. and Grimes, R. 1998. *Clinical Legal Education*. Oxford: Blackstone Press.

Brayne, H. and Grimes, R. 2004. *Mapping Best Practice in Clinical Legal Education*. [Online] Coventry: UK Centre for Legal Education. Available at: http://www.ukcle.ac.uk/research/projects/clinic.rtf [accessed 22 July 2010].

Chandler, S. and Robotham, P. 2006. Extending the Comfort Zones: Loosening the Clinical Straight Jacket, *International Journal of Clinical Legal Education Conference*. London: Institute of Advanced Legal Studies.

Chavkin, D.F. 1998. Am I My Client's Lawyer?: Role Definitions and the Clinical Supervisor, *SMU Law Review* 1507–46.

Clinical Legal Education Organisation (CLEO). 2007. [Online] Available at: http://www.ukcle.ac.uk/resources/teaching-and-learning-practices/clinical-legal-education-stream [accessed 6 August 2011].

Condlin, R.J. 1997. Learning from Colleagues: A Case Study in the Relationship between 'Academic' and 'Ecological' Clinical Legal Education, *Clinical Law Review* 3: 337–438.

Critchlow, G. 1990. Professional Responsibility, Student Practice and the Clinical Teacher's Duty to Intervene, *Gonzaga Law Review* 26: 415–18.

Cruikshank, D. 1996. Problem Based Learning in Legal Education, in *Teaching Lawyers' Skills*, edited by J. Webb and C. Maughan. London: Butterworth, 190–91.

Freire, P. 1970. *Pedagogy of the Oppressed*. New York: The Continuum Publishing Company.

Freire, P. 1972. *Cultural Action for Freedom*. Harmondsworth: Penguin.

Freire, P. 1994/2004. *Pedagogy of Hope*. New York: The Continuum Publishing Company.

Hancox, N. 2005. *What Lawyers Want: Comparing Academics with Practitioners*. [Online] Coventry: UKCLE. Available at: http://www.ukcle.ac.uk/interact/lili/2005/contributions/papers/hancox.html [accessed 22 July 2010].

Hess, G.F. 2003. Learning to Think like a Teacher: Reflective Journals for Legal Educators, *Gonzaga Law Review* 38: 129–31.

Joy, P.A. 2003–4. The Law School as a Model Ethical Law Office, *William Mitchell Law Review* 35–50.

Joy, P.A. and Kuehn, R.R. 2002–3. Conflict of Interest and Competency Issues in Law Clinic Practice, *Clinical Law Review* 493–578.

Kolb, D.A. 1984. *Experiential Learning: Experience at the Source of Learning and Development*. Englewood Cliffs, NJ: Prentice Hall.

Kovach, K.K. 1998. The Lawyer as Teacher: The Role of Education in Lawyering, *Clinical Law Review* 4: 359–90.

Krieger, L.S. 2005. The Inseparability of Professionalism and Personal Satisfaction: Perspectives on Values Integrity and Happiness, *Clinical Law Review* 11: 425–38.

Macrate, R. 1992. Legal Education and Professional Development – An Educational Continuum 213. *Report of the Task Force on Law Schools and the Profession: Narrowing the Gap*. Chicago: American Bar Association.

Martin Berry, M. 1995. Clinical Supervision: Walking that Fine Line, *Clinical Law Review* 2: 137–47.

Nicholls, N.C. 2005. Modelling Professionalism: The Process from a Clinical Perspective, *Widener Law Journal* 4: 441–8.

Norwood, M. in Stuckey, R. et al. 2007. *Best Practices for Legal Education. A Vision and a Road Map*. Clinical Legal Education Association. Columbia: University of South Carolina.

Pakman, M. 2000. Thematic Foreword: Reflective Practices: The Legacy of Donald Schön, *Cybernetics & Human Knowing* 7(2–3): 5–8.

Plowden, P. 2004. *Clinical Legal Education: Theory, Practice and Possibilities.* [Online] Coventry: UK Centre for Legal Education. Available at: www.ukcle.ac.uk/resources/clinic/plowden.html [accessed 20 July 2010].

Quigley, W.P. 1995. Introduction to Clinical Teaching for the New Clinical Law Professor: A View From the First Floor, *Akron Law Review* 28: 463–71.

Reekie, R. 1991. Creating Painters: The Art of Being a Clinical Law Teacher (Part 1), *Journal of Professional Legal Education* 9(2): 137–48.

Schön, D. 1983. *The Reflective Practitioner*. New York: Basic Books.

Schön, D. 1987. *Educating the Reflective Practitioner: Toward a New Design for Teaching and Learning in the Professions*. San Francisco: Jossey-Bass.

Solicitors Regulation Authority. 2007. *Training Framework Review.* London: Law Society.

Sylvester, C., Hall, J. and Hall, E. 2004. Problem Based Learning and Clinical Legal Education: What Can Clinical Educators Learn from Problem Based Learning, *International Journal of Clinical Legal Education.* Northumbria Law Press.

Tarr, N.W. 1993. Current Issues in Clinical Legal Education, *Howard Law Journal* 37(1): 31–2.

Toll Hoffman, P. 1986. The Stages of the Clinical Supervisory Relationship, *Antioch Law Journal* 4: 301–12.

Webb, J. and Maughan, C. 1996. *Teaching Lawyers' Skills*: London: Butterworth.

Appendix

Safety and Satisfaction in the Apprenticeship Process:
Supervisors' Questionnaire

These questions are designed to reveal the emotional impact of supervision on supervisors. The questionnaire takes approximately six minutes to complete. There is a separate sheet at the end that asks for your details and will be detached from the rest of the questionnaire when the answers are analysed.

1. Do you hold a Practising Certificate, or are you a practising barrister?
   Yes No
2. What supervision do you carry out: (tick all that apply)
   a) Advice only b) Casework c) Representation d) Advocacy
   e) Mediation f) Streetlaw g) Other, please describe
3. How many contact hours per week do you supervise students? (One only)
   a) up to 7 b) up to 14 c) up to 21 d) up to 28 e) up to 35
4. How many non-contact hours do you supervise written work? (One only)
   a) up to 7 b) up to 14 c) up to 21 d) up to 28 e) up to 35
5. Which is most important to you – your duty to the client or your duty to your students? (Tick only one)
   a) The client b) The student
6. Did you feel any of the following emotions on answering question 5: (Tick all that apply)
   a) Confusion b) Frustration c) Impatience d) Satisfaction
   e) Irritation f) Concern g) Conflicted
7. Which of the following best describes your style of supervision? (Tick all that apply)
   a) I approve every piece of written work the student does for the client.
   b) I observe the student/client interview.
   c) I observe the representation done by the students.
   d) I listen to the phone calls made by the student with the client.
   e) I listen to the phone calls made by the student with the other party.
   f) I listen to phone calls made by the student to the Court or Tribunal.
   g) I review the client file regularly and give written feedback to the student.
   h) I conduct preparatory meetings with students before the client interview.
   i) I conduct de-briefing meetings with the students after the client interview.
   j) I conduct post-case reflective meetings with the students.
   k) I ask the student to research the law and produce a first draft on their own.
   l) I ask the student to amend draft documents without suggestions.

m) I ask students to amend documents with suggestions for amendments.
n) I ask students to prepare skeleton arguments without suggestions from me.
o) I ask students to prepare skeleton arguments with suggestions from me.

8. How do you feel if a student withdraws from clinic or streetlaw? (Tick all that apply)
   a) Frustrated b) Concerned c) Annoyed d) Sympathy e) Anger
9. How do you feel when a successful outcome is achieved for the client? (Tick all that apply)
   a) Happy for the client b) Happy with the students c) Proud
   d) Satisfied
10. How do you feel if students have made a major error on a case? (Tick all that apply)
    a) Nervous b) Concerned for the client c) Concerned for the students
    d) Confident you can use this as a learning experience e) Anxiety
    f) Stressed g) Guilt
11. Which of the following best describes you? (Please choose only one)
    a) Legal practitioner b) Clinician c) Educator d) Academic
    e) Lecturer f) Trainer
12. What comments would you like to make about your role as supervisor?

Thank you for completing this questionnaire. Please complete this separate page about you.

Chapter 5
Instead of a Career: Work, Art and Love in University Law Schools

Anthony Bradney

> Everything I have taken to heartily has somehow turned into a scrape. My painting is the last scrape; and I shall be all my life getting out of it.
>
> George Eliot *Daniel Deronda* (1967: 518)

> For the perfect friendship which I am talking about is indivisible: each gives himself so entirely to his friend that he has nothing left to share with another.
>
> Michel de Montaigne 'On Affectionate Relationships' in *The Complete Essays* (2003: 215)

Introduction

In his discussion of the alienation of labour, Marx demonstrates the fact of that alienation by pointing out, *inter alia*, 'that as soon as no physical or other compulsion exists, labour is shunned like the plague'; this, however, is not the attitude that some legal academics have towards their work.[1] McMorrow and Baldwin's survey of retired legal academics in the USA found that 32.9% of those surveyed reported that they spent some of their time researching and writing (McMorrow and Baldwin 1991: 416). Similar survey evidence for university law schools does not exist for the United Kingdom.[2] However, on an anecdotal basis it is clear that some legal academics in the United Kingdom continue their research

1 Marx (1959: 72). Riesman, in a discussion of Freud's view of work, argues that 'Western industrial culture' has a specific attitude to work; only in this culture, he suggests, is work 'sharply set off against love, against pleasure, against consumption, against almost every sort of freedom' (Riesman 1954: 312). Marx's view of work can be similarly categorised as a description of labour within Western capitalism. Catephores contends that the idea of the alienation of labour is something that has only a transient place in Marx's thinking (Catephores 1972: 124). Even if all of this is so, the idea is still valuable for this chapter.

2 However, in a study done for the Dearing Committee report on higher education, 51% of respondent academics said that the most important reason for them doing research was because they enjoyed it (*The National Committee of Inquiry into Higher Education: Report 3* 1997: Table 3.3).

and writing after, and sometimes long after, their formal retirement.[3] Since significant payment is rarely associated with publishing research, it is clear that the normal inducement that leads people to work, that, as Marx puts it, the worker 'receives *means of subsistence*', is not the reason for this labour.[4] If academics continue to want to do their work after they have retired it seems likely that the financial motivation that Marx notes was never the most important reason for their work even before their retirement. Their labour is thus not alienated in the various senses that Marx uses.[5] It is not 'external to the worker, ie, it does not belong to his essential being'; instead the labour is 'the satisfaction of a need' and the labour therefore does not belong to another.[6] Put simply, for academics such as these their research and writing is about what Sennett calls 'craftsmanship', 'doing something well for its own sake'; the '*activity itself, not its exchange value, is ... [the] primary goal*'.[7] This is not to say that such academics are necessarily entirely uninterested in financial or other returns; on the contrary, because of their focus on their work, they may be able to negotiate financial rewards beyond those achieved by other academics. Notwithstanding this, it remains the case that the work, not the financial reward, is the thing that motivates them.[8]

3 Leverhulme Emeritus Fellowships exist specifically for academics such as these. See http://www.leverhulme.ac.uk/grants_awards/grants/emeritus_fellowships/ [accessed 14 June 2010].

4 (Emphasis in the original) Marx (1959: 71). McMorrow and Baldwin's study also showed that considerable numbers of legal academics continued to teach after retirement, with 46.6% reporting that they taught full-time and 5.93% saying that they taught part-time (McMorrow and Baldwin 1991: 415). However, since academics were paid to do this teaching, continuing to teach after retirement does not necessarily demonstrate a personal attachment to teaching. This is not to say that no legal academics find teaching compelling. It is, however, harder to show that this is so in the case of teaching than it is in the case of research. Evans, in his study of academics in modern language departments, based on interviews with academics in such departments, is more unequivocal in his views. He writes that '[u]niversity teaching ... is rarely a vocation' (Evans 1988: 90).

5 In her study of academic identities Henkel notes the claim made by scientists, that they 'are somewhat unusual people in that they work because they want to, not because they have to. If you are doing for the money, you might as well go and work for Pedigree Petfoods where you would get paid twice as much' (Henkel 2000: 201). Many academics would correctly contend that they could use their knowledge and skills in a job outside academia that is more highly paid. However, accepting a lower salary for your labour does not, in itself, demonstrate the same attachment to the work that doing it for no payment at all does, particularly when university employment carries with it considerable non-pecuniary advantages such as more flexible working hours that might, for some, make it more attractive than other areas of employment.

6 Marx (1959: 72 and 73).

7 (Emphasis in the original) Sennett (2006: 104); Gorz (1989: 137–8).

8 Bauman, citing Rorty, writes that 'the corridors of academia are filled with two kinds of people – some of them "busy conforming to well understood criteria for making contributions to knowledge", and the others trying "to expand their own moral imagination"

In this chapter I want to explore some of the things that follow from the fact that some legal academics do their research for its own sake, looking at the consequences that it has not only for them but for those around them.

The Motivation to Work

The fact that some legal academics' labour is not alienated may seem to be a pure unalloyed good and because of this not therefore needing any further inquiry. Law schools get dedicated workers and those workers are able to fill their lives with the thing that they find most compelling. In fact, even at this elementary level, whether this is the case is debateable. Non-alienated workers in university law schools do not necessarily find all aspects of their work equally attractive; for example, very few academics, whatever their general motivation to be academics, find administrative work interesting.[9] Dedicated researchers may make even more recalcitrant administrators than those academics who take a more instrumental attitude towards their work precisely because of the attractions that research and teaching have for them. Alienated labour's dominant concern when at work is with the price that it is being paid for its labour; unappealing jobs can be made more appealing by the offer of higher financial reward and thus academics can be convinced to undertake administration.[10] When, however, the '*activity itself, not its exchange value, is ... [the] primary goal*', additional payments to do something other than that activity may prove to be an ineffective incentive. Highly motivated academics are in this way not necessarily congenial colleagues. This point has a significance that is deeper than just academic attitudes towards administration; instead it goes to the heart of how these academics view their careers.

The concept of a career in relationship to employment is one that has a relatively short history, Williams, amongst others, dating it back only as far as the mid-19th century.[11]

---

and read books "in order to enlarge their own sense of what is possible and important – either for themselves as individuals or for their society"' (Bauman 2005: 13). It is the latter group who are likely to find their work non-alienated because the work is personal to them rather than being done according to the usages of others.

9 Becher and Trowler (2001: 148). Those few that do like administration sometimes note their own eccentricity (Henkel 2000: 240).

10 'Wages are a direct consequence of estranged labour' (Marx 1959: 81). The most obvious example of this attempt to provide extra financial incentives for undertaking administration in universities are the extra payments that are made to academics who take up offices such as head of department or pro-vice-chancellor.

11 Williams (1988: 53). See further Brown, van Leeuwen and Mitch (2004). For a discussion of the way in which the word career is used in sociological analysis, see Evetts (1992).

> Careers have traditionally been seen as providing a set of organizing principles around which white-collar employees within bureaucracies have been able to structure both their professional and private lives. The 'psychological contract' between employed and employee was based upon loyalty and commitment to the organization in exchange for the incremental increase in authority, status, and financial remuneration associated with a corporate career. [12]

Academics in this sense do have careers; salary grades and promotion ladders in universities constitute a career structure.[13] However, the concept of a successful academic career, seen from the perspective of the 'subjective career', 'how employees actually … [experience] their work and their careers', is not consistent with this structure.[14] None of the informants in Cownie's ethnographic account of university law schools regarded holding a chair, the top of the academic promotion ladder and usually the most highly paid academic salary grade, as being the key to being a successful academic. Even those few who thought it an important component of success regarded publishing well-received research as being more important; for the majority either publishing research or the effect that one had on one's students were the sole indicators of success (Cownie 2004: 94 and 92–4). In such a context, matters conventional to most areas of employment such as the concept of 'career management' and still more the argument that 'the career has been regarded as a fundamental element in the development process [of the individual] …' (Newell 2000: 218) have, at best, a tenuous hold in academic life.

Jackall, writing about the careers of managers in the corporate sector of employment, argues that the managers try to 'master the shared assumptions, the complex rules, the normative codes, the underlying institutional logic that governs their world' (Jackall 1988: 38):

> [M]anagers are continually tested even as they continually test others. They turn to each other for moral cues for behaviour and come to fashion specific situational moralities for the specific significant others in their world. What matters in the bureaucratic world is not what a person is but how closely his many personae mesh with the organizational ideal; not his willingness to stand by his actions but his agility in avoiding blame; not his acuity in perceiving falsity or errors but adeptness at protecting others; not his talent, his abilities, or his hard work, but how these are harnessed with the proper protocol to address the particular exigencies that face his organization; not what he believes or says but how well he has mastered the ideologies and rhetorics that serve his

12 Edwards and Wachman (2005: 64). However, the concept of a career has never just applied to white-collar employment. See, for example, Savage (1998) on 19th-century railway workers.

13 On academic careers, see Becher and Trowler (2001: ch. 7), Henkel (2000: Part IV) and Strike and Taylor (2009). On careers for academic lawyers, see Cownie (2004: ch. 4).

14 On 'career structures' and 'subjective careers', see Evetts (1992: 4–6 and 10–11).

> corporation; not what he stands for but whom he stands with in the labyrinths of his organization. (Jackall 1988: 193)

It is the career itself that has priority for its own sake, not the work that is being done. Such attitudes have comparatively little place in academic life, especially in the case of those academics who are the focus of this chapter. The highly influential English critic F.R. Leavis was only appointed to a full lectureship at the University of Cambridge at the age of 52 and was not promoted to Reader until the age of 64. He was never given a chair by Cambridge and became a professor only on his appointment at the University of York after his retirement from Cambridge.[15] Whilst he deeply resented his treatment by Cambridge, he made little or no attempt to alter his behaviour in order to secure preferment (MacKillop 1995: passim). This is not to say that committed academics never have any concerns about matters such as their reputation or the impact that they have made. Steiner's general musings on his reputation in his memoir, *Errata: An Examined Life*, and his specific regret about 'the absence of any school or movement originating in my work' belies any such suggestion (Steiner 1997: 153–6 and 155). However, whilst Jackall's managers are concerned about their reputation because of the impact that this might have on their career, the academic concern seems to be with one's work being seen as important.[16] Academic politics clearly exist and those who are dedicated to academic life may be as likely to engage in them as anyone else. However, the nature of those politics is different from the politics of other areas of employment; to use Jackall's phrase, what you 'stand for' is much more at the centre of these politics and the career manoeuvres that are open to Jackall's managers are not so open to those academics whose work is non-alienated.[17]

Work and Love

Even though the legal academics who are the subject of this chapter are likely to disdain conventional careers because of their devotion to their work, even highly motivated academics are rarely just highly motivated academics; most, perhaps

15 For a study of Leavis' life, see MacKillop (1995).

16 Thus, for example, Foucault's relationship with Sartre was ambivalent because, at least in part, both sought to establish intellectual ascendancy (Miller 1993: 44–5). Reputation and even fame was important but it was reputation and fame as regards ideas.

17 On academic politics see Brown (1982). This is not to argue that academics never seek careers in the conventional sense. However, when they do so their work will be alienated in its nature and, whatever their success in their own terms, it would seem from Cownie's analysis above they will not be seen as being successful by the majority of their fellow academics.

all, also seek relationships of varying degrees of intimacy with other people.[18] Put simply, for such people, how compatible is their attachment to their work and their desire for love and friendship?

Freud is reputed to have said that '[a]ll that matters is love and work' (*Oxford Dictionary of Quotations* 1992: 294). Although this remark is widely attributed to Freud, no source has ever been found. There is no common agreement as to exactly what it was that Freud said. Thus, for example, Eriksen writes 'Freud was once asked what he thought a normal person should be able to do well ... Freud is reported to have said, "*Lieben und arbeiten*" (to love and work)' (Eriksen 1956: 222). Both the context that Eriksen gives to the statement and its different formulation from that which is given in the *Oxford Dictionary of Quotations* arguably changes its meaning.[19] For this reason, amongst others, it is not just what Freud said but what he meant that is open to debate. However, notwithstanding its somewhat opaque nature, Freud's observation provides a useful starting point for the relationship between non-alienated labour and friendship and love in law schools.[20]

Freud understood love as meaning something wider than simply sexual love:

> The nucleus of what we mean by love naturally consists ... in sexual love with sexual union as its aim. But we do not separate from this – what in any case has in the name 'love' – on the one hand, self-love, and on the other, love for parents and children, friendship and love for humanity in general.[21]

His dictum on the importance of work and love has to be understood in this context. Eriksen interprets Freud's remark thus:

---

18 The fact that even academics who treat their work as art will also seek intimate relationships is important. Johnstone notes that 'Dewey criticised the notion that each person has just one vocation. So, for instance, nobody is a lawyer and nothing else. A person may have a special career as a lawyer, but will also be a member of a family and various other associations, and will participate in other organised activities. To let one special vocation become too dominant is dangerous; it leads to becoming undeveloped as a human being' (Johnstone 1999). This argument mirrors Eriksen's interpretation of Freud's dictum on work and love below.

19 The *Oxford English Dictionary of Quotations* lists the remark as having been made in English rather than German.

20 Some of Freud's observations form part of the structure of argument in this chapter. This is not to say that the chapter constitutes a 'Freudian' analysis of the problems discussed. However, whilst I find many aspects of Freud's work profoundly unsatisfactory, 'everyone mines every book for the things that are useful to him ...' (Calvino 1986: 50).

21 Freud (1955: 90). Later in the same essay he writes 'language has carried out an entirely justifiable piece of unification in creating the word "love" with its numerous uses, and that we cannot do better than take it as the basis of our scientific discussions and expositions as well' (Freud 1955: 91).

> [w]hen Freud said 'love', he meant the expansiveness of generosity as well as genital love; when he said love *and* work, he meant a general work productiveness which would not preoccupy the individual to the extent that his right or capacity to be a sexual and a loving being would be lost. (Eriksen 1956: 222)

On this account thus work and love together is what one should give one's life to. Whether this is possible for those academics in law schools who are devoted to their work in the way that is outlined above depends on what both work and love demand from them.

Work as Art

Freud's own attitude to work was ambivalent. On the one hand he regarded work as central to human activity. '[E]very civilization rests on a compulsion to work and a renunciation of instinct ...' (Freud 1961a: 10; see also Freud 1961a: 7–8). However, notwithstanding the importance that he saw work as having, Freud's attitude towards the great majority of it was similar to Marx's notion of alienated labour.[22] He regarded most work as forced labour; for the mass, he wrote, it was impossible 'to dispense with coercion in the work of civilization' (Freud 1961a: 7). His general arguments about work are thus not relevant to the subject of this chapter. However, for Freud, not all work was coerced:

> One gains the most if one can sufficiently heighten the yield of pleasure from the sources of psychical and intellectual work. When that is so, fate can do little against one. A satisfaction of this kind, such as the artist's joy in creating, giving his phantasies body, or a scientist's in solving problems or discovering truths, has a special quality. (Freud 1961b: 79; see also Freud 1957)

Work of this kind seems to approximate to the kind of creative work that is done by the kind of legal academics described above. For the purposes of analysis in this chapter we might therefore usefully substitute Coetzee's more limited observation that '[o]nly love and art are ... worthy of giving oneself to without reserve' (Coetzee 2002: 85) for Freud's broader dictum, understanding art in this

---

22 Lichtheim comments more generally that 'the link [between Freud and Marx] appears to lie in a critique of civilization which differentiates between the inevitable degree of repression common to all forms of culture, and the surplus repression peculiar to bourgeois society' (Lichtheim 1972: 69). Riesman argues that Freud's attitude towards his own work, which stressed the fatigue and effort that it involved, 'had a profound influence on the whole psychoanalytic method. For he assumed, as a matter of course, that any answer which came without arduous toil must be wrong' (Riesman 1954: 321). On Freud's attitude to his own work more generally see Riesman (1954: 319–26) and Jones (1964).

context to involve a wide range of intellectual and aesthetic pursuits that are creative in their nature.[23] In order to see whether or not the integration of work and love is possible for legal academics, we thus need to inquire into what work seen as art requires from them.

George Eliot's novel *Daniel Deronda*, in which several artists and would-be artists figure, is a useful resource for reflecting on what it means to be an artist.[24] One thing that distinguishes the various artists and putative artists in *Daniel Deronda* is the different attitudes they take towards their art. Deronda's mother, Leonara Charisi, 'a great singer, and I acted as well as I sang', has Deronda brought up without knowledge of her existence because 'I meant to be free and live for my art. I had to be parted with you. I had no bonds' (Eliot 1967: 688 and 702). 'I wanted to live out the life that was in me, and not to be hampered with other lives' (Eliot 1967: 688). 'I loved the life of my art …' (Eliot 1967: 696). 'You see I had no life left to love you with' (Eliot 1967: 703) she tells Deronda when she first meets him after their separation at his birth when he is in his early 20s and she is dying. Later, in a second and final meeting a few days later, she says to Deronda, '[h]ad I not a rightful claim to be something more than a mere daughter and mother? … Acknowledge that I had a right to be an artist …' (Eliot 1967: 728). Charisi's position is an extreme one, her life being made even more difficult and complex by being born into a traditional Jewish family where there was:

> a pattern cut out – 'this is the Jewish woman; this is what you must be; this is what you are wanted for; a woman's heart must be of such a size and no larger, else it must be pressed small, like Chinese feet; her happiness is to be made as cakes are, by a fixed receipt'. (Eliot 1967: 694)

23 Seeing the work as science would not change the analysis below. See footnote 26.

24 One of the would-be artists in the novel, Gwendolen Harleth, is a central character. Indeed, Leavis argued that the novel should be split into a good part and a bad part and that the good part should be entitled *Gwendolen Harleth* (Leavis 1962: 102 and 144). (For a critical account of both Leavis' method of reading literature and his specific reading of *Daniel Deronda*, see Belsey 1982.) Nonetheless, even given the significance of Harlach to the novel, the novel is about something much larger than the question of how to be an artist. Mintz has suggested that '[t]he late works of George Eliot are preoccupied with the question of work, especially in its relation to the middle classes' and more particularly with work as a vocation or calling (Mintz 1978: 2 and 4–6). In *Daniel Deronda* he sees the '[t]he vocational impulse' as being 'decisively split into "good" ambition and "bad" ambition' (Mintz 1978: 151). In a similar fashion, Preyer writes about the novel's concern with 'the yearning for a saving vocation' (Preyer 1960: 35). Toker argues that '[i]n *Daniel Deronda* the concern with vocation involves the dialectics of the pursuit of social, national, or communal progress on the one hand and the agenda of self-perfection on the other …' (Toker 2004: 565–6). Such readings enable the different parts of *Daniel Deronda* to be read together, reflecting Eliot's own demand that 'everything in *Daniel Deronda* … be related to everything else' (Demaria 1990: 22). Following Mintz's reading enables the position of artists in the novel to be seen as a particular example of a more general phenomenon.

Her life is both a personal and individual rebellion against the demands of a father who 'never thought of his daughter except as an instrument' (Eliot 1967: 726) and also the pursuit of that which is necessary to live the life of an artist. Yet her attachment to her art is matched by others in the novel who are in somewhat easier circumstances. Julius Klesmer's description of the life of the artist is one that is full of 'arduous, unceasing work – and uncertain praise' (Eliot 1967: 297–8). Charged with suggesting that the life is unappealing, he replies:

> I am not decrying the life of the true artist. I am exalting it. I say, it is out of the reach of any but choice organisations – natures framed to love perfection and to labour for it; ready, like all true lovers, to endure. To wait, to say, I am not yet worthy, but she – Art, my mistress – is worthy, and I will live to merit her. An honourable life? Yes. But the honour comes from the inward vocation and the hard-won achievement ... (Eliot 1967: 298)

Klesmer's concern is with 'the true artist'. He tells Bult, a politician, indeed a 'mere politician':

> [n]o man has too much talent to be a musician. Most men have too little. A creative artist is no more a mere musician than a great statesman is a mere politician. We are not ingenious puppets, sir, who live in a box and look out on the world only when it is gaping for amusement. We help rule the nations and make the age as much as any other public men. We count ourselves on level benches with legislators. And a man who speaks effectively through music is compelled to something more difficult than parliamentary eloquence. (Eliot 1967: 284)

Later in the novel he says, '[m]y rank as an artist is of my own winning, and I would not exchange it for any other' (Eliot 1967: 292). Charisi and Klesmer share a belief in both the value and the difficulty of artistic endeavour. Moreover they also share a belief in being 'compelled' to live the 'life that was in me'. In *Daniel Deronda* what makes a 'true artist' is not simply ability and application. Whilst Klesmer might well doubt whether Gwendolen Harleth can follow his injunction to 'subdue your mind and body to unbroken discipline' in training to become a singer and an actress as she says she wishes to do, more fundamentally there is the problem that she is concerned not with 'excellence' in her art but instead with the pursuit of a career (Eliot 1967: 299).[25] Mirah Lapidoth, a more immediately sympathetic character than Gwendolen Harleth, has been trained to be a singer and actress and has talent (Eliot 1967: 252 and 541). On first hearing

25 Klesmer does, however, also put considerable store in training and application. He tells Harlaeth '[w]henever an artist has been able to say, "I came, I saw, I conquered," it has been at the end of patient practice. Genius at first is little more than a great capacity for receiving discipline' (Eliot 1967: 300).

her sing, Klesmer says, '[l]et us shake hands: you are a musician' (Eliot 1967: 452). Nonetheless he cautions her to 'be modest', warning her that her ability extends only to performing in no 'larger space than a private drawing-room', though 'here in London that is one of the best careers open' (Eliot 1967: 452). Her own declared aim is to 'get my bread' from her performances; in the view of her future husband she lacks 'ambition' and 'her nature is not given to make great claims' (Eliot 1967: 452 and 728). She has ability and resolve but can only be a 'mere musician', not a 'true artist'. Her labour, unlike that of Charisi or Klesmer, will always be alienated.

The dedication and ambition that Charisi and Klesmer bring to their art is something that others have discussed. Charles Lamb and Gabriel García Márquez are writers separated by both centuries and culture. Nevertheless they are in agreement about what writing demands. In his essay *Sanity of True Genius*, Lamb, first published in 1833, writes:

> the true poet dreams being awake. He is not possessed by his subject, but has dominion over it. In the groves of Eden he walks familiar as in his native paths. He ascends the empyrean heaven, and is not intoxicated. He treads the burning marl without dismay; he wings his flight without self-loss through realms of chaos 'and old night'. (Lamb 1885: 336)

Márquez's language is more prosaic but his argument is the same. When asked what inspiration is his, he says:

> It's a word that which has been discredited by the Romantics. I don't see it as a state of grace nor a breath from heaven but as the moment when, by tenacity and control, you are at one with your theme. When you want to write something, a kind of reciprocal tension is established between you and the theme, so you spur the theme on and the theme spurs you on too. There comes a moment when all obstacles fade away, all conflict disappears, things you never dreamt of occur to you and, at that moment, there is absolutely nothing in the world better than writing. (Mendoza 1983: 34)

Both Eliot's evocation of the work of artists and the views of writers such as Lamb and Márquez emphasise the focus that the pursuit of art requires: a focus that must be maintained not just for hours or days but for a lifetime.[26] If the work of non-alienated labour is seen in this light, what space and time is then left for love?

---

26 The same is true if the work is seen as science rather than art. '[A]n inner devotion to the task, and that alone, should lift the scientist to the height and dignity of the subject he pretends to serve. And in this it is not different with the artist' (Weber 1948: 137).

Love and Friendship

The title of the 28th essay in Montaigne's *The Complete Essays* is usually translated into English as 'On Friendship' (see, for example, Derrida 1997: 2). However Screech, in his 2003 translation, notes of the French title of the essay, 'De l'amité', that the meaning of amité 'includes many affectionate relationships', and that:

> [s]everal terms are needed in English to render these different senses; they include friendship, loving-friendship, benevolence, affection, affectionate relationships and love. The basic meaning of amité is rooted in aimer (to love) ... (Montaigne 2003: 205)[27]

As with love for Freud, amité for Montaigne covers a broad terrain and, in both instances, not all meanings of the terms are of equal significance.

In his essay, having discussed lesser forms of amité such as the relationship between children and their father, Montaigne distinguishes between common friendship and special friendship. Common 'friendships are no more than acquaintances and familiar relationships bound by some chance or some suitability ...' (Montaigne 2003: 211). In special friendship, by contrast, 'if it were possible for one to give to the other it is the one who received the benefaction who would lay an obligation on his companion. For each of them, more than anything else, is seeking the good of the other ...' (Montaigne 2003: 214).[28] Such special friendship is the highest form of amité for Montaigne. 'Let nobody place those other common friendships in the same rank as this ...' (Montaigne 2003: 213).

Montaigne stresses the depth of obligation that such friendship entails:

---

27 Screech himself translates the title as 'On Affectionate Relationships' (Montaigne 2003: 205).

28 Montaigne (2003: 214). Montaigne's distinction is similar to that drawn by Aristotle between friendship where friendship provides 'some good or pleasure' and perfect friendship where friends 'wish well to their friends for their sake' (Aristotle 1980: 195 and 196). See similarly Cicero's remarks that '[i]t is not so much the advantage gained through a friend, as the love of the friend itself that delights one. What comes from a friend becomes pleasant precisely when it is done with good will' and that 'the finest and most natural form of friendship, [is] the sort which is desired in itself and for its own sake ...' (Cicero 1990: 53 and 63). This link is not coincidental. In his essay Montaigne uses his friendship with La Boétie as an example of the special friendship that he is writing about. Gray observes of La Boétie and Montaigne that '[b]oth were formed intellectually by the Ancients and lived in a humanistic environment. It was inevitable that their feelings should owe perhaps even more than they themselves realized to the ideas on friendship which the Renaissance had inherited from the Greeks and Latins' (Gray 1961: 203). For a discussion of Aristotle's concept of perfect friendship, see Price (1989: ch. 4).

> In this noble relationship, the services and good turns which foster those other relationships do not merit even being taken into account … [J]ust as I feel no gratitude for any good turn I do to myself: so too the union of such friends, being truly perfect, leads them to lose any awareness of such services, to hate and to drive out from between them all terms of division and difference, such as good turn, duty, gratitude, request, thanks and the like. (Montaigne 2003: 214)

Goodrich argues that:

> [f]riendship … begins with listening to the interiority of difference, to the corporeal and sensible expressions of the friend. Friendship lies in an attentive and critical appreciation of difference. That at least is its beginning. (Goodrich 2003: 49)

Key to this is the notion of being attentive. Friendship takes time. If one, in Aristotle's phrase, 'seeking the good of the other' time is needed to learn as fully as possible what that 'well' is (Aristotle 1980: 214). Goodrich, drawing on Nietzsche, suggests that:

> [t]he friend is initially an unfamiliar and to some extent will always in part be unknown, different, a potentiality rather than a possession. This is the source of the possibility of continuing to learn, of friendship growing or growing apart. Friendship is a knowledge of, as well passion for, the friend. It is learned over time, an erudition *in eroticis*, a temporality as well as intensity that leads eventually, through love, to friendship. (Goodrich 2003: 49)[29]

However, as we have seen above, time is precisely what the academic as artist does not have. Work as art drives out everything else.

The opposition here between work as art on the one hand and friendship and love on the other hand is not the same as, nor is it even related to, the familiar problem of work–life balance.[30] Here the academic is not simply seeking to maintain an appropriate boundary between work and life outside of work in the difficult context of what Collier calls 'the *indeterminacy* of academic labour' (Collier 2002: 21, emphasis in original). Instead they are caught in the tension that arises from the fact that they want to explore their art to the fullest extent that is possible whilst at the same time acknowledging the absolute sovereignty

---

29 See also Goodrich's argument that what is necessary for friendship is 'a process of learning, a coming to know the friend over time' (Goodrich 2003: 47). Montaigne writes that only ordinary friendships 'require so much prudent foresight in long preliminary acquaintance' (Montaigne 2003: 212). However, even if this is so, both the obligations of friendship and learning what those obligations are in this particular friendship takes time.

30 On work–life balance in the law school see Bradney (2003: 194–203) and Cownie (2004: 113–18).

that their closest relationships have over them. Both rightfully demand everything of them. 'Both thought (knowledge, *Wissenschaft*, imagination given form) and love ask too much of us. They humble us' (Steiner 1997: 44). This tension cannot be resolved and because of it academics who see their work as art will necessarily fail in both their love and their art.[31] This is not to say that they might not have happy, successful relationships and also produce a host of new ideas.[32] Nevertheless, they will constantly fall short of what they should do in both arenas.[33]

Conclusion

On first appearances the dedication that non-alienated legal academics bring to their work simplifies their lives. Their concentration on their art provides a focus that others do not have. Were academics hermits this might be so. However their general desire to enter into affectionate relationships means this is not so. Their focus on their art brings with it particular complexities and contradictions that are not to be found in other lives.[34] There is a burgeoning literature on academics in both universities in general and university law schools in particular, some of which has been referred to above, that has begun to explore the nature of academic life. The analysis in this chapter suggests that not all academic lives are the same. Analysis of academic lives needs to take account not only of familiar matters such as issues of gender and differences resulting from disciplinary background but also the various ways in which academics connect with their work. Academics as a body have common titles and job descriptions. They do not, however, have common lives.

31 Freud saw all life as failure. 'Life as we find it, is too hard for us; it brings too many pains, disappointments and impossible tasks. In order to bear it we cannot dispense with palliative measures … ' (Freud 1961b: 75). He saw the pursuit of art and science as being one of those palliative measures (Freud 1961b: 75).

32 This is confirmed both *by Daniel Deronda* and the real lives of many of those academics and writers quoted above. In *Daniel Deronda* Klesmer marries Catherine Arrowpoint, who gives up her inheritance in order to be his wife and who is, in Klesmer's view, 'a thorough musician, and has a soul with more ears to it than you will often get in a musician' (Eliot 1967: 291–2 and 542). F.R. Leavis was married to the English critic Q.D. Leavis for 49 years whilst Gabriel Garcia Marquez married his wife Mercedes in 1958 (MacKillop 1995: 107; Martin 2008: 239).

33 This is not to say that I in any way resile from believing in the desirability of seeking to unite vocation and avocation in one's life (Bradney 2003: ch. 8). However, what is desirable is certainly not necessarily easy and may always, in its perfect form, be just beyond the horizon.

34 These lives will have their own complexities and contradictions.

References

Aristotle. 1980. *The Nicomachean Ethics*. Oxford: Oxford University Press.
Bauman, Z. 2005. *Liquid Life*. Cambridge: Polity Press.
Becher, T. and Trowler, P. 2001. *Academic Tribes and Territories*. Milton Keynes: SRHE and Open University Press.
Belsey, C. 1982. Re-reading the Great Tradition, in *Re-Reading English*, edited by P. Widdowson. London: Methuen, 121–35.
Bradney, A. 2003. *Conversations, Chances and Choices: The Liberal Law School in the Twenty-first Century*. Oxford: Hart Publishing.
Brown, J., van Leeuwen, M. and Mitch, D. 2004. The History of the Modern Career: An Introduction, in *Origins of the Modern Career*, edited by D. Mitch, J. Brown and M. van Leeuwen. Aldershot: Ashgate, 3–41.
Brown, W. 1982. *Academic Politics*. Tuscaloosa, AL: University of Alabama Press.
Calvino, I. 1986. *The Uses of Literature*. San Diego: Harcourt Brace Jovanovich.
Catephores, G. 1972. Marxian Alienation – A Clarification, *Oxford Economic Papers* 24(1): 124–36.
Cicero. 1990. Laelius, On Friendship, in Cicero *On Friendship and The Dream of Scipio*. Warminister: Aris and Philllips Ltd.
Coetzee, J.M. 2002. *Youth*. London: Secker and Warburg.
Collier, R. 2002. The Changing University and the (Legal) Academic Career: Rethinking the Relationship Between Women, Men and the 'Private Life' of the Law School, *Legal Studies* 22(1): 1–32.
Cownie, F. 2004. *Legal Academics: Culture and Identities*. Oxford: Hart Publishing.
Demaria, J. 1990. The Wondrous Marriages of *Daniel Deronda*: Gender, Work and Love, *Studies in the Novel* 22(4): 403–19.
Derrida, J. 1997. *The Politics of Friendship*. London: Verso.
Edwards, P. and Wachman, J. 2005. *The Politics of Working Life*. Oxford: Oxford University Press.
Eliot, G. 1967. *Daniel Deronda*. Harmondsworth: Penguin Books.
Eriksen, E. 1956. Growth and Crises of Human Personality, in *Personality in Nature, Society and Culture*, edited by C. Kluckhon and H. Murray. New York: Alfred A. Knopf.
Evans, C. 1988. *Language People*. Milton Keynes: Open University Press.
Evetts, J. 1992. Dimensions of Career: Avoiding Reification in the Analysis of Change, *Sociology* 26(1): 1–21.
Freud, S. 1955. Group Psychology and the Analysis of the Ego, in *The Standard Edition of the Complete Psychological Works of Sigmund Freud: Volume XVIII*. London: Hogarth Press.
Freud, S. 1957. Leonardo di Vinci, in *The Standard Edition of the Complete Psychological Works of Sigmund Freud: Volume XI*. London: Hogarth Press.

Freud, S. 1961a. The Future of an Illusion, in *The Standard Edition of the Complete Psychological Works of Sigmund Freud: Volume XXI*. London. Hogarth Press.
Freud, S. 1961b. Civilization and its Discontents, in *The Standard Edition of the Complete Psychological Works of Sigmund Freud: Volume XXI*. London: Hogarth Press.
Goodrich, P. 2003. Laws of Friendship, *Law and Literature* 15(1): 23–52.
Gorz, A. 1989. *Critique of Economic Reason*. London: Verso.
Gray, F. 1961. Montaigne's Friends, *French Studies* XV(3): 203–13.
Henkel, M. 2000. *Academic Identities and Policy Change in Higher Education*. London: Jessica Kingsley Publishers.
Jackall, R. 1988. *Moral Mazes: The World of Corporate Managers*. Oxford: Oxford University Press.
Johnstone, G. 1999. Liberal Ideals and Vocational Aims in University Legal Education, *Web JCLI* 3. [Online] Available at: http://webjcli.ncl.ac.uk/ [accessed 16 June 2010].
Jones, E. 1964. *The Life and Work of Sigmund Freud*. Harmondsworth: Penguin Books.
Lamb, C. 1885. *The Essays of Elia*. Edinburgh: William Paterson.
Leavis, F.R. 1962. *The Great Tradition*. Harmondsworth: Penguin Books.
Lichtheim, G. 1972. Freud and Marx, in *Freud: The Man, His World, and Influence*, edited by J. Miller. London: Weidenfeld and Nicolson, 55–69.
MacKillop, I. 1995. *FR Leavis: A Life in Criticism*. London: Allen Lane, The Penguin Press.
Martin, G. 2008. *Gabriel García Márquez: A Life*. London: Bloomsbury.
Marx, K. 1959. *Economic and Philosophic Manuscripts of 1844*. London: Lawrence and Wishart.
McMorrow, J. and Baldwin, A. 1991. Life After Law School: On Being a Retired Law Professor, *Journal of Legal Education* 41(1): 407–19.
Mendoza, P. 1983. *The Fragrance of Guava: Conversations with Gabriel García Márquez*. London: Verso.
Miller, J. 1993. *The Passion of Michel Foucault*. London: HarperCollins.
Mintz, A. 1978. *George Eliot and the Novel of Vocation*. Cambridge: Harvard University Press.
de Montaigne, M. 2003. *The Complete Essays*. Harmondsworth: Penguin Books.
Newell, H. 2000. Managing Careers, in *Personnel Management: A Comprehensive Guide to Theory and Practice*, edited by S. Bach and K. Sisson. Oxford: Blackwell Publishers, 218–38.
Oxford Dictionary of Quotations. 1992. Oxford: Oxford University Press.
Preyer, R. 1960. Beyond the Liberal Imagination: Vision and Unreality in 'Daniel Deronda', *Victorian Studies* 4(1): 33–54.
Price, A. 1989. *Love and Friendship in Plato and Aristotle*. Oxford: Clarendon Press.
Riesman, D. 1954. *Individualism Reconsidered and Other Essays*. Glencoe, IL: The Free Press.

Savage, M. 1998. Discipline, Surveillance and the 'Career': Employment on the Great Western Railway 1833–1914, in *Foucault, Management and Organization Theory*, edited by A. McKinley and K. Starkey. London: Sage, 65–92.

Sennett, R. 2006. *The Culture of the New Capitalism*. London: Yale University Press.

Steiner, G. 1997. *Errata: An Examined Life*. London: Weidenfeld and Nicolson.

Strike, T. and Taylor, J. 2009. The Career Perceptions of Academic Staff and Human Resource Discourses in English Higher Education, *Higher Education Quarterly* 63(2): 177–95.

The National Committee of Inquiry into Higher Education: Report 3: Academic Staff in Higher Education: Their Experience and Expectations. 1997. London: The National Committee of Inquiry into Higher Education.

Toker, L. 2004. Vocation and Sympathy in *Daniel Deronda*: The Self and the Larger Whole, *Victorian Literature and Culture* 32(2): 565–74.

Weber, M. 1948. Science as a Vocation, in *From Max Weber: Essays in Sociology*, edited by H.H. Gerth and C.W. Wright. London: Routledge, 129–56.

Williams, R. 1988. *Keywords: A Vocabulary of Culture and Society*. London: Fontana.

Chapter 6
What do Academics Think and Feel about Quality?

Chris Maguire

> Ostensibly the aim of quality assurance may well be to improve service provision but in reality it is a subtle form of panoptic power, control and surveillance over the academic labour process.
>
> (Worthington and Hodgson 2005: 96)

This chapter explores the thoughts and feelings about quality of 10 academic staff who teach on the Graduate Diploma in Law (GDL) programme at the Institute of Practice (IoP).[1] The study seeks to analyse and evaluate their perception, identify any trends within the group and compare those trends, or lack of them, with the literature in the area. The effect of quality on the academic microenvironment has not been studied in depth (Ratcliff 2003: 128). While there is a growing field of research on the mechanics of quality in higher education, and in particular the effectiveness or otherwise of external audit, there is little systematic research on academics' views about quality and its impact on the affective domain of academic labour. The work of Becher and Trowler (2001) on academic identity and Morley (2003) and Deem (1998, 2004), among others, on academics' perceptions of quality and the effects of quality on academic labour provide the foundations for further empirical research. In what follows I use the word 'quality' deliberately broadly to avoid narrow definitions that may limit respondents' responses, and interpret its meaning loosely to include all possible references that the respondents may associate with it.

Constructing Quality

Quality within higher education is not only a contested concept; it is a field of battle within the lived experience of the academic community. The battle lines are not straight nor straightforward. Divisions are not only arranged simply between the proponents and opponents of quality, between collegiality and new managerialism, between Newmanian liberals and economic, neo-conservatives but also between academics themselves – across hard/soft and urban/rural subject divides, between researchers and teachers, the established and the new. Consequently, the field of

1 The IoP is a pseudonym.

battle is not a neat Napoleonic grid but a Venn diagram of liquid alliances and guerrilla activity.

Practical conceptions of quality centre on quality audit, assurance, compliance and enhancement processes encapsulated in local, national and European frameworks. For the purposes of UK higher education, these are articulated through the Quality Assurance Agency's Academic Infrastructure, which provides direction and guidance on standards, level, content, provision and support.[2] The instruments contained within the Academic Infrastructure are the primary reference points in the articulation of higher education institutions' own governance and regulatory models.

However, quality has gained both an instrumental and emotional character that goes beyond the merely practical. While for some commentators within the literature quality is perceived as a set of practical tools and mechanisms to measure academic provision (Liston 1999; McCaffrey 2004), others perceive it more politically as a technology of leadership (Neave 1998; Brown 2004), as a central plank in the ideology of new managerialism (Morley 2004; Deem 1998, 2004) and a paradigm of power, oppression and performativity (Lyotard 1984; Foucault 1995; Deem 1998, 2004).

While similarities with aspects of modern practices and current issues are notable, current discourses on quality centre on the association of quality with the rise of the audit society (Power 1997) and governmental control for economic rather than educational reasons. The audit society itself is a product of the complexity and speed of social, political and economic change in Western society since the end of the Second World War, and in particular since the 1960s when post-war rebuilding and optimism gave way to increasing international competition, the need for a knowledgeable and technically skilled population and the prioritisation by government of economic development over any other social or political agenda (Lyotard 1984). With it came the focus on value for money, the 'rise of the evaluative state' (Neave 1988), audit and quality. Quality itself, interpreted as the articulation and protection of standards, striving for improvement and maintaining efficiency is, of course, a self-evident good, like motherhood and apple pie:

> As abstract principles or as points of rhetoric, they are unassailable. [But] Where the controversy arises is their operational, legislative and financial consequences for the individual establishments that go to make up the nation's system of higher education. (Neave 1988: 7)

This is ironic given that among the catalysts that facilitated greater government intrusion into higher education institutions have been the scandals arising from the financial mismanagement and poor academic leadership of a number of

---

2 See www.qaa.ac.uk/academicinfrastructure/default.asp and in particular the Framework for Higher Education Qualifications, the Codes of Conduct, and Subject Benchmark Statements.

institutions from across the sector (Shattock 2006: 81). Morley recognises the validity of quality as a democratising force: 'it seeks a better deal for students and society; better information, greater diversity and choice, product specification and risk management' (2004: 2). For Morley quality is the convergence of three policy technologies that underpin educational reform: markets, managerialism and performativity. Quality becomes a 'powerful meta-narrative … [and] parades as a cultural logic and universal truth and therefore continually extends its domain' (2004: 2–3). It reforms the academic habitus, feeding upon the emotional commitment of individual members of staff, exploiting feelings of loyalty, anxiety, guilt, desire and shame, leading to a psychic economy wherein the act of auditing academic labour has had 'a profound impact on reconstructing academic conditions of work and academic identities' (2004: 31). Morley characterises this reconstruction as deeply negative in both its emotional consequences for individual academics and in its essential goal of maximising the performance of the organisation.

In doing so she highlights a central issue: do the frameworks, technologies and instruments of quality lead to a culture of quality or a culture of bureaucracy? It has not been demonstrated that quality assurance as defined above is a necessary or indeed a sufficient condition for a quality culture (Yorke 2000). Consequently, quality requires a wider interpretation than that encapsulated by terminology associated with the mechanisms of compliance and assurance. Quality may also be seen as an agent of innovation and transformation.

Deming's approach to quality, as applied in the car industry in the early–mid-20th century is drawn from the Japanese 'Kaizen' philosophy, which was instrumental in leading to the development of the philosophies and technocracies of total quality management (TQM). Kaizen espouses a commitment to striving for continual improvement in the belief that performance can always be enhanced through incremental, innovative and transformative improvements (Liston 1999: 9, 157). Kaizen seeks to create a harmonious and dynamic organisation through an inclusive approach where every member of the organisation is valued and contributes to improvement. Kaizen was influential in the development of TQM, particularly in recognising and attempting to marry the hard concepts of production and delivery with the soft concepts of motivation and empowerment. The extent to which TQM achieves this marriage is contested. Power queries the extent to which TQM differs from more traditional forms of programmatic interventions such as Taylorism and Fordism. He notes that:

> It is argued that TQM preserves hierarchies and that ideals of flexibility reproduce the subordination of labour … TQM … represents a particular project of attempting to create and regulate an internal order. (Power 1997: 58)

Yorke recognises the development of TQM from a manufacturing industry to internal servicing but argues that it must develop further if it is to meet the needs of learning and teaching in higher education. He sees TQM having greatest potential if it is 'built in at the front of the process, rather than "inspected in" after the event'. He cites curricula design as an example where TQM would have an impact. However, he considers that 'this cannot be achieved without detailed collegial discussion about ends and means' (Yorke 2000: 24).

Yorke's caution and appeal to collegiality regarding the adoption of TQM is countered by other commentators' enthusiastic support and adoption of an industry-based lexicon. Venkatraman cites Lundquist, who considers that the 'customer focus, process orientation and continuous improvement philosophies of TQM adopted in industry is very much applicable in education', and Srikanthan and Dalrymple, who describe 'courseware as products, the current and prospective students as users of products and the graduates as output with employers as their users'. And finally, Hammersley and Pinnington, who argue that 'realistically, in higher education, TQM appears to be a systematic and a streamlined philosophy for quality management and management of change' (Venkatraman 2007: 4, 5).

Venkatraman (2007: 8) sets out the core values for adapting TQM to an educational environment:

- leadership and quality culture
- continuous improvement and innovation in educational processes
- employee participation and development
- fast response and management of information
- customer-driven quality, and
- partnership development, internally and externally.

Though some aspects of the language of these values may require unpacking, none of them are unfamiliar in the language and documentation of higher education and can be found within the precepts of the QAA's Codes of Practice. Indeed, it may be argued that higher education has moved beyond this articulation of TQM to the adoption of even more explicit industry practices such as patenting, industry partnerships, spin-off companies, consultancy, income generation and the evaluation of impact. This is demonstrated further in Venkatraman's examples of TQM practices which have been or can be imported into higher education. However, here lies the rub; questions of control, engagement and trust remain to be addressed.

It may be argued that quality assurance mechanisms are not about 'high standards, but those which are uniform, predictable and verifiable' (Power 1997: 58). Badly applied they may lead to a culture of inspection and intimidation. The imposition of a culture of continual improvement may be perceived as a Sisyphean task, under a panopticon of surveillance and intrusion, where the status quo is forever inadequate and academics labour under 'the uncertainty and instability of being judged in different ways by different means, through different agents ... a recipe for ontological insecurity' (Ball 2004: 144) and a Kafkaesque nightmare of unwritten rules and unidentified offences.

Halsey refers to academics as 'an occupational group losing its long established privileges of tenure and self government ... hampered in its control of the syllabus' (1992: 269). Individuals feel objectified: 'I didn't feel like an academic, I felt like the prey to the QAA', and reduced to the extent that they 'desire to avoid innovation for fear that the assessors won't like it' (academic respondents cited in Morley 2003: 98–9). Morley goes on to argue that the psychic economy of quality introduces compliance into a culture that ought to be much more innovative and experimental. She claims that academics are, then, presented as intimidated into asking 'am I doing it right?' and not 'am I doing the right thing?' (Yorke 2000: 27; Morley 2003: 99). For many commentators this is key: academic labour should not be systematised like manufacturing. Quality audit seeks to measure that which is not measurable (Bradney 2002: 4). For example, Dearlove (2002: 262) claims that the effect of the quality movement has been the 'proletarianisation' of academic labour and a loss of academic autonomy and trust. For some this may be justified. In Cownie's (2004) study of cultures and identity in UK law schools, subjects commented on the changes between the 1970s and the present day:

> Has it changed? God, yes! ... I referred to it at that time as the last bastion of English amateurism – nobody taught us how to teach ... if the students thought you were a good teacher, all well and good; if they didn't, well, nobody seemed to be particularly bothered about it. It was all pretty laissez-faire. From that position, we have now entered something which I consider to be excessively regulated, incredibly bureaucratic, terribly frustrating. (Cownie 2004: 160)

Quality, then, particularly in its audit form, raises issues of trust versus verification in a society that has evolved from being duty-based before the Second World War to being rights-based after it. Power (1997: 2) asks can one imagine a society where nothing was trusted. Or a society in which nothing was checked?

> What we need to decide as individuals, organisations and societies is how to combine checking and trusting. What kinds of activities should be checked? How much explicit checking is enough? How does checking affect those who are checked and when does the demand for monitoring become pathological? (Power 1997: 2)

Checking is then both a verification and substitution of trust. But where the object of investigation resists checking and verification because of its intangibility, the verification process reverts to a second order of trust, either through the employment of external expertise to verify the attestations of the internal experts, or those of the institutions' internal control mechanisms. In such cases, Power warns, audit is in danger of reducing quality to what is auditable and of providing 'certificates of comfort' generated by 'shallow rituals of verification' (Power 1997). Quality is then transparently practical, politically fraught and deeply emotional. It plays within the field of higher education that is itself diverse, changing, fractured and fissiparous (Becher and Trowler 2001; Arnoldi 2007).

Quality and the Conditions of Academic Labour

Lyotard's work provides a lens through which to encapsulate and summarise these debates and the variety of attitudes and approaches they indicate. Charting the cultural changes arising from the reconstruction of Europe after the Second World War through the 'resumption of economic world war in the 1960s' (Lyotard 1984: 12) to the economic downturn in the early 1980s, he explores the evolution of knowledge as a tool of homogeneity and otherness, or as the search for truth and knowledge as a commodity within a globalising economy. In relation to the latter he explores access to knowledge, the identity of knowledge producers, who creates and owns it, the types of knowledge and applications that are valued, their legitimation and their socio-economic implications and leverage, and the consequential effects on the focus and value of academic labour and the control of that labour by non-academics.

Lyotard predicted an agenda of performativity and the new managerialism that was to invade the academy. However, perhaps what is most salient in Lyotard's writing is a question on the lips of every academic and on the conscience of every new-managerialist: what difference does the technocracy surrounding quality make? And to what extent does the process of measuring the quality of the educational process inhibit the process itself? Lyotard takes the performativity question of 'what is your argument worth, what is your proof worth' (1984: 54) and raises it to a meta-question: 'What is your "what is it worth?" worth?' This is what Lyotard characterises as the crisis of determinism. Using examples from mathematics, quantum theory and micro physics, he argues that the notion of a stable system within which performance can be predicted, if all variables are known, is a fallacy because it is not possible to know all the variables without 'an expenditure of energy equivalent to that of the system to be defined' (1984: 55). Lyotard argues that knowledge of a system and the variables within does not entail certainty, but in fact may increase uncertainty – the more one discovers of the movement of elements of the system, the more one may be aware of the unpredictable and the contradictory. If this is true, to what extent can the technocracy have a positive effect? Or rather, does the very act of measurement and intrusion into the academic process of labour lead to 'stifle[ing] the systems or sub systems they control and asphyxiate themselves in the process' (1984: 56). Power takes this further, arguing that where performance cannot be demonstrated, 'the nature of the management system becomes itself the mark of effectiveness' and the object of verification (Power 1997: 59).

However, it is not simply the control of academic labour that is in question but the changing balance and identity of that labour. Academic labour has traditionally comprised (in traditional order of preference) research, teaching and administration.

With the massification of higher education and the publication of the Dearing Report (1997),[3] teaching itself has attracted more attention and scrutiny. In some cases this has resulted in a rise in the focus on teaching and the esteem in which it is held, both by institutions and individual academics. However, in other cases, the appearance of increased attention to and valuing of teaching is hollow and reveals only recognition by institutional management of the importance of public relations in the market of student (consumer) choice (Cownie 2004: 162). What it has resulted in is a polarising of the components of academic labour with groups of academics and groups of institutions focusing more explicitly on research or teaching and associated duties of academic citizenship and pastoral support of students. This is particularly highlighted by the burden of administration which is allocated often inequitably between academic staff and which some studies put as having increased threefold between the 1960s and 1990s (Cownie 2004: 85).

Within the literature, attitudes to quality are informed by the effects it is perceived to have on the conditions of academic labour and individual status and survival. Of importance here are Bourdieu's notions of cultural capital, pedagogic authority and symbolic violence. In considering these further it is important to bear in mind the language used to describe the modern academic and the changes to the creation, location, identity and application of knowledge discussed by Lyotard and characterised as 'performative', 'socially distributed' and 'contextualised' (Arnoldi 2007: 49). Academics are now knowledge workers: an ambiguous term that has connotations of both elitism and proletarianism.

In Bourdieu's terms, in the field of higher education, cultural capital is presented as academic capital and intellectual capital. These are the key drivers underpinning the aspirations and values that characterise academic labour. The value of academic and intellectual capital in acquiring cultural and eventually symbolic capital varies in relation to the field, department and institution in which it exists. Academic capital, in particular, is constrained by the specific values, culture and customs of the institution and the value and status they accord an appointment. In contrast, intellectual capital is, as Henkel (2005) comments, a product of the individual's reputation, which goes beyond institutional borders, is independent of institutional grace and favour, and therefore carries greater symbolic capital.

The conditions of academic labour that are afforded by the values of academic freedom and autonomy and the role of the academy *vis-à-vis* society are themselves elements of cultural, social and symbolic capital that impact upon academics' orientation to quality. Indeed, the perceived intrusion of governmental agendas into higher education through the agency of quality and the consequent erosion of academic autonomy and authority may serve to highlight further elements in Bourdieu's theory of capital. The evolution of the knowledge society in the last 40 years or so has shifted pedagogic authority from the academy to the state. Quality, then, may be viewed as a form of symbolic violence (violence enacted

---

3 The National Committee of Enquiry into Higher Education. 1997. *Higher Education in the Learning Society*, chaired by Sir Ron Dearing.

through non-physical forms of oppression, subjugation or constraint) against the academy itself, in which the language of quality is a form of linguistic capital and semantic fog that serves as a legitimated mechanism of control and exclusion. However, as Ball reminds us:

> *We* sit on peer reviews, *we* write the accountability reports, *we* assign grades to other departments, *we* berate our colleagues for their 'poor' productivity, *we* devise, run and feed departmental and institutional procedures for monitoring and improving 'output'. (Ball 2004: 145)

The academy is then both the victim and the perpetrator, leading to alienation of self, denial and schizophrenia.

Ball cites the cases of teachers' reactions to external regimes of accountability and quality from a study conducted by Jeffrey and Woods in 1998. The cases are littered with the language of division and opposition, of 'them' and 'us', of being forced to 'play the game', and of being ashamed for doing so:

> My first reaction was 'I'm not going to play the game', but I am and they know I am. I don't respect myself for it ... why aren't I making a stand? (Jeffrey and Woods 1998: 160, cited in Ball 2004: 147)

Ball refers to this as the alienation of self driven by performativity which results in 'inauthentic practice and relationships' (Ball 2004: 147). However, inauthenticity is subjective and may be contested. For example, drawing on the work of Jeffrey and Woods, Ball cites the case of Chloe, who after criticism of the school's SATs results resolved to improve them. She achieved the second best set of results in the LEA by changing her curriculum. However, it is implied she did this against her professional will and judgement. 'She justified this by saying that she was "now just doing a job"; and had withdrawn her total involvement to preserve her "sanity". "The results were better because I acted like a function machine"' (Ball 2004: 147).

The conflict in values and personal/professional effectiveness is acute in this example. Chloe feels inauthentic despite having achieved impressive results for her students. Is Chloe's professional arrogance of such a level that the validity of her approach to teaching is more important than her students' results or is there a disconnection between what is valuable in the education of students and what is valued through their assessment so that what Chloe now does in the classroom educates her students less but enables them to achieve better results? If that is the case it would be an example of doing things right, but not doing the right thing (Yorke 2000: 27), either for the students or for the articulation of values.

Performativity, then, becomes performance. This is never clearer than in the set-pieces of quality: institutional review, programme approval and the machinations of senior committees, where the projection and management of a protective image is of the first importance. Ball (2004) describes these 'rituals', 'grandiloquent statement' and 'spectacular events' as 'fabrications'. Cownie's (2004) respondents talk about 'gearing up' for reviews, the review being a theatrical presentation of how things should be rather than how they are. A theatrical set is constructed. Like a Jonsonian masque, the institution's staff present an ideal in the tradition of Castiglione rather than the *realpolitik* of Machiavelli. The playing out of such events suggests either a disconnect between the reality of the limitations of academic labour and those standards and aspirations imposed upon it by politics, commerce or competition; or that there is a collusion in the mythology of excellence which can be used to both inspire academics to greater efforts and labour and promote the academic unit (whether department, institution, region or state) as competitive.

The Context of the Study

The research undertaken for this study was carried out at the Institute of Practice (IoP) and focuses on tutors delivering the Graduate Diploma in Law (GDL). Given the commonality of the GDL in the legal HE sector it may be tempting to extrapolate from the responses of the respondents within this study to the sector in general. However, as Ward says: 'No two Law Schools, for sure, are the same ... localised practices of orientation and enculturation, of "belonging, experience, doing and becoming", assume defining importance' (Ward 2010). One could add that no two legal academics are the same.

Cownie, drawing on Toma, highlights the effect that paradigm has in causing academics to view 'the purposes of their work differently, apply different evaluative standards, rely upon different methods and frameworks and accept different values' (Cownie 2004: 20). In the case of academic lawyers there are distinct theoretical approaches to law (doctrinal, socio-legal, critical-legal) which are also further informed by the extent to which they are placed within a liberal or vocational context. Though Cownie discounts this approach to stratifying the sample in her own study because of the difficulty in separating and distinguishing practice by individual academics, these approaches to law assist in describing the IoP and in providing a context for the data drawn from its staff who are the respondents of this study. The IoP is a private law school, largely specialising in doctrinal law applied within professional and practice contexts. The students on the GDL will, at this stage, be focused on a career in legal practice. This context may distinguish the IoP as being at one pole of the liberal/professional, academic/applied axis. Cownie's study focuses on legal academics working in academic as opposed to vocational departments, and although the GDL is part of the academic stage, it is focused on preparation for practice and would fall into Cownie's category of vocational legal education. She suggests that the 'professional experiences and concerns of these legal academics are frequently very different, therefore, from legal academics engaged in the "academic stage" of legal education ...' (Cownie 2004: 19). However, going beyond paradigm, or as

Becher and Trowler (2001) may more traditionally refer to it, subject specialism, there is evidence to suggest that attitudes to quality are also influenced by the value attached to the major components of academic labour: research, teaching, administration and, more latterly, third stream activities and funding.

If this is true, this study explores a part of the legal education sector that is not covered in Cownie's broader study, but which may provide a distinctive response to that presented in her work. Indeed it argues that in a diversifying higher education system where the common denominator is the response to a changing, competitive market and mechanisms of governance and financing, all views are valid and equally representative

Research Approach

Sample

The approach adopted for the sample construction was to ask for volunteers from the Graduate Diploma in Law programme. Ten tutors were then selected to create a stratified purposive sample from among a larger group of volunteers who had expressed an interest in taking part in the study. The selection criteria aimed to achieve a sufficient breadth of experiences and roles within the group to enable judgements to be made as to whether orientation to quality was affected by either of these two variables. The participants were selected on the basis that they fell within one of the following three groups: 1) tutors with up to three years' experience but no or very limited management responsibility; 2) experienced tutors with some management responsibility, e.g. module or programme management; 3) senior tutors (programme leaders and above) with significant management experience and responsibility. The selection criteria also sought to ensure that the group was equally divided by gender. The group stretched from a new tutor with one year of experience, through programme leaders, to a professor and a dean. Within this group some participants were closely orientated to a teaching career and valued that over academic management, whereas others, although still closely engaged in teaching or pedagogy, had chosen academic management routes to promotion. At least two of the respondents were research-active within their subject area and these and others were active in research into pedagogy and regularly gave papers at conferences.

The Interviews

All respondents were invited to take part in semi-structured interviews. A common list of 10 set questions was followed in a semi-structured format, which allowed for the respondent to expand on points and digress on to issues he or she considered more important. Supplementary questions, which supported or clarified the primary questions, were used to encourage respondents to enlarge on their initial answers. Interviews lasted between 17 and 55 minutes and were recorded onto DVD. The DVDs were transcribed, including the noting of noticeable pauses and phatics.

The Interview as a Space for Construction

The interview itself, both as a process of questioning and a space for reflection, appeared to enable respondents to work through their beliefs about and attitudes to quality. Typically, at the beginning of each interview respondents were unclear as to how to describe quality and their attitudes to it appeared to reflect this vagueness. As the interview progressed the initial vagueness gave way to greater clarity and assertions about quality and the respondents' attitudes and relationships to it. In part this was no doubt a result of the subsequent questions that assisted in focusing the minds of the respondents. However, analysis of the interview transcripts reveals that the respondents' attitudes towards quality changed during the course of the interview and they became better at articulating their understanding of quality. This suggests that the act of considering the issues raised by the questions led to reflection and review of their initial attitudes and the recognition of inconsistencies in their accounts, within the timeframe of the interview. Some respondents volunteered remarks to this effect:

> That was interesting I have never thought about these issues philosophically before. (Rufus)

> I was thinking the quality regime as being the design process but of course it's not just the design process it is the collecting of student feedback as well. (Pip)

In other cases it was revealed through contradiction: 'I'm not sure there's much development going on [by] the teaching staff' (Beth). But as she later states: 'That's a good idea. Where did it come from? I don't think it came from quality at all. I think it came from us' (Beth). This comment also highlights the conception of quality as 'not us'.

Analysis of the Data

The interviews were all transcribed and then analysed. The data was analysed through a combination of thematic analysis: line by line, open coding and axial coding (Strauss and Corbin 1998). A number of prior themes were implicit in the approach to the study and informed the questions that were asked. These themes included whether the respondent understood local and national approaches to quality, whether they were positive or negative about quality, whether they felt quality was internal or external to their work, whether it was imposed on them or owned and influenced by them, whether it helped or hindered their work and whether it attacked or protected them, how they reacted to quality and how they used it.

Findings from the Data

Constructions of Quality

A significant issue that emerged during the study was predicted by one of the respondents: 'People have very different notions about what quality means' (Rufus). The diversity of meanings that the respondents attached to quality and the extent to which these meanings were informed by their emotional response to the term played out in three categories: quality as an aspirational concept, quality as a standard or benchmark, and quality as a regime of audit, assurance and enhancement.

In response to the first interview question, 'What do you understand by the term quality?' responses included:

> I'm going to struggle with the broadness of that. (Jacques)
>
> A somewhat meaningless term. (Seb)
>
> I think it's a sort of overused term probably that tends to attach to too many things now … (Kit)

These reactions support Williams' contention that quality and quality assurance, in the form articulated by the Government in the 1992 White Paper *Higher Education: A New Framework*, lacked clarity of definition and purpose and betrayed 'what confusion there must have been in the minds of civil servants and ministers about the whole topic' (Williams 2010: 6–7). That imprecision together with a lack of intellectual underpinning was, Williams goes on to say, the cause of the discrediting of quality in the 1990s and, despite reforms and greater clarity since 2001, the cause of continued uncertainty, vagueness and disregard in the minds and attitudes of academics.

Seb comments that quality is in the same category as 'adding value': 'a word that people want to believe in but can't quite pin down. I think that it only works if you can somehow put measurables on it and can somehow give it a precise definition' (Seb).

The participants in this study may agree with many of Bradney's sentiments about the burden of quality audit; however, they would disagree that it seeks to measure 'that which is unmeasurable' (Bradney 2002). While accepting that there is something at the heart of academic labour that is not susceptible to audit, they do not accept that the provision that supports and delivers the student learning experience cannot be evaluated and, where appropriate, enhanced. Gabriel's comments on the nature of quality illustrate this view. For him quality is: 'a generic term … one that can be seen from the student's point of view'. This reference to an external viewpoint is repeated by other respondents who consider quality to be about the 'actual experience a student has in terms of the educational process' (Rufus). Seb adds that 'it should cover the end product and the process', where the process includes everything from 'first contact with Admissions through to getting their results and graduating'. This 'customer service' approach is reflected in the respondents' views that quality is both an academic and an administrative matter. This is endorsed by their references to benchmarks and standards against which the student experience and the level of service will be judged. A senior member of staff expressed a similar view in more general terms: 'It's a way of making sure that we don't just talk about quality, but make sure there's some kind of empirical evidence to prove that we are doing it … It's very utilitarian' (Gabriel).

The utilitarianism of quality is reflected in the following comment: 'I suppose my first response to the phrase quality is good; we charge more for that. It costs more to produce. It costs more to train to a quality standard' (Jacques). However, he continues: 'I, I struggle with quality, what … I don't … quality of, how what is quality?' The fractured construction of this statement reflects Jacques' struggle to locate quality in a consistent or meaningful context. He continues: '… someone who pays £20,000 for education … is doing something very different very different from someone who perhaps pays a former polytechnic £3,000'. Challenged as to what the difference is, he responded: 'Well, what they're paying … different levels of quality. I wouldn't say there's a defined level of quality. I'd be looking at a continuum of quality'. This type of response may be more typical of, though not unique to, a private sector rather than a public sector provider. For the private sector, price differentiation is central to survival and success; too low a price risks low profit margins and brand damage, too high a price risks reduced sales and revenue. The higher the price that one is able to charge is a reflection of quality and status, not simply because of brand image but because of what is perceived to be the cost of providing a quality programme. For the private sector employee, bred on a market economy, price is the first indicator of market position, and market position defines the status of the institution and with it the cultural (and more specifically academic) capital of the academics who work there. Other approaches to standards of quality are considered more opaque. This theme is taken up by other respondents in relation to the application of quality as a consistent and interpretable set of standards.

> … is there really a standard across the education sector … I know universities are independent in that they have to maintain their own quality within their organisation but, you know, what is the quality of a degree from Cambridge University compared to the quality of a degree from, you know, a newer university … how does the marketplace compare those two degrees? (Beth)

As the market cannot apply price, it applies criteria relating to reputation measured through demand. Jacques adopts the same criterion for his course:

> I suppose the end product that we are looking for is to provide a legal education which people will pay us substantially more for than many other providers in the market … and I think whether we actually provide quality or not is determined by [laughs] the number of students through the door.

It is, then, demand that demonstrates quality and, as demand is dictated by service, choice and price, it may be argued that a customer service ethic is essential, one which places the student as customer and the customer as king – an approach that some in the academy would see as the undermining of standards and validity.

However, Pip's differentiation between quality and quality assurance highlights difference between mechanisms and values. Quality assurance is about 'regulation and bureaucratic hoops'. Quality itself is a value linked to integrity, to delivering what you say you are going to deliver: 'what the students are expecting and need' (Pip). She welcomes aspiration to quality but also feels it can be a deception:

> when I hear people want to aim for quality I feel good because I'm likely to be on the same page but I've heard a lot of the bandying around of the word quality which is just outright lies and so now I've begun to think that it's a word that people use because they think it sounds good and not because they have any true integrity that links to quality.

Quality assurance, then, protects integrity and, consequently:

> I actually believe in various things that are part of the quality assurance regime … To the extent that the regime links to the actual product as in the course. I think that it can contribute very strongly and in fact without it what else would a degree be? It would just be whatever we wrote down on a piece of paper.

Pip introduces two important caveats about quality: it is only meaningful if it protects integrity and to do so it must link to and support the enhancement of the product, e.g. the programme or the student experience of it, avoiding meaningless bureaucracy and it must involve people whose focus is on the quality and integrity of the product. This draws out a truism of private sector practice, brand credibility and reputation dictates success or failure. Providing a well-researched, carefully designed and well-aligned product satisfies the dark side of the corporate soul in growth, profits and security. Rufus sums this up pithily: 'Quality does what it says on the tin', meaning that the programme meets the expectations of those paying for it, where meeting expectations is a positive standard and where that standard is meaningful and measurable.

Thus, from coding the data in terms of what is envisaged by 'quality' it appears that awareness of quality is built on a platform of uncertainty about what quality is, how it is measured and beliefs about whether it can be measured systematically either within an institution or across the sector.

Quality and the Affective Conditions of Academic Labour: Ownership, Protection and Otherness

A central theme to emerge from the data analysis was how ownership of the concepts and instruments of quality affect academics' orientations towards this process; how ownership or imposition are perceived to affect the conditions of academic labour and therefore the construction of the academic habitus.

There is not a simple relationship between ownership and acceptance, and imposition and resistance. Nor is there a clear delineation between the 'academic' and the 'outsider' or the 'other', either in terms of the academic community, a tribe or as an individual academic. Commonly expressed notions of the academic community being 'us' and the Government, QAA, executive management and quality apparatchiks being 'them' or 'the other' (Morley 2004) is not supported in the data. The fissiparous diversity of values and behaviours identified by Becher and Trowler (2001) are replicated to a smaller scale within my sample, and those values and behaviours can be seen to change depending on the context of academic labour and the threats to the cultural capital enjoyed by the academic community, sub-group or individual academic.

In broad terms, where the academic perceives that they 'own' or at least 'control' the mechanisms of quality, then quality and its mechanisms are seen as a positive, inherent, necessary and common-sense aspect of academic labour. Where the mechanisms of quality lie outside the immediate control of academics but are applied within a partnership model, or where a dialogue is present, there is, largely, a significant degree of support for, or at least acceptance of, quality and its instruments. Where the instruments are seen to be outside the control or influence of academics they are perceived as external, bureaucratic and threatening and their contribution to quality, and indeed, the value of the quality being sought through the instruments is contested. The threat emerges from three aspects of the instruments' externality. First, that the instruments serve aims or values of quality which are not necessarily shared by the academic; second, that the instruments have a controlling or constraining effect or facilitate a judgemental culture which, in turn, inhibits academic freedom, creativity and the process of academic labour; and third that the instruments are bureaucratic and burdensome, thereby diverting resources of academic labour and creating 'bureaucratic meaninglessness' (Pip). There are also echoes here of Bourdieu's 'cultural arbitrary' and, because of the implications of imposition, 'symbolic violence'.

Quality as a concept was viewed by most respondents as a self-evident good. The most positive expressions of quality arose from its perception as a value, such as integrity, or as a mark of distinction, both in terms of providing a well-regarded product and meeting student and stakeholder expectations. 'It differentiates you from your competitors' (Jacques). There were also benefits in terms of staff morale and professional self-respect: 'I'm a pro. I'm teaching to a standard that I think is really good … and I guess recognised by outsiders as being a kind of benchmark …' (Kit).

However, other positive expressions about quality resulted from misrecognition. The quality regime was either not apparent to some respondents or those elements of which the respondents were aware were not recognised as external to academic labour but inherent to it. In the first case both junior academics and their senior managers readily admitted that junior members of staff were unlikely to be aware of the quality regime or the network of instruments operating around them:

> I doubt you'll find many junior members of staff who are aware of the quality regime. (Rufus)

> I'm not really aware of quality mechanisms. (Justine)

Even some senior members considered that the mechanisms of quality were not as apparent as they would like:

> I'd like it more transparent … sometimes it's so hidden you don't always know they're there. (Gabriel)

This raises a number of questions: is this because the quality regime does not impact upon junior staff in the same way as senior staff, or is it because the actions and leadership of the senior staff mediate the perception of the quality regime, or is it that the quality regime is embedded to such an extent that its mechanisms appear natural, or are aspects of it deliberately hidden?

Ball's notions of 'rituals' and 'routine' (Ball 2004: 144) are relevant here. While the rituals and spectacular events of the theatre of quality are recognisable as such by all staff, they will usually be outward facing, and junior staff, if involved at all, will be to an extent protected from the inquisitional elements. The staging of the event, complete with rehearsals, will usually have had a team-centric approach. Junior staff will not therefore feel too exposed. Senior staff, in contrast, will be aware of the event as a decisive moment of judgement, not only of the programme or matter under consideration but of the management of it and their performance in support of it at the event itself (Morley 2003: e.g. 89–90). The 'routine' of quality may be more hidden. The preparation of minuting of meeting notes, reports, data analysis, etc., are less visible aspects of quality audit which become apparent in visible events when they are part of the evidence base to be judged and critiqued.

There is also evidence to suggest that at least some aspects of the quality regime become embedded within academic labour: that acceptance of quality instruments (such as scheduled team meetings, student feedback on teaching, statistical monitoring of results and moderation) through time, use or recognition of their utility may have led to transference and acquisition; to them now being conceived as owned by 'us' rather than 'them' and therefore not being an instrument of quality but a component of academic labour: 'the procedure for marking was naturally standardised without anyone saying you have to do it … just seemed natural' (Beth).

A senior member of staff reflects that: 'As a junior, a lot of stuff that came from quality just seemed a naturally good idea and would not have been recognised as part of a quality regime' (Seb).

As perceived components of academic labour, introduced, owned and applied by academics, and without the political baggage of external (or inexpert) surveillance, judgement and threat, such quality instruments carry a greater validity and acceptance than other instruments and approaches achieve.

Even when quality is recognised as external to and imposed on the academic habitus, its authenticity may be valued as a protection of or as an aid to academic labour:

> I generally think they [quality mechanisms] are all appropriate. I think one of the attractive things about IoP … is that it has always had a very utilitarian approach to any activity … it's very much geared towards a particular objective. (Gabriel)

Gabriel's comment echoes the point made by Pip, that quality works and is accepted if it is executed appropriately by the right people and is relevant. Who the 'right people' are is unclear. From the point made above and the literature on collegiality and new managerialism, a simple answer would be 'academics'. However, this is qualified by Pip to refer to people of integrity who share a common set of values and aspirations in relation to the student experience. This would exclude not only some members of senior management who for Pip sometimes may lack 'buy-in' and appreciation of the importance of longer-term reputational build over short-term market gains, but also some academics, such as Cownie's professors, who refer to the 'laissez-faire' approach to teaching quality and the fact that 'nobody ever seemed to fail probation' (Cownie 2004: 161–2). Holding the same values is, then, an important component in providing a constructive and supportive working environment and may go beyond tribal or academic identity and centre on facilitating the process of academic labour.

Quality may also be an obstacle and a threat. While recognising the need for consistency that had been imposed on a multi-site programme Berne comments:

> I'm not sure the teaching would have been as enthusiastic as it might have been had the tutors been given complete free rein to do what they wanted. (Berne)

Modern programme design entails the prescription of a common and consistent set of outcomes at programme and module level. The outcomes must be aligned with an authentic and valid assessment diet and the learning and teaching strategy must provide each student with a fair and appropriate opportunity to achieve the learning outcomes. Such an approach is student-centred and transparent, and aims to provide a consistent and appropriate learning experience. However, for some academics it is at the expense of their academic freedom to teach what and how they wish (Bradney 2002: 5).

Beth queries whether quality has the power to achieve consistency in delivery or even whether it should, and in doing so highlights the gap between regulatory intention and individual practice and the areas for academic resistance:

> How do you really know what goes on in that classroom? What's the experience? I don't see how you possibly can … and that's a good thing because you don't want automatons in the classroom. Just because something is on paper doesn't mean it's actually happening in practice. (Beth)

Beth's statement raises some core issues. She echoes both Lyotard (1984) and Bradney (2002) in querying the extent to which the core academic performance can be measured in any meaningful and consistent way without endangering the vitality of that performance and, like Chloe, reducing it to a dispirited, mechanical act, the replaceable 'dividual' rather than individual (Ball 2004: 144). Finally, she captures the risk of the disconnection between the ideal and the real, between what is aspired to on paper and may even be presented in the theatre of quality events, and that which is achievable in the affective heart of practice.

In contrast, Berne comments that the quality stimulus has positively impacted on her teaching:

> It's improving all the time. We are making more moves not just to teach the same thing but to improve on it … on the teaching side they're getting a lot more than students a few years ago. (Berne)

However, it remains open to question whether this is a result of quality mechanisms achieving a performative balancing act, a wider re-valuing of teaching within the academy under a social policy agenda, or the affective disposition towards teaching and students of the respondents in this study.

People, as Rufus and other respondents go on to elaborate, are central to whether a quality regime supports a successful quality culture. The former is not a sufficient condition for the latter. As Yorke has indicated, the development of a quality culture within higher education institutions has lagged behind the implementation of quality assurance practices. A key element of a quality culture is that it 'places a requirement on managers to *add value* to the work of those who are at the forefront of attempting to satisfy external stakeholders' (Yorke 2000: 21). This is echoed by Rufus:

> For those new to them, the technical demands of quality and the rationale behind them require significant induction and support. (Rufus)

Pip highlights people in the origination of those technical demands:

> All of our learning and teaching and our assessment strategies and everything should be something that is informed by and comes through … the right kinds of people. (Pip)

Gabriel notes the impact of affective management approaches:

> It's [the quality regime at IoP] not so much someone coming in and imposing artificial standards, it's facilitative. (Gabriel)

For Berne, however, in the past, academic freedom had meant complete independence:

> I had complete freedom to teach what I wanted in the way I wanted and there was no one to tell me what to do … Then in the last year or two they started bringing in controls … I remember being very resentful to the person who was telling us what to do [who] got terrible feedback and thinking your students are complaining about you … it's clearly not working. (Berne)

That independence caused Berne some difficulty when settling into working with a team because 'I lost the control and a lot of authority by being part of a team', and with it confidence, which only returned when the team began to function properly, inviting communication and working within a framework.

Conclusions

While the respondents in this study certainly express their criticism about quality, these appear to be matters mainly relating to efficiency, effectiveness and communication. There are few echoes of the conclusions of Morley (2003, 2004) or Deem (1998, 2004) that quality is 'a culture and a mode of regulation, or even a system of "terror" in Lyotard's words, that employs judgements, comparisons and displays as means of control attrition and change' (Deem 2004: 143).

The penultimate question of the interview asked respondents what changes they would make to the quality regime at IoP if they could. Despite Beth's early remark that 'quality always raises your hackles', the respondents' concluding comments were, perhaps surprisingly, positive and constructive:

> Oh that's a tricky question, what changes would I make? I'm not sure I would. I mean, I know I've said it's a pain and stuff like that, but I can see it's a necessity, and I think we are able to work around the awkward bits, like having the freedom with innovation and development. (Beth)

> I can't think of any quality mechanisms that intrude on my academic freedom. (Berne)

> I wouldn't change anything. (Rufus)
>
> It all looked like a load of bureaucratic nonsense … now I have a very different view. I would beef it up. (Pip)
>
> It needs some teeth, a lot can be done. (Seb)

The literature on the 'psychic economy' of quality (Ball 2004; Bradney 2002; Cownie 2004; Dearlove 2002; Deem 1998, 2004; Morley 2003, 2004; Worthington and Hodgson 2005) highlights the destructive effect of quality on academic identity and the process and outcomes of academic labour. In particular, quality is charged with contributing to the erosion of academic autonomy, independence and creativity and replacing these values and qualities with consistency, compliance and conformity.

My small-scale study does reveal echoes of the work of Becher and Trowler (2001), with respondents individually or collectively adopting techniques and adjusting position in relation to maintaining control over instruments that affect or threaten their habitus. For them quality is an aspiration, a value and a set of mechanisms. Influence, participation and control over the interpretation of those values and application of those systems are central to their perception of their cultural capital within the academy: their control over their own labour, their career trajectory and their sense of self-worth. For early career academics, whether they are in a collegiate or new-managerial environment is irrelevant (Ward 2010). What is important is that that environment is safe and supportive. This is perhaps particularly true of the respondents in this study, who may have never experienced a collegial environment because the IoP is their first academic position, such as Kit, or they have come directly from practice, such as Rufus. Some among them may consider collegiality a golden-age myth and agree with Wragg that:

> the prospect of a university Senate trying to decide what to do with a free kick on the edge of the penalty area is too awful to contemplate. (Cited in Watson 2000: 10)

What is salient about academics' orientations to quality is the (mis)recognition of quality mechanisms and the extent to which they are recognised or not, depending upon whether they are owned or not owned by the academic community; whether they are self-evidently necessary as an aspect of the demonstration of the value of academic labour and therefore an aid to and a protection of it; or whether they are an externally imposed instrument of bureaucracy, control and threat. From this study it appears that externally introduced mechanisms of quality will generally evoke the latter, whereas once it is conceived as positive it is appropriated into academic labour, or guardedly accepted depending on the approach and values of the intermediary prescribing it.

It is also notable how orientation to quality differs with seniority. Counter-intuitively, perhaps, it is the senior academics who express the most resentment towards quality in its externalised form; while the most junior academics are far less aware of it and more likely to (mis)recognise it as an innate part of academic labour.

The implication of this for further research is the extent to which leadership of quality supports or inhibits academic labour and to what extent servant leadership as a philosophy and approach is an antidote to the more widely perceived threat of quality as an adjunct to new managerialism and a governmental, social and economic policy agenda rather than an inherent and even invisible part of academic labour.

References

Arnoldi, J. 2007. Universities and the Public Recognition of Expertise, *Minerva* 45: 49–61. Springer.

Ball, S.J. 2004, Performatives and Fabrications in the Education Economy: Towards the Performative Society', in *Sociology of Education*, edited by S.J. Ball. London: Routledge.

Becher, T. and Trowler, P. 2001. *Academic Tribes and Territories*. Buckingham: SHRE and Open University.

Bourdieu, P. 2004. The Forms of Capital, in *Sociology of Education*, edited by S.J. Ball. London: Routledge.

Bourdieu, P. and Passeron, J.-C. 1977. *Reproduction in Education, Society and Culture*. London: Sage.

Bradney, A. 2002. *An Invitation to Hell*. Paper given at the Society of Legal Scholars Conference, Leicester.

Brown, R. 2004. *Quality Assurance in Higher Education: The UK Experience since 1992*. London: RoutledgeFalmer.

Cohen, L., Manion, L. and Morrison, K. 2007. *Research Methods in Education*. London: Routledge.

Cownie, F. 2004. *Legal Academics: Culture and Identities*. Oxford: Hart.

Dearlove, J. 2002. A Continuing Role for Academics: The Governance of UK Universities in the post-Dearing Era, *Higher Education Quarterly* 56(3).

Deem, R. 1998. New Managerialism and Higher Education: The Management of Performances and Cultures in Universities in the United Kingdom, *International Studies in Sociology of Education* 8(1).

Deem, R. 2004. Globalisation, New Managerialism, Academic Capitalism and Entrepreneurialism in Universities, in *The RoutledgeFalmer Reader in Higher Education*, edited by M. Tight. London: RoutledgeFalmer.

Foucault, M. 1995. *Discipline and Punish: The Birth of the Prison*. New York: Random House.

Halsey, A.H. 1992. *Decline of Donnish Dominion: The British Academic*. Oxford: Oxford University Press.
Henkel, M. 2005. Academic Identity and Autonomy in a Changing Policy Environment, *Higher Education* 49: 155–76.
Hoecht, A. (2006). Quality Assurance in UK Higher Education: Issues of Trust, Control, Professional Autonomy and Accountability, *Higher Education* 51: 541–63.
Kloot, B. 2009. Exploring the Value of Bourdieu's Framework in the Context of Institutional Change, *Studies in Higher Education* 34(4).
Kvale, S. 1996. *Interviews: An Introduction to Qualitative Research and Interviewing*. London: Sage.
Lea, M.R. and Stirer, B. 2009. Lecturers' Everyday Writing as Professional Practice in the University as Workplace: New Insights into Academic Identities, *Studies in Higher Education* 34(4).
Liston, C. 1999. *Managing Quality and Standards*. Buckingham: Open University Press.
Lyotard, J.-F. 1984. *The Postmodern Condition: A Report on Knowledge*. Manchester: Manchester University Press.
Marshall, J.D. 1999. Performativity: Lyotard and Foucault through Searle and Austin, *Studies in Philosophy and Education* 18: 309–17.
McCaffrey, P. 2004. *The Higher Education Manager's Handbook*. London: RoutledgeFalmer.
Morley, L. 2003. *Quality and Power in Higher Education*. Maidenhead: SHRE and Open University Press.
Morley, L. 2004. *Theorising Quality in Higher Education*. Bedford Way Papers. London: Institute of Education.
National Committee of Inquiry into Higher Education. 1997. *Higher Education in the Learning Society*. London: HMSO.
Neave, G. 1988. On the Cultivation of Quality, Efficency, and Enterprise: An Overview of Recent Trends in Higher Education in Western Europe, 1986–1988, *European Journal of Education* 23(1/2).
Power, M. 1997. *The Audit Society: Rituals of Verification*. Oxford: Oxford University Press.
Ratcliff, J.L. 2003. Dynamic and Communicative Aspects of Quality Assurance, *Journal of Quality in Higher Education* 9(2).
Rowland, S. 2001. Is the University a Place of Learning? Compliance and Contestation in Higher Education. Inaugural lecture. [Online] UCL. Available at: www.ucl.ac.uk/calt/profiles/sr-inaugural.html [accessed 10 May 2011].
Shattock, M. 2006. *Good Governance in Higher Education*. Maidenhead: Open University Press.
Silverman, D. 2001. *Interpreting Qualitative Data*. London: Sage.
Stone, L. 1999. Education Reform through an Ethic of Performativity: Introducing the Special Issue, *Studies in the Philosophy of Education* 18: 299–307.
Strauss, A. and Corbin, J. 1998. *Basics of Qualitative Research*. London: Sage.

Szanto, T.R. 2005. Evaluations of the Third Kind: External Evaluations of External Quality Assurance Agencies, *Journal of Quality in Higher Education* 11(3).

Tight, M. (ed.) 2004. *The RoutledgeFalmer Reader in Higher Education*. London: RoutledgeFalmer.

Venkatraman, S. 2007. A Framework for Implementing TQM in Higher Education Programs, *Quality Assurance in Education* 15(1): 92–112.

Volkwein, J.F., Lattuca, L.R., Harper, B.J. and Domingo, R.J. 2006. *Getting in Sync: The Impact of Accreditation on Student Experiences and Learning Outcomes*. Paper presented at the meeting of the Association for Institutional Research.

Ward, I. 2010. Rumours Once Heard. Unpublished.

Watson, D. 2000. Managing in Higher Education: 'The Wicked Issues', *Higher Education Quarterly* 54(1).

Web, J., Schirato, T. and Danaher, G. 2002. *Understanding Bourdieu*. London: Sage.

Williams, P. 2010. The Lord Upjohn Lecture 2009. Quality Assurance: Is the Jury Still Out? *The Law Teacher* 44(1).

Worthington, F. and Hodgson, J. 2005. Academic Labour and the Politics of Quality in Higher Education: A Critical Evaluation of the Conditions of Possibility of Resistance, *Critical Quarterly* 47(1–2): 96–110.

Yorke, M. 2000. Developing a Quality Culture in Higher Education, *Journal of Tertiary Education and Management* 6: 19–36.

PART III
Affect and Learning

Chapter 7
From Socrates to Damasio, from Langdell to Kandel: The Role of Emotion in Modern Legal Education

Alan M. Lerner

Introduction

Critical thinking and analytical rigor are essential to teaching and learning law, and to the development of sound legal principles. (Socrates and Langdell were correct in that.) The role of the emotions and personal values of those involved in constructing law, and representing clients is an often unrecognised, but equally powerful element in the process. Understanding this dynamic will contribute significantly to the constructive development of the law, more effective teaching and learning, critical judgement, more effective lawyering, and the development of a morally and ethically grounded role identification, i.e. to all that it means to be a lawyer in a modern democratic society.

Law's critical purpose is to guide the behaviour of individuals and institutions. Making law, through legislative enactments, executive regulations or judicial decisions, and the work of lawyers is, essentially, making decisions – choosing among various options for the creation of policy and rules, and advising clients, and advocating for them in various forums – through the exercise of judgement.

Socrates argued that people would do 'the good' if only they took the time and made the effort, perhaps with the help of an interlocutor such as himself, to reason it out. Langdell argued that law was a science, and as with the natural sciences if one carefully and objectively analysed the raw evidence in its original state – primarily the decisions of appellate courts in the Anglo-American common law system – one could reason one's way to the 'right' answers as to what the law should be. Thus, it seemed, Socrates and Langdell were a match made in heaven for the development and the teaching of law; Socratic examination of appellate court decisions to learn to discern the right from the wrong, the good from the bad in law. Perhaps that is why, following Langdell's tenure as Dean of the Harvard Law School, the formal academic law school so quickly and thoroughly replaced apprenticeship as the accepted means to educate future lawyers (Sullivan et al. 2007).

Indeed, Langdell's model, now the overwhelming model for traditional law school teaching in the US, especially in the first year, became the stuff of legend, spawning movies, books, not to mention reminiscences we all share at law school reunions. And, given that legal academia is populated by those who participated in the rites of passage of Socratic analysis of Langdell's sources of the legal elements and compounds, with little or no leavening from the actual practice of law, so it must always be.

Not So Fast, However

Over the past 20 years, advances in neuroscience have led to the confirmation of theories previously advanced by some psychologists that our cognitive processes, indeed our very perceptions – what we see, hear, feel and taste – and our mental reactions to those stimuli, are significantly affected by our emotions and values – and, importantly, without our consciousness of the process or the effect. Since time immemorial the law has, both expressly and by necessary implication, been based upon values and taken account of the emotions of actors and those upon whom their actions impact. In this regard, at least since Cassius and Brutus made their respective closing arguments to the citizenry of Rome, few would argue that the emotions of the legislators or jurors are irrelevant to either enacted legislation or the decisions of jurors. Moreover, our close examination (now freed from the constraint of our expectation that law is all, and only, about reasoning from objective observation) will reveal, though it be treason, that despite the noble goal of reasoned decision-making by judges, and the best efforts of our judicial officers at achieving that goal, judicial emotions and values are inextricably intertwined with, perhaps unwittingly leading to, the results of their decisions. Further examination reveals some of the varied ways that the profession of lawyering necessarily enmeshes us in emotional considerations of our clients, third parties, including the judges and jurors identified above, and ourselves. That being so, and given the role that emotions and values play in the law and the work of lawyers, to ignore or denigrate emotional and value-based considerations in legal education does our students, and the clients and communities they will serve as lawyers, a disservice. Hence, to teach our students reasoned analysis we should strive to integrate considerations of emotions and values into our legal educational model.

Emotion and Values in the Formulation of Law and Public Policy

> William Roper: So, now you give the Devil the benefit of law!
>
> Sir Thomas More: Yes! What would you do? Cut a great road through the law to get after the Devil?

> William Roper: Yes, I'd cut down every law in England to do that!
>
> Sir Thomas More: Oh? And when the last law was cut down, and the Devil turned 'round on you, where would you hide, Roper, the laws all being flat? This country is planted thick with laws, from coast to coast, Man's law, not God's! And if you cut them down, and you're just the man to do it, do you really think you could stand upright in the winds that would blow then? Yes, I'd give the Devil benefit of law, for my own safety's sake! (Bolt 1962: Act 1, Scene 4)[1]

More believed that law, based as it was on reason, rather than personal passion or prejudice, was the safety of all, and the only sure protection from despotism. Yet, in the formulation of public policy, as expressed through law, and in the determination of disputes under law, the force and power of emotions, values and beliefs are manifested in both subtle and obvious ways. This section will examine examples of the pervasiveness of values and emotions in public policy formulation in the context of: constitutions, statutes, common law and the decision-making process of courts.

Emotions and Values in Legal Doctrine

Constitutions, statutes and regulations The values of most societies are embedded in the words of their constitution and legislation, which define the structure of its government, the relationship between the government and the people, and to some extent the relationships between and among its citizens. The Preamble to the US Constitution, for example, identifies, among others, the following goals and values of the document, 'to form a more perfect union, establish justice ... and secure the blessings of liberty ... '. Among the signal goals of the Constitution are to publicly announce and render compelling and enforceable certain basic values of society embedded in its text, thus providing guides for individual and institutional behaviour. And while both over time and across the population at any given moment there may be differences as to the meaning and application of those values, there is broad consensus that they remain common values. For example, although there is disagreement about what 'process' is due to persons accused by the government of planning terroristic acts, there is broad agreement that the guaranty of 'due process of law' is fundamental to the values of the country. Similarly, there is broad consensus that 'the right of the people to keep and bear

1 Unfortunately for More, his acute cognitive skills, his extensive knowledge of the law, and his faith that the thicket of the law would keep him safe, were ultimately unable to protect him from the King's desire to divorce and remarry, and Cromwell's and the Lords' desire to please their King. Apparently, emotion triumphed over cognition.

arms shall not be infringed' (*United States Constitution, Amendment 2*). Yet, there is intense disagreement as to exactly what that right entails.[2]

Laws that mandate the separation of powers among different branches, or geographical subdivisions of the government, that declare or limit universal suffrage, provide or fail to provide for universal health care, encourage or limit education of children, that provide financial security for the elderly or infirm, that permit the death penalty, etc., as well as the absence of such laws, are reflections of the values of the society. And while such laws might appear to be dispassionate guidelines for the orderly organisation and operation of any modern society, underlying many of those laws is an ongoing and often heated contest as to whether they accurately reflect the society's shared values.

Equally rooted in values are debates about when, to what extent, and how, if ever, the law should intervene in the so-called 'free market'. More concretely, while we like to see the triumph of reasoned justice in the law, often the source of the law is better explained by looking at the values of society. Compare, for example, the 'reasoned analysis' in *Plessey v. Ferguson* [1896], holding that a Louisiana statute mandating the separation of 'White' and 'Black' persons into different cars on passenger railroad trains did not violate the Equal Protection clause of the Fourteenth Amendment to the US Constitution, with that in *Brown v. Board of Education* [1954]. Critical to the outcome of both cases was the Court's assessment of the meaning of legally enforced segregation. In *Plessey*, the Court stated:

> Laws permitting, and even requiring, their separation, in places where they are liable to be brought into contact, do not necessarily imply the inferiority of either race to the other, and have been generally, if not universally, recognized as within the competency of the state legislatures in the exercise of their police power. The most common instance of this is connected with the establishment of separate schools for white and colored children, which have been held to be a valid exercise of the legislative power even by courts of states where the political rights of the colored race have been longest and most earnestly enforced.
>
> We consider the underlying fallacy of the plaintiff's argument to consist in the assumption that the enforced separation of the two races stamps the colored race with a badge of inferiority. If this be so, it is not by reason of anything found in the act, but solely because the colored race chooses to put that construction upon it. (1896: 544)

---

2 See *District of Columbia et al. v. Heller* [2008], affirming the Circuit Court's holding that the Second Amendment, while not an unlimited right, does protect an individual right to possess a firearm and to use that arm for traditionally lawful purposes, such as self-defence within the home.

In *Brown*, the Court analysed the same issue, but to a different outcome, holding that laws requiring the separation of African Americans from Whites are unconstitutional:

> To separate [Black primary and secondary school students] them from others of similar age and qualifications solely because of their race generates a feeling of inferiority as to their status in the community that may affect their hearts and minds in a way unlikely ever to be undone. The effect of this separation on their educational opportunities was well stated by a finding in the Kansas case by a court which nevertheless felt compelled to rule against the Negro plaintiffs:
>
> 'Segregation of white and colored children in public schools has a detrimental effect upon the colored children. The impact is greater when it has the sanction of the law; for the policy of separating the races is usually interpreted as denoting the inferiority of the Negro group. A sense of inferiority affects the motivation of a child to learn. Segregation with the sanction of law, therefore, has a tendency to (retard) the educational and mental development of Negro children and to deprive them of some of the benefits they would receive in a racial(ly) integrated school system'. (1954: 494)

The moment before *Brown v. Board of Education* was decided, the law had not changed; but society's values had. And the law followed. Similarly, in *Bowers v. Hardwick* [1986], the Supreme Court held that Georgia's anti-sodomy statute did not violate the fundamental rights of gay persons. Yet, in *Lawrence v. Texas* [2003], only 17 years later, the Court overruled that decision. Again, the law followed the recognition of a shift in society's values.

Obscenity is another common instance of the values conflict being decided in favour of letting values rule. The First Amendment states that the government 'shall make no law ... abridging the freedom of speech ...' (*United States Constitution, Amendment 1*). Obscenity has been held to fall outside that protection (*Roth v. United States* [1957]). Yet, what is 'obscene'? The Supreme Court has established a three-pronged test to determine when something is obscene, and thus outside the protection of the First Amendment, including whether the act violates 'contemporary community standards'.[3] Few would argue that some things that might violate 'contemporary community standards' in the US 'Bible Belt' would not cause even a raised eyebrow in many, if not most, major US cities. Yet, those

---

3 See *Miller v California* [1973], establishing a three-part test for obscenity: (1) whether the average person, applying contemporary community standards, would find that the work, taken as a whole, appeals to the prurient interest; (2) whether the work depicts or describes, in a patently offensive way, sexual conduct specifically defined by the applicable state law; and (3) whether the work, taken as a whole, lacks serious literary, artistic, political or scientific value.

local values may trump the constitutional protection against the government's potential to restrict freedom of speech and expression.

In looking at some of the daily activities that society values as proper hygiene, health alone does not account for our behaviour or laws. Disgust is a factor driving many human behaviours, from bathing to brushing teeth to covering body odours. Disgust also acts as a powerful legal tool, leading in some cases to criminalising sodomy, public nudity, pornography, incest or cannibalism. Disgust is the emotional reaction to the prospect of contamination entering the self. And, while there is a particularly sensitive cognitive reaction to disgust as it affects the mouth, the idea that the self can become contaminated through the nose, skin and genitals have an equally severe cognitive reaction. It is possible that disgust and contaminants remind us of our vulnerability and mortality and extend to other objects, allowing for psychological contamination. The strong emotional force of disgust is a reaction to the notion that the self will become the offensive contaminant, which drives our decisions to rid society of what each individual or the collective society views as offensive. The development of statutes which punish violators helps society to rid itself of the unwanted possibilities that the self may be contaminated by issues society deems 'lustful, erotic, shameful or morbid' (Nussbaum 2004: 87–94).

Intent and reasonableness in the criminal law One of the mechanisms statutes use to reflect societal values is the analysis of the emotional state of an individual actor at a relevant point in time. While there is a moral and legal duty to refrain from wrongful conduct, the mental or emotional content of the behaviour can be critical to the legal analysis. Did the actor purposefully violate the law, or was there some emotional force that overcame her reason? Identifying the actor's state of mind may help to inform society of the danger the person poses to society, and whether the perpetrator is more or less 'like us', i.e. entitled to our empathy, and thus a less harsh response.[4] We certainly don't want to condone intentional malefactors, lest they and others choose to repeat such conduct without fear of retribution, and certainly do not like to think of ourselves as engaging in such conduct. Conversely, perhaps we can identify with the emotionally distraught actor, recognising that in some contexts our emotions may conspire to push us to act in ways that we would not otherwise. Thus, criminal law accords different levels of culpability and community response to acts depending on whether the perpetrator is found to have had a specific intent to cause harm,[5] a general intent

4 See Berreby (2005) (we tend to treat much more favourably those with whom we find a way to identify ['us'], while demonising those we identify as 'them').

5 Specific intent is defined as the intent to accomplish the precise criminal act that one is later charged with (Garner 2004).

to act where the action caused harm,[6] or acted 'with reckless disregard of the consequences',[7] merely negligently,[8] 'in the heat of passion',[9] or in self-defence.[10]

Even where a perpetrator's state of mind does not enter into the question of guilt or innocence, it may be relevant to the appropriate punishment. Also, the victim's state of mind may enter into the determination of guilt or innocence, as in an allegation of 'assault' (whether the victim was put in fear) or criminal fraud (whether the victim was sufficiently misled into parting with something of value), or in consideration of the penalty. One could argue that victim impact statements are little more than efforts to sway the emotions of the sentencing judge, or to satisfy the emotional needs of the victim and his or her family, etc., to express their grief and loss resulting from the crime.[11]

Emotions and values in civil doctrine The state of mind of the parties may also be relevant in civil law. In tort law, one of our favourite characters is 'the reasonable man or woman', a standard by which we decide what is acceptable behaviour. Divergence from the standard of reasonableness allows the court to assess blameworthiness in tort law and authorise a legal remedy for the victim of such conduct. Emotional consequences can also give rise to liability and a right of recovery even in the absence of physical harm, as in intentional or reckless infliction of *emotional* harm.

But, reasonableness may be in the eye of the beholder. In *Scott v. Harris* [2007] the Court held that a police officer was immune from suit for damages from the plaintiff, who was rendered paraplegic as a result of the officer's violent attempt to arrest him for traffic offences and fleeing to avoid arrest. Based upon a video taken from a camera mounted on the officer's dashboard, the Court held (8–1) that no reasonable person could conclude that the officer used excessive

---

6 General intent is defined as the intent to perform an act even though the actor does not desire the consequences that result (Garner 2004).

7 Recklessness involves the actual awareness of a risk and the culpable taking of that risk (Garner 2004).

8 Negligence involves blameworthy inadvertence (Garner 2004).

9 'Heat of passion' is the rage, terror or furious hatred aroused by some immediate provocation that is so extreme that for the moment one's action is directed by passion rather than reason. The heat of passion can serve as a mitigating circumstance at common law that would reduce a murder charge to manslaughter (Garner 2004).

10 Self-defence is the use of force to protect oneself, one's family or one's property from real or threatened attack; a *reasonable* amount of self-defence is justified where a person believes there is the danger of imminent bodily harm or that force is *necessary* to avoid danger (Garner 2004).

11 'Victim impact' evidence includes information that reveals the individuality (personal characteristics) of the victim of the crime and information revealing the emotional impact of the crime on the victim's survivors. The Supreme Court has held that the Eighth Amendment does not bar the statement, but the Fourteenth Amendment will limit the statement when it is unduly prejudicial. See *Payne v. Tennessee* [1991].

force. Subsequently, researchers asked a diverse sample of approximately 1,500 persons from across the country to view the same video and determine whether the officer's conduct was reasonable. Although approximately 85% of the respondents agreed with the Supreme Court majority, those that disagreed fell clearly into identifiable ethnically and demographically specific groups, suggesting that what was reasonable police conduct to some groups was not seen as reasonable by others (Kahan 2008).

Judges – The Neutral Decision-makers

The Supreme Court of the United States, James Madison wrote, should be an institution where 'constitutional interpretation must be left to the reasoned judgment of independent judges rather than to the tumult and conflict of the political process' (Hughes 1932). This notion of the neutral decision-maker aligns nicely with the concept of rationality and 'equal justice under law',[12] but how realistic is it? Supreme Court decisions are the result of 'justices who draw on emotion and experience, as well as intellect, in shaping their judicial responses' (Ray 2002: 11) and when judges are confronted with ambiguous facts that touch on charged issues they, like everyone else, 'fall back on their emotions or intuitions' and thus 'practice cultural cognition' (Posner 2006; Kahan, Hoffman and Braman 2009). While the neutral, unbiased decision-maker may be an appropriate aspiration, it is unrealistic, if not impossible, to ask a judge to ignore his or her life experience and the 'social intuitions', i.e. values they have come to develop as their own (Posner 2006; Guthrie, Rachlinski and Wistrich 2007; Kahan, Hoffman and Braman 2009; Lazarus 1991).

If we think that the words in a judge's opinion – published only after the opportunity for examination of the record, discussion with colleagues, drafts, reflections and editing – are emotion-free, we need to think again.

In *Texas v. Johnson* [1989], a case in which the defendant burned an American flag in a political protest and was prosecuted for violating a statute that prohibited flag desecration, the Court, in an opinion by Mr Justice Brennan, held that disturbing people's comfort, even making them angry, by displaying contempt for the 'symbol of national unity' was quite within the noble purposes and protections of the First Amendment.

Justice Rehnquist's dissenting opinion is little more than an appeal to the emotion of the readers. 'The significance of the flag, and the deep emotional feelings it arouses in a large part of our citizenry, cannot be fully expressed in the two dimensions of a lawyer's brief or of a judicial opinion', he wrote (1989: 602). Whether one agrees with Justice Rehnquist, it would be very difficult to ignore the power of his emotions in relation to his view of what the law means.

Two pages of his dissent are dedicated to poetry, song and anecdotes, to show the emotional reaction of society in situations where a national symbol is

12 The 'value' carved on the façade of the Supreme Court Building in Washington, DC.

destroyed, because it was his belief that the flag inspires society. Set out as his first bit of historical evidence of the uniqueness of the flag is Ralph Waldo Emerson's 'Concord Hymn' describing the first battle of the Revolutionary War:

> By the rude bridge that arched the flood
> Their flag to April's breeze unfurled,
> Here once the embattled farmers stood
> And fired the shot heard round the world.[13]

And what is poetry if not an appeal through emotions? And, if logic does not answer the question but poetry does, is not Justice Rehnquist's appeal to poetry an implicit acknowledgment that emotion can be more powerful than logic? Mr Justice Rehnquist values the deep feelings [the flag] arouses in a large part of the population as of greater constitutional consequence than he would the defendant's desire to use the flag to express opposition to the government. Fair enough. Yet, is that choice not founded in emotions, rather than on language or logic?

While acknowledging that he had an emotional reaction to the flag burning, Justice Kennedy stated that he could override his emotional intuitions in order to fulfil his legal obligation (Guthrie, Rachlinski and Wistrich 2007). He suggests thereby that his feelings have not affected his ability to reach the correct 'legal' result. To some, Justice Kennedy merely, perhaps unnecessarily, identified the emotional pull of the state's argument, but ultimately relied solely on his cognitive powers – reading the relevant texts, and the authorities, applying the law to the facts, etc. – to reach a decision consistent with the law. Another possible view is that it is purely emotion, rather than rigorous legal analysis, that moved the Justice; he values preserving a strong First Amendment more than protecting against the temporary discomfort that some citizens may experience from viewing the desecration of the flag.

But it is not only in the area of fundamental rights, but also in interpreting the words of a statute, that issues of value and emotion arise. In *Ledbetter v. Goodyear Tire and Rubber Company* [2007], the Supreme Court ruled that the claim of the plaintiff that she was the victim of discrimination in pay was filed after the time allowed by the statute of limitations, and thus must be dismissed. Plaintiff acknowledged that the decision to pay her at a discriminatory rate was beyond the limitation period; but argued that because she received the discriminatory pay within the statutory period, her claim was timely ([2007]: 623–4). Writing for the majority, Justice Samuel Alito, purporting simply to apply the words of the statute, ruled that the statute of limitations began to run from the 'discreet act' of

13 Justice Rehnquist's dissent also quoted John Greenleaf Whittier's poem, 'Barbara Frietchie', and the National Anthem. The Justice made no small effort to offer these examples as well as a direct analysis of the 'shock and disgust' servicemen feel at having the flag desecrated.

discrimination – the employer's decision which resulted in unequal pay. 'We apply the statute as written', he said (642). Justice Alito would have us believe that in the interpretation of this statutory language, there is no room for the Court to make choices; but, is that really so?

The relevant statutory language is as follows:

> It shall be an unlawful employment practice for an employer … to discriminate against any individual with respect to his compensation, terms, conditions, or privileges of employment, because of such individual's race, color, religion, sex, or national origin … (*Civil Rights Act of 1964* §2000e-2(a))
>
> A charge under this section shall be filed within one hundred and eighty days after the alleged unlawful employment practice occurred. (§2000e-5 (e))

Taking Justice Alito's approach, the question is when did the unlawful employment practice occur? Did it occur when management decided to pay women less than it was paying men; when the plaintiff was hired at the lower rate; when she received her first discriminatory pay check; or, perhaps every time she was paid less than a male doing the same job? Justice Ginsburg dissented.[14] After briefly stating the salient facts, and the holdings in the lower courts, she began her discussion as follows:

> Pay disparities are … significantly different from adverse actions 'such as termination, failure to promote … or refusal to hire', all involving fully communicated discrete acts, 'easy to identify' as discriminatory. … It is only when the disparity becomes apparent and sizable, *e.g.*, through future raises calculated as a percentage of current salaries, that an employee in [plaintiff's] situation is likely to comprehend her plight and, therefore, to complain. Her initial readiness to give her employer the benefit of the doubt should not preclude her from later challenging the then current and continuing payment of a wage depressed on account of her sex … ([2007]: 645)

Justice Ginsburg then argued that, based upon the statutory language, the applicable precedents (those relied on by Justice Alito and the majority), and the inherent difference between discrimination in pay from those involving hire, fire and promotion, as discussed above, each pay cheque given to the plaintiff at the discriminatory rate constituted a 'discreet act' of discrimination. Thus, she concluded, the plaintiff's claim was timely.

Justice Alito's opinion purports to focus almost entirely on the words of the statute (whose meaning had caused disagreement among judges in several US Courts of Appeal before this case arose), and how the decision might comport with prior, though at least arguably distinguishable, precedent. Justice Ginsburg's

---

14 Justices Stevens, Souter and Breyer joined in the dissent.

opinion relies heavily on how the statute plays out in the workplace it was intended to regulate, in deciding how to interpret the words of the statute. Justice Ginsburg spent much of her professional life before her appointment to the US Court of Appeals representing plaintiffs, many of them women, in pursuing claims of employment discrimination. Justice Alito spent virtually his entire professional career working for the Government as a prosecutor and judge. Might the difference of experience and values have played some part in the differences between their conclusions?

These opinions, by some of our most respected Justices – whether acknowledging the role of emotion or denying it – expose, with unusual clarity, the role of emotions and values in judicial decision-making, even lifting the curtain to reveal the internal struggle of one Justice to reconcile his conflicting values of patriotism and freedom of speech (*Texas v. Johnson* [1989]: 420).

I will argue, and seek to demonstrate below, that both views represent 2,500 years of the mistaken belief that emotions and reason are entirely separate functions, and both ignore the reality that emotion, intuition, values, culture or whatever we call the pre-conscious relatively automatic first response of our brains to the need for a decision in a matter of importance, whether we like or acknowledge it, powerfully informs our cognitive process and thus our decision-making. And, I will argue, all of us, in every walk of life, and on every tribunal face similar conflicts of values and internal, emotional struggles from time to time. Combining conscious consideration of one's emotion and intuition with careful legal analysis can contribute to achieving a more fully informed, and therefore better reasoned and more appropriate, decision (Guthrie, Rachlinski and Wistrich 2007; Haidt 2001; Kahan and Braman 2006).

But first, allow me to refer briefly to the impact of emotion in lawyering and legal practice.

The Role of Emotion in the Work of the Lawyer

The Lawyers' Professional Relationships

Experienced lawyers understand that relationships including those between lawyers and clients, lawyers and adversaries or negotiating partners, and between lawyers and decision-makers involve interpersonal skills as to which emotions and emotional understanding are the foundation.

Lawyers help clients solve problems that the clients think they cannot solve adequately alone. However refined the legal 'question' is when presented to the lawyer, it occurs within the context of the client's life, whether personal or business, and solving the problem usually involves making choices between and among different paths of action. Making choices involves human emotions and values (Lazarus 1991). And, while lawyers are usually willing to acknowledge that their client's emotions and values are part of the lawyer–client relationship, they seldom acknowledge the role of their own emotions and values in their role as lawyer and counsellor.

Positive rapport and trust are fundamental to any constructive relationship between lawyer and client, lawyer and adversary or negotiation partner, and lawyer and decision-maker, in particular. In the lawyer–client relationship, information-sharing and respect for the judgement of one person to the other are keys to success. Trust affects the completeness and accuracy of the information transmitted from client to attorney. Where there is little trust and confidence, the attorney is more likely to receive misinformation or partial information. Also, if the client doesn't trust and respect the lawyer, she may be less able to accept her analysis and recommendations – the very thing for which she engaged counsel.

In providing counsel to clients, lawyers are asked to understand the social and emotional dynamics in the client's life (Brooks and Madden 2010). Factors outside of winning a case or receiving a maximum award, such as ongoing business relationships, reputation, family values, the impact on third parties, cultural elements, future relationships or even the stress and diversion that the legal matter is imposing on other aspects of the client's life or business, could determine whether engaging in the legal process, even to a successful legal outcome, is really a success for the client.[15] Anticipating, accurately perceiving and appropriately reacting to the client's context, emotions and values will enhance an attorney's relationship with the client and improve the likelihood of an outcome that advances all of the client's goals.

Lawyering skills No knowledgeable person would deny that analytical thinking is critical to the success of a lawyer. Yet, it is but one of many essential tools. Planning, communication, information-gathering, counselling, problem-solving, negotiation, conflict resolution, mediation, assessing the emotions of others and advocacy in dispute resolution, selecting a jury, framing a storyline for the presentation of one's case at trial, oral argument to an appellate court, etc., may be required whenever a client seeks legal help. Each of these involves interpersonal skills and thus an understanding of the role of emotions and values both to what is expressed and what is not. Lawyers need to understand that human pronouncements can *mean* more, or less, than they *say* (Amsterdam and Bruner 2000). They need to understand the power of their client's story and how to tell it. Moreover, whenever the legal issue involves a dispute or a negotiation, it is fair to expect that the other party will have different priorities and offer different

15 Collaborative law, a relatively new approach to domestic relations law disputes, employs a model of lawyering in which the lawyers seek to learn all that they can about the various concerns, needs and goals of their clients in an effort to help them resolve the dispute by agreement, without the necessity of litigation. To incentivise this process, the attorneys agree and advise their respective clients in advance that they will not represent the clients in litigation if amicable resolution is not achieved. This approach is especially valuable when children are involved in a marital dispute. See Tesler (2001).

interpretations of the perceived facts. The lawyer who is not finely attuned to perceive and understand how her client's, third parties' and her own emotions impact on her representation of her client is unlikely to do the best job that her analytical skills would lead one to expect.

Emotion, Values and Decision-making – The Heart of the Matter

At least since the Langdellian revolution that led legal education out of the law office and into the law schools in the US, it has been an article of faith in legal education that the core of legal education is teaching students legal analysis – thinking like a lawyer – ... a purely cognitive exercise, wholly apart from the emotions or values of the student, lawyer or judge, and certainly of the law professor.[16] University-based, baccalaureate-level legal education in Europe has also proceeded from the related premises that the transfer of knowledge and the teaching of tools of cognitive analysis are the essence of legal education (Duncan 2004; Bortoluzzi 2010). The second revolution in legal education, sprung from the law and economics movement, not only reinforced that dichotomy, but argued that most, if not all, questions of legal policy were best answered by the rational use of economic cost–benefit and risk analysis (Hanson and Yosifon 2003).

But what if the result of our legal analysis was predetermined, or at least strongly guided, by mental forces of which we are not aware? What if emotion actually plays a major if not controlling role in how we measure and reason out the expected costs and benefits of any policy?

The past 40 years have seen a revolution in our understanding of the workings of the human brain, through experimentally based cognitive psychology, advances in scientific research and discoveries of the cellular structure of learning and memory, and the subsequent collaboration of neuroscientists and cognitive scientists to create the new 'science of the mind' (Kandel 2006; Damasio et al. 1994; Damasio 1994). Spurred by technology such as functional magnetic resonance imaging (fMRI), which permits scientists to measure neural activity in discreet parts of the brain, scientists have learned, among other things, about the sequence of processing that our brains pursue when stimulated by receipt of outside data. These advances have permitted us to peek behind the curtain that has, heretofore, separated what we do and say – how we appear to the outside world and often to ourselves – from our innermost motivations and the processes of our minds. Heady stuff, indeed!

A brief review of some of these discoveries and their implications for human decision-making may be helpful to understanding their importance in educating

16 But see Lesnick (1990), arguing that the choice of curriculum and the content of our syllabus for a given course contains numerous implicit decisions about what is important and not important for our students to learn in their quest to become lawyers – lessons which they absorb.

lawyers and why teaching legal analysis as a purely cognitive act to the exclusion of all consideration of emotions and values dilutes the value of the teaching and undermines the lawyering, judging and policy-making to which it leads.

The 'Chicken and Egg' Problem with Emotion and Cognition

The debate juxtaposing cognition and emotion – whether emotion precedes cognition, or vice versa, what each is within the human experience and how they interact – has been played out over centuries.

However, modern research has made clear that both emotion and cognition significantly impact human decision-making, especially those decisions that implicate social and moral questions. But exactly how do we acquire, store and use whatever information is lodged in our brains to assist us in making such judgements? As law teachers, if we have any hope of preparing our students to perform as ethical, professionally responsible actors after they leave our classes and become lawyers, and public citizens, we must come to appreciate the answers to those questions because they are the crucial connection to understanding the relationship between learning, legal education and moral judgement. We start by reviewing the process by which we develop, store and use memory more generally.

Learning and Memory: The Basis for all our Choices

After evolution and genetics, what we know is a result of learning; '[w]e are who we are because of what we learn and what we remember' (Kandel 2006: 10, 116). It is from our memories alone that we have a conception of who we are, and what knowledge, experience and beliefs form part of our lives. We can have that conception only as it relates to the environment in which we exist (Schacter 1996). Memory records our never-ending interaction with our environment. Thus memory informs our responses to stimuli from our environment. Our brains are always receiving, recording and responding to new stimuli – incoming data transmissions, i.e. sensory signals – and thus changing, that is, learning (Schacter 1996: 40–42; Caine and Caine 1994).

Explicit and implicit long-term memory Explicit memory is that which is formed primarily from intentional learning. We study, listen to our teachers and the discussions in class, we get feedback, we repeatedly stimulate the same neural pathways, we strengthen the synaptic connections, we create long-term memory. Good news!

Such memories include automatic skill sequences. Memorisation of the multiplication tables, the steps to turn on one's computer or car, touch typing and specific athletic skills are types of explicit memory.[17] Most learning of law school course material (think: contracts, property, civil procedure, etc.) is done explicitly

17 See Richard Roche (Chapter 2, this volume).

– reading, taking notes, listening to lectures, discussing, re-reading, etc. Memory acquired by explicit learning moves easily between memory and conscious activation. When adequately learned (i.e. embedded in memory) memories are thus valuable in survival situations (e.g. law students learn whatever is required to pass law school and bar admission exams; and to respond 'on their feet' in court), because when triggered by the appropriate stimulus the skills and memories laid down in that system of memory can quickly be called into play and we can expect the learned standard response even without conscious prompting (Sylwester 1995).

Explicit memory has its limitations, however. Because the material was explicitly studied as a unique focus to create a memory of itself, rather than as part of a broader experiential context, its memory involves only a few of one's senses and a few neural pathways, with minimal connection to other memories (Caine and Caine 1994: 42–4).[18] Usually, it involves fewer rather than more of our senses – ears/listening, or eyes/reading. And the more of our senses that are engaged in the processing of receiving the stimuli, the more neural stimuli we receive, and the more neural pathways and synaptic connections our brains create of the experience. (Ever wonder why you remember video better than audio, or actually remember the lecture better if you take notes – even assuming that you can stay awake for the entire lecture without taking notes? Who among us remembers anything that they studied in order to pass the bar examination?) Fortunately, explicit memory is not our only tool for long-term learning.

> Cognitive activity is taking place all the time, even in sleep, as manifest by dreams; perhaps it occurs as long as we are not comatose but we cannot really be sure. (Lazarus 1991: 127)

In contrast to memory created explicitly, memory that develops from our participation in our environment without any explicit effort to learn is referred to as 'implicit' memory (Caine and Caine 1994: 44–7). We could not function without implicit learning and memory. Daily doses of Socratic teaching in class after class – not explicit study – leads to implicit learning of the legal analytic thinking process – what law professors and deans refer to as 'learning to think like a lawyer'.

As with most good things, however, implicit memory has its limitations. We bring to every problem a host of intuitions, beliefs and assumptions. These are concepts that we have built on implicit memory accumulated over the years, and we seldom, if ever, reconsider them without some strong external impetus. When the patterns of memory we draw on to create meaning from discordant data are implicit memory, we are not conscious of the analytical work that our brains are doing. Our tendency to establish meanings, to draw conclusions, i.e. to

18 See Schacter (1996: 170) for a demonstration of this with amnesic patients.

conceptualise, from implicit memory, and thereafter to make judgements based on those concepts, may lead us to act without the application of critical judgement.[19]

As Dr Thomas Lewis has characterised it:

> Implicit memory warps our window on the world. (Lewis, Amini, and Lannon 2000: 118). While *explicit memory* serves itself up for conscious reflection, *implicit memory* does not. That is why it escapes our notice ... [We] acquire wonderfully complicated knowledge that we cannot describe, explain, or recognize ... The brain never permits naked reality to intrude into consciousness; all inbound sensory impressions pass through a process that sands the rough edges off an inhospitably complex universe ... All experience comes to us through similar layers of invisible and occasionally dubious deductions. Our internal realities are mock-ups of unparalleled persuasive power ... Behind the bright, analytic engine of consciousness is a shadow of silent strength, spinning dazzlingly complicated life into automatic actions, convictions without intellect, and hunches whose reasons follow later or not at all. (Lewis, Amini and Lannon 2000: 138–9)[20]

In the face of this endless flow of new information, how do we 'separate the wheat from the chaff', that is, how do our brains decide what to retain in long-term memory and what to 'let slide away'?

Making choices Evolution has prepared us for learning by giving us a brain of extraordinary computational and storage capacity that can absorb information both implicitly from our environment and from explicit efforts to learn, and it has given us built-in, hard-wired tools to decide what to retain, where to store it and when and how to use it as needed:

> [B]ecause the environment is enormously complex and not everything can be attended to, and because it is often ambiguous, we attend to and process it

19 For example, in 1998, Professor Susan Sturm and I developed a first-year elective course designed to teach problem-solving to law students in the second semester of the first year by creating a series of simulations in which they would be placed in a role and asked to create a solution to the problem. See Lerner (1999: 109–11, notes 2–30). In the first role-play in which the students were assigned to represent one of four parties engaged in a dispute, we asked them to prepare a letter to their respective clients explaining the case and making a recommendation as to what the client should do. Although the problem did not say that litigation had been started, or even was contemplated, by any party, every student assumed that they were already in litigation in court and addressed only the potential litigation strategies in their letters to their clients (Lerner 1999: 123–4).

20 Scientists have found important similarities in the processing of socially significant information by non-human primates and that of humans. Given the fact that non-human primates live in sophisticated social systems, as do humans, the findings strongly suggest that human systems of social cognition are conserved through evolution (Lewis et al. 2000).

> selectively in ways that are, in a sense, programmed by goal hierarchies and what we believe about ourselves in the world. (Lazarus 1991: 135)

Eric Kandel proved that repetition is one consideration; we learn implicitly, as well as explicitly, about things that are repeatedly in our environment (Kandel 2006). Repetition eventually commands our attention because it both produces experience and connects with previous experience, understandings and meanings, building on existing patterns of neural connections. Repetition also tells our brains that whatever phenomena we are experiencing is not simply a passing fancy, but something to be reckoned with; it is likely to be back.

Kandel also demonstrated that in mice, as in men, emotions, e.g. motivation, drive attention and implicit learning (2006: 307–16).

A breakthrough in our understanding of the relationship between emotion and cognition both as to how our brains learn to select what to retain in long-term implicit memory and how we use that information in decision-making occurred in 1994. In his groundbreaking book, *Descartes' Error*, Antonio Damasio posited that because we are individuals and social animals our brains must be hard-wired to learn how to survive and thrive as a physical individual, and as a member of a social order, a community. Without that knowledge, our brains would not be equipped to make critical decisions, often without time for reflection that would permit us either to survive as individuals or thrive in a social context. We cannot rely on explicit learning, i.e. studying and thinking, to acquire this knowledge. Rather, it must be learned on an ongoing basis from our interaction with our environment. He concluded:

> One might say, metaphorically, that reason and emotion 'intersect' in the ventromedial prefrontal cortices, and they also intersect in the amygdala … [T]here is [also] a region of the human brain, the complex of somatosensory cortices of the right hemisphere, whose damage also compromises reasoning/decision making and emotion/feeling, and, in addition, disrupts the process of basic body signaling …
>
> First, these systems are certainly involved in the processes of reason in the broad sense of the term. Specifically, they are involved in planning and deciding.
>
> Second, a subset of these systems is associated with planning and deciding behaviors that one might subsume under the rubric 'personal and social' …
>
> Third, the systems we have identified play an important role in the processing of emotions. (1994: 78)

Emotions thus play a critical role in the creation of long-term implicit memory by directing our brains to pay attention to what is going on in our lives that is important to our well-being.

We need only to look around to see the proof of Damasio's hypotheses and Kandel's laboratory research. Children begin to learn to identify those that keep them safe and warm, those that communicate lovingly, and not – from experience; they learn to manipulate their environment by direct communication from the moment they are born – from hearing, observing, attempting to influence their environment and observing the outcomes. Throughout their early years, they learn to distinguish between 'us and them', about religion, politics, style, how people address each other, about who is responsible for good things and bad things, right and wrong, class and race, girls and boys, whether education is important, whether the police are your friends, whether the 'free market' is really 'free' and whether it is your friend, whether people who need financial assistance from the government are 'unfortunate' or 'looking for handouts', well, just about everything. And, they – we – don't learn all of that by studying it. Rather, we have learned it because it is ever present in our environment, in the conversation at home, at the playground, at school with peers and teachers, in religious centres, and, increasingly, from television and other electronic media. And, we have learned it because attending to the cues and the consequences of our social environment is critical to survival and success:

> [I]n every society, people talk about and evaluate the actions of other people, and these evaluations have consequences for future interactions. Many of these evaluations occur against the backdrop of specific cultural practices, in which one praises or criticizes the skills or talents of an individual (e.g., 'she is a daring chef'). But an important subset of these evaluations are made with respect to virtues or goods that are applied to everyone in the society … or to everyone in a certain social category … These virtues are obligatory in that everyone (within the relevant categories) is expected to strive to attain them. People who fail to embody these virtues, or whose actions betray a lack of respect for them are subject to criticism, ostracism, or some other form of punishment.
>
> The most important cognitive content in the emotion process consists of *knowledge* (that is, beliefs about how things work in general and in the specific adaptational encounter) and *appraisals* of the significance of the person-environment relationship for personal well-being, whether about a specific encounter or life as a whole. Perceptions of our thoughts, action tendencies, bodily changes, and the subjective feel of the emotions we experience are additional contents of cognition that are part of the emotional process and contribute to knowledge and appraisal … (Haidt 2001: 818)

Thus, we are highly motivated to learn everything we can from our environment as we grow up – at home, in school, in the playground, at our religious venues, etc. These implicit learnings are either reinforced – and thus strengthened – or not reinforced, and thus left to atrophy. Those that are reinforced become part of our base of 'knowledge', i.e. 'what we believe about ourselves in the world' (Lazarus 1991: 135).

All of our experiences occur within some emotional context and thus include some emotional content. The memory of the experience may include memory of the emotion and 'emotionally important contexts can create powerful memories' (Pinker 1999: 96; Sylwester 1995). Our encounter with the environment is a movie whose scenes are continually changing and generating feedback about the psychological situation, our appraisals of the situation and its relationship to our goals and self-image. Feedback from the environment or from one's own actions and reactions constantly needs to be evaluated. Thus, emotions are always active. Goal hierarchies and what we believe about ourselves in the world are matters of emotion; they are neither generally part of our consciousness nor part of our intentional analytical processing. Moreover:

> Emotions ... express the intimate personal meaning of what is happening in our social lives, and combine motivational, cognitive, adaptational, and physiological processes into a single complex state that involves several levels of analysis. ... [E]motion cannot be divorced from cognition, motivation, adaptation, and physiological activity. When we react with an emotion ... our attention and thoughts, our needs and desires, and even our bodies [are likely to be engaged]. The reaction tells us that an important value or goal has been engaged and is being harmed, placed at risk, or advanced. From an emotional reaction we can learn much about what a person has at stake in an encounter with the environment or in life in general, how that person interprets self and world, and how harms, threats, and challenges are coped with. (Lazarus 1991: 135)

Emotion tells us that something is important to us; it captures our attention; thus, emotion drives the selection process that creates our implicit memory.

Decision Time: Putting it All Together

So, our brains are filled with memory (being supplemented even as you read this); how do we use all of that memory to make decisions? The realisation that the neural pathways for all learning are similarly structured, and at the same time exquisitely specialised and distinct, and that the greater part of our learning and memory – the information that we have available for our decision-making – is acquired implicitly, brings us back to the question of how our brain's decision-making system works.

Just Like the Chicken and the Egg – Almost

All decisions imply choice making; but what is the process by which we make choices?[21]

The process, as described by Antonio Damasio in 1994, is that when new data arrives, which requires that we make a decision, our brain, using the emotional centres of what has been collectively referred to as the 'limbic system', seek out related information in memory, in order to understand and effectively utilise the new information and reach the 'right' decision. '[D]eciding well is selecting a response that will be ultimately advantageous to the organism in terms of its survival, and of the quality of that survival. Deciding well also means deciding expeditiously, especially when time is of the essence, at least deciding in a time frame deemed appropriate for the problem at hand'. Damasio concluded that our brain's 'first responders' are those that are based in our biological and emotional memory (1994: 189).

Return for a moment to the discussion of how we learn implicitly – on a continuous and ongoing basis from our environment. Recall that the implicit 'lessons' we are constantly learning which are reinforced either by repetition or emotional importance increasingly become available to be considered, consciously or subconsciously, as part of our affective, automatic, process of appraisal of new data as it arrives. These 'lessons' come to form our 'attitudes', our 'mindsets' towards people, ideas, etc. – our values. And our values are important to us because they help us define ourselves and provide guidance for our moral decision-making and our general social cognition (O'Brien and Oyserman 2009; Festinger 1957; Brehm, Fein and Kassin 2002).

So powerful are these intuitions, predilections, mindsets or values in helping us define and feel good about ourselves that they affect what we think, see and hear, our actual perceptions.[22] And we go to great mental lengths to make sure that our

21 For a thoroughly readable review and explanation of the current state of neuroscience concerning human decision-making, I recommend Jonah Lehrer, *How We Decide*, 2009.

22 See Darley and Batson (1973). A study that demonstrates the power of motivation in affecting our perceptions involved second-year students at a religious seminary who were told that they had to give a practice sermon on the topic of The Good Samaritan. Immediately before the time scheduled for their assignment they were required to be across the campus from the location at which they were to deliver their sermon. Some of the students were told that they had plenty of time to get across the campus and still be on time, while others were told that they were running late and needed to hurry in order to get to their assigned location on time. Along the way, each passed by a person slumped in a doorway, looking disheveled. Overwhelmingly, those that thought that they had plenty of time stopped to see if they could help the person, while those who thought that they were late, did not. Later, when questioned about what they had seen, those that felt that they had adequate time described the person as appearing to be in distress; while those that thought that they were running late, and did not stop, described the person in terms of appearing

perceptions – the external evidence – are reconciled with our internal, emotional predisposition – our attitudes and values (Darley and Batson 1973). Dan M. Kahan and colleagues refer to this as a 'psychological disposition' of which we are not consciously aware, that predisposes us towards privileging certain positions and denigrating or even disregarding others even before we know all of the evidence or hear the rational arguments on the matter (Kahan and Braman 2006: 149–50; Kahan 2008; Bandes 2008; Huang 2008; Kunda 1999).

In positing his hypothesis in 1994, however, Damasio was clear that our emotional brain and its high-speed reactions 'do not deliberate for us. They assist the deliberation by highlighting some options (either dangerous or favorable), and eliminating them rapidly from subsequent consideration. ... Think of it as a biasing device ... ' (1994: 174, 200–1; Bechara and Damasio 2005: 52, 367–8).

Damasio's 1994 hypothesis has been re-examined by psychologists and neuroscientists repeatedly and in a variety of contexts. Their conclusions are consistently in line with Damasio's hypothesis:

> Emotions are a major factor in the interaction between environmental conditions and human decision processes, with these emotional systems ... providing valuable implicit or explicit knowledge for making fast and advantageous decisions. ... The process of deciding advantageously is not just logical but also emotional. (Bechara and Damasio 2005: 368)

There can be little doubt that, like the chicken and the egg, our implicitly built, pre-conscious emotional brain and our cognitive, reasoning brain are in a continuous process of interaction. Thus, while our emotional processes may react first, the relationship between decision-making and emotion is better characterised as interplay rather than as a dependency of one on the other.

Nevertheless, the work of Freud, as well as that of the modern scholars, makes clear that in individual situations, in our daily lives, the 'shadow of silent strength' from our emotional minds informed by our implicit learning carries tremendous power to direct, indeed to pre-empt, our rational decision-making and action – the very things for which our cognition and analytical abilities exist.

---

to be drunk, or on drugs. See also Kunda (1999: 124), reporting on a study in which two groups of individuals were shown a video of a husband and wife interacting together. The difference between the two groups was that one group was told that the woman was a librarian, while the other was told that she was a waitress. Some of the activities and attributes of the woman were consistent with stereotypes of waitresses (e.g. drinks beer, affectionate with husband), and some with those of librarians (e.g. wears glasses, listens to classical music). When the observers were questioned after viewing the video, they recalled the attributes consistent with the stereotype of the person that they expected to see, while not recalling the attributes that were more similar to the other.

Conclusion

Reflect for a moment on the section in which I have tried to identify some of the more salient areas of legal doctrine and the practice of law which either explicitly or implicitly implicate our emotions and values. From the most fundamental structure of government, to the basic laws, the systems for resolving disputes, and the process of negotiating transactions, indeed everything about the law, and that lawyers are called on to do, involves, in every culture and society, emotions. Consciousness of the role of our emotions is thus critical to an honest and as objective an application as we are capable, of the knowledge and skills that we strive to instil in our students. Anything else is simply surrendering to one's own bias and missing the opportunity to grow. Thus, teaching our law students that the members of their profession that they should seek to emulate are dispassionate analytical machines is to do them a disservice. If we want our law students to make the most of their cognitive powers, we need to help them understand the power of their emotional minds. We need to re-examine what it means to teach them to 'think like [the] lawyers [we would like them to become]' and integrate awareness of the role of their, and everyone else's, emotions in making the right decisions.

References

Amsterdam, A. and Bruner, J. 2000. *Minding the Law: How Courts Rely on Storytelling, and How Their Stories Change the Way We Understand the Law – and Ourselves*. Cambridge, MA: Harvard University Press.

Bandes, S. 2008. Emotions, Values, and the Construction of Risk (Response to Kahan, Two Conceptions of Emotion in Risk Regulation), *University of Pennsylvania Law Review*, PENNumbra [Online] 156(3): 421–34. Available at: http://www.pennumbra.com/conversations/?aid=166 [accessed 9 July 2010].

Bechara, A. and Damasio, A. 2005. The Somatic Marker Hypothesis: A Neural Theory of Economic Decision Making, *Games and Economic Behavior* 52(2): 336–72.

Berreby, D. 2005. *Us and Them: Understanding Our Tribal Mind*. New York: Little, Brown and Co.

Bolt, R. (ed.) 1962. *A Man for All Seasons*. New York: Vintage Books.

Bortoluzzi, C. 2010. A New European Model of Legal Education as One of the Traditional Elements of the New European Common Law, *Global Jurist* [Online] 10(1). Available at: http://www.bepress.com/gj/vol10/iss1/art3/ [accessed 20 July 2010].

Bowers v. Hardwick, 478 U.S. 186 (1986).

Brehm, S., Fein, S. and Kassin, S. 2002. *Social Psychology*. Boston: Houghton Mifflin Company.

Brooks, S. and Madden, R. 2010. *Relationship Centered Lawyering: Social Science Theory for Reforming Legal Practice*. Durham, NC: Carolina Academic Press.

Brown v. Board of Education, 347 US 483 (1954).

Caine, R. and Caine, G. 1994. *Making Connections: Teaching and the Human Brain*. Menlo Park, CA: Addison-Wesley Publishing Company.

Civil Rights Act of 1964, Title VII, 42 USC § 2000e (2006).

Damasio, A. 1994. *Descartes' Error: Emotion, Reason, and the Human Brain*. New York: Penguin Books.

Damasio, H., Grabowski, T., Frank, R., Galaburda, A. and Damasio, A. 1994. The Return of Phineas Gage, Clues about the Brain from a Famous Patient, *Science* 264(5162): 1102–5.

Darley, J. and Batson, D. 1973. From Jerusalem to Jericho: A Study of Situational and Dispositional Variables in Helping Behavior, *Journal of Personality and Social Psychology* 27(1): 100–108.

District of Columbia et al. v. Heller, 128 S.Ct. 2783 (2008).

Duncan, N. 2004. Gatekeepers Training Hurdlers: The Training and Accreditation of Lawyers in England and Wales, *Georgia State University Law Review* 20(4): 911–45.

Festinger, L. 1957. *A Theory of Cognitive Dissonance*. Stanford, CA: Stanford University Press.

Garner, B. (ed.) 2004. *Black's Law Dictionary*. St. Paul, MN: West Publishing Company.

Guthrie, C., Rachlinski, J. and Wistrich, A. 2007. Blinking on the Bench: How Judges Decide Cases, *Cornell Law Review* 93(1): 1–43.

Haidt, J. 2001. The Emotional Dog and its Rational Tail: A Social Intuitionist Approach to Moral Judgment, *Psychological Review* 108(4): 814–34.

Hanson, J. and Yosifon, D. 2003. The Situation: An Introduction to the Situational Character, Critical Realism, Power Economics, and Deep Capture, *University of Pennsylvania Law Review* 152(1): 129–346.

Huang, P. 2008. Diverse Conceptions of Emotions in Risk Regulation (Response to Kahan, Two Conceptions of Emotion in Risk Regulation), *University of Pennsylvania Law Review*, PENNumbra [Online] 156(3): 435–47. Available at http://www.pennumbra.com/conversations/?aid=166 [accessed 9 July 2010].

Hughes, C.E. 1932. *The Court and Constitutional Interpretation*. [Online] Available at: http://www.supremecourt.gov/about/constitutional.aspx [accessed 8 July 2010].

Kahan, D. 2008. Two Conceptions of Emotion in Risk Regulation, *University of Pennsylvania Law Review* 156(3): 741–66.

Kahan, D. and Braman, D. 2006. Cultural Cognition and Public Policy, *Yale Law and Policy Review* 24(1): 149–72.

Kahan, D., Hoffman, D. and Braman, D. 2009. Whose Eyes do you Believe? *Scott v. Harris* and the Perils of Cognitive Illiberalism, *Harvard Law Review* 122(3): 837–906.

Kandel, E. 2006. *In Search of Memory: The Emergence of a New Science of Mind*. New York: W.W. Norton & Company.

Kunda, Z. 1999. *Social Cognition: Making Sense of People*. Cambridge, MA: MIT Press.

Lawrence v. Texas, 539 U.S. 558 (2003).

Lazarus, R. 1982. Thoughts on Relations between Emotions and Cognition, *American Psychologist* 37(9): 1019–24.

Lazarus, R. 1991. *Emotion and Adaptation*. New York; Oxford: Oxford University Press.

Lazarus, R. 1999. The Cognition-Emotion Debate: A Bit of History, in *Handbook of Cognition and Emotion*, edited by T. Daigleish and M. Power. Chichester, England: John Wiley & Sons, 3–20.

Ledbetter v. Goodyear Tire and Rubber Company, 516 US 618 (2007).

Lehrer, J. 2009. *How We Decide*. New York: Houghton Mifflin Harcourt.

Lerner, A. 1999. Law & Lawyering in the Workplace: Building Better Lawyers by Teaching Students to Exercise Critical Judgment as Creative Problem Solvers, *Akron Law Review* 32(1): 107–53.

Lesnick, H. 1990. Infinity in a Grain of Sand: The World of Law and Lawyering as Portrayed in the Clinical Teaching Implicit in Law School, *UCLA Law Review* 37(6): 1157–97.

Lewis, T., Amini, F. and Lannon, R. 2000. *A General Theory of Love*. New York: Random House.

Miller v California, 413 U.S. 15 (1973).

Nussbaum, M. 2004. *Hiding from Humanity: Disgust, Shame, and the Law*. Princeton, NJ: Princeton University Press.

O'Brien, B. and Oyserman, D. 2009. It's Not just What You Think, But also How You Think About It: The Effect of Situational Primed Mindsets on Legal Judgments and Decision Making, *Marquette Law Review* 92(1): 149–72.

Payne v. Tennessee, 501 U.S. 808 (1991).

Pinker, S. 1999. *How the Mind Works*. New York: W.W. Norton.

Plessey v. Ferguson, 163 U.S. 537 (1896).

Posner, R. 2006. The Role of the Judge in the Twenty-first Century, *Boston University Law Review* 86(5): 1049–68.

Ray, L. 2002. Judicial Personality: Rhetoric and Emotion in Supreme Court Opinions, *Washington and Lee Law Review* 59(1): 193–234.

Roth v. United States, 354 U.S. 476 (1957).

Schacter, D. 1996. *Searching for Memory: The Brain, the Mind, and the Past*. New York: Basic Books.

Scott v. Harris, 550 US 372 (2007).

Sullivan, W., Colby, A., Wegner, J. et al. 2007. *Educating Lawyers: Preparation for the Profession of Law*. San Francisco: Jossey-Bass/Wiley.

Sylwester, R. 1995. *A Celebration of Neurons: An Educator's Guide to the Human Brain*. Alexandria, VA: Association for Supervision and Curriculum Development.

Tesler, P. 2001. *Collaborative Law*. Chicago, IL: American Bar Association.

Texas v. Johnson, 491 US 397 (1989).

United States Constitution.

Zajonc, R. 1980. Feeling and Thinking: Preferences Need No Inferences, *American Psychologist* 35(2): 151–75.

Zajonc, R. 1984. On the Primacy of Affect, *American Psychologist* 39(2): 117–23.

Chapter 8
Legal Understanding and the Affective Imagination

Maksymilian Del Mar

Introduction

When we learn the law, we learn emotionally; further, what we are learning has emotional content. Teachers of the law can tap into the affectivity of both the mode and the content of learning more or less effectively. Certainly, the learning experience can be greatly enhanced by teachers becoming more aware of the role of the emotions in learning law. The devil, of course, is in the detail. The focus of this chapter is on bringing out some of these details by way of offering an account of the relationship between legal understanding and the affective imagination.

The chapter is divided into three parts. In the first, the relationship between understanding and the imagination is examined. More specifically, it is argued that the content of concepts – as well as that of terms and phrases generally – is inherently ambiguous, necessarily incomplete and always shot through with unforeseen possibilities. It follows that conceptual understanding depends to a large extent on one's willingness and ability to creatively and actively explore possible instantiations of the concept. This account of the importance of the imagination applies to understanding in the general sense, but also to the more specialised understanding required by legal practice. The second part of the chapter then turns to the affective dimension of this imagination and thereby also to the importance of the affective imagination for legal understanding. A specific example is examined: it is shown how the understanding of the concept of 'concerted practice', which is a central concept for competition law (or anti-trust law in the United States), can be enhanced by the affective exploration of its possible affective instantiations. In the third and final part, the lessons of the first two parts of the chapter are brought together and summarised, and some concrete recommendations are made for the development of the affective imagination in the teaching of law.

Understanding and the Imagination

One of the issues faced by all attempts to provide an account of legal understanding is just how to characterise the role of legal language. Even if one emphasises skills, embodied practices, active and creative habits, socially distributed forms of cognition, and so on, one needs to face the language question. After all, legal language is specific: there are particular terms and phrases that have been included in statutes and that courts have used in justifying their decisions, and it is these terms and phrases that are expected to be made reference to in the making of legal claims, arguments and decisions. Further, these terms and phrases typically have long histories, which in common law systems means that they will tend to be associated with a rich pedigree of cases.

One might think, then, that especially in cases where there is a long line of authoritative cases, the meanings of these terms and phrases is relatively stable. And yet, as every legal student and lawyer quickly discovers, despite, in many instances, a distinguished history of application, the meaning of terms and phrases is incredibly difficult to pin down. Of course, if we could pin down the content of legal rules, principles or tests, then the task of teaching the law would arguably be easier: knowing the content of legal language, all that would be left for us to do would be to devise increasingly more effective methods for passing that content on (e.g. we could try various forms of visual representation of the content, or other kinds of multi-sensory transmission). As it happens, however, all previous efforts to find a method thanks to which we could exhaustively determine the meaning of the terms and phrases contained in legal instruments, such as the argument that all terms and phrases have a core and a penumbra (as famously argued by H.L.A. Hart 1961), or the claim that meaning is determined by the purposes of the rules (as Lon Fuller 1958 famously replied to Hart), as well as many other more recent theories, have left much to be desired. There are always counter-examples to these determinative strategies, i.e. to these attempts at providing an exhaustive account of the complete content of legal language.

This is not the occasion to refer to these strategies, and the accompanying objections, but, keeping them in mind, it may be time to seriously consider the possibility that perhaps no term or phrase, and thus also no legal concept, or any other manifestation of legal language, has a content that can be pinned down and made complete. Language, we might say, is inherently ambiguous, and this includes legal language; the terms and phrases by which legal rules, principles and tests are constructed are shot through with possibilities not yet considered and unforeseeable; all legal language is necessarily and unavoidably incomplete. Furthermore, it may be that it is precisely for all these reasons that legal language is so useful and rich a regulative resource.[1]

To see the inherently ambiguous and necessarily incomplete nature of language consider the following non-legal example. Take the sentence, 'there is coffee in the

1 I acknowledge, of course, the literature on the indeterminacy of legal meaning, especially in contemporary Anglo-American legal theory. Nevertheless, what is meant here by the 'inherent ambiguity and necessary incompleteness' of language may differ somewhat from the sense in which 'the indeterminacy of legal language' is used in that literature. I do not have space in this chapter to enter the exegetical discussion here.

coffee cup'.[2] If you try to draw this sentence you will find yourself having to make (or making in the course of drawing) decisions as to, e.g. how much coffee there is to be in the coffee cup, what shape the cup is to have, what kind of handle it is to have, etc. In addition, if you were to make the cup, you would have to decide on other things too, e.g. how heavy it was to be, whether the coffee in it was to be hot with steam pouring from it, what material exactly the coffee cup was to be made from, how strong the coffee would be, etc. What is interesting is that these are not decisions you need to make when you restrict yourself to a linguistic expression, e.g. when communicating the sentence to another person, writing the sentence down, or even perhaps when reading the sentence. Of course, there is a long debate as to the latter, i.e. as to whether when you read or hear a sentence, you construct internal images in your mind that correspond to your associations of cups with coffee in them; some people argue you do this necessarily, others say you may do this on occasion but not necessarily so. Similarly, there is a long debate as to whether when you communicate a sentence to someone you intend certain detailed specifications of it. But even if you do construct and/or intend reasonably detailed internal images, it is doubtful that your construction/intention will be as detailed as you will dicover it needs to be when you draw or make the cup. Whatever one's stance on these debates, it seems uncontroversial to suggest that sentences can be and are ordinarily used without detailed specification, and thus also without those details being agreed upon. Language is so useful for communication precisely because it is inherently ambiguous and necessarily incomplete; furthermore, communication via language flourishes in conditions of heterogeneous rather than homogeneous potential specification.

Let us dwell on this last point a little longer. Language allows itself to be understood in many different ways, and this is incredibly useful, not only in everyday social interaction – imagine that we had to agree on detailed specifications with respect to each term or phrase – but also in the context of specialised practices, such as law. For it is precisely because language is inherently ambiguous and necessarily incomplete, thereby offering opportunities for being refreshed by different specifications (new shapes of coffee cups, differently tasting coffee, etc.), that it connects up with the everyday life of a community. In other words, it is thanks to the inherently ambiguous and necessarily incomplete content of language that persons, including both legal officials and others involved in disputes, are able to infuse legal language with their own experiences and find some guidance in it for everyday life.

Of course, legal language is not completely open-ended; the meaning of legal terms and phrases is disciplined in all kinds of ways. One way in which it is disciplined is that, at least in the common law tradition, we associate certain terms and phrases with certain cases. Some theorists have referred to these associations as facts or fact-complexes (Samuel 2003) or typical narrative images

2 This example is a variation on one offered by Dretske (1981); it is recounted and discussed in Camp (2007).

(Jackson 2000). On this view, at any one time, in any one community, there is a stock of such fact-complexes or typical narrative images, consisting in a line of cases considered authoritative, and it is these that discipline the meaning of a certain term or phrase. But even on this view of how meaning is disciplined, we quickly come to see the need for the active and creative construction of analogies between such fact-complexes or typical narrative images. Consider, for instance, the development of the law of negligence from *Donoghue v. Stevenson* to *Grant v. Australian Knitting Mills* (discussed in Samuel 2003). In the first case, as is well known, Mrs Donoghue was said to have suffered nervous shock on account of discovering a snail in her ginger beer (manufactured by the defendant). In the second, Mr Grant suffered acute dermatitis as a result of wearing underpants (also manufactured by the defendant), which contained an excess of a chemical harmful to human skin. There is nothing inherent in the neighbour principle, i.e. nothing within the concept or proposition itself, which determines that the two cases are related. Instead, persons – in this case, legal officials – are engaged in the active and creative construction of a likeness between aspects of the facts, e.g. between the harm (nervous shock and acute dermatitis), the means (ginger beers and underwear) and the subjects (consumers and manufacturers).

Further, even these fact-complexes or typical narrative images (from here on in referred to simply as pictures) are inherently ambiguous; their content, too, like the content of linguistic terms, is necessarily incomplete and shot through with possible and unforeseeable instantiations. For instance, what typically occurs on some novel facts emerging is that the authoritative cases are themselves reinterpreted or reframed. Thus, depending on the facts before one, one may ask questions one had previously not asked about the facts of the leading case, e.g. returning to *Donoghue v. Stevenson*, what kind of injury or damage is nervous shock? Does it matter that Mrs Donoghue is an elderly woman? What kind of product is a ginger beer? (Samuel 2003: 197–8). There is no 'core' picture, no 'one' picture, in *Donoghue v. Stevenson* such that it determines the meaning of the neighbour principle and thus also subsequent applications. It is almost the other way round: novel facts sometimes make us reinterpret and reframe what we thought the neighbour principle consisted in, including the pictures that we might have previously thought constituted the 'facts' of the leading case.

Once again, content and meaning slip from underneath our feet; what we find instead is a dynamic, ever-changing, ever-developing activity of understanding, which must be open to its own revision, and which is required to be active and creative in the construction of pictures and analogies between them. Thus, to recall, on the one hand legal understanding consists in, and is thereby disciplined by, a certain range of pictures that are, in any one legal community, associated with certain terms or phrases. Nevertheless, even though these pictures, as authoritative associations, do discipline the meaning of terms or phrases, they do not exhaust them, and we can greatly enhance legal understanding by exploring the infinite possibilities for the further active and creative construction of analogies or for the reframing and transforming of the content and meaning of both terms and phrases and their accompanying pictures. It follows that the exercise of the imagination is vital to understanding generally, but also to the specialised understanding of law.

One theorist who has stressed the vital role of imaginative thinking in the course of practical reason is Amelie Rorty (2010). Rorty claims that all reasoning, including the kind of critical and practical reasoning that we associate with constructing legal arguments and making legal decisions, requires imagination, i.e. it requires us to be able to entertain possibilities that we had not previously considered. It is helpful to set out some of Rorty's suggestions as to how these possibilities might be explored, for they also provide an indication of the kinds of possibilities she has in mind:

- generating or enlarging alternative options for action
- generating or enlarging unconventional conceptions of the affordances of objects and situations (e.g. treating an academic appointment as an experimental adventure)
- specifying the sensory and phenomenological details of options
- shifting perspectives on a situation
- revising descriptions and interpretations of perceptions (e.g. seeing a person as eager rather than aggressive, ingenious rather than cunning, collaborative rather than manipulative)
- developing and specifying the implications of analogies (e.g. working through the details of historical analogies: 'Remember Munich' or 'Remember Vietnam')
- tracing the ramifications of competing policies (e.g. tracking the long-range consequences of the consequences of redistricting voting eligibility)
- varying some of the variables that define or compose situations or contexts (e.g. rearranging the seats of an inner-city classroom to change the dynamics of student interactions)
- specifying the details of hypothetical thought experiments (e.g. Parfit's accounts of mind-body switches, Thomson's Trolley Problem, Hardin's Life Boat Ethics
- role-playing, modelling, pretending, simulating

(Rorty 2010: 438)

For Rorty, then, all of these are ways of exploring possibilities, and thereby also engaging in imaginative practical reasoning (for more pedagogically oriented details of her view, see Rorty 2009). And it is this imaginative dimension of practical reasoning that, she argues, has been unduly neglected in our understanding of what practical reason entails. Her list, it must be said, is a little confusing, for when she refers to 'working through the details' or 'specifying the details' of analogies or thought experiments it is not clear whether she acknowledges that this is a never-ending task; it is unclear, in other words, it is not clear whether she would agree that there are no inherent details in any analogy or thought experiment; one does not 'work out' or 'discover' their details: one explores possible ways of further specifying them. Nevertheless, Rorty's contribution is important, and can be most useful in the teaching and learning of understanding.[3]

There have also been some legal theorists and legal educators who have recognised the vital role for 'imagining otherwise' in legal reasoning. Neil MacCormick, in his justly celebrated *Legal Reasoning and Legal Theory* (1978), spoke of the importance of hypothetical reasoning – asking 'what could have happened?' and 'what might happen?' – in the construction of legal arguments and the making of legal decisions. Nevertheless, the theoretical resources are rather thin and much more work needs to be done.[4]

From what has been said above, there are at least four stages to the teaching and learning of legal understanding: first, one has to provide students with the terms and phrases that are used in legal argumentation and justification; second, one has to direct students to authoritative cases, which provide pictures that, in any one community, are associated with those terms and phrases; third, one must enable and encourage students to explore the pictures of already available cases, including the infinitely different ways in which they can be reframed and specified; and fourth, one should also enable and encourage students to explore the possibilities of other everyday experiences that one could associate with certain terms and phrases, for, as we noted above, the inherent ambiguity and necessary incompleteness of language allows for precisely this infusion of law by everyday life. It is the third and fourth steps that I have been urging we need to focus more on. It is also these third and fourth steps that are required should we accept what has been said above by way of the vital role of the imagination in understanding.

However, from the perspective of this chapter and this book, it is the next step that is the really crucial one. This next step consists in acknowledging the affective dimension of the imagination. This affective dimension manifests itself in a number of ways. First, it is there in the pictures associated with legal terms and phrases: these are, after all, pictures of human drama, shot through with affectivity. Second, we confront and experience these pictures affectively; to the extent that we remember them, we remember them emotionally. Third, when we enable and encourage students to explore possibilities, particularly in relation to the pictures we associate with terms and phrases, we ought to set up these explorations in such a way that they facilitate affective exploration of affectively charged possibilities for further specifying or reframing those pictures. It is time to see more concretely how this exploration can be facilitated in the context of a specific example.

3 Another possibly fruitful resource here is the literature on informal logic: see, e.g. Johnson-Laird (2008); see also Toulmin (2001), who pleads for refocusing accounts of reasoning away from rationality (e.g. conforming to the rules of logic) and towards the more context-sensitive notion of reasonableness.

4 I mention some more interdisciplinary resources in the conclusion.

Affective Possibilities, Experienced Affectively

Let us now focus on a specific legal concept and bring out the affectively imaginative dimensions involved in understanding it.

One of the biggest issues in competition law, or anti-trust law in the US, is how and when persons can be said to have acted in concert. This is required to be established in many competition laws, e.g. those prohibiting price-fixing. There are all sorts of evidentiary issues here, e.g. what is to count as proof of having acted in concert, but in fact, before the evidentiary issues can arise, courts or legislatures must establish tests thanks to which the parties can furnish proof. These tests are not, however, easy to formulate. After all, what exactly does it mean to say a group of subjects (e.g. representatives of companies, or the companies themselves) have acted in concert, or were engaged in 'concerted practice' (Article 81 of the *EC Treaty*)? It should be added that we are to assume here that we need to establish concerted practice in the absence of evidence provided by an explicit agreement, e.g. a legally enforceable contract. In the case of European legislation, the *EC Treaty* does not define 'concerted practice' and this has accordingly been left to the courts and scholars.

Courts and scholars have produced a variety of definitions. A standard definition in the literature (according to Black 2005: 141) is that concerted practice is 'a form of co-ordination', but as Black says, 'this is unhelpful', for it merely replaces one vague concept, 'concerted', with another, 'co-operation'. Other scholarly definitions include: 'some form of direct or indirect contact', 'some meeting of minds or consensus between the parties to co-operate rather than compete' (Faull and Nipkay, quoted in Black 2005: 142), and 'a concordance of wills leading to collusive outcomes' (Philips, quoted in Black 2005: 142). According to Black, efforts by US courts are equally 'obscure', e.g. the courts refer to 'unity of purpose' or 'common design and understanding' or 'common purpose' (Black 2005: 142).

Of course, these definitions are, in some sense, an improvement on the mere phrase 'concerted practice'. However, as Black notes, they provide precious little guidance to advocates seeking to make an argument on behalf of their client or to judges needing to make a determination. Noticing these inadequacies, Black then tries to develop a model of concerted practice; in other words, he tries to develop a test for determining how to prove instances of 'concerted practice'. His model is based, in large part, on the notion of reliance, and he presents the following analytical schema of the concept of reliance:

> X, in doing Ax, relies on Y to do Ay where:
> (I) X does Ax;
> (II) X has the goal Gx;
> (III) If X does Ax, Gx is achieved if and only if Y does Ay;
> (IV) X believes (III);
> (V) X believes that Y does Ay;
> (VI) (I) is true because (II), (IV) and (V) are true.
>
> (Black 2005: 150–51)

Arguably, Black's analytical scheme of reliance, and his further argument that reliance plays a central role, or ought to play a central role, in our understanding of the concept of 'concerted practice' is an improvement on the definitions mentioned above. And yet, there are aspects of it that are dissatisfying. What would count as evidence of someone 'having a goal', or someone 'believing' that someone else has done something? Black's analytical schema is an improvement on the definitions, for it helps us to analyse the relations between the actors in a more detailed way, but the content of the terms and phrases referred to in his analytical schema is just as difficult to pin down as any other term or phrase.

It is instructive what Black does from here. Perhaps equally dissatisfied with such 'pure' or 'cold' analysis, Black proceeds to offer an example of reliance in action. He takes the example from Neil MacCormick's *Legal Right and Social Democracy* (1982). Let us look at how MacCormick formulated the example:

> Suppose that Jones had been swimming from a beach at the foot of a cliff on a stormy day. He has failed to notice the speed with which the tide is rising, and is now in such a position that a desperate dash along the beach will perhaps enable him to reach the path up to safety before he is cut off by the tide. Macdonald happens just then to be strolling along the cliff-top carrying a few hundred feet of stout climbing-rope. He spots Jones's predicament and lowers the rope down the cliff-face to him. Jones sees what he is doing and waits for the rope to reach himself, thus losing time so that he can no longer conceivably reach the path before the tide comes in. He then starts to climb the rope. (MacCormick 1982: 198; quoted in Black 2005: 151)

Immediately upon quoting this example, Black says that it is but an instance of his schema; he says that his 'model is exemplified by a case imagined by MacCormick' (Black 2005: 151). Putting it this way suggests that Black first comes up with a model and only then constructs an example. But it may be, instead, that it is such examples that do the driving; in other words, it is on the back of certain examples that we construct models or schemas, such as Black's. Of course, MacCormick's example is also a generalisation – in this case, a description – of an experience of reliance. Arguably, however, the example gives us a much better sense of the notion of reliance than Black's analytical schema. Why is that?

For a start, consider the narrative construction of the example. It is written in such a way that it builds up emotional tension; we, as the readers of the example, want to read on to see what will happen; emotionally, we are hooked: what will happen to Jones? Will he survive? Will someone save him? How will someone do that? Oh, with a rope – oh, will Macdonald lower the rope quickly enough? Oh, will Jones catch in time? Oh, will Macdonald hold on to it? Oh, can Jones trust Macdonald? Second of all, notice the language that MacCormick uses: 'stormy day', 'desperate dash', 'strolling along', 'predicament' ... all of these terms are shot through with emotional content; they help to create the sense of tension and suspense, and also relief at the end. We experience the affective content of MacCormick's example in an affective manner. Arguably, it is for this reason that we get a much better sense of the notion of reliance from MacCormick's example than from Black's model.

Black goes on to provide an analysis of MacCormick's example:

> (I*) Jones waits for the rope
> (II*) Jones has the goal of avoiding drowning
> (III*) If Jones waits for the rope, he avoids drowning if and only if Macdonald holds the rope
> (IV*) Jones believes (III*)
> (V*) Jones believes that Macdonald will hold the rope
> (VI*) Jones waits for the rope because he has the goal described in (II*), and the beliefs described in (IV*) and (V*)
>
> (Black 2005: 152)

All the emotion has disappeared here. We have nothing left of the tension and suspense. We no longer have any of the emotional descriptions used by MacCormick. Instead, all we have is the rather 'cold' or 'dry' characterisation of Jones going through an inferential process, deciding whether to trust Macdonald or not. If anything, this analysis will mislead us about the concept of reliance.

Notice, further, that MacCormick's example suggests, as a result of the use of emotional language, various other emotions that may be experienced in the vicinity of the experience of reliance. Jones may experience a sense of vulnerability, fear and the taste of death. Macdonald may also experience fear, for he may feel scared about taking on the responsibility for trying and possibly failing to save Jones. He may experience the temptation to pretend he has not seen Jones. All of these, and many other possible emotional experiences, are part of the understanding of the concept of reliance. And yet, it is precisely these that are missing from Black's schema, including his analytical reading of MacCormick's example. Of course, I am to some extent 'reading into' MacCormick's example, and that is precisely the point. Thanks in large part to its narrative construction and use of language it invites the further affective exploration of affective possibilities. MacCormick's example is certainly an improvement on Black's model; it is not a mere 'exemplification' of it. It is an improvement because of its use of affective language and an affectively charged narrative, and this enables us to experience not only the notion of reliance in an affective manner, but also possibly surrounding affective experiences.

However, we might also be able to improve on MacCormick's example, and thereby provide even better opportunities for students to experience the affectivity of certain concepts in an affective way. We might be able to do so by, for instance, allowing students to enact the scenario. In doing so, one need not even give students a particular script that they must simply 'express'; this already can be very helpful, but in the spirit of facilitating exploration one can go further. What one can do is provide students with just the bare bones of the scenario, leaving it essentially unfinished, thereby enabling the students to improvise and explore possible ways of going on. One might facilitate this by giving each student a secret instruction. For instance, one can instruct one student to pretend he is drowning. One can instruct another student that she is to walk over by where this other student is pretending he is drowning (though one would not tell this student in advance what to expect). One may also place a rope somewhere in the vicinity of the event, as well as perhaps other props. Then let the students improvise and experience the scenario. Perhaps some will walk on by, ignoring the 'drowning' student. Perhaps others will panic, not knowing what to do. Perhaps others will grab the rope and decide to help the drowning student. In doing so, they may experience a variety of emotions, all of which are possible, and thus part of the contingent tapestry of the emotional experience of a concept (in this case, reliance).

Reflection can certainly be built, and perhaps ought to be built, into this process. The students who improvise can be given tape recorders or notebooks and asked to reflect on their experience, paying particular attention to their emotions. Others may be asked to draw or otherwise describe the scene, also paying attention to the emotions at play. The reflective process can then be further supplemented by the teacher indicating how the experience of reliance may be surrounded by various possible emotional experiences, especially as these appear in the descriptions of facts in relevant cases. In this way, a teacher can provide students with a multi-sensory, affective experience of (of course always only some of) the affective dimensions of a concept. By making it multi-sensory, this kind of exercise further enhances the experience of those affective dimensions. Further, just as in the case of the sentence, 'there is coffee in the coffee cup', so with a particular legal concept, rule, principle or test: the more we have to explore it in multi-sensory ways (and not simply visualise, for instance, or further describe linguistically), the more possibilities we explore. In acting out 'the facts' of leading cases – as one might do, in this area, by asking students to enact the leading 'concerted practice' cases – one comes to experience the various possible ways in which the facts can be affectively reframed or reinterpreted.[5] By building in improvisation, and not

5 Another interesting way to proceed here might be to take a 'biography' of a recent case, which will typically place the case in social and historical context, as well as telling the lives of the persons involved (including the parties, the advocates and the judges), and to explore all of this in a multi-sensory affective manner. *Donoghue v. Stevenson*,

enactment of pre-existing scripts, one further connects legal concepts to the great variety of ways in which we deal with, and experience, the scenarios that life itself throws to us.

You may feel that all this is a bit fanciful, and all too far from the life of the law. I would beg to differ. The life of the law is, to a great extent, about the emotional life of a community; about its emotional relationships, its troubles and temptations, its conflicts and forms of resolving them. The life of the law is sewn into the emotional fabric of the lives of persons and groups. If a lawyer cannot understand this, he or she not only will never understand the law, but also will not be able to represent his or her client, persuading the court, for instance, that this is or isn't a case of 'concerted practice'. A lawyer must be able to understand affectively – i.e. to explore the infinitely possible affective dimensions of – the pictures that are associated with certain terms or phrases (as these consist in some line of authoritative cases).

Affective Teaching

The above two sections have already yielded some specific recommendations for the affective teaching of the affective dimensions of legal understanding, including providing opportunities for students to exercise the affective imagination. In this part, I shall briefly attempt to systematise these recommendations, thereby also offering somewhat of a summary of what has been discussed above.

I have stressed throughout the vital role of imagination in understanding. Imagination, as I have conceived it, consists in the willingness and ability to conceive otherwise, i.e. to reframe or reinterpret, to relocate one's attention, to reorganise one's sense of order, to redraw the categories under which one classifies objects and properties, and so on. We need this imagination in the practice of law for we constantly need to confront our knowledge with novel, unforeseen and unforeseeable events; indeed, our knowledge is itself already much more dynamic and open than we think; it is much more tentative and fragile, much more amenable to change, for if it was not, it would not be useful to us; it would lock us in, rather than prepare us, though never wholly adequately, for come what may. We need imagination to be able to see novel facts as novel, and we need imagination to be able to transform our knowledge in light of that novelty. More specifically, we need the ability to construct new analogies, new likenesses, between pictures, and to enrich our understanding of the infinitely various ways in which persons emotionally experience the infinite variety of events and relations that life itself offers us. Law is certainly a distinct practice, with its own language and its own set of authoritative associations, but it is not so distinct as to be wholly separated from the way our understanding and knowledge works, and

mentioned above, would be a good place to start; for a recent 'biography' of the case, see Chapman (2009).

from the affective dimensions of the resources of understanding and knowledge, including the ever-changing experience of everyday life. Perhaps we should say this: life, including the legal life, has infinitely more imagination than we do; but what we should take this to mean is that we must try to keep up with it, rather than hide away from it.

In the second part of this chapter, I argued that a vital aspect of the imagination, including the imagination that is required for legal understanding, is affective in character. We need, therefore, to consider how we can assist and encourage students to develop this affective dimension of the imagination, as well as helping them to see its relevance and importance for legal understanding. One way in which we can do so is to help students affectively explore the affective content of, or the affective possibilities opened up by, the pictures contained in cases. Examples such as MacCormick's show us the power of narrative, which is to a large extent an affective power, and thus its capacity to help us understand some of the complexity of certain concepts, which may (as in the case discussed above, with the concept of reliance) play an important role in understanding certain legal rules, principles or even whole areas of the law. In drawing on narrative, we can also have recourse to the growing literature on exactly how we experience narratives emotionally; the work of Martha Nussbaum is exemplary here (especially her *Love's Knowledge*, 1990), but there are also more recent contributions, such as that of Jenefer Robinson (2005; for a recent and helpful summary, see Robinson 2010). Of course, there are going to be aspects of this literature that will clash with the account of understanding offered in this chapter, and so it will be vital not to approach this literature uncritically. For instance, I would disagree with the following suggestion made by Roger Scruton:

> … in responding to literature, we are responding sympathetically to an imagined situation, and we do this by 'imitating' or, more properly, rehearsing the motives that would lead us to sympathise towards the real-life version of the characters and feelings described. In rehearsing these motives we are 'learning to feel', and the true work of art is the one that teaches us what to feel, so that we know what to feel towards situations of the kind that it portrays. (Scruton 2010: 100)

It is important to emphasise that I am not suggesting that we use narratives and dramatic rehearsals to teach students *what* to feel, or to teach them to recognise emotional patterns in legal concepts, or to be affectively attuned to spotting legal issues, or anything of the sort. Further, I do not believe that art or literature teaches us 'what to feel' in certain kinds of situations; nor even that it portrays 'certain kinds of situations'. Instead, I would argue that all art and literature provides us with opportunities for experiences, often highly emotional experiences. Art and literature do not necessarily determine what those experiences will be like; nor do works of art and literature necessarily contain inherent and unchanging messages that we only learn to recognise or respond to in certain ways. Rather, art and literature encourage us to suspend our judgement or realise its difficulty; they enable us to explore, in an affective manner, the infinite variety of possible affective stances or attitudes in the work of art or a literary text. It is in their generation of possibilities that art and literature help us to exercise the imagination, including its affective dimension. But if the imagination and its affective dimension is to be further encouraged and developed, then we should not limit our use of it in teaching to students' appreciation of the inherent ambiguity of art or literature; in addition, we should also enable and encourage students to actively and creatively produce imaginative works, whether by improvising from initial scenarios, or by drawing on other multi-sensory forms of exploration and expression.

In legal education, the trick is to find a balance between, on the one hand, passing on the sense in which the uses to which legal language can be put is disciplined – as above, by associations with pictures contained in authoritative cases – and, on the other hand, the sense in which legal language is inherently ambiguous and necessarily incomplete. Legal education cannot afford to focus solely on teaching students to recognise certain factual patterns and applying rules contained in statutes or expressed in cases to those factual patterns. It must also give students the ability to explore legal language and the pictures we associate with certain terms and phrases. Part of the ability to explore does involve relying on such resources as specific rules, principles or tests, as well as purposes, including policy purposes of areas of the law, or the law more generally. On the approach to language adopted in this chapter, rules and other linguistically expressed resources do not necessarily determine what we see; they are not necessarily destructive of our imagination. Rather, they can often serve us well in our exploration. By bringing to mind a rule or principle, etc., we did not initially think relevant, we can often reframe and reinterpret what we originally thought were the 'facts of this case' or 'the picture of actions and events given in this case' and in this way can open new ways of seeing, which can, in turn, help us to establish a new analogy or likeness that may assist our argument or decision.[6]

But we can also go much further than using rules, principles or policies in helping students develop their imagination, including their affective imagination. As I have noted above, we can create conditions under which students can improvise together, draw or make things together – thereby exploring in a multi-sensory fashion, exercising their whole bodies and not just performing certain cognitive operations. If we are to help students develop their imaginations, on the back of recognising the importance of the imagination for legal understanding, we may have to introduce 'multi-sensory, affective playgrounds' into law schools. These playgrounds would be physical spaces where, e.g. the facts of leading cases can be explored in dramatic fashion, or where certain important concepts (e.g. as

6 This enabling capacity of language has been stressed by Andy Clark. Clark is an advocate of recognising the embodied and embedded dimensions of cognition, but he has also been careful not to lose sight of the importance of language. For a discussion in the context of moral judgement, see Clark (1996).

reliance above) can be explored in a number of multi-sensory ways. Imagine a space, with multi-sensory resources, where students can come together in groups to express their understanding of the neighbour principle, e.g. in a group painting, or a short film, or even a song. Of course, such exercises can also be, and may need to be, supplemented by more traditional reflective exercises, where students draw links between their imaginative expression and leading cases and scholarly literature. One of the great pedagogical benefits to such a playground is that it can involve, to a much greater extent, students who learn in a variety of different ways, sometimes simply as a result of the disproportionate development of one sense rather than another. The other benefit, of course, is that it connects the study of law to the incredible creative and imaginative capacities of students, as well as to their experiences of everyday life.

Conclusion

I have so far said little about the reference made to the importance of the imagination in other domains, and it is certainly outside the scope of this chapter to delve into these uses in detail. Nevertheless, it is important to recall that there have been significant previous efforts in other domains, for we can usefully draw on these in making a more developed case for the importance of the imagination in legal understanding. Interestingly, many of these previous efforts have also drawn links between imagination and emotion. Aaron Ben Ze'ev, for instance, in a paper entitled 'The Thing Called Emotion' (2010), has suggested that 'human life concerns not only – or even mainly – the present but rather, and to a significant extent, the realm of imagined possibilities in both past and future circumstances' (Ben Ze'ev 2010: 43). This is connected to Ben Ze'ev's thesis that 'emotions typically occur when we perceive positive or negative significant changes in our personal situation' (Ben Ze'ev 2010: 42), e.g. when we are surprised or something ruptures the familiar course of events. The cognitive value, not to mention the enjoyment, of literature and the arts is often premised precisely on the way they help us exercise the capacity to imagine possibilities – enabling us to be absorbed, including absorbed emotionally, in alternative worlds. For example, Matthew Kieran has spoken of how in reading literature we are taught to suspend judgement, and to affectively encounter an unfamiliar world, including the characters within that world, in a non-evaluative way (Kieran 2010). Roger Scruton, in a paper entitled 'Feeling Fictions', has argued that insofar as we understand imagination to be 'the capacity … to entertain thoughts without affirming or asserting them' (Scruton 2010: 96), imagination is vital to the way in which we experience fiction.

It is also precisely this sense of waiting, of suspending judgement, that theorists of the moral life have said is so important, e.g. Simone Weil, and later Iris Murdoch (1970) following Weil, had this sense in mind when she used the term 'attention'. The idea in Weil and Murdoch is not only to suspend evaluation, but also to silence one's own fantasies. For Weil and Murdoch, both great art and the moral life require quietening the self's projection of all too familiar categories and fantasies. At other times, it is said that this is a matter of not so much suspending judgement, as recognising, in suspending it momentarily, how difficult it is: this is a theme in Martha Nussbaum's work on the moral value of literature (Nussbaum 1990; of course, Nussbaum is also famous for her work on the emotions, see Nussbaum 2003). This ability to think otherwise and transform our understanding, including our ability to see the suffering of others that may otherwise be invisible to us, has also been stressed by James Tully. Weaving together Nietzsche, Wittgenstein and Foucault, Tully argues that the ability to imagine otherwise is vital to the practice of political philosophy in the public sphere (Tully 2009; see especially Chapter 3). Finally, a recent book has argued for the vital role of counterfactuals (a kind of 'imagining otherwise') in the context of the social sciences (see Lebow 2010). In short, there are many interdisciplinary resources we can draw on in advocating for a more robust role of the imagination.

The overlap here between narrative, aesthetic perception and the moral life, as well as the frequent reference made to the emotions in this context, relies heavily on the exercise of the imagination. It is precisely by focusing on the ways in which the imagination is vital for understanding, but also for the moral life, and even for specialised practices such as law, that we may be able to bring together theories and practices of sensory experience and the emotions. In doing so, we may also enhance our understanding of teaching and learning, and, over time, thereby construct a legal pedagogy that is a great deal more responsive to the creativity of our students and the great variety of ways in which they learn.

References

Statutes

Treaty Establishing the European Community (Treaty of Amsterdam 1997), 'The EC Treaty'.

Cases

Donoghue v. Stevenson [1932] AC 562.
Grant v. Australian Knitting Mills [1936] AC 85.

Books and Articles

Ben Ze'ev, A. 2010. The Thing Called Emotion, in *Oxford Handbook to the Philosophy of Emotion*, edited by P. Goldie. Oxford: Oxford University, 41–62.

Black, O. 2005. *Conceptual Foundations of Antitrust.* Cambridge: Cambridge University Press.

Camp, E. 2007. Thinking with Maps, *Philosophical Perspectives* 21: 145–82.

Chapman, M. 2009. *The Snail and the Ginger Beer: The Singular Case of Donoghue v. Stevenson.* London: Wildy, Simmonds and Hill Publishing.

Clark, A. 1996. Connectionism, Moral Cognition and Collaborative Problem Solving, in *Mind and Morals: Essays on Ethics and Cognitive Science*, edited by L. May, M. Friedman and A. Clark. Cambridge, MA: MIT Press, 109–27.

Dretske, F. 1981. *Knowledge and the Flow of Information.* Cambridge, MA: MIT Press.

Fuller, L. 1958. Positivism and Fidelity to Law – A Reply to Professor Hart, *Harvard Law Review* 71(4): 630–72.

Goldie, P. (ed.) 2010. *Oxford Handbook to the Philosophy of Emotion.* Oxford: Oxford University Press.

Hagberg, G. and Jost, W. (eds) 2010. *A Companion to the Philosophy of Literature.* Oxford: Blackwell.

Hart, H.L.A. 1961. *The Concept of Law.* Oxford: Clarendon Press.

Jackson, B. 2000. Literal Meaning: Semantics and Narrative in Biblical Law and Modern Jurisprudence, *International Journal for the Semiotics of Law* 13(4): 433–57.

Johnson-Laird, P.N. 2008. Mental Models and Deductive Reasoning, in *Reasoning: Studies in Human Inference and Its Foundations*, edited by L. Rips and J. Adler. Cambridge: Cambridge University Press, 206–22.

Kieran, M. 2010. Emotions, Art and Immorality, in *Oxford Handbook to the Philosophy of Emotion*, edited by P. Goldie. Oxford: Oxford University, 681–703.

Lebow, R.N. 2010. *Forbidden Fruit: Counterfactuals and International Relations.* Princeton: Princeton University Press.

MacCormick, N. 1978. *Legal Reasoning and Legal Theory*. Oxford: Clarendon Press.

MacCormick, N. 1982. *Legal Right and Social Democracy*. Oxford: Clarendon Press.

Murdoch, I. 1970. *Sovereignty of Good*. London: Routledge.

Nussbaum, M. 1990. *Love's Knowledge: Essays on Philosophy and Literature*. New York: Oxford University Press.

Nussbaum, M. 2003. *Upheavals of Thought: The Intelligence of the Emotions*. Cambridge: Cambridge University Press.

Robinson, J. 2005. *Deeper than Reason: Emotion and its Role in Literature*. Oxford: Oxford University Press.

Robinson, J. 2010. Emotion and the Understanding of Narrative, in *A Companion to the Philosophy of Literature*, edited by G. Hagberg and W. Jost. Oxford: Blackwell, 71–92.

Rorty, A. 2009. Educating the Practical Imagination: A Prolegomena, in *Oxford Handbook of the Philosophy of Education*, edited by H. Siegel. Oxford: Oxford University Press, 195–209.

Rorty, A. 2010. A Plea for Ambivalence, in *Oxford Handbook to the Philosophy of Emotion*, edited by P. Goldie. Oxford: Oxford University, 425–44.

Samuel, G. 2003. *Epistemology and Method in Law*. Aldershot: Ashgate.

Scruton, R. 2010. Feeling Fictions, in *A Companion to the Philosophy of Literature*, edited by G. Hagberg and W. Jost. Oxford: Blackwell, 93–105.

Toulmin, S. 2001. *Return to Reason*. Cambridge, MA: Harvard University Press.

Tully, J. 2009. *Public Philosophy in a New Key*. 2 Vols. Cambridge: Cambridge University Press.

Chapter 9
What Students Care About and Why We Should Care

Graham Ferris and Rebecca Huxley-Binns

This chapter presents an account of the relationship between emotion, reason, law and ultimately legal education as complementary rather than antagonistic. We do not deny the potential for irrationality and destructive behaviour in our emotional lives. However, the familiar image of a dramatic clash between cognitive thought and feeling obscures the more normal, and in fact necessary, co-operation of reason and emotion in the human animal. It is our view that the co-operation of reason and emotion should be acknowledged as an intrinsic element of module design in legal education.

We argue here that education should be undertaken for some object of value to the learner. There is no need to suppose that one sole object must be universally adopted. We believe that an intuitive appreciation of the need to connect with something of importance in our students is very common among those working in higher education and has been articulated in literature (Dewey 1895; Rubin 1973; Biggs 2003; Gardner 2006). Any novelty in our position is derived from insisting that those delivering education should explicitly and deliberately consider the importance not solely of the cognitive outcomes desired (Ferris 2009), but the purposes of learners, meaning the things they do or might value, or care about, or strive for. Whilst the choice of purpose is that of the learner, we can use our experience and knowledge of teaching law in higher education to facilitate purpose, choice or value adoption or rejection. It is acknowledged that people care, and the fact that people care about things matters, in general and in the design of legal curricula.

Methodology

Our relevant expertise is practical and centred in legal education. Accordingly, our method has been to seek independent supports for tentatively articulated intuitive hypotheses to which our experience led us (Gardner 2006; Putnam 2000). Of course this method leads to a danger of self-fulfilling prophecy, selecting from the evidence only that which supports the hypothesis and rejecting that which is obstructive. In the words of Popper (2002: 124):

> if we are uncritical we shall always find what we want: we shall look for, and find, confirmations, and we shall look away from, and not see, whatever may be dangerous to our pet theories. In this way it is only too easy to obtain what appears to be overwhelming evidence in favour of a theory which, if approached critically, would have been refuted.

Another danger is that we may confuse repetition across sources with independent supporting evidence confirming our hypothesis. Given the restraints on space we can do little more here than introduce the disparate approaches that we have identified supporting the necessary linkage between what may be termed affect, or what we care about, and human action and specifically human learning. To summarise we would argue that: the philosophical work of Harry G. Frankfurt; the neurological work recorded by Antonio Damasio; the data on law student distress in law school in the USA; and the general body of work produced by self-determination theory researchers all provide evidence that is supportive of our main hypothesis that legal education is most effective and enjoyable when reason and emotion co-operate.

There remain problems of interpretation, reasoning and integration of the material selected here into an educational context. Synthesis of work produced in disparate fields is inherently hazardous. There are constant dangers of misapplication of ideas and terms outside the areas where they have been coined and refined. There is no way to avoid risks in such an enterprise, and our guide has been to try and follow the advice of Harry G. Frankfurt (1999: xi): 'Surely one need not have been trained in any very distinctive philosophical tradition or skill in order to be able to think clearly, to reason carefully, and to keep one's eye on the ball'. Where there is no scholarly discipline that can be adhered to, as material that spans disciplines is being brought together, there seems little option other than to fall back onto the general disciplines of rational discourse and reasoning (Ferris and Lunt 2010).

Why is What People Care about Important?

Harry G. Frankfurt has been writing about 'volition', or will, for many years. His aim is to establish a discourse of 'what to care about' to complement traditional accounts in philosophy of what to believe (epistemology) and what to do (ethics). A philosophy of volition raises issues of what it means to be a rational free agent. Such agency is characterised by self-reflection upon what desires are condoned and adopted, and what desires are resisted and rejected. Frankfurt talks of first-order and second-order desires, and it is second-order desires that distinguish rational free agents and other creatures. In short, a first-order desire is what is normally referred to as a desire: 'I want to eat the bun'. However, we also have a capacity for reflective self-evaluation that is manifested in second-order desires, so we might want to want to eat the bun, or we might not want to want to eat the bun. Thus, second-order desires have first-order desires as their subject matter (Frankfurt 1998: 12): 'Someone has a desire of the second order either when he wants simply to have a desire or when he wants a certain desire to be his will'.

When we are content in what we want to want then we are 'wholehearted', and being wholehearted makes us feel free in acting upon our approved desires. What we want to want is in turn determined by what we care about, as what we care about is what we identify ourselves with, and that in turn gives a reason to want some desires and to reject others in order to be true to who we want to be. Thus, it is important to us what we care about.

If Frankfurt is correct then his analysis is potentially an important analytic tool for understanding, and facilitating, learning success. It provides an account of effective agency at the highest level of generality – and could thus be used to exploit for educational purposes any theoretical work that is concerned with agency. Essentially, Frankfurt claims that we can and do endorse or resist our own impulses; that we can act with or against the grain of our own willed character. One familiar phenomenon both authors have encountered in our educational practice can be illuminated by this insight – the very high motivation many students attracted to clinical models of legal education bring to their clinical studies. Students attracted to clinical courses typically want to be what they think a professional lawyer is. This is a second-order desire – they will and endorse all desires that serve this end. If a live client is involved there is an ordinary common first-order desire, to satisfy and please the person they interact with. This desire is endorsed by the desire to be a lawyer who serves clients and the student acts wholeheartedly, and with an efficacy and perseverance that wholeheartedness entails. The student feels this educational experience is useful and that doing the job well is worth the effort in its own right. Frankfurt gives us an analytical handle on this process, and therefore the possibility of reproducing its positive effects elsewhere in the curriculum.

If effective education is in part about the relationship between what students care about (second-order desires) and the curriculum then this has consequences for the design of an effective curriculum. For example, anecdotal evidence suggests that on entry to law school students care about myriad things: some care about righting wrongs in society, some want to serve by protecting the innocent or giving the downtrodden a voice. Others care about their earning potential by the age of 40. Motivation is harnessed by students doing what they perceive as being important to themselves. The things students feel are important are those that they care about. However, we cannot assume that all students know what they care about – as people are not inherently imbued with self-knowledge (Frankfurt 2004: 14):

> In designing and managing their lives, people need to confront a number of significant issues. They must make up their minds concerning what they want, which things they want more than others, what they consider to be intrinsically valuable and hence appropriate for pursuit not just as a means but as a final

> end, and what they themselves will in fact pursue as final ends. They have to determine what it is they care about.

Wanting a certain desire to be one's own is a second-order volition. Frankfurt contends that where a person is fulfilling a desire and the desire is one he embraces, then that person is truly free, or 'is enjoying as much freedom as it is possible for us to conceive' (Frankfurt 2004: 20). What we care about dictates our self-regard and our motivation for action, it colours all aspects of our inevitable and necessary involvement with our own emotions.

It is the very fact that our students do care about some things that makes a difference to the quality of their learning experience. Failure to address affect in curriculum design and teaching delivery is to divorce the purely cognitive elements of the taught course from the students' humanity. How often do students react to the outcome of a case with the exclamations, 'That's not fair'? It is the reflexive decision to care and to embrace congruent and resist incongruent desires that marks us as human (i.e. as rational free agents). If what we care about as teachers is that our students become autonomous learners, we must acknowledge and accept that the students' personhood, including their cognitive processes, abilities and perceptions, is driven by what they care about, and therefore not necessarily by what we care about. We should have regard to what our students care about when designing a curriculum and, if necessary, reduce the size of the syllabus to give a voice to the 'it's not fair' emotional response. We should plan with an eye to capturing student engagement. We tend to design in the light of what we regard as essential knowledge for understanding, but we cannot predetermine how our students will be able to respond to the curriculum in order to reach understanding. We must facilitate their journey, and their journey is laid out by what they care about, which may be different for each of them.

We can teach all of our students the same thing in the same way. However, they will not all learn the same thing in the same way. Frankfurt tells us that the student's sense of self is informed by what they care about, and that what they care about is not a given quality – he throws a new light on the old insight that people have to become. Education can ignore this process, can obstruct this process or can try to harness this process. However, if Frankfurt is right, what we cannot do is be immune from the influence of this process.

If we care about our effectiveness as educators we need to care about the fact that our students care about things. There are ways we can make space in a curriculum for whatever it is students do care about. Consider the way Michael Sandel makes use of the intuitive moral sense of his student audience in his justice lectures (Sandel 2006). He seeks out and asks about the students' response to ethical problems; he is inviting his students to think about what they care about and validating that reflective process in higher educational practice.

Frankfurt enjoins us to think about the will, volition, as an independent subject for enquiry. He argues that caring about things is contingent; as a matter of logic it is quite possible to conceive without contradiction of a person who cares about nothing, not even themselves. However, this theoretical schema may not be a reliable reflection of the world. The major concepts fit together well enough: that what we care about guides our agency over time, that we engage in meta decisions about what we want to care about, that we may be bound involuntarily by our own caring about something, that questions of what we should care about are subject to rational discourse – although not necessarily to any transcendent solution (it is probably not possible to arrive at any universal answer, because what we care about is bound up with who we are). However, they raise two empirical questions. Is it possible for someone to not care about anything whilst still having cognitive functions and emotions: is this independence of reflective volition a reality? And if so, would it really matter if the ability to care were broken?

Men Who Could Not Care

Damasio has uncovered the neurological basis of the ability to care. He has confirmed empirically the intuition of Frankfurt that the ability to care about something is vital to a fully functioning human being – that it is not possible to be fully human with cognition alone, reason without purpose is not a viable proposition.

Pressure of space demands we deal with this issue briefly. However, mere familiarity with the neurological malfunctioning of Phineas Gage and the patient Damasio refers to as Elliot suffices for the purposes of this chapter (Damasio 2006). Damasio describes patients who do not care about anything, despite being cognitively functional in all respects and quite capable of understanding and moral reasoning. And these patients were severely compromised. Frankfurt's analysis suggested that volition organised around what we care about and the second-order desires that caring entailed was functionally independent of, although obviously linked to, cognition. That Damasio's work seems to identify a capacity to care that is both functionally and organically isolatable is a remarkable coincidence, and *prima facie* a powerful confirmation of the explanatory power of Frankfurt's analysis. It is not only language that Frankfurt has subjected to analysis – the language reflects a functional and organic reality.

Thus, Damasio confirms the existence of capacity for reflective volition as a separate organic entity in the individual organism. However, this may not render the issue of importance for legal education – it matters to individuals that they care about things, and that they can identify the things they care about, and that they care about the right things for themselves. However, this does not itself entail any imperative demand upon legal educators. What it does identify is a potential hazard for unselfconscious educational activity unaware of the importance of this process of maturation and acting in concord with the will – a potential for institutional frustration of the process that mimics the effects of the organic damage Damasio was concerned with.

To be free rational agents, Frankfurt argues, we need to form second-order desires and to seek to act in accordance with those of our first-order desires that we endorse. Where we are able to act in concord with our second-order desires we are wholehearted, which is a very positive outcome. Where we have formulated second-order desires but are beset with conflicting first-order desires that are contrary to our willed desires, we are conflicted and this is a less happy outcome. When we avoid such conflict by having only first-order desires we are less than fully human, merely 'wanton' (Frankfurt 1998: 16 and 176) and in empirical terms we are in the sad position of Phineas Gage, unable to live a meaningful life. Our colleague Julie Higginbottom has counselled hundreds of law students, and she assures us a significant number volunteer that they chose law because they wanted to 'make a difference'. This strongly suggests these students felt legal study would be relevant to matters they cared about. However, our curriculum pays little regard to such inchoate and naïve desires. If the forming and holding of second-order desires is important then this institutional indifference might have a harmful effect.

Therefore, we turn to the effects legal education has been found to have upon students. The question is whether there is reason to worry that legal education might be hindering students' development of a useful and meaningful approach to what they care about – is there substantial reason to fear that neglect of students' values in law school might be having a deleterious effect on our students?

The Law School Experience in the USA: When Doing Nothing is to Tolerate Harm

The comparable research on this topic in the UK is relatively sparse. However, in the USA over the last 30 years there has been worryingly consistent evidence that law school undermines the well-being of students (Daicoff 1997, 2002). The seminal work in this area was two linked studies reported in two articles by Benjamin and Shanfield (Shanfield and Benjamin 1985; Benjamin et al. 1986). These studies established the problem as a feature of American law school – rather than American professional education (*cf* Enron and Redmount 1957; Solkoff 1968; Solkoff and Markowitz 1967; Heins et al. 1983) or the peculiar nature of an institution's intake (Hedegard 1979), or an artefact of poor empirical administration or analysis. The first study compared law students with medical students, and found unanticipated differences between them. In the second study, the researchers were able to make longitudinal comparison of cohorts of law students, and extend the study to one cohort before it entered the law school, and to one (different) cohort two years after graduation and entry into the profession. As the researchers used personality and diagnostic questionnaires that were well established and validated, they were able to compare law students with a normalised population, as well as with their medical comparators. The study was based in the University of Arizona and the numbers of students completing the questionnaires administered (320) represented a return rate of over 70% (Benjamin et al. 1986). As the study took place over four years (1981–4), it was possible to compare a cohort's scores over time, so that the self-reported psychological health of a cohort in different years of study could be compared.

The studies found, in broad terms, that there was clear evidence that law school was damaging to law students' self-reported mental health. Thus, before going to law school students were healthier than after. In numerical terms the pre-law students were within the normal range for self-reported depression (around 3–9%) when first tested, but between 17% and 40% of students post-commencement at law school reported depression, and between 20% and 40% reported increased symptoms other than depression (Benjamin et al. 1986: 247). It was not that people prone to the psychiatric symptoms reported were attracted to law school and bringing their problems with them. The levels of reported symptoms shot up after entry into the first year. Nor was the problem caused by the difficulties and discipline demanded by all forms of professional education. The law students reported significantly higher levels of distress than the medical students on all the subscales, consistently across different types of distress and at statistically significant levels (Benjamin et al. 1986: 69). Unfortunately, the problem was not merely one of adjustment to the new law school regime; the higher scores for depression, obsessive-compulsion, anxiety and paranoid ideation remained high, and indeed tended to increase, over the course of the three years of study (Benjamin et al. 1986: 240). Finally, it would seem that the problems experienced in law school followed the students into the profession. Although self-reported symptoms tended to lessen a little upon entering the profession, the reduction was not statistically significant and the graduates of law school never recovered their pre-law school state of mental well-being.

We should note the inherent limitations of the study: it relied upon self-report; it concerned a single institution; the battery of tests was applied over a short period of time (15–20 minutes); the cohorts were not identical across time; not all cohorts were tested at each stage of the study. However, it is reasonable to regard the study as establishing a *prima facie* case for the harmful effects of American law school upon the mental well-being of law students. Furthermore, the study has not been out of line with other research. In the words of Daicoff (1997: 1407): 'At least since 1970, studies have found that law students report an unusually high level of stress, psychiatric symptoms, substance abuse, anxiety, depression, and internal conflict soon after beginning law school'. Therefore, we are looking at what appears to be a real problem.

Of course with complex social problems there is a country mile between identifying a problem and settling upon a causative analysis. There have been various attempts to account for the phenomenon of law student distress. The US relies heavily upon the Socratic or case book method of instruction and this has been identified as a stressful form of instruction (Shanfield and Benjamin 1985: 70). In more general terms the relatively heavy workloads, the highly competitive nature of law school, the relatively low contact time between students and staff due to student numbers, and cost, create a learning environment that is less supportive than medical school. We cannot with confidence ascribe causation. However, the personal motivations of the law student as a learner have been identified as a possible cause of law student distress in several commentaries (Benjamin et al. 1986: 250), and have been tested for causative effects in studies by Sheldon and Krieger (2004, 2007) informed by self-determination theory. This research allows us to explore whether law student distress is linked to Frankfurt's concerns around the formation of second-order desires and the acting upon concordant first-order desires, which he described as being wholehearted.

Of course, it is possible to give an account of how a devalued study of law might undermine feelings of well-being, given that law is a source of normative meaning for many people. Schiltz has written with great force and power on the importance of values and personal motivation for the learning, teaching and practising of law (Schiltz 1999). Thus, Frankfurt must be taken as one voice in the contemporary discourse on the role of values in legal education and life. However, as noted above, his account is sufficiently generalised to serve as a bridging theory. It also avoids reliance upon any particular content. Frankfurt makes no attempt to prescribe what we should care about and does not rest his account on any account of development, thus avoiding suspicion of importing substantive values through the qualities inherent to a healthy developmental outcome. Two difficulties with accounts such as that of Schiltz have always been: to avoid the discussion getting bogged down in the nature of the values that should imbue legal education; and to move from a hunch that subjective alienation is a factor towards a research model that allows the hunch to be formally stated and tested empirically. Frankfurt points us in the direction of second-order desires, things we identify ourselves with, and avoids the problem of what those values should be by working at a very high level of generality. He allows us to generalise. A group of humanistic psychologists have developed in self-determination theory a similar concern with the importance of how we regard the ends of our activity to Frankfurt's. What Frankfurt calls identification with second-order desires (in an account that is concerned with the arrival at a second-order desire, and the coherence of the idea of a second-order desire, and only then with the importance and effects of holding second-order desires) Sheldon and Krieger call autonomous motivations (those things one does because one wants to do them and not because someone else wants one to do them – the locus of perceived cause being the crucial issue). In effect Sheldon and Krieger transform the deeply felt hunch of Schiltz and the conceptual concerns of Frankfurt into a set of empirically testable hypotheses about law students.

Sheldon and Krieger replicated aspects of their study at two law schools, the Florida State University and an unnamed urban privately funded college in the mid-west. Several of the questionnaires were also administered once to psychology undergraduates at the University of Missouri, which gave a comparison group for the law students at the commencement of their legal studies. A comparison of the Floridian law students on the first day of term and the Missouri undergraduates showed the law students reporting slightly better subjective well-being and having slightly more intrinsic values (2004). However, when the tests were repeated for the law students they had suffered statistically significant drops in subjective well-being, intrinsic values and autonomous motivation. The unnamed comparison law school also suffered a drop in subjective well-being and autonomous motivation that was statistically significant. Thus, the deleterious effects of the first year of legal studies upon students' well-being was confirmed. The prolongation of the research over the second and third years of study found no recovery in subjective well-being nor intrinsic values or autonomous motivation; there was, however, a slight numbing of all valuation by the second year.

Of course correlations do not show causation, but they can support or undermine theories about causative relationships. Two of the hypotheses that the Sheldon and Krieger research was designed to test were: (i) that autonomous motivation and intrinsic values would be positively correlated with subjective well-being; and (ii) that students with higher scores for autonomy and intrinsic values would have better academic performance holding other factors equal. Motivation was considered autonomous if the students reported acting for reasons they felt identified with, rather than acting in response to what were perceived as the demands of others. Intrinsic values are those that are considered to reflect the needs of the holder and valued in their own right; extrinsic values are those that are valued for the social rewards they are associated with, satisfying needs only indirectly (Kasser 2002: 128; Sheldon et al. 2004). Both hypotheses were supported by the findings. Thus, the study shows that student distress (as measured by subjective well-being) occurs at the same time as students feel less autonomous, and shift their values away from intrinsic and towards extrinsic values. Self-determination theory suggests that this coincidence of measurable changes is linked by a causative relationship, specifically that the loss of felt autonomy and shift in values is causative of some of the loss of subjective well-being. This loss of subjective well-being is in turn associated with earlier findings of mental health vulnerability (Sheldon and Krieger 2007).

The US research on student distress indicates the danger of ignoring the affective aspect of legal education. It seems clear that law school can be linked to unwanted changes in the emotional state of students. Also, the negative effects seem to be carried over into practice, undermining the American legal profession. It would be rash to generalise the research and assume similar problems in the UK and elsewhere. However, it would be just as rash to assume in the absence of careful investigation that no such problems exist elsewhere. Certainly at the anecdotal level several of the observed characteristics of the impact of legal education on the law student are familiar to us from our professional experience. The American experience gives the lie to the convenient assumption that if we neglect the emotional aspect of our students then we will do them no harm. However, the research goes further than that. The work by Sheldon and Krieger suggests that one cause of the problem law schools in the US have encountered is the loss of felt autonomy around values (and a shift from some values to others). This, of course, if correct, is a startling practical example of the importance of what we care about, and fairly obviously there is overlap between Frankfurt's second-order desires with which we identify and the autonomous motivation that reflects the agent's sense of doing what the agent desires to do. However, to assess how much genuine support self-determination theory provides for Frankfurt's analysis we need to give consideration to the origins and conceptual structure of the self-determination theory that informed the research of Sheldon and Krieger.

Origins of Self-Determination Theory: How Rewards can Undermine Performance

In the early 1970s several researchers including Deci (1971), Kruglanski et al. (1971), and Lepper and Greene (1975) independently verified experimentally a phenomenon that ran against the grain of the dominant model of learning based on operant conditioning. The anomalous finding was that rewards could *reduce* subsequent engagement in an activity, rather than reinforcement (reward) leading to behaviour modification in the direction of the reinforced behaviour (motivating continued participation in an activity). Reward could lead to disengagement from an activity that had been initially intrinsically interesting and attractive. The studies gave experimental and empirical confirmation to the intuition that educational institutions with their structures of control and assessment could create boredom and imaginative disengagement. In the words of one of the early studies (Lepper and Greene 1975), the use of rewards risked turning play into work.

The origins of self-determination theory are located in the attempts by researchers to explain this demotivating effect of the giving of reward (summarised in Deci and Ryan 2002). Other studies showed the similar demotivating effects of deadlines, supervision and some forms of feedback, although the effect did not always follow verbal rewards in the form of positive feedback (Amabile, Dejong and Lepper 1976; Lepper and Greene 1975; Deci 1971; Deci, Koestner and Ryan 1999a, 1999b). It was hypothesised that the demotivation was caused by the way a learner perceived and understood the reward, hence cognitive evaluation theory. The theory proposed that the learner understood that the reward meant that the task was being undertaken to further the purposes of the reward-giver rather than being an activity chosen by the learner for the learner's own purposes. In the terms used by self-determination theorists the perceived locus of causation was shifted by the reward, from the learner to an external agent. The learner was no longer choosing but was being manipulated; hence the valued quality in an action known as 'autonomy' was being taken away. The result was the previously intrinsically desirable activity became less attractive, as it was associated with being controlled by an external agent.

Cognitive evaluative theory explained the loss of intrinsic motivation for interesting tasks – the experimental anomaly – and also why a reward that was unexpected, and therefore not perceived as intended to manipulate the learner's behaviour, did not undermine intrinsic motivation (Lepper and Greene 1973;

Amabile, Dejong and Lepper 1976); and why a reward that was perceived as an integral part of the activity, was not demotivating, as it also was not perceived as intended to control the learner's behaviour (Kruglanski et al. 1975). Finally, it explained why verbal feedback would be perceived as sometimes demotivating (when it was perceived as controlling) and sometimes as not demotivating (when it was perceived as supportive) (Deci 1971; Deci, Koestner and Ryan 1999a). More interestingly, it suggested a mechanism that might have effects outside of the circumstances of the original experimental anomaly, and possibly provide a key to successful motivation.

Development of Self-determination Theory

Cognitive evaluation theory was merely a part of a developing model of human motivation, but it was foundational, and it identified autonomy as an important and valued feature of people's experience. When the model expanded its explanatory ambitions, autonomy was identified not simply as something valuable but as one of three psychological needs people have. The other two are a need to feel competent and a need for relatedness (Deci and Ryan 2002). Obviously many activities are not interesting for themselves but because of their role in some greater purpose. Thus, one might learn the legal citation system in order to find law reports, but few of us derived genuine pleasure from distinctions between square and round brackets that had to be learned. To broaden its usefulness and potential application, self-determination theory posits a continuum of autonomous motivation. On the self-caused (autonomy) side of the scale, in addition to intrinsic motivation, it includes 'identified' motivation, which exists whenever a person has made a purpose her own, so she has become identified with it. On the extrinsic or externally caused end of the scale are 'introjected' motivations, things done to please others, and because failure to do them brings shame or guilt, and finally externally imposed motivation, which responds to the rewards and punishments of others (bosses, teachers, or even the nebulous pressures of society or fashion, etc.). Identified motivation – the adoption as one's own of aims, values or things felt to be important – can be understood as a successful adoption of a second-order desire. Although, whether one might be said to have reached a second-order desire in some cases of introjected motives is more difficult to decide. For educational purposes the theory pushes us in two directions: towards trying to encourage student values that will make study purposeful (an aspect we will not pursue here); and trying to give room for student autonomy, as this will be responsive to student motivations and therefore responsive to what they care about.

Thus, with these ideas in mind we can understand what Sheldon and Krieger (2004) meant when they referred to the importance of *why* we care about things. If we care about a task because of its intrinsic attractiveness then motivation is not problematic. Koestner and Losier (2002: 102) suggest that if the attraction is partially due to novelty, or aspiration to mastery of an activity which requires dull perseverance in practice, then we might require some help from identified purposes that can motivate us when an activity is not fun but is necessary to an important personal goal:

> The distinction between intrinsic motivation and internalization revolves around the way an individual becomes drawn to an activity. To the extent that an activity is inherently rewarding, such as recreational activities are for many people, it is likely that processes related to intrinsic motivation will energise and direct a person's involvement with the activity. However, to the extent that an activity lacks intrinsic appeal but is highly valued by one's social group, as may be the case with many school related tasks, it is likely that internalization will have to provide the basis for effective self-regulation. In this case it is the perception of the activity as valuable or meaningful that drives one to engage and persist in it.

Consider the possible ways in which these insights can be used to explain the high motivational responses we have observed in optional courses designed around mooting, that generates a spillover effect into performance in other courses. For some students there is an intrinsic attraction to the presentation of oral argument in a competitive setting – mooting has a performance joy and a game-like aspect – and this could explain initial high motivation. However, it is internalised motivation that can explain persistence in subordinate tasks and spillover effects. Mooting has ethics that may be internalised by students, and in turn motivate. A natural mooter may not enjoy close reading of cases, and yet the desire to win according to the rules of the game may motivate an interest in interpretative technique as an instrument to the desired outcome. Similarly, as mooting is concerned with persuasion, reasoning can become interesting, as logically compelling arguments have a persuasive quality. Here intrinsic satisfaction in one activity can through internalisation lead to motivation for what had before seemed dry and pointless tasks. Once alerted to the ambiguities of interpretation and the varieties of valid and invalid reasoning, the 'rightness' of careful reading and sound reasoning becomes apparent and themselves provide motivation that is likely to improve performance elsewhere. This is not to suggest that close reading and an attention to argumentative form suddenly become intrinsically motivating (activities undertaken for their own sake). It is to suggest that if the student has a reason for valuing the activities, if the student cares whether they have read carefully and reasoned soundly, the satisfaction of doing something the student considers valuable will provide a motivational force.

It is not the 'what' of values we are concerned with here (although self-determination theory does posit that some values are more desirable than others) but why we value things (Sheldon et al. 2004). If students feel that the activities they are engaged in further their own valued purposes then they can call upon the emotional and motivational resources needed to overcome difficulties. If they feel useless (an attack on competence) or socially isolated (an attack on relatedness) or if they feel they have to comply with the demands of the institution (an attack upon autonomy), they risk becoming demotivated, alienated and unhappy. We have seen that in the United States this risk may have been realised, and there are worrying indications that in the United Kingdom, not just law school, but major features of our entire educational system are generating exactly the type of unintended consequences that self-determination theory warns us of.

Frankfurt insists upon the importance of what we care about, and identifies a sense of wholeheartedness that we feel when we are happy with our endorsed desires. Self-determination theorists started from an insight into the importance of why we feel we are doing things – for ourselves or for others. They too developed a concept of the person who is happy with what he desires, which they describe as self-concordance. Before we leave self-determination theory it is useful to reflect upon one more study in this tradition. Numerous studies have supported the proposition that teachers who provide support to their students' autonomy can have beneficial effects on the students (for example, see Reeve 2002). A recent study by Roth et al. (2007) investigated the relationship between the degree of autonomy felt by teachers in their work and the perceptions of the children they taught of how autonomy-supportive the teachers were. The research found that those teachers that felt more autonomous not only felt a greater sense of personal accomplishment and less exhaustion but were perceived by the children they taught as more supportive of the children's autonomy. Although it is but one study of 132 teachers in Israel, it confirms an intuitive feeling that the best teachers are those that enjoy the job, and self-determination theory tells us that we are likely to enjoy the job if we feel autonomous in our professional life.

Conclusion

Clearly good curriculum design cannot prevent depression. However, a well-designed curriculum enhances autonomy. A student (and also a teacher) who feels she is acting autonomously in her studies is likely to have higher subjective well-being and perform better academically. So if curricula are designed to enhance autonomy, we're all better off, and happier, and more productive.

Application of the insights to be gained from Frankfurt and the self-determination theorists does not demand a year zero approach to the curriculum. One final example of a small but significant change towards autonomous action was made in the coursework assessment for the final year option of the law of evidence. We started with a standard problem question concerning the cross-examination of a complainant in a rape case, where the facts were deliberately provocative, but the complainant's previous sexual history was borderline relevant. However, instead of asking for a traditional discussion of the question, students were asked to decide, as trial judge, on the admission of the evidence. Students repeatedly sought and received assurance that they could use the first person, and that provided the law relied on was stated clearly and accurately, there was no 'right' answer in respect of the decision to admit. More students got higher marks in that assessment than ever before; and of the six that got firsts, three admitted the previous history and three did not! We have now adopted this 'role-play' aspect as part of our formative and summative assessment practice. Students take on the role of first instance or appellate judges and practise in seminars where other roles may be played by counsel for the Crown and defence. The point of this is to develop students' competence and confidence and improve their autonomy as learners. Improved performance came from a change in the student standpoint. By role-playing and deciding from the perspective of a judge rather as a discursive academic exercise, the students found meaning in the assessment and they performed better.

As curriculum designers and deliverers of legal education our role is not to provide mass counselling. However, we can provide mass choice or alternatively insist upon uniformity. We can make room for students to share what they value or dismiss such discourse as irrelevant, and we can leave room for explorations of the young person's relationships to his family, class, profession, society and world, or not. Attention to affect in legal education does not entail any need to talk mildly and avoid offence to imagined sensibilities. Whilst we should not attempt to impose our value systems upon the student body, we are more serviceable to them if what we care about is reflected in what and how we teach. If we feel autonomous we are likely to enhance student autonomy. In practical terms it is not difficult to enhance choice for students, nor is there any externally irresistible reason to abjure value discourse in law schools. However, we are still struggling with the simple truth that what we care about determines both what we do and how we feel about it.

References

Amabile, T., DeJong, W. and Lepper M. 1976. Effects of Externally Imposed Deadlines on Subsequent Intrinsic Motivation, *Journal of Personality and Social Psychology* 34: 92–8.

Benjamin, G.A.H., Kaszniak, A., Sales, B. and Shanfield, S.B. 1986. The Role of Legal Education in Producing Psychological Distress among Law Students and Lawyers, *American Bar Foundation Research Journal* 225–52.

Biggs, J. 2003. *Teaching for Quality Learning at University*. 2nd edition. Maidenhead: Open University Press.

Daicoff, S.S. 1997. Lawyer Know Thyself: A Review of Empirical Research on Attorney Attributes Bearing on Professionalism, *American University Law Review* 46, 1337–427.

Daicoff, S.S. 2002. *Lawyer Know Thyself: A Psychological Analysis of Personality Strengths and Weaknesses*. Washington, DC: American Psychological Association.

Damasio, A. 2006. *Descartes' Error*. London: Vintage Books.

Deci, E.L. 1971. Effects of Externally Mediated Rewards on Intrinsic Motivation, *Journal of Personality and Social Psychology* 18: 105–15.

Deci, E.L., Koestner, R. and Ryan, R.M. 1999a. A Meta-Analytic Review of Experiments Examining the Effects of Extrinsic Rewards on Intrinsic Motivation, *Psychological Bulletin* 125: 627–68.

Deci, E.L., Koestner, R. and Ryan, R.M. 1999b. The Undermining Effect is a Reality After All – Extrinsic Rewards, Task Interest, and Self Determination: Reply to Eisenberger, Pierce, and Cameron (1999) and Lepper, Henderlong, and Gingras (1999), *Psychological Bulletin* 125: 692–700.

Deci, E.L. and Ryan, R.M. 2002. *Handbook of Self-determination Research.* New York: University of Rochester Press, 3–33.

Dewey, J. 1895. Interest in Relation to Training of the Will, in *The Philosophy of John Dewey*, edited by J. McDermott. Chicago: University of Chicago Press, 421–42.

Enron, L.D. and Redmount, R. 1957. The Effect of Legal Education on Attitudes, *Journal of Legal Education* 9: 431–43.

Ferris, G. 2009. We Should Look to Legal Theory to Inform the Teaching of the Substantive Law, *Web Journal of Current Legal Issues 3*. Available at http://webjcli.ncl.ac.uk/2009/issue3/ferris3.html [accessed 28 June 2010].

Ferris, G. and Lunt, C. 2010. Law and Nature by David Delany, *Nottingham Law Journal* (19)2: 54–63.

Frankfurt, H.G. 1998. *The Importance of What We Care About.* Cambridge: Cambridge University Press.

Frankfurt, H.G. 1999. *Necessity, Volition, and Love.* Cambridge: Cambridge University Press.

Frankfurt, H.G. 2004. *The Reasons of Love.* Princeton: Princeton University Press.

Gardner, H. 2006. *The Development and Education of the Mind.* Abingdon: Routledge.

Hedegard, J. 1979. The Impact of Legal Education: An In-depth Examination of Career-relevant Interests, Attitudes, and Personality Traits among First Year Law Students, *American Bar Foundation Research Journal* 791–868.

Heins, M., Fahey, S.N. and Henderson, R.C. 1983. Law Students and Medical Students: A Comparison of Perceived Stress, *Journal of Legal Education* 33: 511–25.

Kasser, T. 2002. Sketches for a Self-determination Theory of Values, in *Handbook of Self-Determination Research*, edited by E.L. Deci and R.M. Ryan. New York: University of Rochester Press, 123–40.

Koestner, R. and Losier, G.L. 2002. Distinguishing Three Ways of Being Highly Motivated: A Closer Look at Introjection, Identification, and Intrinsic Motivation, in *Handbook of Self-Determination Research*, edited by E.L. Deci and R.M. Ryan. New York: University of Rochester Press, 101–21.

Kruglanski, A.W., Friedman, I. and Zeevi, G. 1971. The Effects of Extrinsic Incentive on Some Qualitative Aspects of Task Performance, *Journal of Personality* 39: 606–17.

Kruglanski, A.W., Riter, A., Amitai, A., Bath-Shevah, M., Shabtai, L. and Zaksh, D. 1975. Can Money Enhance Intrinsic Motivation? A Test of the Content-Consequence Hypothesis, *Journal of Personality and Social Psychology* 31: 744–50.

Lepper, M., Greene, D. and Nisbett, R. 1973. Undermining Children's Intrinsic Interest with Extrinsic Reward: A Test of the 'Overjustification' Hypothesis, *Journal of Personality and Social Psychology* 28: 129–37.

Lepper, M. and Greene, D. 1975. Turning Play into Work: Effects of Adult Surveillance and Extrinsic Rewards on Children's Intrinsic Motivation, *Journal of Personality and Social Research* 31: 479–86.

Popper, K. 2002. *The Poverty of Historicism*. London: Routledge.

Putnam, R.D. 2000. *Bowling Alone*. New York: Simon & Schuster.

Reeve, J. 2002. Self-determination Applied to Educational Settings, in *Handbook of Self-Determination Research*, edited by E.L. Deci and R.M. Ryan. New York: University of Rochester Press, 183–203.

Roth, G., Assor, A., Kanat-Maymon, Y. and Kaplan, H. 2007. Autonomous Motivation for Teaching: How Self-Determined Teaching May Lead to Self-determined Learning, *Journal of Educational Psychology* 99: 761–74.

Rubin, L.J. 1973. Schooling and Life, in *Facts and Feelings in the Classroom*, edited by L.J. Rubin. East Grinstead, UK: Ward Lock Educational.

Sandel, M.J. 2006. *Justice: A Journey in Moral Reasoning*. [Online] Available at: http://athome.harvard.edu/programs/jmr/ [accessed 9 July 2010].

Schiltz, P. 1999. On Being a Happy, Healthy, and Ethical Member of an Unhappy, Unhealthy, and Unethical Profession, *Vanderbilt Law Review* 52: 871–951.

Shanfield, S.B. and Benjamin, G.A.H. 1985. Psychiatric Distress in Law Students, *Journal of Legal Education* 35: 65–75.

Sheldon, K.M., Ryan R.M., Deci, E.L. and Kasser, T. 2004. The Independent Effects of Goal Contents and Motives on Well-being: It's Both What You Pursue and Why You Pursue It, *Personality and Social Psychology Bulletin* 30: 475–86.

Sheldon, K.M. and Krieger, L.S. 2004. Does Legal Education have Undermining Effects on Law Students? Evaluating Changes in Motivation, Values, and Well-Being, *Behavioural Sciences and the Law* 22: 261–86.

Sheldon, K.M. and Krieger, L.S. 2007. Understanding the Negative Effects of Legal Education on Law Students: A Longitudinal Test of Self-determination Theory, *Personality and Social Psychology Bulletin* 33: 883–97.

Solkoff, N. and Markowitz, J. 1967. Personality Characteristics of First-year Medical and Law Students, *Journal of Medical Education* 42: 195.

Solkoff, N. 1968. The Use of Personality and Attitude Tests in Predicting the Academic Success of Medical and Law Students, *Journal of Medical Education* 43: 1250.

Chapter 10
The Body in (E)motion: Thinking through Embodiment in Legal Education

Julian Webb

There is more reason in your body than in your best wisdom.

Friedrich Nietzsche, *Thus Spake Zarathustra*

The piano begins to play. Susannah stretches out her arm, rising and falling to the cadences of the music, tracing the pattern of the dance she has created and now performs for the camera. In the 'black space' rehearsal room, Hari, Joanne and Yasmeen are practising a short play they have written: an imagined trial scene set within the plot of Shakespeare's *Coriolanus.* They must perform it shortly in front of their tutors and peer group, and submit the script with a reflective evaluation of their performance as part of their coursework. In a seminar room in Taipei, a group of students are working under the supervision of the faculty's artist in residence, each focused on drawing the features of the person sitting opposite them. For this exercise there is one rule only – they must not look down at the paper as they draw. Eight months earlier, in the quad of the Old College in Edinburgh, a group of lecturers, oblivious to the curious gaze of the Sunday morning tourists, are intent on creating the experience of being the inanimate objects around them: a bicycle, one of the stone pillars, a decorative lamp post … .

One thing all these individuals have in common is that none of them are teaching or studying the performing or visual arts as such. Susannah is a medical student, part of the Out Of Our Heads project at Bristol University which encourages students to engage with medical issues through the creative arts, and formally assesses their output.[1] Hari and his friends[2] are a mix of law and English undergraduates, following a course called 'On Trial: Shakespeare and the Law', which is taught jointly by Carol Rutter and Paul Raffield at the University of Warwick, utilising the resources of the CAPITAL Centre.[3] The students and

1 Susannah McMahon, *A Dance Trapped in a Diseased Body*, online at www.outofourheads.net/oooh/handler.php?id=412.

2 Unlike Susannah, 'Hari' and friends are fictional identities; a representation of all or any of the students following this course.

3 The CAPITAL Centre (Creativity and Performance in Teaching and Learning) was established as a joint venture between Warwick and the Royal Shakespeare Company as

academics in Taipei and Edinburgh are also lawyers – though in both cases working on projects facilitated by visual and performing arts practitioners.[4]

So, why this interest in moving beyond the confines of traditional learning and teaching in the disciplines? What do we think can be gained from these kinds of experiences? To answer these questions, I intend to take us, briefly, through some of the problems that can be identified with conventional legal education approaches, to consider why higher learning has become detached from the body, to relocate emoting, feeling and thinking as processes that occur through the body, and to think through some of the implications of 'embodied' learning for legal education.

The Poverty of Learning Law: Once More without Feeling

If the 'taking … seriously' formulation hadn't become so overused, it would be tempting to subtitle this chapter 'taking feelings seriously', since that is pretty much what it is about. That we so often use the word 'feeling' or 'feelings' to describe our affective or emotional responses[5] to a situation is no coincidence. The presence of 'somatic markers' or a 'feeling of what happens' (Damasio 2000: 40–42) points to the strong connection between bodily feelings, emotions and learning.[6] Such markers aid future learning and decision-making by providing signals that direct us towards or away from different behaviours (Damasio 1994, 2000; Carter and Pasqualini 2004), and play a significant part in the further connection between emotion and reason. In short, an emphasis on feelings is consistent with an integrated and adequately complex view of learning that cannot be based on cognition simply understood as a process of *mind.*

Unfortunately this complex view of cognition exists largely beyond the realm of legal and, for that matter, much higher education. While some of us may worry that legal education has lost its soul (Watt 2006), most quite happily disregard the absence of a body. This, of course, is part of a larger issue, which is the tendency

part of the HEFCE Centres of Excellence in Teaching and Learning (CETLs) initiative. It includes two dedicated performance spaces as part of its resources on campus. See http://go.warwick.ac.uk/capital. In July 2010 the CAPITAL Centre will become part of Warwick's new Institute for the Advancement of Teaching and Learning.

4 In the latter case, as participants in the final conference and workshop in the Arts and Humanities Research Council project *Beyond Text in Legal Education*, organised by Zenon Bankowski and Maks Del Mar at Edinburgh – see http://www.law.ed.ac.uk/beyondtext/.

5 In this chapter I will tend to use affect and emotion largely as synonymous. Nevertheless I share the view of other writers that affect has increasingly become used, particularly in the social sciences and humanities, distinctively to stress the embodied, pre-linguistic and pre-personal location of affects as a 'different kind of intelligence about the world' – Thrift (2004: 60); see also Papoulias and Callard (2010).

6 It also follows that, at the risk of stating the obvious, the somatic is understood here as a unified mind–body experience.

of the law school to pay very little attention to the issues of affect and emotion more generally. Indeed, I am tempted to go further than that and suggest that the overriding sense of law school is of a place that is largely intolerant of affect. Students' emotional responses are closed down when we tell our students (directly or by implication) that their emotional responses to injustice don't 'count'. The repetitive tedium of much of the literature (look at the law textbook reviews on Amazon to see what many of our students think of them), and some of the teaching, only adds to this effect.

This doesn't of course exempt law school from having affective consequences, but it does mean that much of it is negative in affective terms. Law school has thus been variously described as 'at best sense without any sensibility' (Murphy 1990: 67); 'an institutionally managed trauma [that] gives birth to a **conforming** or believing **soul**' (Goodrich 1995: 901); 'a sausage factory', and an experience through which 'you lose some of your personality' (students quoted by Webb 1995: 193). It 'tells you that to become a lawyer means to forget your feelings, forget your community, most of all, if you are a woman, forget your experience' (Mackinnon 1987: 205).

I suspect this doesn't make law school a hugely happy place for us teachers either. Gerald Hess, a US law professor, sums up the emotional impact thus:

> In what now seems like another life, I taught second grade. Most of my second graders walked in the first day with new shoes, fresh crayons, and little backpacks. They were excited about school and eager to learn. From me they expected patience, wisdom, kindness, inspiration, and support. My number one goal was for them to leave second grade with those same feelings and expectations. Some of the third-grade teachers did not care much about my goal; they wanted students who understood the basic stuff in the second-grade curriculum, who conformed to elementary school norms, and who were ready to buckle down to do important third-grade work. Nevertheless, I was able to achieve my primary goal with most of my students.
>
> I now teach law school. My first-year students enter with new books, the latest computers, and big backpacks. Many of them have the same excitement and expectations as my second graders. When I allow myself to think about this, I conclude that my number one goal in my law school classes ought to be the same as for my second graders. But I don't think about this very often because I have failed so miserably at achieving this goal with law students. The law school experience systematically beats those feelings and expectations out of many of them. (Hess 2002: 75)

Although it is still a marginal interest, there is at least some evidence of a growing awareness of the role of emotion in the US legal education literature (e.g. Meltsner 1983; Harris and Shultz 1993; Silver 1999; Coleburn and Spring 2000; Hess 2002). That it has not received the same level of attention so far in the UK is, one suspects, in part because the dysfunctional impacts of law teaching are perhaps rather less severe and less obvious on this side of the Atlantic.[7] This does not, however, make the affective domain any less relevant.

The argument developed in this chapter takes as its starting point the assumption that emotion matters for at least three reasons:

1. A proper understanding of legal (or any other system of) reasoning 'requires us not just to allow emotions into the classroom, but to learn how to examine them, learn from them, and incorporate them into rational argument' (Harris and Shultz 1993: 1787).
2. A deep understanding of the context and dynamics of conflict resolution requires both an appreciation of the role of emotions in disputes and conflicts, and the capacity to deal appropriately with those emotions (see Coleburn and Spring 2000; Ryan 2005).[8]
3. If legal education is to function effectively as a humane and liberal education, it needs to give students space consciously to undertake a reasonable level of 'self-work': that is, the development of greater self-awareness, and the social skills and capacities often associated with discourses of 'being' and 'becoming' (Batchelor 2006; Webb 2002).

A focus on these three aspects of legal learning is integral to any claims that a legal education may be transformative as well as informative. Where this chapter attempts to go beyond the arguments made by most earlier writers looking at affect and emotion in legal education is to suggest that taking these things seriously obliges us to address far more concretely the role of the body as a critical site of and context for learning; or, to put it in other words, to acknowledge that learning law is an actively *embodied* process.

Dancing on the Mind:[9] Why Mind/Body Dualism and Objectivism Don't 'Work'

To understand why much Western (legal) education has paid so little attention to embodiment, we need to move into some quite difficult conceptual territory and be aware of the impact of two shibboleths within the Western rationalist tradition:

---

7 The evidence indicates that US legal education, with its extensive reliance on the Socratic method, has substantial negative consequences for students' physical and psychological well-being and their sense of self. A useful summary of much the research is found in Dammeyer and Nunez (1999) and Krieger (2002). For evidence that this is not just a US phenomenon, see Kelk et al. (2009).

8 There is also a particularly strong linkage being developed between the need for emotional literacy/intelligence among lawyers and the rise of so-called 'therapeutic jurisprudence': see, e.g. Gould and Perlin (2001); King (2008).

9 'It is discouraging to try to penetrate a mind like yours. You ought to get it out and

the tendency to separate the body from the mind, and to assume that the world is as it is and can be viewed or explained independently of embodied understanding.

Dualism

'Mind/body dualism' as the name suggests sees the mental and the physical as different, albeit connected, realms. The distinction may be defined as a difference in the properties or *qualia* of mind vs body, what Daniel Dennett (1993: 29) calls 'mind stuff', or, in the stronger versions of dualism, in the belief that the thing 'mind' in and of itself is intrinsically different from another thing called 'body'. Dualism is often typified by reference to Cartesianism, though in fact it is a view that has dominated Western thought from at least the time of the ancient Greeks to Kant. Nevertheless the Cartesian position offers a useful and historically significant ideal type. To put it briefly: for Descartes (1989) the mind is the site of consciousness and the seat of reason. It is largely opposed by the body, which acts as an external force which must be controlled if I am to think clearly and act according to reason. The Cartesian emotions are a state of consciousness, but they are largely determined by feelings – bodily forces that constantly challenge our capacity to think and act rationally.

This may all sound both intuitively very plausible (not least because it is an explanation we have become used to), and rather abstract, until we recognise some of the core problems created by certain interpretations and conclusions of dualism. First, although dualism was certainly on to something in conceptualising mind as distinct in some way from brain, it went too far. Logically, dualism doesn't just separate everything inside the head from the rest of the body, rather it requires us to believe that there really is some kind of ghost in the machine, separate from the matter and impulses that make up the brain, and, moreover, that this property or thing we call 'mind' is non-physical. This, of course, 'elevates' phenomena like mind and consciousness to the status of the metaphysical – things that occupy no space at all, and, by implication, are not necessarily constrained by the limits of the physical world. The metaphysical nature of mind has increasingly been challenged, not just by philosophers such as Ryle (2003), but by a growing body of neuroscientific evidence that has demonstrated the ways in which mind is in and of the brain, even in the context of events, such as out-of-body experience (Ehrsson 2007; Lenggenhager et al. 2007), which seem to demonstrate mind at its most free-ranging.[10]

---

dance on it. That would take some of the rigidity out of it'. Mark Twain in Twain and Paine (2003: 182).

10 Lenggenhager et al. (2007) thus report an experiment during which a volunteer would be filmed from behind, and the video image of their body projected onto a head-mounted display that they were wearing. The experimenters would then stroke the volunteer's back, an action the volunteer could see being performed to their virtual body. The multisensory conflict this caused induced in many respondents an experience of

Secondly, dualism is also problematic insofar as it appears to support the view that there can be an independent realm of cognitive activity. This is really a very old idea. As we have seen, reason has long been separated from 'the passions' and frequently elevated above them. However, the cognitive and affective domains are not really so distinct. Cognition involves a variety of processes: what we traditionally think of as cognitive work – the cool, rational, thinking through a problem, and a much more immediate, 'gut-feeling' response to a situation – what Paul Thagard (2006) evocatively calls 'hot thought'. Which predominates? The answer is essentially the latter. Does that make us intrinsically bad decision-makers? Not at all. Evocative though it is, Thagard's imagery is (if taken purely at face value) misleading. When we think of decisions shaped by affect or emotion, there is a risk that we over-dramatise, and focus on those occasions when decisions are shaped by strong emotion – anger, fear, great sorrow, etc., whereas many affects are far more subtle. In many situations, including application of expert knowledge and experience, and in understanding or empathising with the mental states of others, we rely extensively on automatic, habitual or 'tacit' understanding and heuristics (see, e.g. Preston and de Waal 2002; Todd 2001; Reay 2010). In other words, we are working with a knowledge of the world that has become unconscious and effectively embodied in a feeling of what happens. Although they are beyond our conscious control, and certainly can lead us astray, affective and emotional responses are not therefore simply an inferior form of reasoning. In biological terms they are a high-level adaptation, involving complex chemical and neural responses to stimuli. Damasio (1994) clearly demonstrates that individuals who have sustained injury to the prefrontal and somatosensory cortices of the brain, not only have a diminished capacity to experience emotion, but are much less able as a result to make intelligent practical decisions. Whether based on the 'yuck factor' (Shakespeare 2008), on deeply embedded cultural norms and tacit understandings, or on evolutionary imperatives (Todd 2001; Fehr and Fischbacher 2003), feelings and emotions are shaped to protect, and to increase our chances of survival. As Fessler observes:

> In sum, evolution appears to have patterned decision making, and hence behaviour, by shaping eliciting conditions, cognitive consequences, action tendencies, hedonic values, and biasing effects of specific emotions. (Fessler 2001: 193)

Coleburn and Spring (2000: 23) likewise make the point that '[a]lthough feelings can impair the quality of reasoning, their lack is also an impairment, and nothing resembling so-called pure reason is met in human life except in cases of serious pathology'. The corollary to this, the extent to which reason works as

---

the 'self' moving outside their bodily borders and towards the virtual body. The authors concluded that their results indicated that spatial unity and bodily self-consciousness are based on multisensory and cognitive processing of bodily information.

an exercise in 'post-hoc rationalisation', is something that is increasingly being acknowledged in the literature, particularly as regards moral judgement (Haidt 2001, 2002; Prinz 2007).

Lastly, and related to the above, dualism has also tended to treat cognition as a purely internal, 'in the head', process. That cognition might be in part an external process is, at first glance, probably the most culturally counterintuitive of my suggestions, not least because it does seem to question the extent to which mind really is 'brainbound' (Clark 2008). Within the literatures of philosophy of mind and cognitive science, this has become an important, and in some respects hotly contested, topic.[11] Fortunately it is a debate that doesn't have to detain us here for long. The underlying idea that, functionally, the mind and its environment operate as a single causal process is not particularly contentious, and serves as an established tenet of a wide spectrum of theories of 'situated' and 'embodied' cognition (see Robbins and Aydede 2009). One doesn't have to think about it for long to see that this makes, even intuitively, a great deal of sense. For example, I am acutely conscious as I write this that working on a paper is not a purely mental process. It's not just happening in my head. The act of typing itself becomes part of the thought process, not a mere adjunct to it. I move around my study, and around the house, as I try to work out the implications of something I've just read. I sometimes (quite quietly!) verbalise sentences as I write, hearing and 'feeling' the fit and rhythm of the language to the ideas I want to express. Occasionally I even catch myself gesturing as I talk through an idea in my head.[12]

The conclusion is that dualism does not provide an adequately complex or sufficiently plausible account of how mind and body work together. As always the language and metaphors we use are telling; it is perhaps no coincidence that in ancient Greek *psyche* meant not only mind, but breath and blood (Damasio 2000: 30). Even in the academic world the body is never far removed from scholarship and the life of the mind – we commonly talk about the *subject* of study, a *body* of work, or the *corpus* of knowledge. In more everyday contexts we want to get the *feel* for a problem, be *walked through* a process. To understand another person we need to *get under their skin*, or *inside their heads*, or even *walk around in their shoes*.

---

11 For anyone interested in further understanding the disputed territory between 'intra' and 'transcranialists', c.p. Clark and Chalmers (1998), and Clark (2008) with Adams and Aizawa (2009: 78–95). The more radical formulation of the externalist viewpoint, which seems to regard cognition more as an emergent property of brain, body and environment, invites interesting comparisons with Gregory Bateson's earlier conception of an 'ecology of mind' – see Bateson (1972, 2002).

12 There is already research on gesturing which suggests it is dynamically connected to certain thinking processes. For an overview see Roth (2001).

Objectivism

Modern legal education also tends to draw substantially upon a traditional objectivist epistemology. Objectivism[13] can be understood as the possibility of taking what is sometimes called a 'God's-eye-view' of the world. This assumes that it is possible to identify a single rational structure of reality that exists independently of any individual's beliefs, and that right reason will mirror that structure. Objectivism thus involves, strictly, both an ontological and a set of epistemological claims: first that there is a single real world, and secondly that this world can be perceived objectively and described in concepts that correspond to that reality in a clear, universal and context-independent fashion. For present purposes we need not be particularly worried by the ontological claim. Whether or not there is a real world out there that might be capable of objective description, or whether we are really brains in vats/bodies plugged into *The Matrix*, is not a question I intend to lose sleep over here. But the educational consequences of an epistemological objectivism are a rather bigger deal.

The goal of learning in objectivist terms is to enable the acquisition of knowledge and understanding of the world as it really is, that is, in a way that distinguishes the 'essence' of phenomena from our embodied experience and cultural perceptions of them (see Johnson 1987; Varela et al. 1993). Objectivism acknowledges that people have conflicting understandings and beliefs about the world based on differing experiences, but it treats such beliefs as the outcome of the distorting effects of emotion, prejudice, personal bias, and so on. This view obviously has implications for higher education. Learning thus has to build on research that gives a proper account of reality, an account that can only be derived via rigorous application of scientific method and the proper use of logic. Moreover, according to the objectivist standpoint, since knowledge exists independently of instruction, it can be assessed both objectively and independently of that process of instruction. However, in these processes, objectivism may actually reinforce the naïve epistemological starting point that many undergraduates bring to their higher education: namely a dualistic right-wrong mental model which assumes 'right answer exists somewhere for every problem, and authorities know them. Right answers are to be memorized by hard work' (Perry 1981: 79).

The objectivist position has been extensively questioned across the disciplines of philosophy and social and educational theory. Philosophical challenges include the work of diverse thinkers including Dewey and the later pragmatists,[14] the philosopher of science Michael Polanyi (1958), phenomenologists such as Husserl (1970) and Merleau-Ponty (1962), and feminist theorists including Luce Irigary (1996, 2002). In social theory, the attack on objectivism has been carried on by

13 Used in this proper philosophical sense the term is not to be confused with 'objectivism' as the libertarian ideology developed by Ayn Rand.

14 See, e.g. Richard Rorty's claim that 'knowledge is not a matter of getting it right but rather acquiring habits of action for coping with reality' (Rorty 1991: 1).

writers including the prominent social constructionists Berger and Luckmann (1966), who largely reframed the sociology of knowledge, as understanding the processes by which persons actively make sense of their lives and thereby construct a social reality, and later constructionists such as Bruno Latour (1993, 2005), who sees social life as constructed out of a complex interplay of networks comprising features of the physical, biological and cultural worlds. In educational theory, a number of these critiques have come together as part of the assemblage of ideas (rather confusingly) referred to as 'constructivism', which is worth exploring in a little more depth.

The constructivist view treats learning as an active process of personalised knowledge-making, derived from the learner's 'reconstruction' (Dewey 1973) of experience. Constructivists emphasise learning through 'cognitive apprenticeship' (see, e.g. Collins et al. 1989), a process of collaboration in adequately complex real-world problem-solving. Rather than starting with a pre-defined, externalised body of knowledge, constructivism starts with the person and the problem as 'a stimulus for authentic activity' (Duffy and Cunningham 1996: sec. 7.5). Thus, three things can be seen as central to constructivist design principles. First, learning must be grounded in experience (see Barton et al. 2007). In Lave and Wenger's (1991) terminology, learning takes place and needs to be understood in the context of a 'community of practice' which embodies a set of beliefs and behaviours that learners need to acquire in order to participate effectively in that community. Secondly, there is an emphasis on authenticity: the best learning activities are those that involve complex or ill-defined problems that are of real-world relevance and require deep and sustained exploration. Thirdly, not just 'knowledge', but educational design is an emergent outcome of situated action learning (Suchman 1987: 67).

From a constructivist point of view a purely objectivist approach, of itself, limits the potential for meaningful learning. Objectivism tends to decontextualise knowledge, separating it from the practices to which it belongs and in which it originates. It is neither situated nor authentic. In most traditional learning environments knowledge precedes and is independent of action. The questions of how, where and when particular knowledge is to be used tend to be hived off into the area of 'practice'. The result is a silo effect that separates knowledge from questions (including ethical questions – see, e.g. Granfield 1998) about its use; that divides knowledge from skills, and distinguishes critical *thinking* from critical *being* (Barnett 1997: 1). By privileging the knowledge over the learner, objectivism potentially disempowers learners and reinforces the authority of the teacher. Moreover, it also follows that the social consequences of objectivism tend to be elitist and serve those who already have status and exercise power in academia and the professions. Julie Macfarlane (1992: 300), for example, has thus argued in the legal context, that an objectivist epistemology 'secures the position of [academic] experts … [and is] implicit in the idea of a cherished and highly specialist knowledge-base "possessed" by a profession', and that objective knowledge-based assessment also 'favours those who have been educated in a manner which has effectively groomed them for the university experience'.

In conclusion, then, as Mark Johnson (2006: 46) has observed, '[t]o live in our culture is to unwittingly soak up the metaphysical mind/body dualism that pervades our commonsense views of cognition, knowledge, language and values'. Yet, as this all too brief analysis and critique has sought to demonstrate, there are multiple reasons for questioning the dualist-objectivist stance. In educational terms there is thus a case, and I would argue that it is a strong case, for at least supplementing the traditional rationalist approach to learning, or, perhaps better still, reframing it within a far more experiential and embodied approach that discourages the separation of personal, affective, responses from academic and professional life. So what might such an approach look like?

Thinking through the Body: Some Implications of Embodied Learning for Legal Education

Changing Curriculum: The Body as an Object and Con-text of Law

Even if the body has been largely absent from pedagogy, it has at least started to gain a place in the curriculum. This I suggest serves as a useful precursor to taking the body more seriously in legal pedagogy – as a minimum it serves to make the body visible and acceptable as a proper subject (or at least object) of legal discourse.

The body is in fact central to understanding the operation of law. In Michel de Certeau's words (1984: 139), 'a body is itself defined, delimited, and articulated by what writes it. There is no law that is not inscribed on bodies'. This is reflected in a growing body – no pun intended – of scholarship which focuses on how corporeality is made to signify in law, for example, in constructing the sexed or racial specificity of the legal subject (see e.g. Bridgman and Millns 1995; Hyde 1997), or by examining ways in which touch shapes law's objects and limits (Grabham 2009).

The deconstructive treatment of the body-as-text has usefully served to highlight and denaturalise the place of the body in law. But there also seems to be a danger here, in that Foucauldian and Lacanian discursive legacies have perhaps gone too far, to have reduced the body to the status of just another signifier:[15] one of a number of sites on which law is inscribed. This idea of the body as a blank surface to be written upon, or, indeed, of the body itself as a *con*-text, something that acts or exists only with(in) the text of law is ultimately reductive and phenomenologically troubling. As Susannah's dance reminds us, illness brings us face to face with the experience of living with the (diseased) body, rather than

15 C.p. Simon Williams' charting of the retreat from 'biophysical reality' within medical sociology in Williams (2006: 7).

just the medical discourses surrounding that body. Likewise, understanding the relationship between the law and the body surely calls us to engage more directly with the body-as-flesh – flesh shaped by law and flesh that shapes law. This view, in short, requires us to think again about the nature of legal acts and legal actors. Once we begin to think affectively about law, that is, thinking *through the body*, rather than solely with the mind, we may – perhaps must – conceive of law and legal relations in quite different ways.

First, thinking through the body, even more than thinking about the body, forces us to consider the ways in which legal decision-making is shaped affectively. In criminal law, for example:

> The rational decision at each level – whether to arrest, to prosecute, to find guilty, and how to sentence – is connected to an affective response. It becomes crucial, therefore, to understand more about authorities' affective responses to charged issues such as rape, child abuse and wife-assault. We need to know more about how to shift those responses, and we need to try to find out whether the responses are correlated with gender, such that a more gender-balanced judiciary might more reliably generate optimal affective responses. (Nedelsky 1997: 105)

Taking affect seriously might encourage us to ask alternative questions about, and take different approaches to, the apparent failures of rationality that we see in the courts and legal process. For example, does it make more 'sense' of a judge's inability to see something wrong in describing a three-year-old as 'sexually aggressive' (Nedelsky 1997: 103) or suggesting that women who dress 'provocatively' are asking to be raped,[16] if that failure is recognised as affective rather than cognitive? What does the fact that the necessary somatic markers seem to be missing tell us about the potential gaps in our education system, in professional training, and broader social attitudes, and what we might do about that?[17]

Secondly, as Nedelsky (1997: 103) also argues, engaging with the body in law itself requires us to think about difference. Ngaire Naffine observes in a similar vein that:

> True legal actors … are healthy, self sufficient, rational, adult men who are relating to one another at arm's length … The legal actor, they say, is rarely thought of as a suckling baby or a woman giving suck; he is not the frail aged,

16 See, e.g. the outcry caused by Judge Julian Hall, who in sentencing an offender to two years' imprisonment in 2007 for the 'statutory rape' of a 10-year-old girl took account of the fact not only that she looked 16, but 'dressed provocatively' – see http://news.bbc.co.uk/1/hi/uk/6237480.stm.

17 C.p. Temkin and Krahé (2008), who argue that better education about sexual aggression and rape myths can make a difference, and suggest, *inter alia*, making rape education an explicit element of personal, social and health education (PSHE) for 14–16-year-olds, and implementing proper training and guidance for teachers.

> the heavily dependent on the good offices of others … This is not to say that the dependent young and old do not find their way into law and receive law's protection. But they tend to be treated as abnormal, not as typical. They are special or diminished cases of legal persons … (Naffine 2009: 158–9)

A focus on the embodied person, in all her different guises, can thus powerfully expose the ways in which law is partial and unequal in its treatment of those who do not fit its mythic, ideal type of the 'rational', able-bodied male. This in turn enables us to ask important questions about how well law fulfils its espoused purposes (Naffine 2009: 182–4).

Thinking Somatically

Our failure to engage with embodied cognition leaves us operating in a culture that not only teaches students to distrust their feelings, but also does not assist them to recognise when an affective response, or the very tacitness of their knowing, will itself create barriers to communication and insulate knowledge from critical reflection and evaluation. By contrast, if we start from the supposition that thinking is embodied, we can begin to see ways in which the learning process can be enhanced by a more conscious recognition of its somatic character. This is not just an issue of how we teach, but what we teach (and teach with). It is about constructing an affective interface between curriculum and pedagogy. Again, I will offer just a couple of pointers as to what might be achieved.

First, thinking somatically would not only support students to develop their communication and emotional intelligence 'skills', but would also help them achieve 'better' reasoning about legal outcomes. For example, instead of beginning a debate about some aspect of legal policy from the perspective of theory, or an analysis of what the law is, we could use a form of problem-based learning by beginning with a comparison of experiences. This could draw on textual, auditory or visual sources that are sufficiently powerful to generate a somatic response[18] – or, better still, multiple and conflicting somatic responses – that must then be synthesised into a workable solution. The diverse social and cultural backgrounds of our students can also be utilised in this context, albeit with care, to highlight affective differences and denaturalise a given point of view.

Secondly, I would suggest that a greater focus on thinking somatically in legal education has the potential to refocus students' attention, at least to a degree, from simply knowing about the law in an intellectual way to actively caring about what they are learning, and its consequences. This, I have previously argued, is a significant aspect missing from legal education (Webb 2006). A more holistic, or 'ecological', approach to learning should not stop at the level of knowing what, how or why the law is as it is, or even why, technically, it should be otherwise.

---

18 Elspeth Probyn (2004), for example, talks about the value of texts that are 'goose bumpy', a useful metaphor for the kind of affects we are talking about.

Students need to *care* about how and why it is, and why it could – or should – be different. An experience that generates or 'amplifies' (Probyn 2004: 26) an affective response is more likely to engender deep learning: 'emotions command attention and facilitate memory' (Prinz 2007: 305). This can be powerfully achieved, for example, within experiential and clinical forms of learning, as the following reflection from Cindy Nguyen, a clinic intern working with a domestic abuse victim, demonstrates:

> I do not want to be stripped of the power, stripped of the right, to do something. I want to be armed with the knowledge of the right, armed with the knowledge, that not only do I know something, but that I have the right, indeed, I have the obligation to help someone when no one else was willing. At that moment, I not only wanted justice, I wanted retribution. A moment's reflection reminded me that as a part of my summer internship, I was not there to deliver retribution. A second moment's reflection told me that I was not even there to deliver justice. I was but a meager volunteer working in a legal clinic for a summer. What could I do? Yet what could I not do? At that moment while I was writing the woman's declaration, I had never felt so powerless in all my life. What was a college education worth when others were helplessly standing there being victimized by the very persons who presumably love them? As powerless as I may have felt at that moment, my client assured me that I could never truly grasp the emotional impact that this incident had on her. Although I was powerless, she was voiceless. I felt powerless because I felt that I had no capability through which to help her. But she felt voiceless because she did not possess any medium through which protest could even be heard, let alone acted upon. A person's life is fragile, and a person's dignity is no less important. To truly believe in human rights, I had to believe in the human being beneath. It was not that my own personal aspirations in the legal field were categorically ascertained at this moment. On the contrary, my aspirations took a rather hard beating. I understood the meaning behind assisting these victims of domestic violence to seek shelter and protection through legal means. However, it was as if working on the restraining order aspect of the problem was like treating the symptoms of the problem, not the actual source of the problem. For a while after the internship ended, I was paradoxically disillusioned and empowered. I questioned whether I could really make a difference, and the equivocal answer that I got from myself and from my internship compelled me to seek an answer. (Nguyen 2005)

It is significant that it was Nguyen's affective response that triggered her reflection and learning. It was the experience of her own feeling of loss of power that led her to empathise with her client's powerlessness, to identify with the 'human being beneath' the legal problem, and thereby connect with her own commitment to making a difference. It is fostering and maintaining that connection to another human being that seems to me to be essential if we are to enable students to understand that 'law schools are not just places to play with rules' (Economides

1999: 413), but places that encourage genuinely moral thought and the capacity for moral action that underpins a *humane* professionalism (Arthurs 1983; Webb 2006).

Using Performance: Beyond Mimesis and the Mirror of Nature

It is widely recognised that higher education has become increasingly focused on the performative – on what both students and teachers are able to do. Current concerns about UK higher education quality can be seen as a particular instance of this performative agenda. There is, perhaps, a danger that we respond to these debates, and the demand for better teaching, by further reifying a teacher-centred model of learning, and teacher-led curriculum. While I am not suggesting that teaching quality is a non-issue, there is a risk that, in focusing attention on teacher rather than student performance, we address the problem from the wrong angle. As Kirkpatrick and Thorpe (2000) found in the early days of the Australian teaching awards, good teaching was often exemplified by performances in which powerful and confident teachers produced 'spectacle' for resistant and relatively passive students. By contrast, I want to focus on student-centred processes that involve both less (conventional) teaching, and better *learning*.

To do this it helps to go back to constructivism. For Lave and Wenger (1991), appreciating the situated and embodied character of learning is at the heart of their distinction between a learning and a teaching curriculum. While the latter offers learning that is 'mediated through an instructor's participation, by an external view of what knowing is about', the former provides an environment for the 'improvisational development of new practices' (Lave and Wenger 1991: 97).

The embedding of 'real' experiences, simulation and performance in educational processes is central to creating a situated learning environment, as it provides a basis for authentic, embodied, learning. Authenticity may thus be something of a double-edged sword for a higher education that is largely independent of the world of practice, meaning that education can offer little more than a kind of *mimesis* (Barton et al. 2007: 146–8) – an imitation or representation of reality. Personally, I do not find this a strong objection. Authenticity, in this sense, seems to be a bit of a red herring. I suggest it sets the bar too high by reifying a particular reality of practice,[19] but also, paradoxically perhaps, thereby

19 Barton et al. (2007) also question the possibility and desirability of mimesis. I agree, but in doing so I would possibly go further than them in questioning the very possibility of objectively describing a 'world of practice' as such. My reasons for saying this are quite complicated and, though the argument is rooted in the rejection of classical objectivism, it is something of a side issue for this chapter. To summarise the objection briefly, I follow Bateson (1972) in arguing that we can never wholly capture the *ding an sich* of and for itself. Consequently, any attempt to essentialise or objectify a practice, even within its own environment, delivers no more than a representation of that practice. In other words, even if we try to create models and simulations that seem to demonstrate goodness of fit with the observed world, we are still only creating representations (or more properly

sets it too low to deliver the more transformative aims of a higher education. Phenomenologically, I suggest that authenticity needs to be more about exploring potentiality than uncovering actuality. It needs to lead us into Barnett's realm of being, into questions about the possibility for ourselves and our discipline. If legal education is to be transformative, it needs to be about the imaginative creation of possible worlds of law and justice. This kind of authenticity, I suggest, requires two things.

First, it is not enough for legal education simply to 'hold the mirror up to nature', where nature is defined by the parameters of current practice. What we do must be more than a 'rite of reproduction', as Goodrich (1995) has called it. This is not to say that simulation, and clinic, in particular, cannot take on that role, though I suggest the clinical movement has often encountered tensions between its reproductive and transformative aims (see Nicolson 2006; Webb 1999: 295). That said, the best clinical work is capable of making a difference for students as well as clients. 'Clinics encourage a depth of experience that promotes a structural analysis of injustice' (Evans 2008: 333). They can build strong affective commitments in students, and the belief that, sometimes at least, 'the best lawyer is someone who wants to change the law' (student quoted in Webb 1995: 209). Moreover, the rate of advance in virtual environments suggests that some of the greatest potential for transformation may lie in virtual rather than real-world simulations, using 'immersive' learning experiences rather than traditional modes of knowledge transfer (see e.g. de Freitas et al. 2010; Maharg 2007). New-generation immersive games, such as *Fahrenheit* (2005; see Lessard 2009) and *Heavy Rain* (2010) continue to narrow the gap between gaming and film, offering not just increasingly sophisticated levels of interactivity, but a degree of characterisation and plotting that offers emotional depth, and even an element of moral complexity.[20] Sophisticated games can deservedly be regarded as somatic experiences (Tavinor 2005; Nielson 2010), and their educational potential is, I would suggest, enormous.

Secondly, we could do more to explore the potential for other kinds of performance-based learning. It has been said that 'the best judge is one who embraces poetry'[21] – and perhaps we should add playwriting, or painting, or drama, or dance to the list. As I have sought to show throughout this chapter, (embodied) emotions shape much of our daily lives, and exploration of the literary and creative arts has the power to open up and make us more aware of this 'faculty of sensibility' (Ward 2009: 102). The physical engagement of the body can, of

representations of representations) of reality. Ultimately, I don't see this as a problem; indeed, it helps to be aware of our limitations.

20 See for example the trailer to *Heavy Rain*, which markets the game with the strapline 'How far will you go to save someone you love?': http://www.youtube.com/watch?v=JKPPdgBK3r8&feature=related. Thanks to John Davison for drawing this game to my attention.

21 Ward (2009: 101), citing Martha Nussbaum.

itself, bring another level of understanding to academic work. Paul Raffield's courses at Warwick demonstrate how drama and playwriting can operate as powerful learning tools.[22] They enable students to engage with and understand law as a living, ethical, enterprise. Plays, when explored both as text and through performance, in Raffield's words, 'harness intellect to imagination and emotion'. Theatrical warm-up exercises and improvisation can also be used in this process of freeing up the imagination and fostering creativity, capacities which Raffield sees as central to developing students' potential as legal scholars.

Getting Social

Raffield's work draws heavily on the notion of the 'ensemble'. The ensemble, which is also apparent in the paradigm of 'open-space learning' (OSL) being developed by the CAPITAL Centre,[23] serves as a secure but challenging learning environment. Raffield describes the ensemble as a 'mix of laboratory and playground'. 'Playing', he asserts, 'is at the heart of it all'. It is playing in ensemble that opens up the imaginative and ethical potential of the class. This fits with much established learning theory (c.p. Johnson et al. 2007; Matchett 2009), and exemplifies my final point: that an embodied approach to legal learning necessarily (re)constructs it as a social rather than solipsistic pursuit. Cooperative and collaborative forms of learning are powerful; students not only produce better knowledge outcomes than from individualistic and competitive approaches, they

22 The following comments draw on a workshop led by Paul Raffield and Carol Rutter at the CAPITAL Centre Colloquium on 'Creativity and Performance in Teaching and Learning', 19 September 2009, and, whilst preparing this chapter, a subsequent conversation with Paul Raffield in May 2010. My thanks to Paul for his time and generosity.

23 Nick Monk thus describes OSL as: 'an example of what might be recognised as the "workshop model" of teaching and learning. The workshop is the basic unit in pedagogic interaction between facilitator and participant in OSL. It is defined here as a teaching and learning session that takes place in an environment in which participants can engage actively with the learning materials that are that session's focus. Such materials might include text, but they might also include props, objects, and audio-visual materials. Participants work independently, or in small groups, with these materials in order to fashion or create their own knowledge. The workshop allows the participants to become the producers of knowledge. The space itself is fundamental in preventing the reformation of the rigidly hierarchical space of lecture theatre and seminar room. Each of the spaces used for OSL (the rehearsal room, the studio, the reinvention room) exists in its first incarnation "without chairs" which forces any group entering the spaces to address their own physicality in relation to that of the space – there is no longer the security and reassurance of traditionally arranged furniture. The spaces, therefore, are no more seminar rooms and lecture theatres, for the purposes of OSL pedagogy, than they are theatrical spaces. They exist in a space that is always "open", both figuratively and actually. What this permits is a particular freedom in which, if carefully managed by facilitator/tutor, individuals exist as neither performer nor passive listener, but full participant in the discovery and creation of knowledge' (Monk 2010).

become empowered as producers of knowledge, and, potentially, develop a deeper understanding of their own and others' agency. This last issue is the one I want to focus on here.

As we have seen, action is determined at least as much by feeling as by reason. Effective agency is shaped by our ability both to relate to others and to experience our environment in relation to ourselves, that is, as including our own bodily, affective, presence and capabilities. As Gibson (1979: 112) recognised, one of the hardest things for us to see is ourselves, restricting our view! Group learning can provide a two-way mirror. Looking out, we can observe and reflect on others' ways of being in the world, but in the processes of interaction, we are also commonly presented with challenges and insights to our own way of being. Effective groups are marked out by many of the values prized by liberal education: trust (Johnson et al. 2007), tolerance, empathy and a generosity of spirit (Carr 1991). By enabling our students to 'get social' in the classroom, to come together in a more structured and reflective way, group learning can actively support their social and moral development, and – maybe, just maybe – enhance their ability to become 'better' social actors.

Conclusions

This chapter has sought to provide a coherent theoretical explanation and justification of the need to take embodied emotion more seriously in legal education. Emotions matter because they are central to what makes us human and key to unlocking the transformative potential of law school. Drawing on the phenomenological tradition, this chapter has challenged classical dualist-objectivist thinking and its hold on education. It has offered a range of examples of how learning 'through the body' might be introduced into substantive curricula, and experientially through problem-based, clinical and performance-based pedagogies. None of these pedagogies are entirely new to legal education, but are presented here as an encouragement to think differently about them and to explore ways in which they can be used to engage effectively (and affectively) with the embodied nature of learning.

This is not to say that there aren't risks and challenges that need to be considered. Students and teachers may well be sceptical, though there is a growing awareness of the importance of 'emotional literacy' and creativity in both schools and the workplace, and so higher education could, equally, find itself out of synch. But there is also the risk that the economic imperatives driving those agendas will lead to an instrumentalised and reductive vision of affect, much as we saw with the skills agenda in the late 1980s and 1990s (c.p. Hartley 2003), and this is patently not what we need. The way in which academics, individually and collectively, engage with the affective domain will matter; it will make or mar, support or marginalise work on the affective domain. This work will be challenging for teachers, requiring different skills and new knowledge. As with all forms of experiential learning, the teacher is no longer the sole, authoritative, source of knowledge, though she continues to perform a key (and perhaps even more demanding) role in facilitating and holding the space in which learning can happen.

Nevertheless the potential is enormous. A more embodied legal education has the capacity to make learning not just more meaningful, but also more engaging, and, dare I say it, more humane, and maybe even more fun. Could we handle it? As Foucault rather playfully suggests, 'Imagine what would happen if people got into as big a frenzy about learning as they do about sex. Crowds shoving and pushing at school doors! It would be a complete social disaster'.[24] Now there's a prospect.

References

Adams, F. and Aizawa, K. 2009. Why the Mind is Still in the Head, in *The Cambridge Handbook of Situated Cognition*, edited by P. Robbins and M. Aydede. Cambridge: Cambridge University Press, 78–95.

Arthurs, H.W. 1983. *Law and Learning: Report of the Consultative Group on Research and Education in Law*. Ottawa: Social Sciences and Humanities Research Council of Canada.

Barnett, R. 1997. *Higher Education: A Critical Business.* Milton Keynes: Open University Press.

Barton, K., McKellar, P. and Maharg, P. 2007. Authentic Fictions: Simulation, Professionalism and Legal Learning, *Clinical Law Review* 14(1): 143–93.

Batchelor, D. 2006. Becoming What You Want to Be, *London Review of Education* 4(3): 225–38.

Bateson, G. 1972. *Steps to an Ecology of Mind.* Chicago: University of Chicago Press.

Bateson, G. 2002. *Mind and Nature: A Necessary Unity.* Cresskill, NJ: Hampton Press.

Berger, P.L. and Luckmann, T. 1966. *The Social Construction of Reality: A Treatise in the Sociology of Knowledge*. New York: Anchor Books.

Bridgman, J. and Millns, S. (eds) 1995. *Law and Body Politics: Regulating the Female Body.* Aldershot: Ashgate.

Carr, D. 1991. *Educating the Virtues.* London: Routledge.

Carter, S. and Pasqualini, M.C.S. 2004. Stronger Autonomic Response Accompanies Better Learning: A Test of Damasio's Somatic Marker Hypothesis, *Cognition & Emotion* 18(7): 901–11.

Clark, A. 2008. *Supersizing the Mind: Embodiment, Action and Cognitive Extension*. New York: Oxford University Press.

Clark, A. and Chalmers, D.J. 1998. The Extended Mind, *Analysis* 58(1): 10–23.

24 Cited in Probyn (2004: 35).

Coleburn, L.A. and Spring, J.C. 2000. Socrates Unbound: Developmental Perspectives on the Law School Experience, *Law and Psychology Review* 24: 5–38.

Collins, A., Brown, J.S. and Newman, S.E. 1989. Cognitive Apprenticeship: Teaching the Craft of Reading, Writing, and Mathematics, in *Knowing, Learning, and Instruction: Essays in Honor of Robert Glaser*, edited by L.B. Resnick, Hillsdale, NJ: Lawrence Erlbaum Associates, 453–94.

Damasio, A. 1994. *Descartes' Error: Emotion, Reason, and the Human Brain.* New York: G.P. Putnam.

Damasio, A. 2000. *The Feeling of What Happens: Body, Emotion and the Making of Consciousness*. London: Vintage.

Dammeyer, M.M. and Nunez, N. 1999. Anxiety and Depression among Law Students: Current Knowledge and Future Directions, *Law and Human Behavior* 23(1): 55–73.

de Certeau, M. 1984. *The Practice of Everyday Life*, trans. by S. Rendall. Berkeley, CA: University of California Press.

de Freitas, S., Rebolledo-Mendez, G., Liarokapis, F., Magoulas, G. and Poulovassilis, A. 2010. Learning as Immersive Experiences: Using the Four-dimensional Framework for Designing and Evaluating Immersive Learning Experiences in a Virtual World, *British Journal of Educational Technology* 41(1): 69–85.

Dennett, D.C. 1993. *Consciousness Explained.* London: Penguin Books.

Descartes, R. 1989. *The Passions of the Soul*, trans. by S. Voss. Indianapolis, IN: Hackett.

Dewey, J. 1973. My Pedagogic Creed, in *The Philosophy of John Dewey, vol. 2*, edited by J. McDermott. New York: G.P. Putnam.

Duffy, T. and Cunningham, D. 1996. Constructivism: Implications for the Design and Delivery of Instruction, in *Handbook of Research for Educational Communications and Technology*, edited by D.H. Jonassen, 1st edition. New York: Macmillan. [Online] Available at: www.aect.org/intranet/publications/edtech/07/index.html [accessed 5 June 2010].

Economides, K. 1999. Learning the Law of Lawyering, in *Current Legal Problems*, Vol. 52, edited by M.D.A. Freeman. Oxford: Oxford University Press, 392–418.

Ehrsson, H.H. 2007. The Experimental Induction of Out of Body Experiences, *Science* 317(5841): 1048.

Evans, A. 2008. Southern Exposure: Post-liberalism and Moral Recovery in Australian Legal Education, *Law Teacher* 42(3): 329–38.

Fehr, E. and Fischbacher, U. 2003. The Nature of Human Altruism, *Nature* 425(6960): 785–91.

Fessler, D.M.T. 2001. Emotions and Cost-benefit Assessment: The Role of Shame and Self-esteem in Risk Taking, in *Bounded Rationality: The Adaptive Toolkit*, edited by G. Gigerenzer and R. Selten. Cambridge, MA: MIT Press, 191–214.

Foster, J.C. 1981. The 'Cooling Out' of Law Students: Facilitating Market Cooptation of Future Lawyers, in *Governing Through Courts*, edited by R.A.L. Gambitta et al. Beverly Hills, CA: Sage, 177–90.

Gibson, J.J. 1979. *The Ecological Approach to Visual Perception.* Hillsdale, NJ: Lawrence Erlbaum Associates.

Goodrich, P. 1995. Twining's Tower: Metaphors of Distance and Histories of the English Law School, *University of Miami Law Review* 49: 901–16.

Gould, K.K. and Perlin, M.L. 2001. 'Johnny's in the Basement/Mixing up his Medicine': Therapeutic Jurisprudence and Clinical Teaching, *Seattle University Law Review* 24: 339–71.

Grabham, E. 2009. Shaking Mr Jones: Law and Touch, *International Journal of Law in Context* 5(4): 343–53.

Granfield, R. 1998. The Politics of Decontextualised Knowledge: Bringing Context into Ethics Instruction in Law School, in *Ethical Challenges to Legal Education and Conduct*, edited by K. Economides. Oxford: Hart, 299–314.

Haidt, J. 2001. The Emotional Dog and its Rational Tail: A Social Intuitionist Approach to Moral Judgment, *Psychological Review* 108(4): 814–34.

Haidt, J. 2002. 'Dialogue between my Head and my Heart': Affective Influences on Moral Judgment, *Psychological Inquiry* 13(1): 54–6.

Harris, A.P. and Shultz, M.M. 1993. A(nother) Critique of Pure Reason: Toward Civic Virtue in Legal Education, *Stanford Law Review* 45: 1773–1806.

Hartley, D. 2003. The Instrumentalisation of the Expressive, *British Journal of Educational Studies* 51(1): 6–19.

Hess, G.E. 2002. Heads and Hearts: The Teaching and Learning Environment in Law School, *Journal of Legal Education* 52(1–2): 75–111.

Husserl, E. 1970. *The Crisis of European Sciences and Transcendental Phenomenology*, trans. by D. Carr. Evanston, IL: Northwestern University Press.

Hyde, A. 1997. *Bodies of Law.* Princeton, NJ: Princeton University Press.

Irigary, L. 1996. *I Love to You: Sketch of a Felicity within History*, trans. by A. Martin. London: Routledge.

Irigary, L. 2002. *Between East and West: From Singularity to Community*, trans. by S. Pluháček. New York: Columbia University Press.

Johnson, D.W., Johnson, R.T. and Smith, K. 2007. The State of Cooperative Learning in Postsecondary and Professional Settings, *Educational Psychology Review* 19(1): 15–29.

Johnson, M. 1987. *The Body in the Mind: The Bodily Basis of Meaning, Imagination and Reason.* Chicago: University of Chicago Press.

Johnson, M. 2006. Mind Incarnate: From Dewey to Damasio, *Daedalus* 135(3): 46–54.

Kelk N.J., Luscombe, G.M., Medlow, S.D. and Hickie, I.B. 2009. Courting the Blues: Attitudes towards Depression in Australian Law Students and Legal Practitioners, *BMRI Monograph 2009-1* (Sydney: Brain & Mind Research Institute).

King, M.S. 2008. Restorative Justice, Therapeutic Jurisprudence and the Rise of Emotionally Intelligent Justice, *Melbourne University Law Review* 32(3): 1096. [Online] Available at: http://www.austlii.edu.au/au/journals/MULR/2008/34.html#Heading372 [accessed 2 July 2010].

Kirkpatrick, D. and Thorpe, S. 2000. Iconic (Pre)occupations, in *Taught Bodies*, edited by C. O'Farrell et al. New York: Lang, 165–80.

Krieger, L.S. 2002. Institutional Denial about the Dark Side of Law School, and Fresh Empirical Guidance for Breaking the Silence, *Journal of Legal Education* 52(1–2): 112–29.

Latour, B. 1993. *We Have Never Been Modern.* Hemel Hempstead: Harvester Wheatsheaf.

Latour, B. 2005. *Reassembling the Social: An Introduction to Actor-Network Theory*. Oxford: Oxford University Press.

Lave, J. and Wenger, E. 1991. *Situated Learning: Legitimate Peripheral Participation.* Cambridge: Cambridge University Press.

Lenggenhager, B., Tadi, T., Metzinger, T. and Blanke, O. 2007. *Video ergo sum:* Manipulating Bodily Self-consciousness, *Science* 317(5841): 1096–9.

Lessard, J. 2009. *Fahrenheit* and the Premature Burial of Interactive Movies, *Eludamos: Journal for Computer Game Culture* 3(2): 195–205.

Macfarlane, J. 1992. Look Before you Leap: Knowledge and Learning in Legal Skills Education, *Journal of Law & Society* 19(3): 293–319.

Mackinnon, C. 1987. *Feminism Unmodified.* Cambridge, MA: Harvard University Press.

Maharg, P. 2007. *Transforming Legal Education.* Aldershot: Ashgate.

Matchett, N.J. 2009. Cooperative Learning, Critical Thinking, and Character: Techniques to Cultivate Ethical Deliberation, *Public Integrity* 12(1): 25–38.

Meltsner, M. 1983. Feeling Like a Lawyer, *Journal of Legal Education* 33(4): 624–35.

Merleau-Ponty, M. 1962. *The Phenomenology of Perception*, trans. by C. Smith. London: Routledge and Kegan Paul.

Monk, N. 2010. *About Open-space Learning and the OSL Project*. [Online] Available at: http://www2.warwick.ac.uk/fac/cross_fac/capital/osl/repository/about [accessed 2 July 2010].

Murphy, W.T. 1990. Reference without Reality: A Comment on a Commentary on Codifications of Practice, *Law and Critique* 1(1–2): 61–79.

Naffine, N. 2009. *Law's Meaning of Life: Philosophy, Religion, Darwin and the Legal Person.* Oxford: Hart.

Nedelsky, J. 1997. Embodied Diversity and the Challenges of Law, *McGill Law Journal* 42(1): 91–117.

Nguyen, C. 2005. *Undergraduate Summer Fellows Report*. Yale Law School. [Online] Available at: www.law.yale.edu/intellectuallife/cindynguyen.htm [accessed 5 June 2010].

Nicolson, D. 2006. Legal Education or Community Service? The Extra-curricular Student Law Clinic, *Web Journal of Current Legal Issues.* [Online] Issue 3. Available at: http://webjcli.ncl.ac.uk/2006/issue3/nicolson3.html [accessed 2 July 2010].
Nielson, H.S. 2010. The Computer Game as a Somatic Experience, *Eludamos: Journal for Computer Game Culture* 4(1): 25–40.
Papoulias, C. and Callard, F. 2010. Biology's Gift: Interrogating the Turn to Affect, *Body & Society* 16(1): 29–56.
Perry, W.G., Jr. 1981. Cognitive and Ethical Growth: The Making of Meaning, in *The Modern American College*, edited by A.W. Chickering. San Francisco: Jossey-Bass, 76–116.
Polanyi, M. 1958. *Personal Knowledge: Towards a Post-critical Philosophy.* Chicago: University of Chicago Press.
Preston, S.D. and de Waal, F.B.M. 2002. Empathy: Its Ultimate and Proximate Bases, *Behavioural and Brain Science* 25(1): 1–71.
Prinz, J. 2007. *The Emotional Construction of Morals.* Oxford: Oxford University Press.
Probyn, E. 2004. Teaching Bodies: Affects in the Classroom, *Body & Society* 10(4): 21–43.
Reay, M. 2010. Knowledge Distribution, Embodiment and Insulation, *Sociological Theory* 28(1): 91–107.
Robbins, P. and Aydede, M. (eds) 2009. *The Cambridge Handbook of Situated Cognition.* Cambridge: Cambridge University Press.
Rorty, R. 1991. *Objectivity, Relativism, and Truth: Philosophical Papers, Vol. 1.* New York: Cambridge University Press.
Roth, W.-M. 2001. Gestures: Their Role in Teaching and Learning, *Review of Educational Research* 71(3): 365–92.
Ryan, E. 2005. The Discourse Beneath: Emotional Epistemology in Legal Deliberation and Negotiation, *Harvard Negotiation Law Review* 10(1): 231–85.
Ryle, G. 2003. *The Concept of Mind.* Chicago: University of Chicago Press.
Suchman, L.A. 1987. *Plans and Situated Action: The Problem of Human-machine Communication.* New York: Cambridge University Press.
Tavinor, G. 2005. Video Games, Fiction and Emotion, in *Second Australasian Conference on Interactive Entertainment*, edited by Y. Pisan. Sydney: Creativity and Cognition Studio Press, 201–7.
Temkin, J. and Krahé, B. 2008. *Sexual Assault and the Justice Gap: A Question of Attitude.* Oxford: Hart.
Shakespeare, T. 2008. Reason Special: A World Based on Reason, *New Scientist* 23 July. [Online] Available at: www.newscientist.com/article/dn14385-reason-special-a-world-based-on-reason-html [accessed 5 June 2010].
Silver, M. 1999. Emotional Intelligence and Legal Education, *Psychology, Public Policy & Law* 5(4): 1173–203.
Thagard, P. 2006. *Hot Thought: Mechanisms and Applications of Emotional Cognition.* Cambridge, MA: MIT Press.

Thrift, N. 2004. Intensities of Feeling: Towards a Spatial Politics of Affect, *Geografiska Annaler* 86B(1): 57–78.

Todd, P. 2001. Fast and Frugal Heuristics for Environmentally Bounded Minds, in *Bounded Rationality: The Adaptive Toolbox*, edited by G. Gigerenzer and R. Selten. Cambridge, MA: MIT Press, 51–70.

Twain, M. and Paine, A.B. 2003. *Mark Twain's Autobiography, Vol.1.* Whitefish, MT: Kessinger Publishing.

Varela, F.J., Thompson, E. and Rosch, E. 1993. *The Embodied Mind: Cognitive Science and Human Experience.* Cambridge, MA: MIT Press.

Ward, I. 2009. Legal Education and the Democratic Imagination, *Law and Humanities* 3(1): 87–112.

Watt, G. 2006. The Soul of Legal Education, *Web Journal of Current Legal Issues* [Online] Issue 3. Available at: http://webjcli.ncl.ac.uk/2006/issue3/watt3.html [accessed 5 June 2010].

Webb, J. 1995. Where the Action Is: Developing Artistry in Legal Education, *International Journal of the Legal Profession* 2(2/3): 187–216.

Webb, J. 1999. Developing Ethical Lawyers: Can Legal Education Enhance Access to Justice? *Law Teacher* 33(3): 284–97.

Webb, J. 2002. Being a Lawyer/Being a Human Being, *Legal Ethics* 5(1/2): 130–51.

Webb, J. 2006. The 'Ambitious Modesty' of Harry Arthur's Humane Professionalism, *Osgoode Hall Law Journal* 44(1): 119–55.

Williams, S. 2006. Medical Sociology and the Biological Body: Where are We Now and Where do We Go from Here? *Health* 10(1): 5–30.

Chapter 11

Developing Professional Character – Trust, Values and Learning

Karen Barton and Fiona Westwood

Introduction

Traditionally professional character was developed through a lengthy apprenticeship, with the new entrant to the profession learning knowledge, skills and behaviour through working alongside a 'master'.

The bifurcation of legal education into academic and vocational is well documented and researched. Most commentators feel that this has resulted in tensions between the theory of law and its application to real-life situations in practice. For example, 'professionalism' has come to mean adherence to a code of conduct that includes *inter alia* rules covering conflicts of interest, duties to the court and client confidentiality. Inevitably, this is reflected in how the subject of professional ethics, for example, is handled within legal education curricula in the UK, with its emphasis on the content of practice rules over the development of attributes such as 'moral character' (Nicolson 2008). This results in a cognitive approach, similar to that touched on briefly by Eraut (1994: 205) when he talks about a 'sense of commitment to the code of conduct at the time of qualification' in relation to his discussion on the assessment of competence in the professions and in particular in handling competence in ethical issues. In this chapter we wish to move beyond this into looking closely at the role that affect plays in the development of professional character and suggest one way in which this interplay can be more effectively promoted and developed. This point of the importance of developing professional character has been discussed most recently in the Economides and Rogers report, where they comment, '[m]ore might be done to encourage and motivate good behaviour' (2009: 59).

To develop this concept of professional character, we feel that it is important in this introduction to define it specifically and set it in the context of the affective domain. Following Bloom's (1956) *Taxonomy of Educational Objectives*, which established the now familiar hierarchy of cognitive processes referred to frequently in the design of educational learning objectives, Krathwohl et al. went on to establish a similar set of hierarchical objectives in the affective domain. As in the cognitive domain, lower levels of engagement act as prerequisites to higher levels within the more subjective attributes of feelings and emotion. The authors state that the affective objectives 'vary from simple attention to selected phenomena to complex but internally consistent qualities of *character* and conscience' (Krathwohl et al. 1964: 7, emphasis added). According to their taxonomy, at the highest level of 'characterisation' an individual possesses a value system that controls their behaviour or lifestyle. Common examples of how this quality may be exhibited include self-reliance in independent work; co-operation in group activities; professional commitment to ethical practice; and an ability to value others as individuals. In Carter's (1985) taxonomy of objectives for professional education there is a much more explicit attempt to link what he refers to as *knowing*, *doing* and *being* and the importance placed on 'personal characteristics' such as integrity, initiative and emotional resilience. It is clear from his model that in order to reach the highest level of professional development, an individual must acquire suitable knowledge, appropriate skills and necessary attitudes.

In terms of educating professional lawyers, therefore, these models point to the need to develop, within individuals, a commitment to a personal value system which sits comfortably with the value system of the profession as a whole. This ensures that future practitioners do not hold personal values that will be in direct variance with the articulated and espoused values of their chosen profession. This theme is taken up in the US Carnegie Report on Legal Education (Sullivan et al. 2007), where, clearly, the development of habits of the head and hand and heart referred to in their critique of professional legal education map very neatly to the cognitive, skills and affective domains. As the authors note, traditional legal education has tended to over-emphasise development of habits of the head (the cognitive domain) at the expense of habits of the heart (the affective domain) and the result is a lack of preparation for the full dimensions of the legal profession. To this end they propose a 'pervasive' approach to legal education that balances the cognitive, skills and affective domains more effectively to produce a 'more coherent and integrated initiation into a life in the law' (Sullivan et al. 2007: 147). They stress time and again the development of identity and purpose – in other words, professional character – as central to achieving that goal.

Recent external pressures also require the legal profession to revisit the importance of professional character. For example, the legal profession must come to terms with external regulation that sits in judgement of their service quality. Clients are much more demanding of their professionals and more comfortable with challenging the service they receive and the costs related to it. As a result, lawyers need to be able to demonstrate what they have done to meet clients' expectations, as well as receive external criticism and feedback in a constructive way. Self-resilience is therefore becoming increasingly important. Writing from the perspective of management science, 'character' is explained by Finkelstein (2003: 263) as an individual who encompasses 'high ethical standards and deep competence, who desires to succeed by helping others … wise on their own, who can face reality even when it's unpleasant and acknowledge when something is wrong, and who engenders trust and promotes honesty'. This links to service to others and integrity inherent in the definition of all professionals. The importance of affect is now recognised across the business and professional environments with Goleman's (1998) definition of 'emotional competence' including affects of self-awareness, self-regulation, motivation, empathy and a range of social skills, such as influence.

This chapter offers a model for developing professional character within the context of teamworking in student legal firms as an integral element of a legal practice course. This model identifies the importance that developing trust based on shared values has on the student's learning experience. The role of vocational legal education is considered in supporting the repositioning of professionalism as a response to the demands of changes in the external marketplace.

The Effect of the Repositioning of Professionalism and the Role of Legal Education

At the macro level, the repositioning of legal professionalism has been fully debated by a number of commentators, including Abel (1988), Dolliver (1990/91), Nelson et al. (1992), Paterson (1996), Kritzer (1999), Abel (2003) and Flood (2007), and brought about in part by the commercial pressures of growth, deregulation and consumerism. It is argued that these commercial pressures have led to a bifurcation of the profession into very large corporate-like businesses and small, local law practices who operate under different interpretations and applications of the concept of professionalism. Galanter and Palay (1992), Seron (1992) and Sullivan (2005) provide interesting commentary on this issue. Similarly, the contractual basis of relationships with clients is shifting as clients become more informed (Paterson 1996; Westwood 2008) and the introduction of sophisticated knowledge retrieval and management systems allows the commodification of knowledge, with practitioners able to concentrate on high-level work, leaving more routine work to paralegals. This is a trend that has been debated for some time, originally highlighted by Susskind (1996) and taken up by others such as Davenport and Prusak (2000); Pritchard et al. (2000) and Edvinsson (2002).

It is essential to look at the impact that this repositioning has had on individual professionals, not simply in relation to their daily work but also to their motivation and self-esteem (Webb 2002). For example, Sullivan (2005: 6) narrates that, in the USA, lawyers 'now routinely report low satisfaction with their choice of career'. In a survey conducted by Moorhead and Boyle (1995: 246) over half of the trainees surveyed expressed concerns about their future job security, with 'concrete evidence of a marked change from the traditional notion of the solicitors' profession as providing a job for life'. Being a professional is more than simply doing a job (Torstendahl and Burrage 1990) as it requires commitment to 'a calling' and, as a result, it is difficult to distinguish professional ethos from 'who we are as moral persons' (Webb 2002: 133). Loss of job satisfaction therefore results in more than simply concerns about future employability. In addition to the bifurcation described above, the commercial pressures on competing law firms has resulted in firms adopting behaviours such as poaching clients and successful partners, which undermines the ethos of professional collegiality (Kronman 1999: 50) and 'in the absence of social confidence in the value of the work done, ambition must become paranoid and even self-destructive' (Sullivan 2005: 169). As a result, professionals feel isolated and begin to question their self-worth, which in turn threatens the underpinning elements of their profession and their professionalism.

Learning from and working with colleagues is an important part of becoming a practising professional, as it teaches affective 'behaviours such as listening and constructively responding to points of view expressed by others, giving others the benefit of the doubt, providing support to those who need it and recognizing the interests and achievements of others' (Katzenbach and Smith 1993: 21).

Employers and clients now expect lawyers to work collaboratively (Maister 1997; Westwood 2001, 2008). Employers also want employees to adopt a positive attitude to learning as: 'What individuals know on their own is less important than what they can do with others to "add value" to the enterprise; learning becomes collaborative, outward looking and goal oriented rather than an end in itself' (Boon et al. 2005: 481).

In other words all professionals must be able to adopt a 'learning strategy': 'a series of behaviours which enables an individual to structure and motivate his or her work behaviour by setting goals, practising new and desired behaviours, keeping track of progress and rewarding himself or herself for goal achievement' (Van der Sluis 2000: 21).

It is worthwhile at this juncture to look at the role of legal education in supporting the development of professionalism. Educating young professionals is a core element of professionalism as 'it is no exaggeration to say that education remains a dominant feature of professional life, even long after the formal phase of training' (Sullivan 2005: 25). Legal education has therefore an important role to play in developing this collegiality and willingness to learn, or in Webb's (2002: 150) words: 'a more holistic understanding of legal education which acknowledges the role played by volitional and affective dimensions in shaping how individuals learn'.

Mastering the Craft of Lawyering – Head, Hand and Heart

In the Carnegie Report on Legal Education (Sullivan et al. 2007), the authors use the metaphor of a three-stage apprenticeship to describe the complex process of learning how to become a professional lawyer. The first stage focuses on the intellectual or knowledge base of the profession, and what the authors term 'habits of the mind'. The second stage is concerned with the development of expert practice, the skills of the profession or 'habits of the hand'. The third apprenticeship relates to identity and purpose and it is at this stage that the ethical standards and social roles that distinguish the profession are addressed:

the 'habits of the heart'. The authors contend that, in the American law schools at least, where they conducted their research, 'the primary emphasis on learning to think like a lawyer is so heavy that schoolwide concern for learning to perform like one is not the norm' (Sullivan et al. 2007: 22) and they call for a shift in the way that lawyers of the future are educated, both practically and ethically, in order to transform the profession for the better.

Other recent publications also take up this theme of transformation within the current systems of legal education. Maharg (2007: 271), strongly influenced by Dewey's pragmatist approach, advocates 'methods rather than plans' to achieve this. He proposes four key areas where this transformation might be rooted: experience, ethics, technology and collaboration. Stuckey et al. (2007) take a different approach in providing a concrete set of recommendations and roadmap for best practices for legal education in order to prepare law school graduates more adequately for practice. Economides and Rogers (2009) also emphasise the importance of the ethical character of legal practice, while Maughan and Webb (2005: 27) argue that 'to be a competent practitioner thus requires … the ability to develop your own sense of ethics and social responsibility and to make decisions consistent with those values'. The unifying theme is the clear message that a deeper integration of knowledge, skills and values within the legal curriculum is required in order to effect that transformation, and this integration should be underpinned by a renewed focus on professionalism. The Carnegie Report, in fact, adopts the term 'apprenticeship of professional identity' (Sullivan et al. 2007: 128) to encompass both professional ethics and 'the wider matters of morality and character' and calls on legal education to take this formative role very seriously in the 'authentic interests of the profession and the students as future professionals'.

At a practical level, achieving the balance between learning in the knowledge, skills and affective domains within the confines of an academic institution and instructional-based courses is a difficult task and has traditionally been reflected in the teaching and learning approaches adopted at the various stages of legal education. In most legal practice or bar vocational courses, for example, where the emphasis shifts from the academic study of law to preparation for entry to the legal profession, we see traditional forms of instructional learning such as lectures, seminars and essays give way to more experiential forms of learning such as role-plays, simulations and case studies. In theory, these approaches should help shift the balance towards developing the habits of the hand and of the heart that tend to be neglected at the earlier stages of legal education. Nonetheless, finding effective methods to help students learn about professional responsibility and how to 'be' a professional can be problematic for legal educators.

However, a more holistic approach has been adopted at Glasgow Graduate School of Law (GGSL) and the results of our three-year study into the effectiveness of this initiative provide some interesting results, suggesting that it is possible to develop the type of professional attributes and values that we propose are crucial for every new trainee as they enter the legal profession.

For the duration of their Diploma in Legal Practice Course at GGSL, students work in 'virtual firms' on a number of practice-based simulated legal transactions located within the virtual Scottish provincial town of Ardcalloch. The 'transactional learning environment' (TLE), as this model has been named, forms the backdrop for a form of constructivist and situated learning where both conceptual understanding and extended performance are developed. The approach has been disseminated widely in academic journals and the educational benefits of the environment reported (Maharg 2001, 2004; Maharg and Paliwala 2002; Barton et al. 2007).

As we have developed this simulation environment over the years, we have come to realise that it provides more than just a mechanism to practise legal skills and learn about legal transactions within a safe environment. As Sullivan et al. (2007: 196) assert, simulation environments 'can also provide the setting for teaching the ethical demands of practice'. However, we have found that this understanding extends beyond what we might describe as solutions to 'standard' ethical problems relating to issues of professional responsibility or codes of conduct that we might purposefully design into the simulations themselves, such as conflict of interest or solicitor/client relationships. More than simply the virtual town that forms the construct for our legal simulations, Ardcalloch is also a 'real' community of practice comprising fellow students within virtual firms, practitioner-tutors and academic staff, and it is through engagement with this community as well as with the virtual clients and transactions themselves that students come to learn and appreciate the values, attitudes and ethics of the Scottish legal profession (Barton and Maharg 2006).

An important reason for this is the educational rationale underpinning the course design and our key decision to re-align the Practice Management module within the course as a form of meta-narrative for the simulation environment. Rather than studying this subject as an isolated module, students now learn through practical experience about concepts such as time management, risk management and client care through engagement with the virtual community of Ardcalloch; through their work practices and relationships with each other within their virtual firms; and through their relationship with their practice management tutor, who takes on the role of practice manager to the firm. This is an important construct, both for the students and for us. Tutors are able to supervise and advise on the development of key skills and work processes within the firm and, more importantly, help shape students' professional values. In this environment students are exposed to some of the more tacit elements of professional practice that they might usually only encounter previously through work placement or clinical experience. To help foreground some of these elements more explicitly, and to assist students in the process of using their experiences in order to develop their professional identity, there are a number of what we would term practice management support systems that underpin the TLE. These support systems function to 'assist students' self-learning by creating structures and protocols that will help them reflect on and understand better what they are learning from experience, whether or not it is something we intend them to learn' (Stuckey et al. 2007: 173), and include, *inter alia*, activity logs, personal reflective logs, firm calendars, electronic notice boards, task allocation systems, and peer and self-assessment logs. Together, the use of these tools encourages the student firms to adopt sound work practices through delegation of work and the development of effective systems of checks and balances. Moreover, they also assist in promoting an ethical, collaborative approach through honesty in recording achievements and mistakes, as well as evaluation of personal involvement and assessment of others' contribution.

In recent studies, we have focused our attention on the particular role that teamworking plays within the overall concept of the TLE and how we can use this to support students to maximise their learning (Barton and Westwood 2006). Given our reliance on the social nature of learning, it is essential that the student firms find a way to work together effectively: as Maharg (2007: 210) puts it, in 'a relationship of intimate strangers' that 'lies in ethical behaviour and professionalism'. Interestingly, then, in this work we see clear parallels emerging between the characteristics of the most successful virtual firms (or teams) and the qualities of professionalism that we aim to inculcate in our students. As a result we contend that, at a deeper level, students' professional identities and values – their character – can be shaped through this form of learning and enable them to 'envision not just what they will do but who they will be in the profession' (Barton and Maharg 2006: 142).

The Influence of Teamworking and Trust on Professional Character

The original work on which this chapter builds (Barton and Westwood 2006) sets out in detail the methodology and approach that allowed us to develop our four-quadrant matrix describing the characteristics of four types of firm that tend to emerge through working within the Ardcalloch virtual community. This model describes four broad types of group dynamics through consideration of the characteristics of learning and trust in virtual law firms comprising a group of four students. These characteristics were identified through analysis of a three-year study of students' experience of working in these firms during the one-year Diploma in Legal Practice at Glasgow Graduate School of Law.

Learning

Type 2: Legal Eagles **Low Trust High Learning** **Culture** Suspicious, blame, independence, me first, team second **Task** Task focused: debate about details, my way; high engagement, exhausting **Relationships** Insular, abrasive, reluctant, limited listening, suspicious **Work styles** Inflexible, rigid, majority, one upmanship	**Type 1: Learning Community** **High Trust High Learning** **Culture** Inclusive, fair, interdependence, team first, win-win **Task** Task focused: our way; high engagement to get things done, good communications **Relationships** Open, value each other, mutually supportive, honest, shared responsibility, respect **Work styles** Flexible, adaptive, learn from mistakes, consensus, responsive, resilient
Type 4: Dysfunctional **Low Trust Low Learning** **Culture** Suspicious, blame, ego-centred, me first, firm nowhere **Task** Not task focused; low engagement **Relationships** Blame, victimisation, polarised, abrasive, no self-awareness **Work styles** Inflexible, superficial, dictatorial, rigid	**Type 3: Friendly Societies** **High Trust Low Learning** **Culture** Inclusive, cosy, dependence, friends first, firm second **Task** Not task focused; low engagement **Relationships** Like minded, sociable, nice, supportive **Work styles** Superficial, majority, avoid conflict

Trust

Figure 11.1 Learning/trust matrix
Source: Barton and Westwood (2006)

Type 1: Characteristics of Learning Communities (High Trust, High Learning)

First of all there were the firms that we called 'learning communities' that experienced high trust and high learning. Their culture was inclusive and fair. They were willing to rely on each other, putting the aims of their team first, rather than any personal agenda or gain. When differences were aired, they looked for a win–win result. They were task-focused, with a strong commitment to getting the job done. They operated in an open and honest way, respecting each other's strengths and supporting weaknesses, sharing responsibility for mistakes and problems. They learned from mistakes, sought consensus at all times and as a result were responsive and resilient.

Type 2: Characteristics of the Legal Eagles (Low Trust, High Learning)

The 'legal eagles' focused on their individual identity rather than that of the firm. They argued with each other over details, preferring to tackle projects their way rather than accommodate other people's approach. As a result, they spent a disproportionate amount of time and energy on arguing rather than doing. Their relationships were abrasive and argumentative with limited listening. They were inflexible and suspicious of anything new. They sought to score points off each other rather than seek to move the team forward. Whilst they did get the job done successfully, the process exhausted everyone.

Type 3: Characteristics of Friendly Societies (High Trust, Low Learning)

The culture of the 'friendly societies' was inclusive and comfortably secure. They were like-minded and sociable, spending companionable time together at the expense of getting on with their tasks. As a result, their approach was superficial and comfortable, avoiding any conflict or disagreement.

Type 4: Characteristics of Dysfunctional (Low Trust, Low Learning)

This group operated a culture of suspicion and blame, seeking their own agenda at all times with no recognition of the need to work as a firm. Their intra-firm relationships were abrasive and self-seeking, with no awareness of the impact of their behaviour on other firm members. When mistakes occurred, they abdicated responsibility, seeking to polarise discussion and blame others. They were demanding, ego-centred and inflexible.

These characteristics, developed from analysis of the individual students' reflective reports, corroborated by their activity and personal logs, illustrate the importance of culture, task approach, relationships and work styles in allowing them to successfully practise together and build the 'social capital' that consists of 'the stock of active connections among people: the trust, mutual understanding and shared values and behaviours that bind the members of human networks and connections and make co-operative action possible' (Cohen and Prusack 2001: 4).

Parsons (1969: 142) argues that trust is 'the attitudinal ground – in affectively motivated loyalty'. Trust is therefore an essential element of the formation of a successful team culture, as 'to be part of a group is to share values with the others' (Ward and Smith 2003: 96), and has a direct impact on how the group performs, with establishment of trust being a 'pre-condition of superior performance' (Lane 2000: 1).

This in turns confirms how important it is to recognise the impact affect has on students' ability to learn, an issue debated, most famously, by Goleman (1998) but also De Geus (1999) in relation to organisations and Webb (2002) in relation to lawyers specifically. Those firms who were most successful in relation to completion of their projects, marks achieved and tutors' feedback were those who displayed high levels of both trust and learning.

This model demonstrates that it is possible to influence the development of professional character through the active management of teamworking and highlights the importance of self-awareness, personal responsibility and peer review. Through structuring and coaching interventions, some of which are described below, it is possible to directly influence the dynamics of these firms to improve the development of their trust and learning. Analysis of the effect that these had by providing 'scaffolding' (Raelin 2008: 17) supports this influential effect.

Active Interventions to Engage More Deeply

Our aim for 2005–6 and our measure of success was to increase the number of firms that achieved Type 1 characteristics by adopting a strategy aimed at helping the firms engage more deeply in the experiential learning cycle and work together to build trust, for it was apparent from our earlier analysis of the students' learning experiences that more than 50% failed to achieve both high learning and high trust.

Our overarching objectives were to identify the potential firm types at an early stage and use active interventions to encourage:

- the legal eagles to be less antagonistic and develop trust;
- the friendly societies to be 'less friendly' and treat their tasks more authentically; and
- the dysfunctional firms to seek help.

These interventions involved the introduction of formal structuring tools facilitated by the practice manager tutors allocated to each of the firms. We felt early intervention was essential as *de facto* our firms only work together for a relatively short period of time (six months). It was clear from our earlier analysis and direct feedback from the practice managers that many firms displayed symptoms of team problems from the outset, yet it was difficult to identify the underlying causes. For example, our practice managers would express concerns over the performance of particular firms but were unable to find a mechanism to explain this to them adequately. Students similarly said in their reflective reports that from the outset they were uncomfortable about their firm's approach to group working but did not have the tools to raise this with other members or their practice managers.

We therefore decided to require the student firms to articulate and identify as soon as possible both the physical and time constraints they had as individuals that would impact on their availability for teamwork. We also wanted them to have a mechanism to discuss these in a constructive way.

We therefore made a number of structuring changes to the content of the Practice Management module. We invited all of the Practice Management tutors to attend a training workshop where we explained the results of our research and the changes we planned to introduce to the content of the module and the development of their role, as this role was crucial to the success of our interventions. We therefore sourced and distributed a book on coaching styles to allow them to enhance their knowledge of the different styles of coaching. We expanded the content of the introductory tutorial to the module by including the results of our teamworking analysis and asked tutors to explain the four categories of firms and their characteristics to allow students at the outset of the module to be more aware of the ranges of styles of firm working. We introduced the requirement that each firm had to draft and agree a formal written partnership agreement and offered them a style to work from which included draft clauses addressing workload management, dispute resolution, communication and reporting mechanisms, decision-making processes, and so on, which they had to discuss and amend as necessary. It became a mandatory requirement that each firm had to consent and sign the agreement within four working weeks of the start of the module, with the Practice Management tutor acting as a formal witness to that signature. We also developed a written exercise that required them to articulate and agree at least four common values, which had to be incorporated as such in one of the required clauses of the written agreement. This proved to be a key element of the partnership agreement and an important exercise in team-building.

In addition, we developed techniques to allow firm members to better understand each other and their own and team members' style of working, especially in relation to time and workload management. To formalise the opportunity to reflect on each firm members' contribution to the firm's workload, we introduced a confidential, online self- and peer assessment system that required students to reflect on both the quality and quantity of input of every firm member on a weekly basis, including themselves.

Scaffolding to Support Learning

From our initial analysis and our matrix determinants of learning and trust, it was clear that the adoption of a task focus was essential for high learning. In addition, those firms who developed an inclusive culture attained high trust. This mirrors the sociability and solidarity matrix adopted by Goffee and Jones (2003: 275), where 'sociability refers primarily to relations between individuals who ... share certain ideas, attitudes, interests and values and to be inclined to associate on equal terms. ... Solidarity ... describes task-focussed co-operation between individuals and groups'. It was important therefore that our interventions encouraged both a task orientation through completion of the requirement to formalise a written partnership agreement and the development of a supportive culture through the discussion and agreement of common core values.

Discussing and agreeing the contents of the agreement required the members of the firm to plan ahead, to make decisions about how the firm would be organised and how work would be controlled, how communications and time demands would be co-ordinated and how potential problems could be avoided or resolved. The process of identifying options and agreeing choices, we felt, was an important element in articulating and understanding what individual members saw as important, as well as allowing people to agree what the firm would actually do.

Given the relatively short duration of the diploma and the number of client transactions to be completed by each firm, implementation of decisions would be the key to a firm's effective performance. The external and internal time constraints the firms require to work under meant that they had to be able to prioritise decisions, ensure their political acceptability to all the team members and make sure that their way of operating would allow tasks to be completed successfully (Miller et al. 2004). Formalising all of these mechanisms through the written partnership agreement was designed to assist all of this so as to provide a framework to allow individual firms to develop a shared culture and working relationship which would develop organically over time.

Our earlier analysis had shown that some firms did not truly engage in the process of forming a team. For example, the friendly societies had drifted through the first semester of the course paying little attention to how effectively the firm was working and as a result had not even started on what Tuckman (1965) describes as the four-stage team model, whilst the legal eagles had moved rapidly to 'storming' without any attempt at either considering 'forming' or move themselves on to 'norming'. By introducing the requirement to debate and formalise a written agreement at an early stage in their firm relationships, we sought to encourage movement more quickly through the first three of the four elements of Tuckman's model (1965), i.e. 'forming, norming and storming' to his final stage of 'performing', 'in which interpersonal structure becomes the tool of task activities. Roles become flexible and functional, and group energy is channelled into the task. Structural issues have been resolved, and structure can now become supportive of task performance' (Tuckman 1965: 78).

The ceremonial requirement of putting their individual signature to a formal document, witnessed by their practice manager, was to be seen by trainee lawyers as an important step in committing to their firm and their fellow team members. Barker (1993: 415) argues that:

> [p]eer management increases the total control in a concertive system through two important dynamics. The first is that concertive workers have created this system through their own shared value consensus, which they enforce on each other. But in so doing … the teams necessarily create a system of value-based rational rules … . They have put themselves under their own eye of the norm, resulting in a powerful system of control.

It was crucial, therefore, that shared values were an integral part of that agreement. The final partnership agreement required the inclusion of a clause where the core values that the firm members held in common were stated, as '[v]alues are deeply held views, of what we find worthwhile' (Senge et al. 1994: 209). As we argued before, an essential part of establishing trust and community ethos is having values in common (Nicholson 2000; Edvinsson 2002). For professionals, and for legal practitioners in particular, values are profoundly influential in the way that they function: 'the life of the law must not be mere logic; it must also be values. Each lawyer ... must make personal judgments. ... Each lawyer must consciously and constantly assess his or her values and goals in forging rules of law for the future' (Higgenbotham 1987: 815).

All professional bodies impose ethical codes of conduct and standards and 'act as a readily accessible guide to professional behaviour norms' (Nicolson 2005: 605). Controlling professionals must therefore involve identification with these norms and values and the effect of a failing to deliver both personal and professional values can have a direct effect on both the effectiveness of the firm and the stress levels of its members (Westwood 2001, 2008).

The students were first given the task of choosing their individual values. The process of then identifying and agreeing what values they had in common sought to allow them to feel part of a group of people who had similar goals and aspirations, which in turn would motivate them to begin to feel part of and responsible to the firm as a whole. As Moingeon and Soenen (2002: 1) put it, '[i]dentity plays a critical role because it provides meaning, stability and distinctiveness. "Who are we?" is one of the most critical questions organizations and their executives need to address'.

The formalisation of these values as part of the partnership agreement provided a foundation in which both trust and learning could take root. Using this framework would help clarify and address areas of tension, a strategy discussed in, for example, Nicholson (2000) and Ward and Smith (2003) and allow practice managers to find out about these disparities at the earliest opportunity. In addition, and crucially, the development of trust allowed the development of learning, confirming De Geus (1990: 236) that '[t]rust allows space and tolerance, both inside the hierarchy and towards the outside world'. Given that our students did not choose their fellow team members but were allocated them at the outset on a random basis, it was important that they learned to feel secure with each other. Tracy (2003: 254) argues that:

> [t]he most important ingredient in a high-performance work environment is harmony. In an harmonious environment, people can feel happy, safe, respected, and secure. They feel that they can do their job and make mistakes without being criticized, condemned, or threatened with punishment. They feel that they can express themselves freely ... without the danger of being ridiculed. In a high-trust environment, characterized by caring, courtesy and consideration, people feel free to perform at their very best and to put their whole hearts into their work.

This feeling of security was facilitated by their initial discussions. Once values had been established the culture and norms of the group were formed (Schein 1985). Group members then were able to use these articulated values to review their firm's actual behaviour and attitudes. For example, if their firm had identified 'excellence' as one of their agreed values, if their task approach became slapdash and haphazard, the student could articulate their unease through a reference to their written agreement.

With this in mind, therefore, mid-way through the course, the practice manager and the firm were required to review the values selected at the outset and take the opportunity to reflect on how well the firm was living up to the expectations it set for itself. This provided an opportunity for individuals to raise any concerns they had about the firm's effectiveness in the light of adherence to these shared values and allowed discussion and resolution of any potential issues to be carried out in a constructive and supportive manner. In addition, it is important that our firms are able to self-manage. The identification of shared values is an important element of that self-managing as:

> teams will develop behavioural norms that put their values into action in consistent patterns applicable to a variety of situations … Thus, the teams could turn their value consensus into social norms or rules. The teams had manifested the essential element of concertive control: their value-based interactions became a social force that controlled their actions. (Barker 1993: 423)

As a result, to perform effectively as a team, we felt that it was essential that the members had a process to identify the values they had in common.

Building Professional Character and Self-resilience

In the year after we had introduced the interventions described above, our analysis of the firms provided some interesting results (see Table 11.1). In the previous two years that the analysis had taken place, just over 40% of firms were classed as 'learning communities'. In 2005/6 this figure rose to 56%. It was clear that many more firms were exhibiting some or all of the more positive traits of the successful firms described earlier.

The proportion of 'friendly societies' peaked at 31% in 2004/5, then reduced to 18% the following year. The 'legal eagles' peaked at 27% in 2003/4 and then dropped to 14% and 18% respectively. However, a more welcome result in some respects was the shift in 'dysfunctional' firms from 12% and 13% in the previous two years to 8% following the new interventions (see Table 11.1). The small core of firms that were classified in this way tended to have a range of external factors which exerted a strong detrimental effect on one or more individuals within the firm ranging from serious personal problems to extreme work pressures (e.g. individuals trying to hold down near full-time employment while completing the course). In a very few cases, a single individual within the firm was the cause of much of the dysfunction and the attempts of the other firm members, or indeed the practice management tutor, to resolve the issues was not successful. In severe cases, often our only solution is to dissolve the partnership, remove the student who is the disruptive element and allow them to effectively practise as a sole practitioner.

Table 11.1 Comparison of firm characteristics

	2003/4 51 firms	2004/5 64 firms	2005/6 66 firms
Type 1: Learning Community	41%	42%	56%
Type 2: Friendly Society	20%	31%	18%
Type 3: Legal Eagles	27%	14%	18%
Type 4: Dysfunctional	12%	13%	8%

Following the interventions, it was clear to us as student advisors, and confirmed by the consultation with the practice management tutors, that the early discussions and formalisation of the partnership agreement had allowed potential problems to be identified much earlier than in previous years. The practice managers reported that the process of formalisation had been extremely useful and the illustrations of the four types of firms had allowed them to illustrate the potential problems of working in firms as well as the potential solutions.

What was particularly gratifying was the use the students themselves made of the tools we had provided in facilitating their reflection and their overall assessment of their firm performance. As explained in more detail in our earlier article (Barton and Westwood 2006), each student is asked to submit an individual written report at the end of the Practice Management module reflecting on his or her experience of working in the firm. They are asked to comment on the style of work that was adopted, the strengths and weaknesses of that approach and what they would do differently in the future. Our analysis of previous years' reports evidenced that students found it difficult to carry out this reflection (Schon 1987). We saw that this was an important skill we wanted them to develop because 'in order to find points of contact between professionals' education, knowledge and work, one must use other concepts of knowledge – such as the reflective type of knowledge – which can better explain how professional proficiency is embedded in practice itself, with the contextual conditions that are tied to specific situations' (Svensson 1990: 69–70).

We could identify an improvement in their ability to reflect through their use of the descriptors of the four types of firms to explain the journey taken by their firm. The tools effectively provided them with an understanding and vocabulary that allowed them to articulate this process more clearly, even if that journey was a difficult one. For example, in a student report from a firm classified as 'legal eagles':

> Being able to see that although we didn't turn out to be the high trust, high learning 'learning community' that we wanted, our experience (painful though it has been) has perhaps resulted in us learning more. Our firm culture is suspicious and centres too much on blame, but we have managed to remain task-focused and produce high-quality work. According to the theory, that makes us 'legal eagles'. We walk into our traineeships better prepared to deal with conflict and with high hopes that things can only improve.

And in another example, this time from a firm classified as a 'learning community', this student appears to recognise the conflict they felt between remaining focused on their work and the growing bonds of mutual respect and friendship:

> Although my initial reaction was that our firm had great potential to fall within the realms of the friendly society, I passed this off as something which would change given that the induction week was geared towards informality and getting to know your firm. However, even at this stage I was beginning to envisage that there would be cultural and personal differences in attitudes to working style and conduct of personal behaviour. Perhaps I would have been better placed to raise these concerns at the outset?
>
> Our practice manager showed concerns at the start of the semester as to our obvious 'friendly society' that had built up very quickly over the induction weeks and the start of the projects. We are however all very keen workers and were adamant to not let that aspect of the diploma intrude on effective practice management. However, it became difficult at times to separate the bonds, loyalties and mutual respect of friendship from those of the firm environment.

Analysis of the most commonly chosen values across all of the 70 virtual firms showed some interesting results. Each firm had to select a minimum of four values which would be enshrined in their partnership agreement from a list of 31 (adapted from Senge et al. 1994: 210) that were provided. The most common value, chosen by 44% of the firms, was *reliability*. *Work–life balance* was the next most common choice, appearing in 37% of firms' partnership agreements. *Integrity* and *quality* were tied in third place on 25%. The next four most popular values selected were *democracy*, *happiness*, *challenge* and *excellence*, each appearing in partnership agreements for between 15% and 20% of firms. The values which did not appear in any agreement were: change, competition, freedom, friendships, independence, leadership, privacy and status. Recalling that these were student firms who had not yet embarked on their legal careers, it is reassuring to note that there appears to be a sense of shared agreement on the types of values that display a sense of honesty, commitment and respect for others.

In addition, students used the choice of their core values to illustrate, in their reflective reports, the reasons why the firm adopted its way of working and the reasons behind it. In an example taken from a 'learning community' firm, we can see that the values they chose became, for them, a useful and practical mechanism for dealing with problems and potential conflict in a non-threatening and positive manner:

> On establishing ourselves as a firm the four members, myself included, signed a partnership agreement with four core values that we felt it was imperative we upheld, namely: work–life balance, reliability, democracy and happiness. We felt it was essential to our success that these be enshrined in the agreement and on reflection it would appear that they have been upheld to the greatest practical extent possible. We have not gone without our problems and the upholding of our second core value was called into question on a few occasions. At the outset our firm, certain members in particular, had to deal with emotional and personal issues, and as a result impact was made on the working firm. However, the upholding of our first and fourth core value ensured that we were able to deal professionally and reasonably with such issues and relations within the firm strengthened.

When trust was difficult to establish, students were often able to trace this back to the initial value-setting stage, as this example from a firm of 'legal eagles' illustrates:

> My concern for the success of the firm began from its inception because it was insisted that the term 'happiness' was incorporated in to our constitution and I felt strongly that this did not accord with the attempt of professional or commercial verisimilitude of the course. It is ironic therefore that the incorporation of the word 'happiness' was actually to be the beginning of the underlying unhappiness which marred our firm and alienated one of the members right from the start.

The sociologist Richard Sennett defines character as 'the ethical value we place on our own desires and on our relations to others' (1998: 10) and concern as 'the personal traits that we value in our selves and for which we seek to be valued by others' (1998: 10). He goes on to argue that current workplace environments and the associated shift from traditional hierarchical structures and supervision to networks and teamworking does not support the concept of character and that a climate such as this works to corrode trust, loyalty and mutual commitment. We would argue that while this pessimistic conclusion may be true for some of the types of organisations he describes – for example (1998: 77) the mass-production, computerised bakery where the engagement with work and identity within 'teams' can be viewed as superficial or even detached in nature – it is not necessarily so for all models of teamworking activity. It should certainly not be the aim of professional or multi-professional teams within knowledge-intensive organisations such as legal firms where teamworking does not, as Sennett (1998: 99) argues, equate to 'the group practice of demeaning superficiality'. On the contrary, 'we need to develop a new language of and commitment to personal and professional responsibility. Responsibility should be seen as empowering and underpinned by values of honour, integrity and altruism' (Webb 2002: 150).

Conclusions

Within our educational context as described, we supported the development of student learning through the creation of authentic and sustained teamworking practices. Through the careful and supported use of virtual firm practice, we aimed to encourage the characteristics of learning communities, summarised in our earlier description. More importantly we have shown that it is possible to influence a change in the dynamics of our student firms and shift them towards this type of effective teamworking. We therefore used the experience of virtual firms to allow students to experiment with the character of their firms: to allow them to test their identified values against the reality of working together on group projects and of relying on each other to achieve 'competence'.

Our work with students on the Diploma in Legal Practice at GGSL has demonstrated that it is possible to influence directly the student's experience of learning through the introduction of working in a virtual team of lawyers tackling client transactions. It is also possible to allow them to experience, in a community of practice, the characteristics they will need to develop to be a successful practising professional.

It is essential, however, to actively manage this student experience through the use of skilled practitioners who are provided with formalised structuring tools that agree the firm's way of working and the core values they hold in common. This management will allow more students to experience high learning and high trust associated with working in a 'learning community'. Trust allows learning which in turn develops trust. Having values in common allows people to learn from each other in a constructive and collaborative way and so helps develop '[t]he kind of personal maturity that graduates need in order to practice law with integrity and a sense of purpose … qualities such as compassion, respectfulness and commitment' (Sullivan et al. 2007: 146). In other words, character:

> Character will shape [law firms], but these institutions also will shape character. A sufficiently rich account of professionalism thus must be attentive to law firms not simply as collections of lawyers but as social forms that play an important role in constructing and expressing the values of the legal profession. (Regan 1999: 3)

References

Abel, R. 1988. *The Legal Profession in England and Wales*. Oxford: Basil Blackwell.

Abel, R. 2003. *English Lawyers between Market and State*. Oxford: Oxford University Press.

Barker, J.A. 1993. Tightening the Iron Cage: Concertive Control in Self-managing Teams, *Administrative Science Quarterly* September: 408–37.

Barton, K. and Maharg, P. 2006. E-simulations in the Wild: Interdisciplinary Research, Design and Implementation of Simulation Environments in Legal Education, in *Games and Simulations in Online Learning: Research and Development Frameworks*, edited by D. Gibson, C. Aldrich and M. Prensky. London: Information Science Publishing, 115–48.

Barton, K., McKellar, P. and Maharg, P. 2007. Authentic Fictions: Simulation, Professionalism and Legal Learning, *Clinical Law Review* 14(1): 143–93.

Barton, K. and Westwood, F. 2006. From Student to Trainee Practitioner – A Study of Team Working as a Learning Experience. [Online] *Web Journal of Current Legal Issues*. Issue 3. Available at: http://webjcli.ncl.ac.uk/2006/issue3/barton-westwood3.html) [accessed 31 July 2010].

Bloom, B.S. 1956. *Taxonomy of Educational Objectives, Handbook I: The Cognitive Domain.* New York: David McKay Co Inc.

Boon, A., Flood, J. and Webb, J. 2005. Postmodern Professions? The Fragmentation of Legal Education and the Legal Profession, *Journal of Law and Society* 32(3): 473–92.

Carter, R. 1985. A Taxonomy of Objectives for Professional Education, *Studies in Higher Education* 10: 135–49.

Cohen, D. and Prusack, L. 2001. *In Good Company – How Social Capital Makes Organizations Work.* Boston: Harvard Business School Press.

Davenport, T.H. and Prusak, L. 2000. *Working Knowledge – How Organizations Manage What They Know.* Boston: Harvard Business School Press.

De Geus, A. 1999. *The Living Company – Growth, Learning and Longevity in Business.* London: Nicholas Brealey Publishing Limited.

Dolliver, J.M. 1990/91. Law as a Profession; Will it Survive? *Gonzaga Law Review* 26(2): 267–75.

Economides, K. and Rogers, J. 2009. *Preparatory Ethics Training for Future Solicitors*. London: The Law Society.

Edvinsson, L. 2002. *Corporate Longitude – What You Need to Know to Navigate the Knowledge Economy.* London: Pearson Education Limited.

Eraut, M. 1994. *Developing Professional Knowledge and Competence*. London: Falmer Press.

Finkelstein, S. 2003. *Why Smart Executives Fail and What We Can Learn from Their Mistakes.* New York: Portfolio.

Flood, J. 2007. Law Firms, in *Encyclopaedia of Law and Society: American and Global Perspectives*, edited by D. Clark. London: Sage, 924–30.

Galanter, M. and Palay, T. 1992. The Transformation of the Big Law Firm, in *Lawyers' Ideals/Lawyers' Practices – Transformations in the American Legal Profession*, edited by R.L. Nelson, D.M. Trubek and R.L. Solomon. New York: Cornell University Press, 31–62.

Goffee, R. and Jones, G. 2003. Organizational Culture, in *Organization 21C: Someday all Organizations will Lead this Way*, edited by S. Chowdry. New Jersey: Financial Times Prentice Hall, 273–90.

Goleman, D. 1998. *Working with Emotional Intelligence.* London: Bloomsbury Publishing Plc.

Higgenbotham, A.L. 1987. The Life of Law: Values, Commitment and Craftsmanship, *Harvard Law Review* 795–816.

Katzenbach, J.R. and Smith, D.K. 1993. *The Wisdom of Teams – Creating the High Performance Organisation.* Boston: Harvard Business School Press.

Krathwohl, D.R., Bloom, B.S. and Masia, B.B. 1964. *Taxonomy of Educational Objectives Handbook II: Affective Domain.* New York: David McKay Co.

Kritzer, H.M. 1999. The Professions are Dead, Long Live the Professions: Legal Practice in a Post Professional World, *Law and Society Review* 33(3): 713–59.

Kronman, A. 1999. Our Beleaguered Public World, *Journal of Legal Education* 49: 50–57.

Lane, C. 2000. Introduction: Theories and Issues in the Study of Trust, in *Trust Within and Between Organizations*, edited by C. Lane and R. Bachman. Oxford: Oxford University Press, 1–30.

Maharg, P. 2001. Negotiating the Web: Legal Skills Learning in a Virtual Community, in *Web-based Teaching, Learning and Assessment in Law*, edited by P. Maharg, special edition, *International Review of Law Computers and Technology* 15(3): 345–61.

Maharg, P. 2004. Virtual Communities on the Web: Transactional Learning and Teaching, in *Aan het werk met ICT in het Academisch Onderwijs*, edited by A. Vedder. Rotterdam: Wolf Legal Publishers.

Maharg, P. 2007. *Transforming Legal Education: Learning and Teaching the Law in the Early Twenty-first Century*. Aldershot: Ashgate.

Maharg, P. and Paliwala, A. 2002. Negotiating the Learning Process with Electronic Resources, in *Effective Learning and Teaching in Law*, edited by R. Burridge et al. London: Kogan Page, 81–104.

Maister, D.H. 1997. *True Professionalism – The Courage to Care about Your People, Your Clients and Your Career.* New York: The Free Press.

Maughan, C. and Webb, J. 2005. *Lawyering Skills and the Legal Process.* Cambridge: Cambridge University Press.

Miller, S., Wilson, D. and Hickson, D. 2004. Beyond Panning: Strategies for Successfully Implementing Strategic Decisions, *Long Range Planning* 37(3): 201–18.

Moingeon, B. and Soenen, G. (eds) 2002. *Corporate and Organizational Identities – Integrating Strategy, Marketing, Communication and Organizational Perspectives*. London: Routledge.

Moorhead, R. and Boyle, F. 1995. Quality of Life and Trainee Solicitors: A Survey, *International Journal of the Legal Profession* 2(2/3): 217–51.

Nelson, R.L., Trubek, D.M. and Solomon, R.L. 1992. *Lawyers' Ideals/Lawyers' Practices – Transformations in the American Legal Profession.* New York: Cornell University Press.

Nicholson, N. 2000. *Managing the Human Animal.* London: Texere Publishing Limited.

Nicolson, D. 2005. Making Lawyers Moral? Ethical Codes and Moral Character, *Legal Studies* 25(4): 601–26.

Nicolson, D. 2008. Education, Education, Education: Legal, Moral and Clinical, *The Law Teacher* 42: 145–73.

Parsons, T. 1969. Research with Human Subjects and the 'Professional Complex', in *Experimentation with Human Subject*, edited by P.A. Feund. New York: George Braziller, 116–51.

Paterson, A. 1996. Professionalism and the Legal Services Market, *International Journal of the Legal Profession* 3(1/2): 137–68.

Pritchard, C., Hull, R., Chumer, M. et al. 2000. *Managing Knowledge – Critical Investigations of Work and Learning.* London: Macmillan Business.

Raelin, J.A. 2008. *Work-based Learning – Bridging Knowledge and Action in the Workplace.* San Francisco: John Wiley and Sons.

Regan, M.C. 1999. Law Firms, Competition Penalties and the Values of Professionalism, *Georgetown Journal of Legal Ethics* 13(1): 1–74.

Schein, E.H. 1985. *Organizational Culture and Leadership.* San Francisco: Jossey-Bass.

Schon, D. 1987. *Educating the Reflective Practitioner.* San Francisco: Jossey-Bass.

Senge, P., Kleiner, A., Roberts, C. et al. 1994. *The Fifth Discipline Fieldbook.* New York: Doubleday.

Sennett, R. 1998. *The Corrosion of Character: The Personal Consequences of Work in the New Capitalism*. New York: Norton.

Seron, C. 1992. Managing Entrepreneurial Legal Services: The Transformation of Small-firm Practice, in *Lawyers' Ideals/Lawyers' Practices – Transformations in the American Legal Profession*, edited by R.L. Nelson, D.M. Trubek and R.L. Solomon. New York: Cornell University Press, 63–92.

Stuckey, R. et al. 2007. *Best Practice for Legal Education: A Vision and Road Map.* Columbia, SC: University of South Carolina, Clinical Legal Education Organization.

Sullivan, W.M. 2005. *Work and Integrity – The Crisis and Promise of Professionalism in America*. San Francisco: Jossey-Bass.

Sullivan, W.M., Colby, A., Wegner, J. et al. 2007. *Educating Lawyers: Preparation for the Profession of Law*. The Carnegie Foundation for the Advancement of Teaching. San Francisco: Jossey-Bass.

Susskind, R. 1996. *The Future of Law – Facing the Challenges of Information Technology.* Oxford: Clarendon Press.

Svensson, L.G. (1990) Knowledge as a Professional Resource: Case Studies of Architects and Psychologists at Work, in *The Formation of Professions – Knowledge State and Strategy*, edited by R. Torstendahl and M. Burrage. London: Sage, 51–70.

Torstendahl, R. and Burrage, M. (eds) 1990. *The Formation of the Professions – Knowledge State and Strategy.* London: Sage Publications.

Tracy, B. 2003. The Power of Focus, in *Partnering: The New Face of Leadership*, edited by L. Segil, M. Goldsmith and J. Belasco. New York: Amacon, 241–56.

Tuckman, B.W. 1965. Developmental Sequence in Small Groups, *Psychological Bulletin* (63): 384–99.

Van der Sluis, L. 2000. Learning Behaviour and Learning Opportunities as Career Stimuli, *Journal of Workplace Learning* 14(1/2): 15–26.

Ward, A. and Smith, J. 2003. *Trust and Mistrust*. Chichester: Wiley.

Webb, J. 2002. Being a Lawyer/Being a Human Being, *Legal Studies* 5(1&2): 130–51.

Westwood, F. 2001. *Achieving Best Practice – Shaping Professionals for Success*. Maidenhead: McGraw-Hill.

Westwood, F. 2008. *Accelerated Best Practice – Implementing Success in Professional Firms*. Leicester: Troubador.

Chapter 12
Addressing Emotions in Preparing Ethical Lawyers

Nigel Duncan

While on a summer clerkship with a large and well-respected commercial firm, you are (naturally) concerned to make a good impression. It is your second last year of law school and you are desperate for Articles. The partner supervising you decides to give you some of her files to get ready for 'costing'. She asks you to total the number of hours which she has spent on each file and, from her harried expression, it is pretty clear that she is concerned to charge out a significant amount on each file. She asks you to 'round up' her hours to the next hundred in each file, saying that, on average, clients are happy because the main thing they demand is quality work. You know that these clients are entirely satisfied with the firm and that your supervisor is not about to debate the issue with you. *Would you round up the hours as requested?* (Evans and Palermo 2005: 113).

This question was put to several hundred graduates of Monash University as part of research conducted by Adrian Evans and Josephine Palermo into individual values and ethical behaviour. The findings were interesting. A majority (56.6%) of respondents were willing to round up the hours in those circumstances, even though they will have been aware that this would add a considerable sum to the bill eventually given to the client. More insight came from the responses to the researchers' request that respondents identified the values they considered that they were applying in order to come to this decision. The researchers also asked respondents to indicate the values that influenced their decision. These included: employment prospects; loyalty to your supervisor; honesty; professional ambition; client concern.

So it seems that responding ethically to a situation is not merely a question of knowing the rules, or intending to behave well. To understand it requires consideration of individuals' emotional responses to the situation in which they find themselves and the question of their exhibiting moral courage and when that might be particularly difficult. Thus, the affective domain is engaged and those of us who are interested in preparing students for ethical practice as lawyers should be willing to address it.

Professional Ethics in Current Legal Education

The extent to which professional ethics is addressed in legal education varies with jurisdiction, with the structure of legal education and between institutions. It is common for it to be a required subject under one name or another. Thus in the USA, 'professional responsibility' is the only mandatory subject on the JD.[1] The Bar of England and Wales requires 'professional ethics and conduct' to be taught on its Bar Vocational Course (BSB 2008: 8). The Solicitors Regulation Authority requires 'Professional Conduct and Client Care, including Solicitors' Accounts Rules' as an element of its Legal Practice Course (SRA 2004: 3). Australia's 'Priestley 11'[2] includes 'Professional Conduct (including basic trust accounting)'. All of these requirements are relatively similar.

It is worthy of note that the only courses where it is a requirement are those which are regarded as preparation for practice. Thus, in the USA, where the JD is usually the only course students undertake (unless they take specific courses to prepare for different state bar exams), this requirement falls on a degree course. In the UK, where there are discrete professional courses which follow an undergraduate degree, there are no requirements on the LLB, but only on the professional courses. In Australia, law degrees which are not designed to prepare students for practice are not required to meet the Priestley 11. So there is no general requirement that ethics should be part of an academic law degree. Indeed, a recent small survey (Chandler and Duncan 2008) found some jurisdictions (e.g. Japan, Kuwait, Vietnam) where there was no requirement that ethics be addressed at any stage, most jurisdictions where it was required by the professional body, as in the examples above, but also some jurisdictions, such as Poland and Russia, where it was required by the state.

There is little research on the extent to which ethics is in fact taught. The same study found no consistent pattern. What is more, when UK respondents indicated that ethics were addressed on academic courses, this response represented a typical view of the few actively addressing legal ethics:

1 This requirement is contained in Standard 302(a)(5) of the American Bar Association's Standards for the Approval of Law Schools. This standard requires that all law students be educated in the 'history, goals, structures, values, rules and responsibilities of the legal profession and its members'. Interpretation 309-9 elaborates on this goal: 'The substantial instruction in the history, structure, values, rules, and responsibilities of the legal profession and its members required by Standard 302(a)(5) includes instruction in matters such as the law of lawyering and the Model Rules of Professional Conduct of the American Bar Association' (ABA 2010).

2 Eleven compulsory subjects for courses designed to prepare students for admission to practice, introduced in 1992 by the Consultative Committee of State and Territorial Law Admitting Authorities of Australia.

> It would be an exaggeration to say that ethics is taught as a topic in its own right. It is covered in a part 1 module on General Principles of Law and also in Legal Skills. The final year Pro Bono Writing Credit optional module is one where the issue of ethics comes most to the fore, but it is not taught as such on this module, as it is a module where the students prepare an e-portfolio on their PB work. This module is new (started in 2006–7) and increasingly popular. In both the LLB and the LLM there are options in international law and international HR and international mooting where ethics will be covered. There are also LLB options in Discrimination Law and Medical Law which will deal with ethics.[3]

However, those teaching on the professional courses all indicated that ethics were addressed. Thus the division in England and Wales between academic and professional law courses appears to have encouraged most law schools to leave the study of ethics to the professional stage.

The Narrow Deontology of the Dominant Approach

When one turns to the content of the teaching of professional ethics there is considerable variety, but, in spite of this, there remains one dominant approach. This tends to have a group of characteristics which are probably related. One is that the central topic is the ethical rules required by the professional code. Another is that teaching and learning methods adopted tend to be didactic. A third is that assessment tends to focus on memorisation of the rules. Thus the experience for students encourages them to learn what the rules are, rather than to think critically about them. They know that their assessment will be a memory test, so they will be reluctant to spend time on critical study or learning about how the rules might apply in practice. Most courses recognise this, which encourages a didactic approach by teachers, further encouraged by the institutional advantage that this approach can be met in economical, large group classes.

This approach is exemplified by the US Multi-State Professional Responsibility Exam, whose purpose is described:

> The purpose of the NCBE Multistate Professional Responsibility Examination (MPRE) is to measure the examinee's knowledge and understanding of established standards related to a lawyer's professional conduct; thus, the MPRE is not a test to determine an individual's personal ethical values. (NCBE 2010)

The format is 60 multiple-choice questions which are to be answered in two hours and five minutes. Although there is no doubt that multiple-choice tests may set complex and demanding tasks, a test which allows two minutes per answer is clearly not designed to encourage critical or contextual thinking. This has

3 Confidential response to Chandler/Duncan study held by author.

not prevented the development of thoughtful and experiential ethics teaching programmes in US law schools, but they tend to be optional and additional to the didactic courses preparing students for the exam.

In the UK the assessment of 'professional conduct' on the Bar Vocational Course has been more varied. Students are assessed on their practice skills by realistic role-play and drafting activities. Assessors have embedded ethical dilemmas into some of these and students are expected to practise in a way which is consistent with the requirements of the code. In addition, there are strict requirements about attendance and engagement with the course and students who fail to attend sufficiently, or to be sufficiently prepared, may fail the professional conduct assessment. This approach still focuses on code compliance, rather than encouraging a critical approach to the rules, but does at least relate it to practice and personal behaviour. It should be noted, however, that the requirements for the new Bar Professional Training Course[4] provide for assessment of 'Professional Ethics' by multiple-choice test instead, plus answers to short problem questions, to be centrally set and taken as an unseen, three-hour examination (BSB 2010). This appears to be a move towards a narrower approach favouring memorisation and not going beyond code compliance.

One analysis which distinguishes between different approaches to ethical behaviour is that between deontological and teleological approaches. Deontology, named from the Greek for the study of duty or obligations, focuses on rules to decide on action and, in its strict form, would lead to acting according to the rules regardless of the consequences. Many religious codes are dominated by this perspective, holding a holy book to be the divinely inspired source of correct behaviour. Teleology, by contrast, is the study of ends, or purposes. It focuses on the consequences of acts (and is therefore often referred to as *consequentialism*).

Adopting either approach leaves many issues for debate. Deontologists may interpret codes differently or quote selectively from holy books. Consequentialists may disagree as to which consequences carry greater value. However, the point I wish to address here is the essential inadequacy of simply adopting either approach. Deontologists may be criticised for some of the unintended consequences of narrow rule-following. Consequentialists may be criticised for allowing the end to justify the means, when they do something widely regarded as wrong in order to achieve a desirable goal. In practice, few people adopt one perspective to the exclusion of the other. This may be brought to the attention of students by getting them to read judgments where the court is struggling with legislation or case law which has had (arguably) unintended damaging consequences. Where they feel unable to avoid unjust consequences they may finish with a judgment which declares the law as it clearly stands, but express their unease and suggest that this is a matter to which Parliament should pay urgent attention.[5] These judgments, which generally flow

4 The BPTC has replaced the BVC from 2010.

5 Such cases occur regularly. One which I read on the day I wrote this section is *Redmacher v. Granatino* [2009] EWCA Civ 649 concerning the status of pre-nuptial

from the arguments presented to the court by the lawyers appearing before it, are also a powerful reminder that a critical approach to the law may be relevant to practitioners as well as to academic lawyers.

An approach to teaching legal ethics which focuses on learning the codes encourages the narrow deontological approach which, I have suggested, is fundamentally flawed. Students who, when faced with the question 'what should I do in this situation', are encouraged to think only of what the code requires and will be less likely to think of consequences or to balance their understanding of the code with the consequences of simply following it.

That may sometimes be appropriate. There may be situations where it is better to follow the rules than to break them in order to achieve justice in a particular situation. Thus the lawyer defending a client she strongly suspects to be guilty should nevertheless challenge prosecution evidence even if the consequences are the acquittal of a guilty defendant. Here it is (arguably) better for the quality of the criminal justice system that this approach be maintained. However, I would argue that this conclusion is better achieved by considering the norms (the deontological approach) and then undertaking a consequentialist analysis. A purely deontological approach is less soundly grounded.

Furthermore, there are many situations where the code is unclear or may be seen as justifying different actions in different situations. In other situations different provisions of the code may come into conflict. Professional practice is full of situations where judgement must be exercised, and a narrow deontological approach does not prepare students for those demands.

The next section will propose a variety of approaches which may do a better job of educating in professional ethics rather than training a group of narrow deontologists.

Developments Proposing a Broader Approach

Although the dominant approach to teaching legal ethics has been a didactic, code-compliance approach, many alternative methods have been introduced. Most have arisen in the context of degree programmes rather than the shorter professional courses, which tend to leave little time for critique or contextual discussions. This is not the place for a full exposition of the different methods which have been adopted, but this section will briefly summarise some distinctive approaches.

agreements. The reports of the Law Commission and equivalent bodies in other jurisdictions also provide examples of studying existing rules from a teleological perspective in proposing reform.

Best established is the introduction of moral philosophy within a formal study of philosophical principles. This commonly formed an element of jurisprudence or legal theory courses, although these are less common than they formerly were.[6]

An alternative is to include the ethics of the legal profession within a course on the legal system or legal method. This can meet the goals both of a liberal education and of professional preparation by permitting a critical and contextual study of the practice of law as opposed to the black letters of which it is composed.[7]

Law and literature is a significant movement which allows for ethical questions to be explored.[8] A related approach is to use other aspects of popular culture in a similar way: film and television can provide a valuable resource for those wanting to discuss ethical issues.[9]

The clinical legal education movement has been a major source of ideas for introducing legal ethics to students (Duncan 2005; Curran et al. 2005). Role-play and simulation provide many opportunities to introduce students to specific issues within controlled situations (Hartwell 1994). Live clinical models may allow for less control, but add invaluable realism and, with proper supervision and clinical seminars, provide a thoughtful educational experience (Curran et al. 2005).

Exercises have been developed where students consider how they would respond to ethical dilemmas and then explore the values which lead them to their decisions (Parker and Evans 2007).

One new development is a module within a UK degree programme which explores students' careers intentions and how they might most effectively prepare themselves for the demands which lie ahead. This lends itself to addressing professional ethics as an element of that study (Roberts 2009).

All of these potential methods may exist as self-standing modules within programmes, or be combined in various ways. A number of academics have argued for ethics to be taught pervasively throughout a law degree (Rhode 1992). These, however, have been hard to implement for a variety of reasons (1992: 54). A method which combines an element of planned pervasiveness with coherent ethics teaching within modules is what Rhode describes as 'ethics by the continuing method'. This requires a degree of faculty-wide commitment to ensure that the teachers who are expected to address ethics within their course are sufficiently informed, prepared and motivated to do so. One developed approach to this may

6 In 1974/5 John Wilson's survey of university legal education showed 96% of participating law schools provided jurisprudence, 72% making it compulsory. This had dropped to below 80% by 1991/2, 41% making it compulsory (Wilson 1993). In 2004 the proportion of compulsory courses had fallen further to 34% (Harris and Beinart 2005).

7 In 2004, 26% of law schools required study of lawyers' professional responsibilities, and a further 8% offered such a course on an optional basis (Harris and Beinart 2005: 309).

8 The journal *Law and Literature* provides a significant source (details available at http://ucpressjournals.com/journal.asp?j=lal).

9 For guidance on useful films and other resources, see http://lib.law.washington.edu/ref/lawonfilm.html.

be seen in the 'vertical curriculum' developed by Griffith University Law School (Robertson 2005). Here, several themes are actively designed to recur in different contexts and in a progressive manner over the years of a degree programme.

All of these methods have the capacity to get students thinking about values: their own values and those of the profession they aspire to join. Wes Pue points out that we ourselves need to have explored our own values if we are faced with students who question our fundamental values. He says:

> Unless one has struggled hard with value choice, such questions are show-stoppers. In the absence of profound knowledge, faculty responses to difficult value questions are likely to mix inadequate fumbling with blaming the student for their 'inadequacies' as moral beings. We shoot from the hip when we are untrained in the use of sights. (Pue 2008: 285)

We owe it to our students, the profession and its clients to address this issue as effectively as we can.

The following section will explore the input of recent scientific work on the roots of human moral behaviour and the way the brain works in order to inform us as to how we might approach using these and other methods to teach legal ethics in our courses.

Developing Ethical Behaviour

Our Characteristics and Our Experience

If we are to achieve an approach to legal education which prepares students as well as possible for the ethical demands of practice we must consider the nature of the challenges which will face them. The example at the beginning of this chapter is just one of many examples, requiring the student to make a short-notice response to a demand from a superior which he or she may consider unethical. The supervising solicitor's demand clearly contravenes the Solicitors' Regulation Authority's Code of Conduct Rule 1.04 that 'You must act in the best interests of each client' (SRA 2007). But it requires more than knowledge of the rules for the student to take proper action. It also requires courage. This is something we will return to later.

A further example is one which arises regularly in practice:

> You have taken on a case for the Free Representation Unit to advise and represent a client who claims to have been unfairly dismissed for fighting with his foreman. He claims that he was only acting in self-defence. His employer has responded with statements from his foreman and other employees that your client instigated the fight and has a history of losing his temper and acting aggressively. He comes to meet you in the FRU offices. When you begin to

> explain the strength of the evidence against him he responds angrily. You would prefer not to continue with the case but you are acting under the Bar Code of Conduct which prevents you from refusing a case you are competent and able to take on (BSB 2004: para 601). What would you do?

This example is drawn from the experience of one of my students on the City Law School Bar Vocational Course. It is another situation which requires courage but in this case empathy is also a significant factor. The student's relatively privileged background meant that her client's background and experience were radically different from hers. This situation may create a barrier to the level of empathy which would naturally arise with someone with whom one had much in common.

We will turn to look at empathy and courage below, but first it is worth considering recent research which suggests that there are elements of our brains which help us to respond ethically to dilemmas. This is important because this research challenges two tendencies which have suggested that the brain is hard-wired in favour of self-centred responses.

The first of these tendencies arises from the fact that most of us live in societies which are dominated by market principles which tend to encourage competitive, self-centred behaviour. I do not intend to engage in a debate about the propriety of particular political ideologies. After all, most political systems notionally premised on communist ideologies were consistent with a considerable amount of unethical behaviour. Instead I suggest that different ideological systems are exploited by the powerful. Our system happens to be a market-driven one and therefore is the one to which we should respond. These capitalist principles tend to encourage the values of competition and individualism leading to self-centred decision-making. This raises issues about whether they may impose some constraint on the tendency to behave ethically or otherwise.

The second tendency, which has developed out of Darwin's theory of evolution, is the view that the process of natural selection must inevitably produce hard-wiring in human minds which leads to self-interested behaviour. In other words, people are inherently self-centred and competitive, evolved thus as a factor in their survival.[10] These two tendencies combine in a justificatory cycle which may influence the perspectives of many of our students who enter legal education. It also gives us notice of aspects of the nature of the world into which they will go once they have left us. Accepting them in a simplistic way may also raise in students' and teachers' minds the thought that any attempt to encourage ethical behaviour is bound to fail.

10 These are hotly contested areas in which we should be cautious about drawing confident conclusions. 'When you hear another explanation of how a particular human characteristic … derives from our origins as savannah-dwelling lion-fodder, ask a simple question: is this testable? If so (and it often is) it's a scientific hypothesis. Otherwise it's an origin myth' (Ryrie 2009: 40).

Life, of course, is not as simple as this. We recognise that individuals' motivation is far more complex than this. Not only may there be personal advantage in behaviour that supports others, but most individuals appear to have some moral sense which may lead them to behave in altruistic or even self-sacrificing ways. What are the sources for this type of behaviour? They are probably multi-faceted.

Conventional 'survival of the fittest' analyses draw attention to the fact that a great evolutionary advantage is given to groups who can co-operate. This goes beyond the immediate family group (where Dawkins' 'Selfish Gene' concept (Dawkins 1989) may justify co-operation). Gary Olson cites Marc Hauser (2006: 416) as presenting sophisticated studies suggesting 'that large-scale co-operation within the human species – including with genetically unrelated individuals within a group – was favoured by selection' (Olson 2007). So, without calling in aid any altruistic tendencies we may well expect a variety of behaviours which value the interests of others. In the field of legal education, Donald Nicolson has proposed four categories of student:

- *The Sinners*: a very small group, who are already inclined to lie, cheat, bully and oppress others in the service of their clients[11] and themselves;
- *The Saints*: a relatively small group of students with already developed virtuous characters in the sense that they value morality and tend to act accordingly;
- *Thatcher's Children*: possibly the largest group – they are not incorrigibly bad but tend towards amorality and the pursuit of self-interest;
- *The Moral Innocents*: probably the second biggest group – with the right conditions they may develop a sense of ethical professionalism, but otherwise are likely to adopt the current norms of amoral professionalism.

(Nicolson 2008: 161)

He is pessimistic as to the proportion of students 'whose moral characters can be influenced towards that of ethically aware and morally committed professionals' (2008: 162). However, most educators would probably take the view, and I would agree, that their task is not to inculcate a particular ethical view, but rather to encourage and facilitate students to engage seriously in debate about ethical issues so that their own decision-making is informed and challenged.

New research gives us reason to believe that most people's minds will provide a fruitful field for sowing ethical ideas. Neuroscientists report experiments which suggest that moral responses are, indeed, influenced by the hard-wiring of the brain. Michael Koenigs found that 'damage to … the ventromedial prefrontal cortex (VMPFC) increases a preference for "utilitarian" choices in moral dilemmas – judgments that favour the aggregate welfare over the welfare of fewer individuals' (reported in Moll and de Oliveira-Souza 2008: 30). Thus, when people make

11 Admittedly, such behaviour is arguably a morally justified position (see e.g. Nicolson and Webb 1999: chs 6–8), but only if adopted after due reflection rather than as self-serving justification (Nicolson's reference).

explicit moral judgements, the VMPFC is engaged and damage to it appears to reduce prosocial sentiments (2008: 33). This receives confirmation from Moll and de Oliveira-Souza's evidence that the VMPFC is engaged when people 'are passively exposed to stimuli evocative of prosocial moral sentiments (such as a hungry child)' (33). This suggests that this physical site in the brain plays a role, where it is not damaged or compromised, in encouraging empathic responses to others in difficult circumstances.

This, however, is not to say that moral behaviour is biologically determined, merely that biology plays a part in moral decision-making. It is clear from our own everyday experience that if a particular ethical approach can be a trait it varies considerably (like other attributes such as intelligence or physical strength) within the population. Furthermore, the capacity of humans to undertake decisions and actions out of principle rather than any (conscious or subconscious) analysis of interests is well established. This tendency may flow from many sources, including religious convictions, a sense of well-being at doing what is approved by one's peers or simply a feeling of personal satisfaction at taking principled decisions. Modern Darwinists point to evolutionary reasons for the development of all of these tendencies.[12] The only safe conclusion is that both nature and nurture play a part in individuals' propensity for moral decision-making.

Whatever the balance between nature and nurture, the fact that nurture may play a part is of crucial significance for educators. If not, we have no role. How, then, might education influence the moral behaviour of prospective lawyers? The starting point is to inform students of different ethical positions which might be held. Note that this simple proposal already goes further than training which simply seeks code-compliance. It requires discussion and debate. It would be one possible focus for a jurisprudence or legal theory course. It is intellectually challenging and of great value in adding depth and critical context to legal studies. It can be addressed in many ways, for example through studies of philosophy, through literature or through developed problem-based learning. It is an invaluable starting point for a critical view of code provisions and should therefore precede that element of education.

It is not, however, sufficient if we wish to prepare students for the ethical demands of practice. If we accept that these learning methods can assist the student to make informed choices about ethical values we need to go further to assist them to put those values into practice when faced with challenging situations. This requires empathy, courage and experience. We shall consider empathy and courage and then explore the ways in which experiential learning may help with developing them.

12 Wright argues that the passing of genes to future generations may be facilitated, in species which operate in social groups, by such behaviour, thus proposing an amoral source for moral behaviour (Wright 1996: generally and 338–44).

Empathy

The more we share with others, the greater is the likelihood of an empathic response to them. It is easy to feel empathy for close family members, longstanding friends and neighbours, those with whom we share religious convictions, political views or even experiences. As Decety and Lamm say:

> In humans and other mammals, an impulse to care for offspring is almost certainly genetically hard wired. Less clear, however, is whether an impulse to care for siblings, more remote kin, and similar nonkin is genetically hard wired. (Batson 2006: 59–64) The emergence of altruism, of empathizing with and caring for those who are not kin, is not easily explained within the framework of neo-Darwinian theories of natural selection, and thus social learning explanations of kinship patterns in human helping behavior are highly plausible. Indeed, one of the most striking aspects of human empathy is that it can be felt for virtually any target, even targets of a different species. (Decety and Lamm 2006: 1148)

It becomes more difficult when there is greater distance or difference between us. Differences in class, race or education can make empathy less easy to achieve. I do not suggest that these are *necessarily* barriers to empathy. Many people respond empathically in spite of considerable differences, but others may find that they do become barriers.

There may, moreover, be substantial reasons for thinking that the capacity for empathy with different people is expanding over historical time. Peter Singer notes that Plato proposed a moral advance which seems remarkably restricted to us: 'He argued that Greeks should not, in war, enslave other Greeks, lay waste their lands or raze their houses; they should do these things only to non-Greeks' (Singer 1981, quoted in Wright 1996). Observation of the current expansion of moral concern beyond national boundaries leads him to suggest that it may eventually reach a global scope. This may be to a degree speculative. It is not the case today.

In an increasingly globalised world with major migration between countries for economic reasons and as refugees, we are increasingly likely to encounter people with significant differences from ourselves. What is more, the nature of migration means that a high proportion of migrants will find themselves disadvantaged economically and in other ways and are particularly likely to find themselves in legal difficulties.

Migrants are also more likely to have difficulties with the language of their host country. This produces a further difference, which may inhibit empathy. Moreover, the very difficulty of communication may act as a further barrier to empathy, let alone the fact that the struggle to comprehend adds to the lawyer's work and the stress involved in advising and representing the client. Work with relatively marginal clients is particularly likely during the early years of practice, when newly qualified lawyers have the least experience to fall back on. All lawyers should have a sufficient degree of empathy with their clients (and perhaps others) if they are to manage effectively the difficult balance between objectivity and engagement.

Decety and Lamm also provide insights into the mechanisms which permit management of that balance. Their argument is in the section of their article headed 'Self-Other Awareness and Empathy', and concludes:

> … self-awareness and the sense of agency play pivotal roles in empathy and significantly contribute to social interaction. These important aspects are likely to be at play in distinguishing emotional contagion, which heavily relies on the automatic link between perception of the emotions expressed by the other and one's own experience of the same emotion, and empathy that necessitates a more detached relation. We suggest that the nonoverlap in the neural response between self and other frees up processing capacity in the brain for unfolding appropriate future action towards the other. Further, being aware of one's own feelings, and being able to regulate consciously one's own emotions may be what allows us to distinguish empathic responses to others from our own personal distress, with only the former leading to prosocial behaviour. (Decety and Lamm 2006: 1155)

Their reference to 'nonoverlap in the neural response between self and other' is well explained by Ramachandran. He describes experiments using monkeys where the same neuron was seen to fire 'not only (say) when the monkey reached for a peanut but also when it watched *another* monkey reach for a peanut!' (Ramachandran 2007). These neurons are known as 'mirror neurons' and appear not to distinguish between self and the other. How does this link to empathy? Ramachandran describes further experiments with human subjects:

> Neurons in the anterior cingulate will respond to the patient being poked with a needle; they are often referred to as sensory pain neurons. Remarkably, researchers at the University of Toronto have found that some of them will fire equally strongly when the patient watches someone *else* is [sic] poked. (2007)

He describes these as 'empathy neurons'. If his conclusions are correct, they certainly explain our ability to feel for the concerns of others and the work of Decety and Lamm provides some insight into the balancing processes which enable us to maintain those distinctions when taking difficult decisions.

Thus the evidence from neuroscience gives us a basis for understanding both our capacity for empathy and also for limiting our application of it where it might conflict with self-interest or where it might be limited to those who are in some way close to us. How might educators address the importance of developing a broad capacity for empathy in their students? According to Olson, '[c]ultivating empathic engagement through education remains a poorly understood enterprise' (Olson 2007).

Preston and de Waal propose a number of factors which affect the likelihood of empathic behaviour:

> The literature suggests that empathy and helping are determined by the subject's ability to help. Human subjects are more likely to help when the level of need or potential benefit to the object is higher (note that this is also when the probability of reciprocation by the object is highest). Adult human subjects that are trait sympathetic volunteer to help a distressed object when they expect to have control over the procedure or expect to be able to help the object. Thus, it may be more accurate to consider helping behavior as the result of a complex cost/benefit analysis on the perceived effectiveness of helping and the effect of helping on short and long-term goals. If the cost is greater than the benefit, attention can be directed away from the distress to control or subvert empathic processing altogether, making the desire to help less likely. (Preston and de Waal 2002: 25)

So how do we use these insights to inform our approach to the ethical education of lawyers? Clearly we should be developing in them high levels of competence so that they can identify ways of assisting their client and have confidence in their ability to put it into effect. We should also be encouraging autonomy and independence of mind so that they can exercise effective control over the procedures available to them. These characteristics are very much those generally considered to be engaged in practice as a lawyer and are consistent with many of the principles in the codes of practice. They are also to be found in much conventional legal education. They indicate the importance of effective recognition of the cognitive domain for the quality of affective behaviour. However, they are not sufficient.

One paradox is that autonomy, useful for people to be able to act effectively once they have responded empathically, may be challenged by that empathic response. Berlant suggests: 'You want to feel attached to others, but you don't want to be destabilized. Empathy reveals your non-autonomy, and this is a culture that values freedom and identifies freedom with autonomy'. Gibson quotes her as saying that '[y]ou have to train people to act with empathy, to restrain their ambivalence' and continues: '[s]entimental literature—books like *Uncle Tom's Cabin* or films like *Schindler's List*—provides training by demonstrating the consequences of not having empathy' (in Gibson 2006).

This approach has long been proposed by Nussbaum, who suggests that education in the arts and liberal humanities helps students to understand the lives of strangers (Nussbaum 1997). Olson criticises this on the basis that such work rarely addresses the reasons why the disadvantaged face such problems (Olson 2007). If he is right, it draws our attention to the need to combine studies of literature with a critical take on why those people's experience was as it was. This lends itself superbly to legal studies.[13] Similar approaches can be developed using film and other aspects of popular culture.[14]

These approaches involve a combination of learning which takes students into the experience of others with learning about why they face that experience and what might be done about it. They begin to establish links between the cognitive domain which forms the mainstream of most legal education and the affective domain. In this way they may develop their understanding of empathy for the other.

The connection between empathy and similarity with the other raises a further paradox which has been recognised in the context of social work training.

> … close similarities between social worker and client—in religion, background, race, class, education, or family—can make for a trickier relationship. 'It's easy to assume you know what a person is thinking if they're like you', [Teigiser] says. 'You say three things to me and I don't ask anything more because I know it all'. Uncovering a connection with someone completely different, however, requires hard work and lots of questions. 'You and I might have the same objective experience, but it's not about that', Teigiser says. 'Empathy means understanding another person's *subjective* experience'. (Gibson 2006, quoting Karen Teigiser, a colleague of Olson's)

This directs us to another prerequisite for effective ethical education: experience, but first we should consider moral courage.

Moral Courage

Both the ethical dilemmas presented in this chapter require courage for an ethical response as well as the capacity for evaluating which alternative is best and the empathy to be able to engage with the other person's needs. No doubt, individuals bring different degrees of courage to their legal studies and legal practice based on their own inherent characteristics and their upbringing. However, as has been found by studies into other aspects of human character, there may be a role for legal education.

What do we mean by moral courage? Leslie Sekerka defines it as 'the ability to use inner principles to do what is good for others, regardless of threat to self, as a matter of practice' (Sekerka and Bagozzi 2007: 135). He points out how affect

13 See, for example, the journal *Law and Literature*, which provides regular articles in this field predominantly from a US perspective, but providing analysis which is of broader relevance and validity. Details are available at http://ucpressjournals.com/journal.asp?j=lal. See also Hanafin, Gearey and Brooker 2004.

14 See http://lib.law.washington.edu/ref/lawonfilm.html, which is a resource in its own right, and provides details of a number of other sources. See also Greenfield, Osborn and Robson 2007.

acts independently from the judgement of the value of a goal when a decision to act is being taken.

Some instrumental acts will be intrinsically enjoyable or lead to pleasant consequences. Others may be so noxious or unpleasant as to lead to avoidance. The felt affect in response to the consideration of the possible means supplies additional information to a decision-maker on the personal consequences of engaging in goal pursuit (Sekerka and Bagozzi 2007: 138–9). This functions through multiple stages via anticipated emotions, affect towards means, desires to act, felt self-conscious emotions and attachment to a group (144).

This suggests ways in which organisations may improve the likelihood of ethical behaviour and may also provide guidance to law schools in establishing a strong group which espouses ethical values. It may also be useful to students to consider this analysis when reflecting on their own fears and behaviour. Although there is limited empirical work in applying these psychological insights to law students, some work has been done. In addressing it I will focus on the importance of being able to overcome the natural tendency to defer to dominant behaviour, whether from a senior colleague, as in my first example, or from an aggressive client, as in my second.

The prevalence of this tendency was made appallingly clear in the famous Milgram experiments of the 1960s (Milgram 1974). Here experimental subjects believed that they were delivering electric shocks of increasing severity to 'victims' who gave wrong answers. A high proportion continued to levels apparently dangerous or extremely painful for the 'victim' upon being prompted by an authority figure. Steven Hartwell conducted a related experiment in the context of legal education (1990: 141–3). Students were interviewing a 'client' seeking advice in respect of a forthcoming rent dispute hearing. Hartwell was in an adjoining room, available to give advice. Twenty-four students sought advice and were all told that they must advise their client to perjure herself in court. Although the experimenters had expected that the majority of students would reject this advice, which so clearly flouted their ethical code, all but one obeyed it and advised the client to perjure herself.

Hartwell used Kohlberg's theory of moral development to analyse and explain these disturbing results. Kohlberg identified six stages of moral reasoning, which can be simply represented as follows.

There are two 'pre-conventional' stages. The first is fundamentally punishment avoidance and accepts authoritarianism: might is right. The second is self-interestedly instrumental. Thus collaboration between others may be seen as desirable if it brings benefits. These two stages are seen as pre-conventional as they operate independently of the moral conventions of the culture within which the individual lives.

The two 'conventional' stages are based on those cultural conventions. Stage three involves conformity and establishing longstanding trusting relationships. People operating at this level tend to be highly concerned with approval by those close to them. Stage four involves a more conscious acceptance of the rules through which moral conventions are articulated. There is an acceptance of authority and a recognition of the values of maintaining social order.

The post-conventional stages are more concerned with principled moral reasoning. Stage five, which Kohlberg described as 'social contract driven', engages the individual with fundamental moral principles such as justice and equality. This will involve a critical analysis of rules and a recognition that there are competing values of individual rights and collective interests. Resolution of any such conflicts will come through debate and majority decision. Stage six involves reasoning based on universal ethical principles and remains a very abstract concept. Kohlberg found few research subjects who used it consistently, which suggests that it is not common for people to reach this stage.[15]

Hartwell concluded that in order for people to act ethically when faced with such an authority dilemma it would be necessary for them to have attained stage five. This concerned him because:

> Stage 5 moral reasoning is not common. Only highly selective groups of individuals such as students engaged in advanced moral philosophy, regularly demonstrate Stage 5 moral reasoning. Law draws its practitioners unselectively from diverse elements of society. Entrance into law school is not predicated upon the attainment of some stage of moral development. Neither success on the bar examination nor high scores on professional responsibility examinations indicate a high stage of moral reasoning. Even under ideal circumstances, the development of an individual's moral reasoning, as measured by change in a Kohlberg stage, is a very slow process. The notion that the moral reasoning of the legal profession might somehow be elevated to Stage 5, either through training or by selection, seemed unrealistic. (1990: 144–5)

Hartwell also developed a reflective practice in his students in respect of their client interviewing. As this improved they became more sympathetic, but this made them 'more vulnerable to manipulative and aggressive clients' (150). This suggests a real conflict between values generally considered desirable in lawyer interaction with clients.

Hartwell responded with three innovations. He introduced assertiveness training (151). He began to teach the Kohlberg theory of moral development to his students (155), and get them to analyse different responses to dilemmas in Kohlbergian terms. Finally, he introduced simulations whereby students were faced with ethical dilemmas and then had to consider the proper responses, devise rules in respect of those issues and justify those rules (164). His tentative

15 It should be observed that Kohlberg's analysis is not universally accepted. In particular, it has been criticised for an uncritical acceptance of narrow justice-oriented values and a rejection of the values inherent in an 'ethic of care'. See Gilligan (1982). It nevertheless provides a useful schema for categorising moral decision-making and is used in this chapter only with that intention.

conclusions are that there is an improvement in students' scores on a test designed to measure the degree to which they used stage five reasoning. On this basis he qualifies his initial pessimism by suggesting that moral development may be learned. Crucial components are: recognising the fact of a moral dilemma, which can be improved by empathy; developing a capacity for moral reasoning, which can be improved by the use of simulation; and exercising a moral choice, which can be improved by assertiveness training (167).

It is the last of these which is most clearly related to the ability to exhibit moral courage. If combined with measures to develop student competence and appropriate levels of self-confidence, some effective steps can be taken towards developing moral courage.

Implications for Legal Education: Experience

This section will seek to draw together the conclusions reached above and apply them to how we might approach our task as legal educators to recognise the impact of emotions on educating ethical lawyers.

We need to support the development of students' knowledge base and the development of their competency with relevant experience. 'Ervin Staub ... acknowledges that even if empathy is rooted in nature, people will not act on it "... unless they have certain kinds of life experiences that shape their orientation toward other human beings and toward themselves"' (quoted in Olson 2007). We have limited influence over our students' life experience, but in designing their legal education there is a number of things we can do.

The conventional classroom may not, however, be an effective way of achieving these goals. Alan Lerner observes that 'attempts to directly teach thinking and reasoning in a classroom setting generally show little transfer to activities outside the classroom, and because moral judgment involves [more highly emotionally charged] topics than are usually dealt with in courses that attempt to teach thinking and reasoning, the degree of transfer is likely to be even smaller' (Lerner 2004: 673, quoting Haidt 2001).

Most programmes designed to develop ethical practice are based on the theories of Lawrence Kohlberg (1981). Steven Hartwell developed the work described above by designing such experiential courses and conducted research into their impact (Hartwell 1994). This work, based on the development of role-play, found a significant effect on his students' moral development which was not present in students only taking non-experiential courses.

Why should this be?

> 'Experience produces a qualitative change in the mode and content of knowing, which cannot be replicated by the transmission of information or the discussion of cases. ... The way in which ideas are understood after they have been used feels different in a sense that is not fully explained by the fact that they are

> more easily remembered'. This is particularly true of ideas about values, much of whose content is lost when understood in a purely intellectual way. (Myers 1996: 835, quoting Bellow 1973: 391)

Thus it is through being required to undergo appropriate experiences that students 'begin to internalize and make their own moral and ethical judgments' (Myers 1996: 836).

I would endorse this view and also suggest two other advantages of experiential approaches:

- One is that experience of playing either lawyers or (particularly) clients in role-play can develop insight which can help with empathy for those with very different experiences. This may be even more true of working in live clinical settings where students advise and represent real clients.
- The second is that by providing students with experience of realistic and real situations we can help them to avoid 'fight or flight' reactions when faced with the need to respond appropriately in a challenging situation.

The first of these has been addressed above. I will now turn to the second.

Alan Lerner has provided a clear explanation of how understanding this significant issue may be assisted by an understanding of how the brain works.[16] Following MacLean (1978) he explains how the brain may be presented as three distinct but interconnected parts: the most primitive (sometimes known as the 'reptilian' brain); the limbic system; and the neocortex, that part of the brain which is most recently evolved (Lerner 2004: 659).

Lerner describes the limbic system as:

> primarily involved with the emotional system, with evaluating, organizing, and directing incoming data for processing in the brain stem and the cortex, and with our awareness of ourselves, physically and emotionally (ibid). 'It is also involved with certain of our primal activities such as sense of smell, sex, nourishment, and bonding between individuals' (Sylwester, 1995, 43–44). It is capable of mediating our responses to external data through its ability to 'read' and act upon our emotional responses, as well as overriding rational thought. (2004: 660)

This capacity has a profound consequence when we are faced with a novel problem or challenge:

16 A fuller explanation of the gross anatomy and microanatomy of the brain may be found in Roche's contribution to this book and of the brain's significance for emotion (Chapter 2).

> Because the limbic system is involved in all of these activities, emotion is involved with virtually everything that we experience or do. For example, when incoming data indicates a problem, and the limbic system in concert with our rational/emotional brain structures, can discover no appropriate solution or problem solving process, anxiety, even fear, takes over, and the brain activates our fight-or-flight stress response. (Lerner 2004: 660)

The neocortex is described as the part of the brain which:

> does most of the processing of sensory data, and makes language, logical and formal thinking, and planning for the future possible. It is responsible for the creativity that we call science and art (Caine and Caine 1994: 63) and is largely responsible for planning, analysis, sequencing, learning from errors, certain inhibitions to inappropriate behaviors, and capacity for abstraction, including empathy (Caine and Caine 1994: 67). Logical/rational thinking is centered in the neocortex. (Lerner 2004: 660)

The interconnectedness of these parts of the brain is mediated by the limbic system. Its function of directing incoming data either to the neocortex or the primitive brain for processing makes it the key to how individuals respond to stimulus. If we want our students to use their rational and empathic capacities, the neocortex must be engaged. According to Lerner:

> The challenge for legal educators is to help students learn so that, when faced with problems, whether intellectual, moral or both, they avoid resorting solely to the automatic, primitive, flight or fight response, but rather engage their neocortex with all of its power to process sensory data, draw broadly from memory, abstract, identify patterns, analyze rationally, and create new concepts, thus bringing to consciousness a broad range of potentially effective, ethical responses. (2004: 661)

What leads to individuals responding to challenge by engaging their primitive brain rather than their neocortex? It is particularly when faced with stressful situations, with which, unfortunately, legal practice is replete: 'Making choices and exercising judgment produces stress. Making morally charged choices, or choices in situations where one feels personally threatened, produces a high level of stress' (678). This is not necessarily harmful. It leads the body to produce two hormones, adrenaline and noradrenalin, which assist us in thinking and responding effectively. However, where stress is extreme or continuing, the body produces excessive amounts of cortisol, a third hormone which tends to inhibit rational thought. 'Our brain resorts to recall primarily from its more primitive, survival oriented reptilian and limbic systems' (679).

It is not inevitable that this will happen, and it appears that the more we feel capable of dealing with a problem the more likely we are to avoid the reaction

(Caine and Caine 1994). There are a number of ways in which educators can help students to develop the necessary characteristics.

Increase Number of Encounters

One is simply to raise the number of students' encounters with ethical dilemmas. The more often they are raised the more familiar they will become and the less challenging they will appear when encountered in practice. This supports arguments for a degree of pervasive ethics teaching in law courses.[17]

Developing Expertise

Another is to develop expertise in our students.

As described by Gary L. Blasi (1995) and Donald A. Schön (1983), experts seem to be able to leapfrog over several levels of detailed analysis to identify and engage patterns of apparently related information directly to a given problem, and also to matters that are facially different, yet analogous, and thus useful for the solution. Their memories include a combination of a deep body of subject matter data, and 'experience', the accumulated knowledge from actually using the data in various situations over time (i.e. in context). Accessing these memories permits them to compare and contrast the characteristics of the presenting problem with those of the many problems with which they have engaged in the past (Lerner 2004: 686).

There is a considerable literature on the use of experience to develop high standards of competence at complex professional tasks. Schön's (1983) work explores different levels of reflection (reflection on action and reflection in action) to explain the development of expertise. At its highest levels this has been described as 'artistry' and has been applied to legal education (Webb 1995). It is beyond the scope of this chapter to develop the arguments further. Suffice it to say that this literature provides a strong theoretical basis for the value of incorporating active learning methods combined with a self-conscious reflective process. By undertaking a reiterative process which takes students through a cycle of experience, reflection on that experience, planning for further experience which then takes place, perhaps in different contexts (Kolb 1984), students participate in a learning spiral which should assist them to develop expertise or even artistry as lawyers.

This is commonplace in the discourse on higher education and represents the currently dominant approach amongst education theorists. I refer to it here to draw attention to the fact that our increasing understanding of the role of the affective domain is a further encouragement for this approach. Indeed, Avrom Sherr has published research which shows that even where experience fails to

---

17 For approaches to achieving this, see 'Developments Proposing a Broader Approach' section above.

improve lawyers' competence, it does improve their confidence (Sherr 1996). If this is true it will have a direct impact on the way in which the affective domain impacts upon individuals' ability to respond rationally to ethical challenges rather than simply react.

Conclusion

This analysis has proceeded at a relatively general level. I have made no mention of gender differences, an understanding of which could play a significant role in our approach to student learning. Nor have I addressed different perceptions students may hold about personality; whether they are 'entity theorists' or 'incremental theorists' (Maughan 2011). However, while these are further layers of understanding which are worth exploring, I believe that these conclusions are valid and follow the evidence and arguments presented above.

Considering the role of emotions in preparing people to be ethical lawyers provides strong support for a number of educational approaches and developments which have recently been recommended. I shall summarise these here and suggest that the approaches recommended are mutually supportive.

The first relates to the overall curriculum. The inadequacy of narrow code-compliance suggests that ethical issues should be raised often and in different contexts throughout students' legal studies. A degree of pervasiveness therefore needs to be planned for and this requires careful organisation.

The second relates to the type of learning students are exposed to. Students need a foundation of knowledge which they should then be enabled to apply through a variety of experiential learning approaches. What should that knowledge include? I would argue that it requires much of the substantive legal knowledge already reflected in the compulsory parts of most law degrees; a contextual and critical view of how the legal profession operates today; and a critical view of professional norms. This foundation permits a diversity of experiential approaches which have been widely considered, both in respect of the overall law curriculum (Le Brun and Johnstone 1994), skills development (Webb and Maughan 1996; Maughan and Webb 2005) and the development of clinical methods (Brayne, Duncan and Grimes 1998).

Much of this can be achieved in the classroom. The use of problem-based learning, whether simply to reinforce knowledge by its application, or to discover knowledge through the problem-solving process, is increasingly used within legal education.[18] Hartwell's research suggests that there is greater development within the affective domain if that problem-solving is approached through simulation rather than as a pure paper or discussion-based exercise (Hartwell 1994). Another advantage of simulation is the fact that students can take on roles other than that of the lawyer. This may have a role in developing empathy.

---

18 For a critical view of its use in legal education see Cruickshank (1996).

Simulation is also a necessary prerequisite for students undertaking live clinical work. Providing students with real experience may not be possible for all, given the cost and organisational implications of doing so. However, the growth of pro bono work with other agencies provides a means of engaging the resources and experience of others provided effective learning contracts are developed with those providers. Nor is it necessary for student law clinics to be integrated into the curriculum for them to have an impact on ethical awareness and moral development (Nicolson 2008).

The diversity of interest of academic staff is bound to have an impact on the nature of the student experience. It is therefore fortunate that such diversity of approach exists. It enables us to address the analytical, critical academic purposes of the law degree while also assisting individuals to develop the resources necessary for their future involvement in society or even as lawyers. Currently, new resources are being developed to provide an international resource bank and forum for those interested in working in this field linked with opportunities to contribute to that bank and to discussion of issues of mutual interest.[19]

Ultimately, students will retain responsibility for their ethical behaviour. Their values will be their own, rather than ours. However, these values will provide a better foundation for their lives after they have left us, whether as legal professionals or other members of society, if they have been exposed to a variety of learning experiences which have required them to think about those values and to do things with them. This, I suggest, is a valid goal for any higher education. For legal higher education it is best placed in the context of a critical and experiential study of practice as a lawyer in the real social and economic context in which that is situated.

References

American Bar Association. 2010. *Standards for the Approval of Law Schools*. [Online] Available at: http://www.abanet.org/legaled/standards/standards.html [accessed 19 July 2010].

Batson, C.D. 2006. Folly Bridges, in *Bridging Social Psychology*, edited by P.A.M. Van Lange. Mahwah, NJ: Erlbaum, 59–64.

Bellow, G. 1973. On Teaching the Teachers: Some Preliminary Reflections on Clinical Education as Methodology, *Clinical Education for the Law Student* 374 (CLEPR).

Blasi, G. 1995. What Lawyers Know: Lawyering Expertise, Cognitive Science, and the Functions of Theory, *Journal of Legal Education* 45: 313–97.

Brayne, H., Duncan, N. and Grimes, R. 1998. *Clinical Legal Education: Active Learning in Your Law School*. London: Blackstone.

19 Colleagues may wish to participate in and contribute to the forum at www.teachinglegalethics.org.

BSB. 2004. *Code of Conduct of the Bar of England and Wales.* [Online] Available at: http://www.barstandardsboard.org.uk/standardsandguidance/codeofconduct/ [accessed 19 July 2010].

BSB. 2008. *BVC Course Specification Requirements and Guidance.* [Online] Available at: http://www.barstandardsboard.org.uk/assets/documents/2007-8%20Golden%20Book.doc [accessed 19 July 2010].

BSB. 2010. *BPTC Handbook 2010/2011.* [Online] Available at: http://www.barstandardsboard.org.uk/assets/documents/BPTC%20-%20handbook%20version%2001-08-08.pdf [accessed 19 July 2010].

Caine, R.N. and Caine, G. 1994. *Making Connections: Teaching and the Human Brain.* London: Pearson Learning.

Chandler, S. and Duncan, N. 2008. Survey of Ethics Teaching, in *Preparatory Ethics Training for Future Solicitors*, edited by K. Economides and J. Rogers. London: Law Society, 78–86.

Cozolino, L. 2006. *The Neuroscience of Human Relationships: Attachment and the Developing Social Brain.* New York: Norton.

Cruickshank, D. 1996. Problem-based Learning in Legal Education, in *Teaching Lawyers' Skills*, edited by J. Webb and C. Maughan. London: Butterworth, 187–239.

Curran, L., Dickson, J. and Noone, M. 2005. Pushing Boundaries: Designing Clinical Programs to Teach Law Students an Understanding of Ethical Practice, *International Journal of Clinical Legal Education* 8: 104–22.

Dawkins, R. 1989. *The Selfish Gene*, 2nd edition. Oxford: Oxford University Press.

Decety, J. and Lamm, C. 2006. Human Empathy through the Lens of Social Neuroscience, *Scientific World Journal*, 6 September: 1146–63. [Online] Available at: http://www.thescientificworld.com/TSW/Search/searchResults.asp?month=9&YearofPub=2006&JournalTitles=141,43&PageSize=10&volume=6&pageno=1&From=Toc&openaccess=1&jid=141 [accessed 20 July 2010].

Duncan, N. 1997. The Skill of Learning: Implications of the ACLEC First Report for Teaching Skills on Undergraduate Law Courses, *WebJCLI* 5. [Online] Available at: http://webjcli.ncl.ac.uk/1997/issue5/duncan5.html [accessed 19 July 2010].

Duncan, N. 2005. Ethical Practice and Clinical Legal Education, *International Journal of Clinical Legal Education* 7: 7–19.

Economides, K. and Rogers, J. 2008. *Preparatory Ethics Training for Future Solicitors.* London: Law Society.

Evans, A. and Palermo, J. 2005. Australian Law Students' Perceptions of their Values: Interim Results in the First Year – 2001 – of a Three-year Empirical Assessment, *Legal Ethics* 5: 103–29.

Gibson, L. 2006. Mirrored Emotion, *University of Chicago Magazine* 94(4): 1–9. [Online] Available at: http://magazine.uchicago.edu/0604/features/emotion.shtml [accessed 19 July 2010].

Gilligan, C. 1982. *In a Different Voice.* Cambridge: Harvard University Press.

Greenfield, S., Osborn, G. and Robson, P. 2007. *Film and the Law*, 2nd edition. Oxford: Hart.

Haidt, J. 2001. The Emotional Dog and its Rational Tail: A Social Intuitionist Approach to Moral Judgment, *Psychological Review* 108: 814–34.

Hanafin, P., Gearey, A. and Brooker, J. (eds) 2004. Law and Literature, *Journal of Law and Society* 31.

Harris, P. and Beinart, S. 2005. A Survey of Law Schools in the United Kingdom, *Law Teacher* 39: 299–366.

Hartwell, S. 1990. Moral Development, Ethical Conduct and Clinical Education, *New York Law School Law Review* 35: 131–68.

Hartwell, S. 1994. Promoting Moral Development through Experiential Teaching, *Clinical Law Review* 1: 505–40.

Hauser, M. 2006. *Moral Minds.* New York: Harper Collins.

Kohlberg, L. 1981. *Essays on Moral Development, Vol. I: The Philosophy of Moral Development*. San Francisco: Harper and Row.

Kolb, D. 1984. *Experiential Learning: Experience as the Source of Learning and Development.* Englewood Cliffs, NJ: Prentice Hall.

Le Brun, M. and Johnstone, R. 1994. *The Quiet (R)evolution.* Sydney: Law Book Company.

Lerner, A. 2004. Using Our Brains: What Cognitive Science and Social Psychology Teach us about Teaching Law Students to Make Ethical, Professionally Responsible Choices, *Quinnipiac Law Review* 23: 643–706.

MacLean, P.D. 1978. A Mind of Three Minds: Educating the Triune Brain, in *Education and the Brain*, edited by J.S. Chall and A.F. Mirsky. Chicago: University of Chicago Press, 308–42.

Maughan, C. 2011. Why Study Emotion?, in this collection.

Maughan, C. and Webb, J. 2005. *Lawyering Skills and the Legal Process*, 2nd edition. Cambridge: Cambridge University Press.

Milgram, S. 1974. *Obedience to Authority: An Experimental View.* London: HarperCollins.

Moll, J. and De Oliveira-Souza, R. 2008. When Morality is Hard to Like, *Scientific American Mind* Feb/March: 30.

Myers, E. 1996. Simple Truths about Moral Education, *American University Law Review* 45: 823–58.

NCBE. 2010. *Description of the MPRE.* [Online] National Conference of Bar Examiners. Available at: http://www.ncbex.org/multistate-tests/mpre/mpre-faqs/description0/ [accessed 19 July 2010].

Nicolson, D. 2008. 'Education, Education, Education': Legal, Moral and Clinical, *Law Teacher* 42: 145–72.

Nicolson, D. and Webb, J. 1999. *Professional Legal Ethics: Critical Interrogations.* Oxford: Clarendon.

Nussbaum, M. 1997. *Cultivating Humanity*. Cambridge: Harvard University Press.

Olson, G. 2007. Neuroscience and Moral Politics: Chomsky's Intellectual Progeny. [Online] Available at: http://www.dissidentvoice.org/2007/10/neuroscience-and-moral-politics-chomskys-intellectual-progeny/ [accessed 19 July 2010].

Parker, C. and Evans, A. 2007. *Inside Lawyers' Ethics*. Melbourne: Cambridge University Press.

Preston, S. and de Waal, F. 2002. Empathy: Its Ultimate and Proximate Bases, *Behavior and Brain Sciences* 25(1): 1–20.

Pue, W. 2008. Legal Education's Mission, *Law Teacher* 42: 270–90.

Ramachandran, V.S. 2007. The Neurology of Self-awareness, *The Edge*. [Online] Available at: http://www.edge.org/3rd_culture/ramachandran07/ramachandran07_index.html [accessed 19 July 2010].

Rhode, D. 1992. Ethics by the Pervasive Method, *Journal of Legal Education* 42: 31–56.

Roberts, P. 2009. Career Development in the LLB, *Law Teacher* 43: 297–309.

Robertson, M. 2005. Challenges in the Design of Legal Ethics Learning Systems: an Educational Perspective, *Legal Ethics* 8: 222–39.

Roche, R. 2011. Learning and the Brain – An Overview, in this collection.

Ryrie, A. 2009. A Kind of Intellectual Cancer, *Times Higher Education* 21 May: 39–40.

Sekerka, L. and Bagozzi, R. 2007. Moral Courage in the Workplace: Moving To and From the Desire and Decision to Act, *Business Ethics: A European Review* 16(2): 132–49.

Schön, D.A. 1983. *The Reflective Practitioner: How Professionals Think in Action*. New York: Basic Books.

Sherr, A. 1996 The Value of Experience in Legal Competence, *Australasian Professional Legal Education Council Conference Papers* Vol. 1, (Sydney, College of Law): 133–68.

Singer, P. 1981. *The Expanding Circle*. New York: Farrar, Straus and Giroux.

SRA. 2004. *Legal Practice Course – Written Standards*. [Online] Available at: http://www.sra.org.uk/documents/students/lpc/standards.pdf [accessed 19 July 2010].

SRA. 2007. *Code of Conduct*. [Online] Available at: http://www.sra.org.uk/solicitors/code-of-conduct.page [accessed 19 July 2010].

Sylwester, R. 1995. *A Celebration of Neurons: An Educator's Guide to the Human Brain*. Brookline, MA: Zephyr Press.

Van Lange, P.A.M. (ed.) 2006. *Bridging Social Psychology*. Mahwah, NJ: Erlbaum.

Webb, J. 1995. Where the Action is: Developing Artistry in Legal Education, *International Journal of Law and Psychiatry* 2(2/3): 187–216.

Webb, J. and Maughan, C. 1996. *Teaching Lawyers' Skills*. London: Butterworth.

Wilson, J. 1993. A Third Survey of University Legal Education in the United Kingdom, *Legal Studies* 13: 143–82.

Wright, R. 1996. *The Moral Animal: Why We Are the Way We Are*. London: Abacus.

Chapter 13
Space, Absence, Silence: The Intimate Dimensions of Legal Learning

Paul Maharg

> car la musique ne respire que
> dans l'oxygène du silence
>
> (Jankélévitch 1983: 168)

Introduction

One way of thinking about a programme of study is that it creates opportunities or spaces for learning. The spaces are there because a learner has laid aside social, domestic or work life for a time, and created space in his or her life to devote to learning. The spaces are defined by the context of higher education: buildings, campuses, materials for study, formalised relationships with tutors and lecturers, with learning resources, with peers, with online environments. The learning events, though, can occur anywhere in people's lives where they grapple with concepts, issues, knowledge and relationships, engaging and re-engaging with the processes of learning. How are we to construct these spaces so as to ensure effective learning?

We can begin by defining how the space is to be constructed by the materials around it. This means thinking about the construction of, for instance, lectures and tutorials, or resource-based learning. Within this will be key spaces, deliberate absences of information or knowledge, where students construct for themselves the knowledge, skills, values that no one but they can learn. In this sense, well-planned absences are critical learning spaces. Nor are they blanks or vacuums only, for their absence is relational to the presence of the learning object, whatever the object happens to be. This applies not just to legal education but to the learning processes of any discipline. Indeed, spaces of absence – biological, ecological, architectural, theological, legal, historical, social, cognitive, literary, musical, educational – are as we shall see critical to the process of learning, which requires an absence, paradoxically, in which it can be enacted. This chapter argues that it is necessary for legal educational design to create this space of absence, and that the space can be uniquely adapted to the serious play of affect.

The relation between space and object has implications for curriculum design, which we often (mis)take for the distribution of resources for learning. We talk of planning classes, organising courses, but in reality the process is often more akin to finding our classes, deeply enmeshed, within a much larger, homogeneous body of legal information and within conceptual lattice structures, where we identify and frame the information and concepts that we require our students to learn. We set out conceptual teaching, detailing information that students will require to read and master, with associated activities. We fill a curriculum with things, largely readings, discussions, attendances at events (lectures, labs, seminars, workshops). Academics think of curriculum as composed of constructed objects because we see it largely from the point of view of our activity. We seldom think of the spaces in between activities and objects as planned (except in an operational sense – for example bottlenecks in assessment deadlines and the like).

But a curriculum seen from a student point of view often looks quite different. Students are much more aware of the gaps and spaces surrounding such objects in a conventional curriculum: the relation of learning object to intent (why was it put there?), of learning object to other objects, and to the absences and spaces between the objects. Linden West and other adult educators have investigated how curricula look from student perspectives. They point to students' anxiety about the suppression of voice in higher education (HE) curricula. West takes a number of in-depth, longitudinal case studies, whose stories 'highlight the importance of personal narrative in weaving unity and meaning from the fragments of experience and in establishing some sense of self, psychological cohesion and truth' (1996: 15). What West's adult students discover in HE is that within the space, the clearing, they need to integrate prior life experiences with the new and sometimes disturbing experience of learning to read and write the texts of disciplinary genres – texts that both constrain and liberate. The problem is, as West defines it, 'that certain conversations, thoughts and actions are favoured rather than others in a manner which can frustrate the struggle for more integrated learning, selves and stories' (188). Learning a disciplinary discourse is of course a disciplined activity. But the process of learning a discipline need not be separated from the development of our students as persons – indeed the two are closely allied. West pointed this out, drawing from Belenky and others to highlight the gap between private and public lives in HE – a gap that is frequently invisible, in part because the emotional lives of students are unregarded: 'Belenky *et al.* (1986) have documented the fragmenting consequences of privileging rationalistic and abstract understandings while pushing more intuitive and experiential knowledge to the margins' (188).

West's observation is one of many on the subject by educationalists (Stenhouse 1983; Giroux 2001). A key problem inherent in learning to understand and produce any disciplinary text is the gap between the normalising rational power of the discourse – the text as object – and the experiential struggle of the novice to comprehend and to make that powerful discourse part of their own voice – the text as subject. The struggle is not a type of Jacob and the Angel wrestling match: rather, it is a struggle in the writer between attitudes and emotions arising from prior writing experiences, and the need to reproduce the signs of a complex discourse, while negotiating, sometimes suppressing, that prior writing experience. The object on the legal textbook page, so polished, neutral, candid yet arcane, bears little mark of any such struggle: it has been stripped of emotion. Readers and writers, though, come to the text object with prior emotions about the text, about what to do with it, about their organic lives around the text. The student's task of reading and creating discourse is really a microcosm of the whole transitional status of the higher education experience. The past and its affective freight cannot be ignored; present experience beyond the text presses in upon the reading experience; the academic future lies beyond and is dependent on the student's struggle with the text. As West put it, '... reclaiming a past – emotionally, biographically, intellectually and culturally – is essential to claiming a future, built more on one's own terms than upon those of others' (211).

Case Study 1: Affective Sociolinguistics and Student Writing

We can appreciate this if we consider the following extract as a case study, one based on a project on writing conferences (Maharg 2000, 2007). Writing conferences, a form of dialogue about student writing, has a respectable lineage in the domain of composition and compositional studies in US higher education (Harris 1986). In its general form the conference consists of a dialogue between tutor and student; and the broad range of research that has been carried out on it tends to focus on the type and quality of the dialogue, in order to improve feedback and student writing processes (Walker and Elias 1987). This conference, also a research project, was carried out with first-year students on a law course in a Scottish university and aimed to increase the quality of feedback to students on their writing. In the writing tasks set for students in an introductory writing skills module, the writing conference was employed to enable students to think critically about the legal argument tasks that were set for them, using the approaches outlined by Scardamalia and Bereiter (1986: 797–8).[1] The argumentational models students structured and the writing heuristics they experimented with in one unassessed essay were then used in a subsequent assessed essay in the module.[2]

It became clear after the first few conferences, and on studying the transcripts, that it was difficult for students to discuss the structure of their writing without discussing the social and performative aspects of it, within the context of their own experience of text production. The following extract is typical:

1 Scardamalia and Bereiter (1986) base their approach on 'procedural facilitation' rather than on 'substantive facilitation', the intent of this being 'to enable students to carry out more complex composing processes by themselves' (61). The approach is one variant amongst a number. For a summary of others, see Newell and Swanson-Owens (1994).

2 For more details on the methodology, see Maharg (2000: 90–91). This extract was considered briefly in that chapter and is analysed in more detail here.

Interviewer: … do you think … you're unsure about your writing?

Ian: I don't think – not too much. I suppose there is maybe a possibility that I just don't want to be cornered – I don't want when I'm writing the essay to put it as if – I don't want to be cornered to look as if I haven't got a clue what I'm talking about. So you try and cover as much ground as you can, if you know what I mean, so that you don't, you aren't totally wrong rather than following one chain of thought and then 'Oh that's completely wrong'. If you try and make it a little bit more broader then you've got a better chance of not being wrong. But it's maybe just a habit I've got into trying to do that because I think in a lot of the exams I did in the Higher there wasn't maths or anything like theory, it was like Modern Studies, Geography, Economics, English. A lot of essays I had to write in the exam. I think that's what's got me into the habit of it, writing like that so that when the marker comes to mark it, it's not – they can't say 'Oh that's right or wrong'. I've tried to cover myself.[3]

The discussion above shifted from discussion of textual features to discussion of attitude and emotion.[4] As he found his voice Ian began to reveal deep anxiety and uncertainty about his writing, and his ability to master a discourse shifting from first to second person when he describes being wrong. He produced a clear historical account of the reasons why his writing was vague, diffuse and confusing to read – writing that could not commit to an argument. Ian was well aware of this. 'Covering' – the metaphor is apt in its adamic inflection, redolent as it is of the figure of the dark Miltonic Covering Cherub – was the result of the realisation that he could not see a way to produce coherent legal argument; and that this was shameful. He therefore produced strategies to cover that shame, which in turn prevented him from improving his writing.[5] The problem, both sociolinguistic and affective, is not uncommon in student writing, as a number of commentators have observed (Gee 1996).

The interview also revealed how insular Ian's *writing* practice was. No one else was ever involved in the activity: he had never collaborated with others and very rarely received peer feedback. School teachers had adjudicated on his ability

3 The 'Higher' is the Higher examination which is usually taken in the fifth year of high school. The grades obtained are a key determinant of university entrance in Scotland. Student name has been altered to preserve anonymity.

4 Much of the literature on writing conferences describes how this happens in various ways. See for instance Patthey-Chavez and Ferris (1997), where the researchers note that 'the divergent backgrounds students bring to instructional events have a structuring effect that cannot be dismissed solely as teacher bias and self-fulfilling prophecy' (51).

5 It is also an interesting example of Nussbaum's argument (2004), where she critiques the effects that those two emotions play in legal culture, and argues with regard to shame that 'a liberal society has particular reasons to inhibit shame and to protect its citizens from shaming' (15).

to pass or fail essays and mock exams. Writing was used for little else in his life. His writing *practice*, in the sense of his ability to articulate a set of rules about his writing, was based on fear and anxiety, and became silent, inarticulate. It was an absence, a space of dread and frustration for him.

For Ian, the writing conference was a significant moment as regards the quality of his work. We discussed ways to commit to an argument by planning how research and early writing could be used as tools to break out of the covering cycle and into the lifeworld of legal discourse. In a sense the moment was little more than an exploration of feelings that made Ian realise that legal discourse was formed in his mind, that it was not an object on the page; and that rather than treat it as an object or swerve around it, he needed to understand his own representations of what the discourse was to him, and how he managed to write versions of it. But the affirmation that emotion mattered in writing, as he acknowledged later, was something he had not discussed with anyone before. It enabled Ian (to put it in Derridean terms) to substitute for the space of anxiety his own centre of significance as part of the process of writing and legal interpretation.

It was one way to gain confidence and a sense of energy about his writing, which improved across the remainder of the small writing tasks in the module. It is interesting to compare what happened in the writing conference to the research results on the use of neurofeedback and performance. It has been conclusively proven that alpha/theta neurofeedback is successful in treating addictions and in improving the performances of music and dance students (Gruzelier and Egner 2004).[6] Raymond et al. (2005) analysed the effects of such feedback on personality and mood of medical students, revealing that such feedback produced 'feelings of energy and confidence' (291). Such feelings are not always present when other anxiety-reducing techniques such as the Alexander Technique, aerobics or mental skills training are used. It is significant that the researchers asked the students while they were listening to the neurofeedback sounds that they should 'visualise themselves being the sort of person they most wanted to be and solving problems in the best way possible' (288). Perhaps the best approach for Ian and for students in similar dilemmas might be a combination of both neurofeedback and the mini-conference – forms of self-visualisation and guided affective sociolinguistics – that provide a space within the curriculum for them to construct their own integration of lifeworld and discourse.

If this is true of students, the same is true of teachers and teaching. Writing conferences are still uncommon. The cost of such one-on-one dialogue in terms of time and effort is only one reason, however. If his personal 'state of being' was crucial to Ian's writing, it is also important to teachers too. In Chapter 1 of this book Maughan calls for a re-appraisal of the role of tutors; and the chapters in Part 2, focusing on affect in staff experience, reveal how important the processes

6 Neurofeedback is a form of biofeedback that gives information to persons about their brain activity, based upon electroencephalography (EEG). Alpha and theta refer to forms of brain activity that give rise to oscillatory EEG patterns.

of self-identity are to legal educators. This has consequences for the development of the type of writing conference described above. West noted this, adducing the work of Susan Weil:

> Weil has noted the neglect of the personal and emotional in discussions of teaching in higher education and how these are often focused on subject expertise, technical skill and communicative method rather than relationship and states of being.

If they are to be involved in the analysis of text and personal experience at this level with students, teachers need guided experience in developing their individual expertise in dealing with emotion while giving feedback, and in developing areas such as affective sociolinguistics. The dialogue is much more than pointing out surface features of argument that should be remedied. As the literature on feedback shows, this is often neither a useful nor successful strategy to improve student writing (Walker and Elias 1987; Carothers 2008; Värlander 2008). Instead – and just as Ian needed a space to talk about his writing – teachers need a space to learn how to help Ian to do this. It is a space bounded not just by the borders of other work commitments, but bounded also by life commitments.

Space as Absence

There is of course a much more expansive phenomenological context to the concept of space that we must acknowledge if we are to take the idea of educational space seriously. In the arts, particularly philosophy, theology, music and literature, there is a wealth of literature on the subject of absence, whether as space or silence, and the relations between these concepts.[7] In literature, for example, Samuel Beckett's use of silence as an integral part of dramatic performance in *Endgame*, *Footfalls* and *Waiting for Godot* is one instance of many (as is the difficulty it presents for actors – Bryden 1998: 49, quoting Whitelaw 1996). In education the interest has spanned early appreciation of the effects of physical space (Dewey 1933), to the analysis of cultural space (Bachelard 1969; Lefebvre 1991), to the educational use of such cultural space. The space has been mapped (Zembylas and Michaelides 2004). Chan et al. (2001) for instance describe four learning space models in physical space that interact with time and location. Caranfa (2006) argues that the fostering of critical reasoning, the aim of most liberal arts programmes of study, will fail because the project largely excludes emotion and silence from the thinking process. He proposes an aesthetic method to complement the critical. Leander and

7 In theology, see for instance Davies and Turner (2002), Atchley (2007), Muers (2004). In philosophy, see Bindeman (1981), Dauenhauer (1980), Mortley (1986a, 1986b). In literature and music the bibliography is of course extensive, and I shall be drawing on some of this below.

Sheehy, drawing on Bakhtin, Deleuze and Guattari as well as Lefebvre, analyse how space profoundly affects literacy and rhetorical sophistication (Leander and Sheehy 2004). Savin-Baden (2008) explores what learning spaces are, their increasing disappearance in academic life and the resultant dissolution and fragmentation of the academic community; and she argues (rightly, I think) for a reappraisal and revaluing of learning *spaces* in university today.[8] This is even more pressing given that many of the spaces for learning can now be online and virtual, as well as within physical buildings on or off campus.

It is also pressing because, despite the interest in absence as an educational concept, we are in danger of forgetting such spaces in our pedagogic language in legal education. One of the commonest metaphors to describe the way in which learning can be facilitated is to use metaphors from architecture or construction: scaffolding, for example, by which learners are given help, via examples or models, to understand what it is they are supposed to understand or perform (Bruner 1960). Or we talk of 'foundation courses', drawing on the ancient metaphor of learning as a building process. This draws on a related metaphor – that of scholarly work as architecture. This is represented in our buildings – institutes, for instance, which is less of a word, more a network of constellated meaning, rich in connotations – building, foundation, creation, provision, investiture. It surfaces in Quintilian's *Institutes*, which is concerned with the place of rhetoric in a life of eloquence and service. Justinianic law was termed thus, as were, in Scots law, the foundational works of Mackenzie, Stair and Erskine. As a result 'institution' has a real presence, to adopt a theological metaphor, a reality of presence in the world that law most emphatically possesses, but inarticulately; and which law compensates for by adopting the ancient metaphoric icons of architecture, rhetoric and other disciplines. The process lives on today. In our contemporary curricula we talk of modules, in much the same way that modernist architects talked of modular construction units (Gold 2007). Such language, prevalent in the discourse of QA, focuses on specific forms of educational, construction and interactivity. Space, where discussed, is the arrangement of physical space – again, the presence of things. Space itself, especially as absence, is rarely considered.

But space lies at the historical roots of universities. In their medieval origins, the arrangement of offices, chapel and residences around the space of a quadrangle was adopted as an architectural plan by both Oxford and Cambridge and adapted elsewhere (St Salvator's College, St Andrews, for instance). It embodied the collegial foundation; and Wykeham's educational rules for both Oxford and Winchester Colleges were innovative in their day because, like Benedict's Rule, formed almost a millennium before, they imagined community as composed of social and individual, talk and silence (Smith 1952; Leach 1899). In this sense Wykeham's innovations were, in a sense, an early version of a social constructivist environment (Turkle and Papert 1990), where the physical environment was

8 She points out how important are proxemics, positive kinesics, eye contact, etc., to the learning space in *Second Life*, for instance.

designed to stimulate learning, and where environment, rules and learning had space and absence as integral to their design.

Learning: The Presence of Absence

How can we describe the presence of absence? One way is to draw upon another discipline's use of space and silence, namely music. It is commonly said of music that silence is essential to it, where the intervals in sound define the nature and duration of its acoustic. As Andrew Edgar points out, 'silences that anticipate, accompany and succeed the performance of music may be seen to constitute something of the hermeneutic horizon of that music' (Edgar 1997: 311). That hermeneutic horizon of music is extended by an extraordinary work by Jonty Semper, namely *Kenotaphion*, a collection of Remembrance Sunday and Armistice Day two-minute silences.[9] Each sound event begins in the same way, with Big Ben tolling the hour; and each is different: the sound of rain, of birds, of shuffling, coughing, the murmur of distant traffic, the sense of a throng of people, all more or less silent. Some early recordings have voice-overs, but the overwhelming effect is of a dense, intentional silence, the record of a deliberate absence of sound that is magnified by the random quality of the sounds of the urban world captured on the CD.

Semper's artwork is one more in the tradition of modernist minimalism – John Cage's *4'33"* for instance.[10] Nothing could be further from what we think of as earlier representations of the natural world in Beethoven's *Pastoral Symphony* or Vaughan Williams' *Lark Ascending*. Instead of formal representation within a musical structure, there is a capturing of the absence of sound as nearly as it is in the real world, with the constant tension between absolute silence (whether that is actually possible) and the random sounds that define the silence.[11] But it could

---

9 The silences, 70 of them in total, are drawn from the period 1929–2000. For a review, see Kennedy (2001).

10 Cage's famous piece, first performed in 1952, was composed for 'any instrument or combination of instruments'. The instrumentalist would arrange his or her instrument as if about to play, then remain like that for a period of four minutes and 33 seconds. The experience of listening is curious: all audible noise begins to enter the aesthetic frame of the time period set by Cage, and becomes part of the performance, as it does in *Kenotaphion*. There have been a number of theories regarding the length of the piece – it is an ironic comment on the typical length of a pop song, for instance; or the total number of seconds equates to the temperature of absolute zero (-273 degrees C – Rayner 2010).

11 The work of Cage, Semper and others follows in a modernist tradition, one wing of which is the interest in 'found' noise – the work of Marinetti for instance, or Luigi Rossolo, in whose work we can find a whole new genre of music, defined as sound. Rossolo, an Italian futurist, argued that what had been regarded as background noise to modern living, the noise of industrial machinery for example, should be heard as music. He designed machines to compose this music (Rossolo 2005).

be argued that the modernist focus on silence is not new. When Vaughan Williams wrote *The Lark Ascending*, for instance, he deliberately sets the freedom of the violin against the impressionistic orchestration from which it springs; and the cadenzas mimic the disappearance of the lark high into the heavens, as in George Meredith's poem from which the piece takes its title (Vaughan Williams 1925; Meredith 1895). Towards the end of the composition, however, Vaughan Williams makes us aware of the encroaching silence: the orchestration falls away, leaving a sublimely weightless birdsong, which of course ends by fading into silence.

But there is a key difference between sitting in an auditorium and listening to Cage's *4'33"*, and listening to *Kenotaphion*, or indeed any CD. *4'33"* is in real time, the CD is not. Indeed, like every CD, *Kenotaphion* consists of highly choreographed silences. When we listen to any contemporary recorded music, we are in a virtual auditorium where sound is deliberately distributed in the stereo field by sound engineers, composers, artists. Instrumental sounds are foregrounded, backgrounded, pitch can be altered, almost every aspect of sound dismantled and reconstructed. The same is true even of representations of recorded silence such as *Kenotaphion*.[12]

This contextual point is symptomatic of a larger issue. Listening to music, even the way we interpret silence, is a social experience. The acoustical properties of what we hear are always understood within a social context of culture, history, artistic production and the like. As Frith puts it, 'musical organisation requires some kind of social organisation and cultural context before it can be created, understood or otherwise invested with meaning' (Frith 1998: 102). Such cultural context imbues performances of *4'33"* with meaning: the silent musicians can be interpreted as a gesture against bourgeois romantic idealism and its belief that music speaks to us as if direct and unmediated (Revill 1991), where Williams' innocent birdsong is interpreted as a lament for a pastoral, pre-1914 England. *Kenotaphion*'s cultural context challenges us to listen to silence simultaneously in many ways: as distributed sound, as an art form, a historical record, a map of changing urban soundscapes, a public and highly political event. But it is also, inescapably in its context, a mourning, in theme and variations, made private and intense because it is stripped of the visual panoply of the Armistice Sunday remembrance ceremonies.

The relationship of music to silence gives us valuable insights into legal education at a profound level. As the sound of the crowd and our knowledge of the event defines our experience of *Kenotaphion*, so too do the boundaries of disciplinary knowledge and educational experience in encounters such as the case study above. The roles that affect and space as absence play are important not just in writing conferences: they can be used in many forms of experiential learning and

12 And the same difference is present in literature too – for instance, Beckett's *Krapp's Last Tape*. Silence signals doubt and anxiety in the younger Krapp's voice. But the existence of the tape recorder means that there are two sorts of silence in the piece – recorded silence, i.e. the absence of speaking, and silence within speech, that is, between words.

they can be encouraged by the design of the space itself. We can see this happening in other, more unusual learning contexts such as games and simulations.

Simulation as Nearly Real, Nearly Now

If games and simulations are to be effective, we know that they need to engage users in the rule-based activities or scenarios that are the core of the game/simulation. When this takes place in legal simulations, the effect can be dramatic and powerful, where a learner playing the part of a lawyer, for example, enters into a relationship with a client. But yet the client is not a *real* client, as may be the case in a clinical setting. A simulation or game is a 'nearly real' object – certainly not a *mimesis* of reality (for as Barton et al. (2007) point out, such a concept is impossible), but the resumption of certain aspects of a possible reality for the purposes of serious play.

'Nearly real' approaches to educational research such as this can be drawn upon and co-opted by those who advocate games and simulations, not to normalise the position of play strategies within a discipline, but to extend and radicalise the pre-existing research bases, and enable the research to work for transformation of disciplinary or professional teaching and learning strategies. An educational simulation, after all, always has a referent in the world of praxis, and there is an implicit analogy that is made between the world of play on the one hand and the world beyond play on the other. For an educational game player, representations of both are necessary to the game. Moreover, the social aspect of simulation and gaming, as Taylor and others have pointed out, is crucial to the experience of the game (Taylor 2006: 21–67); and designers need to plan the social spaces that students will inhabit, where they can reflect in and on action. Heppell's idea of the 'nearly now', a time that exists between now and not now is a useful description of this space (Heppell 2008). He cites Twitter as a classic instance where a user can step outside the momentary activity to record, reflect upon it. Heppell's notion is interesting because it can be seen as one example of many that attempt to describe the subtle processes of time-shifting that take place almost as a matter of course in our daily lives. Technology allows us to split and reshape time and its representations in many ways (Kern 2003). The effect has been observed increasingly since the late 19th century – Benjamin's classic essay on photography is one early 20th-century example of it (Benjamin 1970). We can see it in the narrative techniques of authors such as Proust, who uses syntax and paragraph structure, as Leo Bersani has observed, to abolish the conventions of novelistic time narratives (Bersani 1965: 91–7).

The concept, though, has deeper resonances. Other commentators on technology and media have observed similar processes in the very processes of reading and writing. Walter Ong, for instance, attempted to create a diachronic phenomenology of the process of distanciation that, according to him, writing brought about in our society. His 14 theses are worth rethinking in terms of

Heppell's 'nearly now'. The seventh observes that writing separates past from present, while the first states that 'between knower and known writing interposes a visible and tangible object, the text' (Ong 1986: 39). Ong thus points to the mediatory qualities of text in its control of the presentation of the world to the knower. Because text is fixed and can be revisited endlessly, it also shapes our dwelling upon the world in part because we enter the timeframe of the text. The type of timeframe and the effects it has on us depends on the text itself, as well as our reading and writing activities in and around the text. That disengagement from the world or from text is necessary to engage with the other: absence, in other words, is essential to presence.

However much one might agree or disagree with Ong's central thesis, his analysis of discourse relations helps give us tools to understand how games and simulations can be used for education. His tenth thesis, for instance, states that 'writing separates academic learning (*mathēsis* and *mathēma*) from wisdom (*sophia*), making possible the conveyance of highly organized abstract thought structures independently of their actual use or of their integration into the human lifeworld' (Ong 1986: 42). Whether or not this is always true of the introduction of writing into human societies, it is certainly the case that writing enables the process to happen much further and faster than would otherwise be possible. That process has of course increased exponentially, as many commentators from different disciplines have pointed out (Carruthers 1990; Barnett 1999; Bolter and Grusin 2003).

Games and simulations demand a form of distanciation and the nearly now. The game does take on something of the nature of a text, similar to Ong's 'tangible object' that is interposed between knower and known; and in this sense present is separated from past. But as Csikszentmihalyi (2002) has observed, games also have the capacity to abolish the sense of passing time, the relations between past and present, and to enable the player to enter a suspended mode, where his or her being is not separated from time. Games thus have an ambiguous identity, protean and problematic, where time and emotion play different roles than they do in a conventional curriculum. How does this affect curriculum design and learning?

Simulation as Diegetic and Configurative Learning

Perhaps the first step is to recognise the play element in games and simulations and to *reframe* the curriculum accordingly. But such a process of enframing the curriculum, while it creates difficulties within conventional curricula, becomes even more problematic when planning experiential learning approaches such as games and simulations within a curriculum.[13] These approaches require a *diegetic*

13 The concept of the frame, deriving from the discourse of art and cartography, is used in many disciplines. See for example MacLachlan and Reid (1996). This concept has a number of similarities with Heidegger's concept of 'enframing' (das Gestell), by which

reading of curriculum activity. Diegesis can be briefly summarised as the narrative of a text – commonly regarded, it includes characters, events, storyline and the like (de Freitas and Oliver 2006; de Freitas and Maharg 2011). Within a film, diegesis includes the many devices associated with cinematography: angle of shot, direction of camera gaze, lighting, narratological features such as flash-back and flash-forward – in other words the myriad devices that create a filmic narrative. Non-diegetic elements can also be part of a film's vocabulary, of course. A soundtrack which is inaudible to the characters in the film is non-diegetic, while a door closing, radio music heard by a character, words spoken by one character to another – these are examples of diegetic sound.[14]

However, approaches to learning that use play, simulation and gaming rely on more than diegetic narrative devices to enable learning. They set up imaginary frameworks, often involving extended role-play, where students, staff and others can interact. The interaction is critical, and separates diegetic activity from what one might call (following Aarseth's useful term) configurative activity (Aarseth 1997). In simulations and games, players are active: they configure the environment. But while such games can be wholly immersive, wholly active – single-shooter games are the classic example – they can also be written so that they involve interpretive and reflective activity as well as action. They are then both diegetic and configurative spaces – in Klevjer's comprehensive description, they are at once 'representation and action, reading and configuration, communication and event, mediation and play' (Klevjer 2006).

To someone who has never encountered such an environment, it can seem strange and alien – as it did to Justice Scalia in the Supreme Court case of *Schwarzenegger v. Entertainment Merchants Association.* In this case a group of 82 scholars in the social and medical sciences filed an amicus brief to the Supreme Court against the California law that banned the sale of certain violent films to minors.[15] Mr Smith, acting on behalf of the respondents, describes to a puzzled Justice Scalia the user interactivity of the game:

---

representation of the object world is not just a re-presentation, but a rupturing as well as a capturing – Heidegger (1977: 19–20). Very often this 'enframing' goes unnoticed because it must do so in order to work its effect – '[w]hat has produced and manipulated the frame puts everything to work in order to efface the frame effect …' (Derrida 1987: 73).

14 The *locus classicus* is Plato's *Republic*, Book III, 392e, where Socrates defines mimetic art as the forms of tragedy and comedy, and diegetic art as those forms such as lyric and epic poetry that relate a narrative to the listener (Kirby 1996: 30–32). Diegesis is in many respects a contrast to mimetic approaches to art, which emphasise imitation or direct representation.

15 The brief, one should point out, does not argue in favour of children playing violent adult games. Rather it advocates an informed understanding of video game research.

> Justice Scalia: The child is speaking to the game?
>
> Mr Smith: No. The child is helping to make the plot, determines what happens in the events that appear on the screen, just as an actor helps to portray what happens in a play. You are acting out certain elements of the play and you are contributing to the events that occur and adding a creative element of your own. That's what makes them different and in many ways wonderful.[16]

The result of the interactivity that Smith describes well above is that the configurative nature of learning from play cannot be pre-planned in the way that highly teacher-centred activities (lectures, seminar readings, themes, etc.) can be. Simulation is of course sufficiently protean to be used for both open-field as well as highly bounded learning activities (Barton and Maharg 2006); but students can often learn more than the limits of competence-based outcomes from such activities (Stenhouse 1983). Play-learning thus needs more designed spaces where students themselves play and reflect upon that play.

This gives rise to a number of design problems. First, if simulation designers are to create a diegetic narrative that is also a configurative environment, they need to consider not just the events that make up the narrative of the simulation. They also need to think about the density of this narrative, its detailing, purpose and intent. Novelists and poets have always been aware of this, and how the deliberate omission of information rather than its baroquely detailed elaboration has specific effects upon a reader. Robert Louis Stevenson, for example, was well aware of the tendency of fictive reconstruction to become hypnotically self-referential: 'How to get over, how to escape from, the besotting *particularity* of fiction. "Roland approached the house; it had green doors and window blinds; and there was a scraper on the upper step." To hell with Roland and the scraper!'[17] The same holds for game and simulation designers. As with the intertwining of music and silence, they need to design spaces in the narrative, gaps and absences where the designed matrix of the narrative allows not just for configurative activity on the part of the learner but for diegetic interpretive reflection as well, and its recording.

---

16 *Schwarzenegger v. EMA*, p.40, 3–12, at http://www.supremecourt.gov/oral_arguments/argument_transcripts/08-1448.pdf. See also SCOTUSblog at http://www.scotusblog.com/case-files/cases/eanf/?wpmp_switcher=desktop.

17 Stevenson (1994–5: 8, 296). It is interesting that Stevenson had just finished recounting in this letter to James how he turned for relief from fiction to *Fountainhall's Decisions*, a collection of 18th-century Scots law reports. He comments: 'There's literature, if you like! It feeds; it falls about you genuine like rain' (296). For some authors, of course, the process of layered detail was endless. Walter Benjamin recounts of Proust:

> From his publisher Gallimard we know that Proust's proofreading habits were the despair of the typesetters. The galleys always went back covered with marginal notes, but not a single misprint had been corrected; all available space had been used for fresh text (Benjamin 1970: 204).

Second, such reflection can be focused on the student's own practice within the simulation. There are many ways of designing this. The reflection may focus only on the user's experience in the game or simulation. It may be bi-focal, on elements of acknowledged good practice that can be compared with the student's own practice. Or it may involve a critique of normalising practice and professionalism, in the light of the student's own experience of the simulation. Two points are critical, however. First, the diegetic interpretive activity can take place within or without the frame of the simulation. Second, the object of analysis – for example, professional legal practice – need not be reified within the diegetic frame of the simulation. Indeed I would argue that simulation is only transformational when allied to an ethical view of social relations that acknowledges the 'broken middle' of the human condition (Maharg 2007, analysing Rose 1996).

Third, the idea that students enter an environment where they play within a designed space is really only enacting what happens when we read text. The concept of the space in narrative that affects our response to text is central to a theory of textual reading called 'reader-response theory' or 'reception theory' (from the original German, *rezeptionaesthetik*). It was developed by theorists such as Rosenblatt (1978), Iser (1978) and Jauss (1982), who explored how meaning derives from the relationship between reader and text and cultural context, and therefore – much as in music production – how the gaps or spaces in the narrative or form are as important to a reader's understanding and engagement as the information that is there on the page. Meaning is thus shaped not by information alone, but by the deliberate absence of information and what readers feel and understand when faced with such a gap.

This is a profound point for all game and simulation designers as well as educationalists; and it could be argued that the educational connection was actually present early on in the development of *rezeptionaesthetik*. The idea of the importance of space originally derived from Roman Ingaarden's concept of the indeterminacies of meaning. In a novel (indeed any text), music text or artwork, an indeterminacy is created by the writer, composer or artist. Rosenblatt was originally a professor of education at Columbia, and was much influenced by John Dewey's concept of transactional meaning creation, as can be seen from the subtitle of her influential text. Her interest in *rezeptionaesthetik* was based upon a phenomenological understanding of relationships between reader and text, which of course included the ways in which text produced and reproduced affective responses in readers. As we shall see in the following case study, the planning of absence is not limited to the creation of fictional narrative or the planning of game designs and curricula: it is as essential a component of communication as silence is to music.

Case Study 2: Communication, Space, Emotion

This case study is a fragment of a discussion forum, within the context of a curriculum-wide implementation of simulation activities within the postgraduate, professional legal educational programme, the Diploma in Legal Practice, described in Chapter 11. For background information and further comment, see Maharg (2004, 2006, 2007) and Barton and Maharg (2007). At the start of the year students are formed into groups of four, each one being a simulated law firm within a fictional town called Ardcalloch. Situated on the south bank of the Clyde, the town acts as a complex simulation of the reality that surrounds actual legal transactions.

In the Personal Injury Negotiation Transaction (PI), the firms act for clients, either the injured claimant or as the insurance company's solicitors, in a personal injury negotiation that extends over 12 weeks. In order to negotiate the case they need to engage in fact-finding by contacting characters and institutions within the virtual community, and by pooling and analysing the factual information they obtain. They then need to carry out legal research on issues such as liability and quantum; set out their negotiation strategy and perform the negotiation, by email and recorded face-to-face meetings. Discussion forums for both sides support students in the complex process of carrying out this legal transaction – a PI solicitor is on both forums to answer student queries and provide information. Postgraduate students are trained to answer emails in the guise of any one of around 12 different fictional characters, and to give the appropriate information to students. They are supported by an online forum where Maharg and the PI practitioner are present (Hennessy was author of the scenario and many other resources associated with the transaction). If they wish, students can meet as a firm with either the PI practitioner or another negotiation tutor to discuss strategy and performance before they negotiate with the other side. This meeting is in effect a form of small-group, salon learning. It is voluntary: there are no face-to-face interventions at all in this module, apart from an introductory and general feedback lecture (students can also, if they wish, obtain feedback on performance from file assessors at the end of the project). The transaction is thus a unique construction of face-to-face and online interventions by staff and fictional characters who form part of the diegetic narrative, and who play essential roles in the configurative role-play.

Table 13.1 is a fragment from a four-person student discussion forum within the firm, on the PI transaction. It occurs early in the process of communication within the firm. Kirsty's first 'hey guys' sets the tone for the rest. Her post ends with a comma, as if the author had hit the send button too early, or had been timed out. She writes a wry apology next, again with the informality that marks conversational discourse online. She then seeks advice from the rest of the firm on a draft letter before it is formally posted to the opposing firm. There are two issues, inter-related. The first is informational largely (she was unsure whether to let the other side know they had no site maintenance records). The second point raises a related issue of specificity, referring to the detail of the legal basis for their claim.

Table 13.1 Discussion forum fragment

Student	Comment	Date & time
Kirsty	hey guys,	20 November 14:23:42
Kirsty	obviously i am not very good at this chat thing since i just posted a post saying hey guys and thats it!	20 November 14:27:33
Kirsty	wot i am trying to say is, i posted my first draft letter to the other firm, although i didnt know whether to tell them that we have no maintenance records, and also, i re read their letter to us and they have already told us the legal basis for their claim but they havent been very specific. do u think i should leave that bit in? [name] x	20 November 14:29:07
Alan	hey guys. cant find my phone at the mo so if you text me I won't get it. If you want to phone about sending off letters I'll be at my parents and their no is [number, possibly landline]	21 November 09:47:17
Alan	Shouldnt we also clarify with the other side the date of the incident cos they said 2008 but the insurance co have confirmed that it was 2007.	21 November 13:49:45

She points out that the other side have not been very specific about the legal basis of the claim, and wonders whether she should ask for more ('do u think i should leave that bit in?'). 'That bit', we must infer, is a reference to the site maintenance records. There are issues of reciprocity of information-sharing raised here in the context of professional practice. There are also contextual issues of confidentiality and negotiation strategy. It is a complex set of issues, raised in casual language that verges at times on textspeak.

Another member of the firm, Alan, then answers the next day, twice within four hours (from two different locations, as it turned out). The first posting deals with communications issues. His second posting returns to a substantive issue of the letter that has been drafted by Kirsty, namely the date of the incident, but without answering Kirsty's points.

Read chronologically, these posts look chaotic. Apart from Kirsty answering her own postings, there is almost no continuity of dialogue here: Alan's point, for instance, does not answer Kirsty. Nor is this an unusual feature of this firm's intra-firm forum. But the discontinuity is not necessarily evidence of chaos and fragmentation. Discontinuity, like silence in music, is an integral part of communications that we have learned to manage so as to mitigate the anxiety that it can cause in human relations. However, new technologies present new problems for us, and I would argue that such problems are easier to deal with if we acknowledge the discontinuity and necessary absence at the heart of the communicational process. We can see this happening in the fragment above on three dimensions – information management, personal voice and social network.

Information management is surprisingly problematic for students, and we can appreciate this if we are aware of the sophisticated wider context of student communications. The firm members are phoning each other and texting. They also email. In other words, the process of communication about a letter draft in the firm is a complex of different communicational methods, only one of which happens to be the forum. In fact, the firm resolved Kirsty's substantive point about information-sharing by phone (though significantly the issues concerning the long-term effects of Kirsty's point on the firm's negotiation strategy were not resolved). The problem for the firm is not one of forum use (in spite of Kirsty's first attempts), or tone of voice, or even spelling, grammar, textspeak and the like, but the very contemporary problem of managing information and voice across the range of communicational platforms they are using. With the possibilities of at least eight widely used channels open to them (IM, email, mobile phone, landline, voicemail, texting, discussion forum, Twitter), the issue of information management is significant. This was a problem for many firms: they lacked the information management tools to be able to gather, track, archive and recall the information they needed. A number of conscientious firms took the long way round to doing this by manually recording key decisions made in the process of communication – in effect stopping the process of information to summarise it. It may be that students need to be aware of the complexity that this brings to problem-identification and decision-making – after all, Kirsty's issues were only partly addressed by the firm across the communications platforms. The situation requires students to clarify issues and persist in raising them until they are resolved.

If the first problematic dimension is that of information management, the second is the problem of managing voice, register and genre on these platforms. There is a wider context to this communicational fragment. It reads like a fragment from a conversation rather than formal written discourse because students are adopting the discourse of webtalk. This creole of textspeak and email abbreviation worked well for the firm. But just as the casual nature of the intra-firm chat forum (compared with the much more formal discourse on the discussion forums used by all firms) can be a strength in bonding the firm, it can also be a weakness, in that it may not be seen to be a register where persistent logical thought can easily be represented. The ligatures of logical argument do not sit easily with the style of speech or attitude it represents. It may be that the answer is not to insist on formal register, but to help students learn a post-Ciceronian digital rhetoric, in which they can achieve flexibility of tone, linguistic precision and argumentational sophistication.

The third dimension is perhaps the most significant – the socialising process. This forum is an important relational space. Within the formal environment of the case management system that students used, the forum allows a back-channel close to the drafting and posting zones, where students can comment on their work and chat about related issues. In simulation terms this is not quite a debrief – it does not take place with a tutor or coach and outside the domain of the simulation. However, it is not the simulation file itself but talk about the file. It represents a separate zone, where students can discuss and reflect on their work, try out identities that are at once professional but cool, make mistakes or learn from others' mistakes, and learn how to communicate consistently and accurately with colleagues, in any register. The process can help to bind the firm emotionally as a working unit, giving them confidence in their work and in each other.

Conclusion

This book is predominantly an exploration of the affective domain, as well as an introduction to the capacities of neuroscientific exploration of brain architecture that may help us understand the process of learning the law and understand ourselves and our activities as educators. As the first three chapters of the book point out, neuroscience has considerable potential for improving legal education, particularly in the affective domain. This is not a new insight: a decade ago, Goodenough (2001) argued for more interdisciplinary research on the subject. But teaching the law involves innovative curriculum design, and is a craft (in that it consists of a repertoire of skills and practices), and an art (in that it is dialogic, creative and intuitive) and is filled with ethical issues and problems. We need to bring together the paradigms of education and educational psychology with the natural science basis of neuroscience. Researchers are already doing so in other domains (Howard-Jones et al. 2005; Howard-Jones et al. 2007); but this is barely a start: we need much more interdisciplinary research on these issues, particularly in legal education.

In addition, this final chapter argues that we need to consider not just our teaching interventions but our deliberate absence as an essential space adjacent to learning objects, a plenitude of silence. Such absence can act like Heppell's 'nearly now'; and in spaces such as this students may not only discuss work and acquire knowledge but through participation they can create affective bonds that are integral to their work on the course and their development of professionalism (Barton and Westwood, this volume). All learning in higher education, I would argue, requires such spaces, but particularly experiential learning, where students may develop their voices as novice professionals, and support each other in their associative responsibilities, as well as analysing the nature of professionalism and its foundational ethics. Compare the sense of collective effort and collective responsibility that is growing in the forum fragment of the second case study above to the isolation, alienation and shame felt by Ian in the first case study – an altogether different space of emptiness. Which of these two spaces do we want our students to inhabit? In this way space as constructed absence can help students to negotiate the transitional passages of higher education or, as Flower put it eloquently, can help them understand how the 'negotiation of inner voices shape[s] the *hidden logic* of the text' (Flower 1994: 55, her emphasis). They also provide staff with a concept that is often missing and forgotten – the space of affective learning, with all the enormous advantages that that brings to the learning process. Neuroscience can help us research that domain, can help give us a language that can express new insights into ancient processes. Together, approaches combining educational and neuroscientific methods may reveal new insights, through exploration of the affective domain, that help us understand ourselves as learners and explore the 'intimate dimensions' of learning. The phrase is Linden West's, and to him I give the last word:

> For adults as well as children, affirmation, holding and inclusion, especially for those on the margins, provides a basis for existential legitimacy, core cohesion and authentic engagement in the world. The problem has been that education and educators have lacked a compelling language to interpret and theorize the intimate dimensions of learning and self-development within a connected and historical frame of reference: or, to state it differently, to interpret what it takes, emotionally, socially as well as intellectually, to keep on keeping on even in the most oppressive and fragmented of times. (West 1996: 208)

References

Aarseth, E. 1997. *Cybertext. Perspectives on Ergodic Literature*. Baltimore and London: Johns Hopkins University Press.

Atchley, J.H. 2007. The Silence of the Secular, *Literature and Theology* 21(1): 66–81.

Bachelard, G. 1969. *The Poetics of Space*, trans. by Maria Jolas. Boston: Beacon Press.

Barnett, R. 1999. *Realizing the University in an Age of Supercomplexity.* Buckingham: Open University Press.

Barton, K. and Maharg, P. 2006. E-Simulations in the Wild: Interdisciplinary Research, Design, and Implementation, in *Games and Simulations in Online Learning: Research and Development Frameworks*, edited by C. Aldrich, D. Gibson and M. Prensky. Hershey, PN: Information Science Publishing, 115–49.

Barton, K., McKellar, P. and Maharg, P. 2007. Authentic Fictions: Simulation, Professionalism and Legal Learning, *Clinical Law Review* 14(1): 143–93.

Belenky, M.F., Clinchy, B.M., Goldberger, H. and Tarule, J.M. 1986. *Women's Ways of Knowing: The Development of Self, Voice, and Mind.* New York: Basic Books.

Benjamin, W. 1970. *Illuminations*. Edited with an Introduction by H. Arendt. Translated by H. Zohn. London: Jonathan Cape Ltd.

Bersani, L. 1965. *Marcel Proust. The Fictions of Life and of Art*. Oxford: Oxford University Press.

Bindeman, S.L. 1981. *Heidegger and Wittgenstein: The Poetics of Silence*. New York: University Press of America.

Bolter, J.D. and Grusin, R. 2003. *Remediation: Understanding New Media*. Cambridge, MA: MIT Press.

Bruner, J. 1960. *The Act of Thinking*. Harvard: Harvard University Press.

Bryden, M. 1998. Beckett and the Sound of Silence, in *Samuel Beckett and Music*, edited by M. Bryden. Oxford: Oxford University Press.

Caranfa, A. 2006. Voices of Silence in Pedagogy: Art, Writing and Self-encounter, *Journal of Philosophy of Education* 41(1): 85–103.

Carothers, A.D. 2008. *A Circle of Response: Addressing the Tensions of Teacher Response to Student Writing*. Masters Thesis submitted to Oregon State University.

Carruthers, M. 1990. *The Book of Memory. A Study of Memory in Medieval Literature. Cambridge Studies in Medieval Literature*. Cambridge: Cambridge University Press.

Chan, T. et al. 2001. Four Spaces of Network Learning Models, *Computers & Education* 37: 141–61.

Csikszentmihalyi, M. 2002. *Flow: The Psychology of Optimal Experience*. New York: Harper Perennial Modern Classics.

Dauenhauer, B.P. 1980. *Silence. The Phenomenon and its Ontological Significance*. Bloomington, IN: Indiana University Press.

Davies, O. and Turner, D. 2002. *Silence and the Word: Negative Theology and Incarnation*. Cambridge: Cambridge University Press.

de Freitas, S. and Maharg, P. 2011. Digital Games and Learning: Modelling Learning Experiences in the Digital Age, in *Digital Games and Learning*, edited by S. de Freitas and P. Maharg. London: Continuum Press.

de Freitas, S. and Oliver, M. 2006. How can Exploratory Learning with Games and Simulations within the Curriculum be Most Effectively Evaluated? *Computers and Education Special Issue on Gaming* 46: 249–64.

Derrida, J. 1987. *The Truth in Painting*, translated by G. Bennington and I. McLeod. Chicago: University of Chicago Press.

Dewey, J. 1933. *How we Think*. Amherst, NY: Prometheus Books.

Edgar, A. 1997. Music and Silence, in *Silence. Interdisciplinary Perspectives*, edited by A. Jaworski. The Hague: Mouton de Gruyter, 311–28.

Egner, T. and Gruzelier, J.H. 2004. EEG Biofeedback of Low Beta Band Components: Frequency-specific Effects on Variables of Attention and Event-related Brain Potentials, *Clinical Neurophysiology* 115: 131–9.

Flower, L. 1994. *The Construction of Negotiated Meaning: A Social Cognitive Theory of Writing*. Carbondale, IL: Southern Illinois University Press.

Frith, S. 1998. *Performing Rites: Evaluating Popular Music*. Oxford: Oxford University Press.

Gee, J.P. 1996. *Social Linguistics and Literacies: Ideology in Discourses*. Second edition. Abingdon, Oxon: RoutledgeFalmer.

Giroux, H. (ed.) 2001. *Theory and Resistance in Education. Towards a Pedagogy for the Opposition*. Westport, CT: Greenwood Publishing Group.

Gold, J.R. 2007. *The Practice of Modernism. Modern Architects and Urban Transformation, 1954–1972*. Abingdon, Oxon: Routledge.

Goodenough, O. 2001. Mapping Cortical Areas Associated with Legal Reasoning and Moral Intuition, *Jurimetrics* 41: 429–42.

Gruzelier, J.H. and Egner, T. 2004. Physiological Self-regulation: Biofeedback and Neurofeedback, in *Musical Excellence*, edited by A. Williamson. Chichester: Wiley, 197–219.

Harris, M. 1986. *Teaching One-to-One: The Writing Conference*. Urbana, IL: National Council of English Teachers.

Heidegger, M. 1977. The Age of the World Picture, in *The Question Concerning Technology and Other Essays*, translated by W. Lovitt. New York: Harper.

Heppell, S. 2008. Back and Forth, *Guardian* 18 March. [Online] Available at: http://www.guardian.co.uk/education/2008/mar/18/link.link27 [accessed 11 December 2010].

Howard-Jones, P.A., Blakemore, S.J., Samuel, E., Summers, I.R. and Claxton, G. 2005. Semantic Divergence and Creative Story Generation: An fMRI Investigation, *Cognitive Brain Research* 25: 240–50.

Howard-Jones, P.A., Winfield, M. and Crimmins, G. 2007. Co-constructing an Understanding of Creativity in Drama Education that Draws on Neuropsychological Concepts, *Proceedings of the British Educational Research Association Annual Conference 2007*, Institute of Education, London.

Iser, W. 1978. *The Act of Reading*. Baltimore, MD: The Johns Hopkins University Press.

Jankélévitch, V. 1983. *La Musique et L'Ineffable*. Paris: Éditions du Seuil.

Jauss, H.R. 1982. *Toward an Aesthetic of Reception*, translated by T. Bahti. Minneapolis: University of Minnesota Press.

Kennedy, M. (2001) CD Art and the Sound of Silence, *Guardian* 9 November. [Online] Available at: http://www.guardian.co.uk/uk/2001/nov/09/maevkennedy [accessed 12 December 2010].

Kern, S. 2003. *The Culture of Time and Space: 1880–1918*. Second edition. Harvard: Harvard University Press.

Kirby, J.T. 1996. Classical Greek Origins of Western Aesthetic Theory, in *Languages of Visuality. Crossings Between Science, Art, Politics and Literature*, edited by B. Allert. Detroit, Michigan: Wayne State University Press, 29–49.

Klevjer, R. 2006. In Defence of Cutscenes. [Online] Available at: http://share.auditory.ru/2006/Ivan.Ignatyev/DiGRA/In%20Defense%20of%20Cutscenes.pdf [accessed 20 August 2010].
Leach, A.F. 1899. *A History of Winchester College*. London: Duckworth & Co.
Leander, K.M. and Sheehy, M. 2004. *Spatializing Literacy Research and Practice. New Literacies and Digital Epistemologies*. New York: Peter Lang.
Lefebvre, H. 1991. *The Production of Space*, trans. by D. Nicholson-Smith. Malden, MA: Editions Anthropos.
MacLachlan, G. and Reid, I. 1996. Framing and Interpretation, in *Rhetoric of the Frame: Essays on the Boundaries of the Artwork*, edited by P. Duro. Cambridge: Cambridge University Press.
Maharg, P. 2000. 'Context cues Cognition': Writing, Rhetoric and Legal Argumentation, in *Learning to Argue in Higher Education*, edited by S. Mitchell and R. Andrews. Portsmouth: Boynton/Cook Publishers, 85–95.
Maharg, P. 2004. Virtual Communities on the Web: Transactional Learning and Teaching, in *Aan het Werk met ICT in het Academisch Onderwijs*, edited by A. Vedder. Nijmegen: Wolf Legal Publishers.
Maharg, P. 2006. On the Edge: ICT and the Transformation of Professional Legal Learning, *Web Journal of Current Legal Issues* 3. [Online] Available at: http://webjcli.ncl.ac.uk/2006/issue3/maharg3.html [accessed 27 February 2007].
Maharg, P. 2007. *Transforming Legal Education. Learning and Teaching the Law in the Twenty-first Century*. Aldershot: Ashgate Publishing.
Meredith, G. 1895. *Poems and Lyrics of the Joy of Earth*. London: Macmillan and Co.
Mortley, R. 1986a. *From Word to Silence. Volume 1, The Rise and Fall of Logos*. Bonn: Hanstein.
Mortley, R. 1986b. *From Word to Silence. Volume 2, The Way of Negation, Christian and Greek*. Bonn: Hanstein.
Muers, R. 2004. *Keeping God's Silence: Towards a Theological Ethics of Communication*. London: Wiley-Blackwell.
Newell, G.E. and Swanson-Owens, D. 1994. Using Intervention Protocols to Study the Effects of Instructional Scaffolding on Writing and Learning, in *Speaking About Writing: Reflections on Research Methodology*, edited by P. Smagorinsky. Thousand Oaks, CA: Sage Publications, 141–61.
Nussbaum, M. 2004. *Hiding from Humanity: Disgust, Shame and the Law*. Princeton and Oxford: Princeton University Press.
Ong, W. 1986. Writing is a Technology that Restructures Thought, in *The Written Word: Literacy in Transition*. Oxford: Clarendon Press, 23–47.
Patthey-Chavez, G.G. and Ferris, D.R. 1997. Writing Conferences and the Weaving of Multi-voiced Texts in College Composition, *Research in the Teaching of English* 31(1): 51–69.
Raymond, J., Carney, C., Parkinson, L.A. and Gruzelier, J.H. 2005. The Effects of Alpha/Theta Neurofeedback on Personality and Mood, *Cognitive Brain Research* 23: 287–92.

Rayner, L. 2010. Letter, *Guardian* 22 December, Letters, 29, col 1.
Revill, G. 1991. *The Lark Ascending*: Vaughan Williams' monument to a radical pastoral, *Landscape Research* 16(2): 24–30.
Rose, G. 1996. *Mourning Becomes the Law. Philosophy and Representation.* Cambridge: Cambridge University Press.
Rosenblatt, L. 1978. *The Reader, the Text, the Poem: The Transactional Theory of the Literary Work.* Carbondale, IL: Southern Illinois University Press.
Rossolo, L. 2005. *The Art of Noises*. Pennington: Pendragon Press. First published 1913.
Savin-Baden, M. 2008. *Learning Spaces: Creating Opportunities for Knowledge Creation in Academic Life.* Milton Keynes: Open University Press.
Scardamalia, M. and Bereiter, C. 1986. Research on Written Composition, in *Handbook of Research on Teaching*, edited by M.C. Wittrick. Skokie, IL: Rand MacNally, 778–803.
Smith, A.H. 1952. *New College Oxford and its Buildings.* London and New York: Oxford University Press.
Stenhouse, L. 1983. *Authority, Education, and Emancipation: A Collection of Essays*. London: Heinemann Educational Books.
Stevenson, R.L. 1994–5. *The Letters of Robert Louis Stevenson.* Eight volumes. Edited by B.A. Booth and E. Mehew. Yale: Yale University Press.
Taylor, T.L. 2006. *Play Between Worlds: Exploring Online Game Culture.* Cambridge, MA: The MIT Press.
Turkle, S. and Papert, S. 1990. Epistemological Pluralism: Styles and Voices within the Computer Culture, *Signs: Journal of Women in Culture and Society* 16(1): 128–65.
Värlander, S. 2008. The Role of Students' Emotions in Formal Feedback Situations, *Teaching in Higher Education* 13(2): 145–56.
Vaughan Williams, R. 1925. *The Lark Ascending: Romance for Violin and Orchestra*. Oxford: Oxford University Press.
Walker, C.P. and Elias, D. 1987. Writing Conference Talk: Factors Associated with High- and Low-rated Writing Conferences, *Research in the Teaching of English* 21(3): 266–85.
West, L. 1996. *Beyond Fragments. Adults, Motivation and Higher Education: A Biographical Analysis*. London: Taylor & Francis.
Whitelaw, B. 1996. *Billie Whitelaw ... Who He?* London: Saint Martin's Press.
Zembylas, M. and Michaelides, P. 2004. The Sound of Silence in Pedagogy, *Educational Theory* 54(2): 193–210.

Index

Note: numbers in brackets preceded by *n* refer to footnotes.